The PRECARIOUS REPUBLIC

Modernization in Lebanon

MICHAEL C. HUDSON

Brooklyn College of The City University
of New York

RANDOM HOUSE · NEW YORK

TO MY PARENTS

Robert Bowman Hudson

AND

Joan Loram Hudson

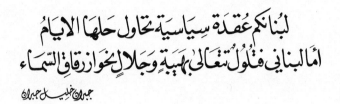

لُبْنَانُكُمْ عُقْدَةٌ سِيَاسِيَةٌ تُحَاوِلُ حَلَهَا الْأَيَامُ
أَمَّا لُبْنَانِي فَتُقُولُ تَغَالَى بِهَيْبَةٍ وَجَلَالٍ لِنُحَوِّرَ زَرِقَاقَ السَّمَاءِ

جبران خليل جبران

Your Lebanon is a political riddle that time tries to
solve, but my Lebanon is hills rising in splendor toward the blue skies.

—*Khalil Gibran*

Acknowledgments

This study was undertaken with the guidance and encouragement of Professor Karl W. Deutsch, to whom I am indeed grateful. I am equally indebted to Professor Samuel P. Huntington and the Center for International Affairs at Harvard University for providing me with a year in a stimulating environment to develop my ideas further and to write the manuscript.

An important source of information was a series of interviews with Lebanese politicians, civil servants, businessmen, and journalists, including the four Presidents of Lebanon since 1943 and four Prime Ministers. The 111 formal interviews, along with numerous less formal conversations, took place over the period 1962–1966. I should like to thank each of these individuals for his generous cooperation. So many other Lebanese helped in so many ways that complete or adequate acknowledgment is impossible. Particular thanks, however, must go to students, professors, and administrators at the American University of Beirut. Although the A.U.B. had no official connection with my study and is in no way responsible for it, the staff's hospitality and informal assistance were gratifying.

I should also like to thank Mr. Michel Abujaoudeh, Professor Leonard Binder, Professor and Mrs. Eberhard Boecker, Miss Laila Chaib, Mr. Jean Chami, Professor Ralph Crow, Professor Rupert Emerson, Mr. Bassem al-Jisr, Professor Walid Khalidi, Professor A. J. Meyer, Mr. George Nasr, Professor Kamal Salibi, Mr. Joy Tabet, Professor William Yale, Mr. and Mrs. George Wahbé, and the Abul-Husn family. Mme. Michel Chiha graciously allowed me access to her late husband's library.

Mr. Robert Erwin, the Center editor, was especially helpful with suggestions for improvement and clarification. Lilian Christmas, Peggy Thompson, and Jane Tatlock typed the various drafts of the manuscript. The Brooklyn College Research Center in Comparative Politics and Administration and the Yale Political Data program provided facilities during the final stages of preparation.

I gratefully acknowledge the permission of Professor William Yale to quote a passage from his papers at the Yale University Library; of the Middle East Institute to include material from my article, "The Electoral Process and Political Development in Lebanon," which appeared in *The Middle East Journal,* 20, No. 2 (1966), 173–86; of Imprimerie Catholique, Beirut, to include the lines from Khalil Gibran that introduce this work; of Mr. Pierre Sadek to reproduce six of his drawings; and of Mr. Joseph Hneineh, who prepared the calligraphy for the dedication.

For financial assistance at various stages of this project, I am grateful to Yale University, the American Community School of Beirut, Brooklyn College of The City University of New York, and the American Philosophical Society.

Finally, special thanks go to my wife, Vera Wahbé Hudson, whose assistance, scholarly and otherwise, was very great indeed.

Many of those who helped may disagree with my analysis; therefore, I wish to emphasize the usual disclaimer: They should not be considered responsible for it.

M. C. H.

Contents

Maps

Tables

The PRECARIOUS REPUBLIC

Introduction

The Lebanese Republic is one of the most unusual states in the world. It is a conglomeration of paradoxes and contradictions. Since it became independent of France in 1943 it has struggled from one crisis to another, avoiding disaster by the narrowest of margins. Lebanon as a polity is archaic, inefficient, and divided; it is also liberal, democratic, and—in general—orderly. It is Arab and Western, Christian and Muslim, traditional and modern. Its precarious survival is a fascinating subject for the student of politics.

This study attempts to answer two questions about Lebanon. How did it succeed in enduring through the dangerous years after independence, and what are its prospects for the future? The answers require an analysis of the relationships between the changing capabilities of its political system and the changing burdens imposed by the environment. Lebanon's present uncertain viability is largely the result of its limited capacity to modernize politically during its first two decades as an independent country. Its future development depends on whether or not its modernizing capacity will continue to bear the increasing weight of external and domestic pressures.

Some readers familiar with Lebanon may be astonished at the idea that the little state is modernizing in a political sense. Economic and social modernization is obvious, but political modernization is not. Indeed, many Lebanese citizens, who equate modernization with improvement or progress, are more inclined to view their political life as regressive or, at best, stagnant. There is considerable truth in such views; indeed, compared with states that rank near it on levels of socioeconomic development, Lebanon is politically underdeveloped.[1] Its executive stability is low, it lacks a modern party

3

system, and its administrative capabilities are deficient. These weaknesses are rendered all the more serious by an apparent increase in the adversity of the Lebanese social and economic environment. They do not augur a bright future for the country. But, if the system is so defective, its apparent success over two decades is puzzling. It is this puzzle that makes Lebanon an interesting political subject.

The Lebanese experience illustrates both the surprising possibilities for modernization in a deeply divided political culture and the strains that such a process imposes on the political system. Beneath the surface of corruption, stagnation, and meaningless change there are indications of growing rationality, complexity, flexibility, participation, and executive power in the Lebanese system. The important issue, however, is not simply the occurrence of these trends but rather their velocity and amplitude. It will be suggested later that these trends are taking place in independent Lebanon but also that they are moving rather slowly. They have been of sufficient scope to permit the insubstantial stability that has made postwar Lebanon prosperous, but they have not left much margin of safety. By the same token, however, their gradualness has forestalled the destruction of the fragile balancing mechanisms that adjust frictions among Lebanon's several primordial communities. The object of this study, therefore, is not only to identify the political changes that are occurring but also to assess their rates of change and to compare them with the changing environmental loads.

Lebanon, the land of Phoenicia, is today a constitutional parliamentary republic of around 2 million people. The country is divided into five provinces—Beirut, Mount Lebanon, North Lebanon, South Lebanon, and the Biqa (see Map 2)—and subdivided into administrative districts. For all its cultural divisions, Lebanon is formally a unitary state, and the provincial governors are entirely responsible to the central government. Local government is largely controlled from Beirut, although municipalities elect officials and have unofficial mayors (*mukhtars*). Although Lebanon's legal system is patterned after the French Code, such matters of personal status as marriage and inheritance fall under the jurisdiction of the several religious courts. Justice by feud and vendetta competes with justice by the Criminal Code.

A parliament is elected by the people every four years, and a President of the Republic is elected every six years by the Parliament. Seats in Parliament are allocated on a sectarian as well as a geographical basis, and by custom the President is a Christian and the Prime Minister a Muslim. The President may not seek re-election. The constitution, written in 1926 by Christian notables in consultation with the French Mandate authorities, gives the President considerable power. The President names the Prime Minister, who in turn selects a cabinet; but, although the Cabinet is theoretically answerable to Parliament, it is in fact answerable to the President. Between 1943 and 1964 Lebanon had three Presidents, seven Parliaments, and thirty-six governments. During the same period it experienced three serious attempted coups d'état and, in 1958, a short civil war in which the United States intervened militarily. The prevailing economic and political philosophy in Lebanon favors unrestricted private enterprise, and the government, like the country in general, derives most of its income from trade.

Lebanon is divided, historically, along sectarian, regional, and family lines. Not only is there chronic suspicion between Christians and non-Christians; there is also incessant rivalry among the various sects within each of the two religions. Local communalism antedates the establishment of the present territorial entity in 1920 by the French, and even today there is tangible cultural distance between the people of the three outlying provinces (North Lebanon, the Biqa, and South Lebanon), which were grafted onto traditional Christian Mount Lebanon by the French Mandatory, and those of the core area of Beirut-Mount Lebanon. No sect, region, or family coalition commands a majority of the population; in fact, it cannot be scientifically or legally ascertained whether Christians or non-Christians predominate in the contemporary Lebanese state, although there is an important myth that Christians exceed Muslims and Druzes in a ratio of six to five. It is difficult to name a political culture more divided along traditional lines. Traditional divisions are to some extent deepened by conflicting foreign pressures: The regional and international ferment of the postwar era is reflected in local politics, complicating further the basic cleavages. Furthermore, since World War II, Lebanon has experienced an extremely rapid rate of social mobilization, which has superimposed potential new political divisions on this fragmented political culture. Although some aspects of social mobilization, notably mass communications, have spread rather widely, such others as population concentration, urbanization, and economic growth have been confined almost entirely to the Greater Beirut area. And, whereas the service sector of the Lebanese economy has blossomed beyond all earlier dreams, the mass-employment sectors—agriculture and industry—have remained relative backwaters. Vulnerable as it is to so many of the burdens that beset all contemporary new states, Lebanon's experience invites comparison not only with neighboring Arab states but also with all fragmented polities undergoing rapid, uneven social change—from Malaysia to Italy, from Nigeria to New York City.

The political system in Lebanon embodies a confusion of elements that render it extremely difficult to classify according to the usual typologies. Lebanon is a democracy, but it is also an oligarchy. One could reasonably place it in four of the five types of new states proposed by Edward Shils.[2] It is stable enough to attract enormous amounts of capital, yet a radio speech or a thrown rock can send the country into turmoil. Reform movements are as routine as corruption. Cabinet crises are chronic. The party system is feeble, yet public opinion is politically volatile. In short, many generalizations about the new states do not apply easily to Lebanon, and those that do contradict one another.

It is understandable, therefore, that the student of Lebanese politics should look away from single-nation models in search of a theory that will explain the Lebanese situation. The field of international politics, strangely enough, offers a model that seems to explain the Lebanese political situation much better: the classical balance-of-power system. In Lebanon, as in the international system, there is no ultimate arbiter of conflict and no monopoly of the instruments of force. This observation may seem strange drawn from a state that possesses full legal sovereignty, international recognition, and a modern army, gendarmerie, and police force. The fact remains, however, that central government control is a tenuous thing, dependent on the agreement of powerful local leaders who themselves command sizable deterrent forces and who can take advantage of certain geographical, cultural, and historical conditions to assert their autonomy if their interests are threatened. Furthermore, in Lebanon, as in the international system, there are several actors, none of whom is strong enough to control the entire system.

The balancing process is observable at four levels: sectarian, regional, personal, and institutional. In a society divided almost equally between Christian and Muslim inhabitants and subdivided along sectarian lines within each religion, Lebanon's domestic tranquillity is based upon a perpetual stand-off among the sects. If, in the normal course of politics, one sect demands and receives additional representation in the Cabinet, other sects will demand it too, resulting in either an enlarged Cabinet or a withdrawal of the original sect's advantage. On a larger scale, if for some reason Parliament were to elect the Muslim Grand Mufti of Lebanon President of the Republic, it is probable that the various Christian sects, which normally are not united, would unite to thwart such a move, and it is possible that they might carry a portion of the Muslim Shiite community with them. One would see a classic balance-of-power maneuver. Similar maneuvers can be observed on a regional scale. If the President of the Republic is a Maronite from North Lebanon, it is less easy for a Sunnite in Tripoli to be Prime Minister than it would be if the President were from Mount Lebanon. If major public-works projects are authorized for Beirut without some compensation for the politicians of South Lebanon and the Biqa, the Prime Minister may find his majority threatened with mutiny from the deputies of those regions. At the level of notables and personalities, the balancing process is clearest. Lebanon's intricate clique politics are reminiscent of eighteenth-century England, characterized as they are by alliance building on the part of semiautonomous personages. One alliance will call into being a counteralliance, as there are enough families with varying degrees of power and ambition in any region to coalesce against the dominant group. The electoral process, at both the municipal and the parliamentary levels, simply legitimizes and institutionalizes this struggle. A prominent example of the balance-of-power struggle among notables occurs in the Druze community between the leaders of two traditional factions; it has not only involved the enlistment of other notables on each side but has also used British-French rivalry, Arab-Lebanese tension, and even the conflict between capitalism and socialism. Fortunately, in terms of general order, there are a great many arenas in which gains and losses can be registered, and the scoring process is not very precise.

It is at the institutional level, however, that the most spectacular balance-of-power plays of recent years have occurred. The President of the Republic has been striving constantly to enhance his power at the expense of other institutions. On two occasions, in 1952 and 1958, such assertions have triggered countermoves by an alliance of parliamentarians and notables with the army.

It will be noted that the main actors in the balance-of-power system may be classified as parochial rather than as modern and that even those, like President and Parliament, that carry nonparochial titles are operating essentially from communal power bases. Nor will it escape the attentive eye why the successful Lebanese politician is pragmatic and unfettered by ideology or program. The logic of the balance-of-power situation requires him to be flexible above all, to make and break alliances with a minimum of embarrassment, and to promote his self-interest, which is tied with traditional bonds to the interest of his local constituency.

THE STABILITY PROBLEM

Americans and Europeans concerned with the development of moderate liberal democracy in the new states often argue that the main obstacle is lack of political stability. This instability may be the result of an entrenched traditional culture that lacks the resilience, education, and personality characteristics for such institutions. It may also be caused by the breakdown of this culture through the forces of "modernization," which creates anomie, inflated expectations, and general disorder. Or it may be explained by the general low economic level. The Lebanese experience appears to support the general point: First came stability, then democracy. Appearances can be deceiving, however. In Lebanon, there is reason to think that the relationship is precisely the reverse: Democratic institutions have been a requisite for political stability, not a result of it. This stability has in turn permitted the conservation of traditional pluralism while allowing a degree of modernization and economic development.

If democracy produces stability, what produces democracy? Students from Alexis de Tocqueville to David Truman have accepted the idea that a proliferation of overlapping private organizations is essential for a moderate democracy.[3] But twentieth-century Lebanon is not analogous to nineteenth-century America. In the first place, the pluralism of Lebanon is basically primordial, that is, traditional, as opposed to the rationalized pluralism of the United States. Cohesive family, clan, and sectarian groups are mobilized to participate politically as autonomous security communities in defense of their own identities; only when these identities are secure can the politics of nontraditional interest groups proceed normally. The nearest American equivalent is found in the pre-Civil War period and is reflected appropriately in Calhoun's theory of the concurrent majority. In the second place, pluralism is not the only pillar upon which the American democracy rests; a second vital condition is public security. With some notable exceptions, American political behavior is predicated upon an assumption that a public interest exists and can be served without severe threat to vital private interests; the American state has won legitimacy by serving this public interest. Lebanon does not enjoy this second condition: Its subcommunities are mutually suspicious, and they do not trust the formal institutions to be powerful or impartial enough to protect their local interests. Formal institutions thus do not engender the kind of positive legitimacy inherent in the Western notion of rule of law. In short, the subnational communities are compelled by the situation to act as if they were states in an international environment. And, paradoxically, because a deeper positive consensus is lacking, institutional procedures must serve as the balancers essential to the condition of stability. In the United States pluralism plus legitimacy (the basis of public security) make democratic practices possible; in Lebanon pluralism plus democratic practices (the mechanism for the balance of power) make public security possible.

THE DEVELOPMENT PROBLEM

If stability were the only issue in politics, the balance-of-power process observable in Lebanon might be judged a complete solution for all states not blessed with positive consensus. Of course, there are other basic issues that affect the stability problem. The question of national development is one of them. National development is a problem for a new political system, in that it requires innovation and rational coordination. In the post-World War II era it is a problem that no state can evade. It is a problem that the process of social mobilization aggravates and ameliorates simultaneously. Because new states lack the infrastructures and human skills requisite for undirected economic "take-off," the problem falls on the sector that generates the demand in the first place: the political system. During its first decade of independence, the Lebanese Republic was spared the full rigors of demands for development, largely because its talented commercial elite successfully influenced the government to institute liberal tariff and monetary policies. These measures, known collectively as the policy of the "free economy," are as politically significant as is the most radical socialist planning. Furthermore, the balance of power operated adequately enough during that first crucial decade to provide the domestic order necessary for a commercial economy. In subsequent years, however, the demands for direct political intervention in behalf of national development have greatly increased; and with these demands has emerged the latent contradiction between the balance-of-power process essential for basic stability and the need for greater central power to provide the newly demanded capabilities.

What does "national development" entail in a state like Lebanon? Insofar as it is confined to the development of water, electricity, and transportation facilities, it does not tax the balance-of-power process unduly. But, when it begins to involve administering a social-security system or decentralizing medical services, it strains the capabilities of the system. Sensitive foreign-policy issues, like those that arose during the Suez War of 1956 and the Arab-Israeli War of 1967, can nearly dislocate the balance, because important minority groups differ sharply over what the national interest really is. All these stresses converge upon the Presidency. As the main repository of authoritative power, the Presidency has become the locus of political modernization, and the conflict between the President and traditional power holders has become increasingly severe. But, just as nuclear technology exerted restraining effects on behavior in the international system, there are factors that check disintegration of the analogous system within the Lebanese Republic. All the sectors in this little system, to the extent that they share an interest in maintaining it, are restrained by the same forces that tend to drive them apart. The demand for socioeconomic growth coupled with a vocal radical socialist movement elsewhere in the Arab world hangs like a sword of Damocles over notables and government alike. Lebanese politicians, who have learned to compromise in order to preserve pluralistic autonomy and stability, are well aware of the advantages of similar accommodation of the new regional forces. Although lacking central control and legitimacy, the Lebanese system thus does in a limited way coordinate itself for national development. Whether or not this rudimentary capability will be sufficient in the long run depends upon a leveling off of the environmental loads.

THE PROBLEM OF SOCIAL JUSTICE

One of the hallmarks of the postwar ferment in the Arab world, one at least as important as national development, has been the increasingly powerful pressure on political systems for fairer representation and more equitable distribution of wealth and status. Insofar as demands for social justice are directly related to the stability problem, the Lebanese system makes sophisticated adjustments in a complex but efficient manner. Justice in confessional terms is thus meted out according to a strict formula: Political and administrative representation by sect is numerically balanced. The distribution of real power is adjusted incessantly through a complex interplay of traditional pressures. Although sectarianism functions primarily to preserve stability, its beneficial effects for social justice are not negligible. A similar argument can be made for the representation of regions and great families, as well as for pro-Western and pan-Arab interests. The essence of ordinary Lebanese politics is the continuous incremental adjustment of these interests.

A second aspect of social justice is political liberty. Lebanon is rightly known for its tolerance of diverse opinions. Almost every political element can be heard in Lebanon and can operate with relative freedom. This salutary situation is doubtless possible as much because of the weakness of central authorities as because of a genuine spirit of tolerance, but whatever its causes it is functional in terms of demands for social justice. Repression is directed only to opinion and activities judged injurious to all the elements in the Lebanese mosaic, and it is frequently ineffective. In the eyes of radical Arab politicians Lebanon may be archaic, but it is hardly despotic. And its liberal characteristics give it considerable moral and political weight.

Beyond this basic liberalism, however, the capacity for institutional adjustment declines; and, as social justice becomes more a matter of income redistribution, class and status equality, and transnational philosophies, it presents a more pressing problem. Liberalism, like the concurrent-majority arrangement, harmonizes with the historical necessities of the balance of power; but redistributive justice, like planned development, does not. Here, indeed, the Lebanese system is weakest. This weakness is becoming increasingly critical because of the rapid political mobilization of both masses and new elites. The latter tend to favor radical reform to an extent that challenges the balance of power. Lebanese notables, no matter how liberal they may be, are loath to undermine their own positions by approving land reforms, progressive taxation, and curbs on the "free economy." Opponents of the new social justice in Lebanon point to the experience of the progressive Arab states, arguing that those states redistribute poverty, not wealth. The comparison, however, has another edge, which many Lebanese notables have also perceived: Elites that have not adjusted to the demands for redistributive justice have perished. The Lebanese establishment, therefore, is confronted with a potential dilemma: To adjust to the new social justice and the newly politicized elements may lead to a derangement of the traditional balance of power, with its attendant instability; not to adjust may invite the total destruction of the political system.

POLITICAL MODERNIZATION

"Like the states of seventeenth-century Europe," Samuel P. Huntington has written, "the non-Western countries of today can have political modernization or they can have democratic pluralism, but they cannot normally have both." [4] Lebanon has shown signs of abnormality. The balance-of-power situation has forced upon it a little of each. In the absence of legitimized central control, a kind of democratic pluralism has been a necessity rather than a luxury. Similarly, under the increasing pressures of modernization, the balance has been altered to accommodate the moderate development of rationalized authority, differentiated political structures, and mass participation. These accommodations must be analyzed, as we have suggested, in a setting of interrelated environmental stresses: Failure to handle the problems of national development and social justice will have adverse repercussions on stability, and by the same token too much success in those areas may be equally disastrous. The critical questions are yet to be answered. How much alteration will such a delicately balanced system sustain without collapsing? How strong are the disintegrative tensions inherent in such a fragmented political culture, shaken as it is by conflicting external and social-mobilization demands? Analysis of these questions is the purpose of this study.

NOTES

[1] Michael C. Hudson, "A Case of Political Underdevelopment," *Journal of Politics,* Vol. 29, No. 4 (November 1967).

[2] Edward Shils, *Political Development in the New States* (1959), mimeo. According to this typology, Lebanon could be described as a political democracy, a "tutelary" democracy, a modernizing oligarchy, or a traditional oligarchy. It could not be described as a totalitarian oligarchy. *Cf.* Leonard Binder's typology in *Iran: Political Development in a Changing Society* (Berkeley: University of California Press, 1962), pp. 44–5. Lebanon falls more often into his "traditional" category than into the "conventional" or "rational" category, but it does not fit easily anywhere.

[3] Alexis de Tocqueville, *Democracy in America,* I (New York: Vintage, 1958), 433–6, chaps. 16, 17; David Truman, *The Governmental Process* (New York: Knopf, 1951), chap. 3, pp. 519–24.

[4] Samuel P. Huntington, "Political Modernization: America vs. Europe," *World Politics,* 18, No. 3 (1966), 412.

PART ONE

Stresses

CHAPTER · 1

Obstacles to National Integration

> Dans un pays comme le nôtre, fait de minorités sensiblement égales et également jalouses de leurs droits, où aucun élément ne peut-être prétendre de constituer une majorité oppressive, où il ne saurait être question de régime de contrainte—la seule paix réalisable est une paix consentie, fondée sur l'entente et la collaboration, sur un état d'équilibre.[1]

The above statement by Charles Helou, written after the fall of the Vichy administration in Lebanon and General Catroux's promise of independence, puts Lebanon's historic problem—and its solution—succinctly. For two decades politicians like Charles Helou, acting within an institutional framework specifically predicated on the idea of equilibrium and the principle of the concurrent majority, have successfully implemented this solution and kept the state from disintegrating. Their success is all the more remarkable when the magnitude of the historic disintegrative forces is properly appreciated.

The fragmentation of modern Lebanon's political culture has two dimensions. One is sociocultural and reflects the multiple, diverse, and often contradictory identifications of its peoples. The second derives from the area's vulnerability to and attraction for foreign political interests. The two are interrelated through the dynamics of internal insecurity and external rivalries. Minority groups with historical memories of old enmities understandably look to outside powers or coreligionists for guarantees, and every traditional group is in some sense a minority group. Regional or international powers

17

at the same time find it possible to cultivate client communities; and modern Lebanon has been strategically desirable enough to prove attractive. Both sociocultural parochialism and external intervention tend to be functionally disintegrative for the political system, insofar as they perpetuate loyalties that conflict with identification with the modern Lebanese entity.

PAROCHIAL TENDENCIES

Political culture, writes Sidney Verba, "consists of the system of empirical beliefs, expressive symbols, and values which defines the situation in which political action takes place. It provides the subjective orientation to politics." [2] To speak of political culture in Lebanon solely in terms of a body of shared beliefs would ignore its diversity and parochialism, crucial characteristics that function both as blessing and curse for the political system. There are several beliefs shared by most Lebanese, but we shall argue that they are mainly derived from shared suspicions and communal orientations and possess only a thin basis independent of these historical memories.[3] Coordinating a set of highly articulated subcultures is, indeed, one of the two fundamental problems confronting the Lebanese political system. It is a problem that most states, old or new, face in some degree but few in such formidable proportions. Religious, communal, and kinship cleavages have made Lebanon politically an area of traditional veto groups. Since the Egyptian occupation (1831–1840), these vertical cleavages have been enlarged and exploited both because of external political interests and by related socioeconomic modernization, and the horizontal stratification has taken on increasing political importance.[4] All the more impressive, therefore, is the signal accomplishment of the modern Lebanese political system: institutionalizing traditional pluralism.

To appreciate why this achievement is so notable it is necessary to discuss two broad aspects of the traditional pluralism prevailing in Lebanon. One, which we shall dwell upon only briefly, is the extraordinarily pervasive influence of families and family alliances in politics; the other is the religious and sectarian fragmentation of the country. Together they constitute a particularly intricate pattern of what Professor Carleton Coon calls the "mosaic culture" of the Near East, and they constitute a crucial intervening variable in the political life of Lebanon.[5] So strong are these factors that Lebanon's political institutions, traditional and modern, have been molded to reflect them. It would be a mistake to underestimate the success of an institutional equilibrium that has averted many a crisis and produced at least a superficial stability. The fact remains, however, that the several "primordial sentiments" dividing the Lebanese polity greatly retard its political modernization by promoting *immobilisme* and hindering the development of rationalized authority structures.[6] They foster political loyalties that ignore the Republic in favor of either local or supranational interests. Indeed, Lebanon's institutional solution only perpetuates and strengthens these divisions.

Political Cliques

The characteristic political pattern in Lebanon, as throughout geographical Syria, is the labyrinthine, shifting factionalism of local notables with their clienteles of supporters. This pattern is part of the traditional culture and social structure of the Near East, in that it merges the political domain with prevailing kinship and semifeudal relations. It also has survived the numerous impositions of imperial power from outside. The extended family is the basic political, as well as social, unit in Lebanon. This structure—patrilineal, patrilocal, patriarchal, and endogamous—comprises the power base of nearly all the important politicians in modern Lebanon, just as it did for the notables during the Tanukh, the Maan, and the Chehab dynasties of the Mamluk and Ottoman periods.[7] Governed as it is by an elaborate hierarchical code of obligations and interwoven into the larger social units of clan, village, and tribe, the family is the primary bulwark of the notable's local autonomy. When notables of different families come together in a clique, they pool their traditional power, and, insofar as they command strong loyalties from their respective families, they become formidable obstacles to the centralizer, rationalizer, or unifier.[8] A French scholar has written of Lebanon: "Les communautés libanaises sont donc en fait non seulement de véritables communautés religieuses mais aussi de véritables nations et des fédérations de familles patriarchales." [9]

The existence of such families, however, only begins to explain the complexities of traditional pluralism in the Lebanon. It is also necessary to consider the lingering influence of Near Eastern feudalism in its varying forms. This feudalism, as Iliya Harik has argued, is significant as a political as well as an economic system; it established formal power relations between notables at every level, from the ruling amir, through the baronial *muqataajis,* the lesser *shaykhs,* and finally the local peasantry.[10] The mechanism establishing this relationship was the *iqṭāʿ* taxation system. Under the Seljuks, in the late eleventh century, the revenue of villages was divided into two categories for taxation purposes. One part, the *khas* or *miri,* went directly to the ruler, but the other, the *iqṭāʿ,* was collected by local officials, partially for their own use and partially for disbursement on projects of the central administration. The *iqṭāʿ,* in effect, was a kind of monetary fief. In the Lebanese mountains especially, the *iqṭāʿ* was more prevalent than were the more direct forms of taxation, and local autonomy was higher than in other parts of the Empire.[11] The *iqṭāʿ* system thus reinforced and perpetuated the local autonomy of the great families from the lesser families and the peasants, while the concomitant absence of effective general power drove the lesser elements to establish allegiance with the local chiefs in return for protection. At the same time the existence of many quite autonomous power centers, a condition reinforced by the mountainous terrain, necessitated the emergence of factional politics and elaborate bargaining processes. For two and a half centuries under the Chehabs, the double *qa'imaqamiyyah,* the *mutasar-rifiyyah,* the French Mandate, and now the independent Republic, family alliances rooted in these socioeconomic patterns have played the dominant political role in the region.[12] The decline of feudalism in the latter part of the reign of the Chehab prince, Amir Bashir II, culminating in the European-guaranteed reforms of 1861, initiated a new phase of the society of the Lebanon; yet even today in Mount Lebanon the shell of the old feudal structure shapes the distribution of power, and old feudal families like the Chehab, Arslan, Jumblat, Talhouk, Khazen, and Karam play an essential role.[13] And in the districts added to Mount Lebanon in 1920 the vestiges of feudalism, economic as well as political, are still evident, although even there new forces are stirring.[14] So deeply ingrained are these particularistic loyalty patterns, so pervasive is the influence of the great families, so intertwined are political and social affiliations that a century of Westernization—both material and intellectual—has not worn them away. The feud is as much a part of Lebanese life in the 1960s as it was a century earlier. It ranges from the everyday vendetta involving family honor to full-fledged clan wars that disrupt national political life. The Maronite families around the town of Zagharta in North Lebanon, for example, periodically engage in battles that require the intervention of a full army brigade. Electoral activity and rational political participation in general are frequently disrupted by family feuds. Even if there were no religious cleavages in present-day Lebanon, there would still be a politics of clique and balance, and there would still be formidable traditional barriers to building a positive identity with the national state.

Religious-Sectarian Cleavages

Albert Hourani has written, "The primary divisions inside the Near East are, as they have been for over a thousand years, religious: whether a man is Moslem, Christian, or Jew, and which branch of the Moslem, Christian, or Jewish community he belongs to." [15] Nowhere is the truth of this statement more apparent than in the Lebanon, and the independent Republic finds this particular manifestation of traditional pluralism an increasingly critical problem.

The sects are politically important because they are traditionally the primary social organizations through which political security has been maintained. In Lebanon the sects have long been organized in semiautonomous communities, and the religious chiefs have had distinct political functions. This form of organization has been particularly strong in the Maronite community, whose clergy were important in undermining the *iqtāʿ* system during and after the Chehab dynasty.[16] These closely knit communities, institutionalized as *millets* under the Ottoman domination, maintain their own personal-status laws and effective internal systems for conflict resolution even in modern Lebanon. In times of trouble one is compelled to identify himself as a Christian or a non-Christian; in ordinary times it is often necessary for an individual to assert or exploit his membership in a particular sect, like the Sunnite (Muslim) or the Maronite (Christian). It is difficult for any outside observer to speak at length about the intensity of sectarian feelings, but it is safe to say that they involve a more complete commitment than do the kinds of religious affiliation common to the West; hence their relevance to politics. Not, however, that the Lebanese in general are highly religious; rather, sectarian affiliations are communal and sect affiliation has a corporate aspect. The two strongest sects, the Maronites and the Sunnites, share a wide range of cultural and ethnic characteristics and outlooks. Indeed, their corporate spirit spills over into the political realm. Strong Maronites regard Mount Lebanon as their territory, and their creed includes a claim to dominion over it; similarly, many Sunnites feel an affinity with the Arab-Muslim world around them and identify with Arab nationalist and unity movements. Mutual insecurity results in incessant competition for power

—the scarcest and dearest value; political tension is the final product.

Because sects are represented in Parliament and administration according to their presumed porportions of the population and because the census that determined these proportions was taken in 1932, there is an understandable reluctance on the part of the elite, with its interest in the status quo, to examine the confessional proportions again. Therefore the real confessional breakdown of the population today is a politically sensitive issue about which little solid information is available.[17] Table 1 presents an official estimate

TABLE 1

LEBANESE POPULATION BY SECT, 1956

Sect	Estimated Population
Maronite	424,000
Sunnite	286,000
Shiite	250,000
Greek Orthodox	149,000
Greek Catholic	91,000
Druze	88,000
Armenian Orthodox	64,000
Armenian Catholic	15,000
Protestant	14,000
Jewish	7,000
Syrian Catholic	6,000
Syrian Orthodox	5,000
Latins (Roman Catholic)	4,000
Nestorean Chaldeans	1,000
Others	7,000
Total	1,411,000

Sir Reader Bullard (ed.), *The Middle East: A Political and Economic Survey* (3d ed.; London: published by Oxford University Press for the Royal Institute of International Affairs, 1958), p. 453.

made in 1956 and may be taken as a rough indicator of the present situation.

The accuracy of these proportions in the middle 1960s is impossible to ascertain; the Lebanese government refuses to divulge its own recent estimates. It is probable, however, that the rate of increase of non-Christians (Sunnite and Shiite Muslims and Druzes) is higher than that of Christians, for reasons that will be discussed in Chapter 3, and that therefore the proportions are changing. In most states such a demographic shift might have scant political relevance, but in Lebanon it challenges the myth that supports the entire intricate governmental structure. According to the myth, this structure is legitimate because it allocates political positions by sect according to each sect's share of total population. The 1932 census found that Christians exceeded non-Christians in a ratio of six to five, and political positions were allocated accordingly. For example, seats in the Lebanese Parliament are distributed precisely on this basis. In the ninety-nine-member Parliaments of 1960 and 1964 the Maronites were allotted twenty seats, the Greek Orthodox eleven, the Greek Catholics six, the Armenian Orthodox four, the Armenian Catholics, Protestants, and Christian minorities one apiece for a Christian total of fifty-four. The forty-five non-Christian seats were distributed as follows: Sunnites twenty, Shiites nineteen, and Druzes six. These proportions have been maintained in all the Parliaments of the independent Republic. The formula, furthermore, provides that the President of the Republic be a Maronite, the Prime Minister a Sunnite, the Speaker of the Chamber of Deputies a Shiite, and the Deputy Speaker and Deputy Prime Minister Greek Orthodox. Cabinet portfolios are carefully distributed among Christians and non-Christians, and key ministries are reserved for particular sects; the Foreign Minister is always a Christian and usually a Maronite; the Interior Minister is usually Sunnite; the Defense Minister is usually Druze. Furthermore, every sect has a fixed share of important administrative posts.

Ingenious as this arrangement is, it has obvious drawbacks. Real power is not easily parceled out according to numerical formula, and the non-Christian sects have long complained that the Christians, and especially the Maronites, are disproportionately powerful. This complaint was an important cause of the 1958 civil war, and one of the results of that crisis was the equalizing of administrative and Cabinet post allocations between the two religions. As long as the real population proportions are debatable, the legitimacy conferred by the myth is frail indeed.

One might ask why such elaborate arrangements are necessary. Part of the answer is apparent to any American who lives in a large city like New York or observes the national political conventions: A religiously and ethnically balanced ticket makes political sense. But political sectarianism in Lebanon runs somewhat deeper than in the United States, and ethnic security is a higher-priority issue. Every sect has memories of historical periods of subservience, and in the relatively short span since the Chehab dynasty there has been

outright conflict. In Mount Lebanon Shiites and Maronites clashed in the eighteenth century and Druzes and Maronites in the nineteenth century. In the twentieth century since World War I, the normal social relations between Sunnite Muslims and Christians, especially the Maronites, have been inflamed and remain tense today. The rise of indigenous "national" feelings in the last two centuries, closely interwoven with sectarian loyalties and exacerbated by outside intervention—political, military, economic, and cultural —has contributed to the contemporary fragmentation of the political culture in Lebanon.

To appreciate the sectarian problem it is necessary to observe the distribution of the major sects and their doctrinal differences.[18] Table 2 presents an estimate of the distribution of the major sects in the districts of Lebanon (see also Map 1). Although each sect is thickly concentrated in certain areas, there is not a single district without visible, if not substantial, minority representation. This distribution begins to make clear why the major sects can retain some political autonomy and how the ecological situation imposes a substantial mutual tolerance: Every sect in effect holds hostages of other sects and is simultaneously vulnerable to reprisals. There is no love lost, for example, between the Sunnites of Tripoli and the Maronites of neighboring Zagharta, but intemperate behavior is deterred by the existence of small minorities of each sect in each place. Similarly, the Greek Orthodox, the Sunnites, the Shiites, and the Druzes, of the Merjayoun district, share a common incentive to live together peacefully, as do the Shiites and Maronites in Kisrwan; the

FIGURE 1. *President of All. Left to Right: Protestant, Armenian Orthodox, Shiite, Druze, Greek Orthodox, Sunnite, Maronite.*

Sunnites and Shiites in Baalbek; the Maronites, Shiites, and Druzes in Baabda; and all the sects found in Beirut. Communal separatism is strong, but living together is a practical possibility as long as the sectarian balance of power remains stable at the national level. The reason that communal identities remain so strong, reinforced rather than obliterated by the communications explosion, is the result of historic doctrinal differences and memories of oppression, both antique and recent.

The Maronites, the largest single sect, composing some 29 per cent of the total population, appeared in northern Syria during the sixth century and were driven into the Lebanese mountains in the early part of the seventh century by the Islamic tribes from Arabia.[19] The patron saint of the Maronite Church is an ascetic monk, Maroun, who seems to have lived early in the fifth century, but its founder was Yuhanna Maroun (*c.* A.D. 707), under whom the sect developed a distinct communal and political organization. Although the Maronites have been speaking Arabic since the fifteenth century, they retain Syriac derivations of the original Aramaic in their liturgy. From their beginnings the Maronites fell into bloody conflict with such rival sects as the Jacobites and later, in the seventh century and after, faced more formidable foes, ". . . holding with one arm the Moslem caliph and with the other the Byzantine emperor."[20] It is said, although many Maronites now deny it, that the sect professed the Monothelite heresy (the doctrine that Christ has two Natures but one Will) between the seventh and twelfth centuries. With the invasion of the Crusaders, however,

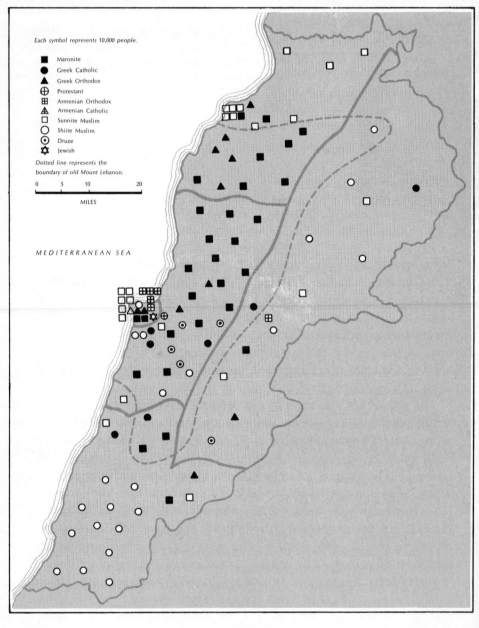

MAP 1

*Ottoman Mount Lebanon and Recent Distribution
of Major Lebanese Sects*

After Pierre Rondot, *Les Institutions Politiques du Liban* (Paris: Imprimerie
Nationale, 1947), p. 32. Reprinted by permission of Institut des Etudes Islamiques
de l'Université de Paris and General Pierre Rondot.

TABLE 2

DISTRIBUTION OF RELIGIOUS COMMUNITIES IN LEBANON, 1950

PERCENTAGE OF POPULATION OF DISTRICT*

District	Maronite	Greek Orthodox	Greek Catholic	Armenian Orthodox	Sunnite	Shiite	Druze
Akkar	18	2	1	0	52	0	0
Tripoli	5	10	0	1	78	0	0
Zagharta	90	3	0	0	6	0	0
Batroun	76	18	2	0	1	3	0
Koura	28	63	0	0	8	4	0
Hermel	3	0	30	0	6	62	0
Baalbek	12	2	4	0	12	68	0
Zahleh	19	10	23	8	24	10	1
Kisrwan	85	2	1	2	1	8	0
Metn	51	9	5	19	0	0	30
Baabda	48	8	3	1	3	18	18
Aley	29	16	3	0	1	2	46
Chouf	34	0	9	0	22	2	31
Saida	8	0	8	0	18	62	0
Jezzine	63	0	16	0	3	5–20	1–5
Rachaya	4	25	2	0	28	0	37
Merjayoun	6	14	5	0	13	45	13
Tyre	6	0	6	2	4	80	0
Beirut	8	11	3	24	24	6	1–5

* Percentages by *caza* (district) are the same as those calculated after the evaluation of population on December 31, 1944. That is the most recent date for which there are figures on confessional distribution for *cazas* as well as *muhafazas* (provinces). Religious data for the entire populations of the *cazas* were not available; therefore the columns for districts do not total 100 per cent. Several of the minor sects have been omitted.

Etienne de Vaumas, "La Répartition Confessionelle au Liban et l'Equilibre de l'Etat Libanais," *Revue de Géographie Alpine,* 43 (1955), 511–603.

the Maronites entered into communion with the Roman Church. The relationship was strengthened in the late sixteenth century and again in the year 1964, when the Patriarch of the Maronites was made a cardinal. By the fourteenth century, Maronites were located in numerous villages from Qadisha in the North to the Nahr (River) Ibrahim in Mount Lebanon, and foreign travelers were impressed with their organizational capacities.[21] Despite harsh Mamluk domination, the Maronites prospered and spread southward and into the Biqa, where they mixed, none too peacefully, with the Shiites, also seeking refuge in the mountains; traces of Maronite-Shiite friction in the Biqa remain to the present day, despite the presence of a common potential Sunnite threat.[22] Farther south the Maronites established relatively friendly relations with the politically dominant Druzes. But during the eighteenth century, as the Maronite community continued to increase rapidly in numbers and wealth, it began to challenge Druze power, and by the middle of the nineteenth century it had largely succeeded in displacing that power. This community's political success, achieved by a militant clergy, which had engendered a strong ethnic, protonational feeling, was an underlying cause of the great massacres of 1860. These massacres climaxed several years of violence in which the Druze nobility resisted with force the changes being pressed by Maronite peasantry and priesthood. They left 11,000 Christians killed, 4,000 dead from destitution, and 100,000 homeless.[23] This dreadful memory helps to explain the unusual cohesion and suspicious outlook of the community today. The massacres precipitated not only the end of feudalism among the Maronites, converting them into a community primarily of small farmers, but also the open intervention of the European powers, which placed Mount Lebanon under the jurisdiction of a Christian governor. This foreign guarantee for the Maronites and, to a lesser extent, for the other Christian sects was strengthened with the imposition of the French Mandate in 1920. With the end of direct foreign protection in World War II, the Maronites, as chief beneficiaries under the old arrangements, were understandably uneasy about independence.

The Greek Orthodox, comprising something over 10 per cent of the population, are the second largest Christian community and trace their origins to the historic split between Byzantine and Roman Christianity in 1054. The Eastern Church developed national churches like the Russian, Serbian, and Greek, each with its own patriarch and autonomous religious jurisdiction. In the nineteenth century the Greek Orthodox Church in the Near East took Arabic for its liturgical language and Arabs for its priests. Many of the Orthodox consider themselves distinctly Eastern, opposed to the Roman Church and the infallibility of the Pope, and some consider themselves purer Arabs than the Sunnite Muslims are, recalling their origins as Arab tribes and inheritors of the original Eastern Empire.[24] Since the end of the Byzantine Empire, Moscow has assumed the spiritual and political importance for many of the Orthodox faithful that France has for the Maronites. The Russian Revolution, however, has weakened, though not obliterated, that historic tie. In modern Lebanon the Greek Orthodox is perhaps the most urbanized and best-educated community. It includes much of the financial elite, yet it also supplies some of the most radical and destabilizing elements. Of all the Christian communities the Greek Orthodox has been the most favorable toward pan-Arab nationalism and the least happy with a political system dominated by a sect in communion with Rome. By the same token it has performed important mediating functions in the crises of the independent Republic.

Lebanon's Greek Catholics are a splinter group of the Orthodox. They were persuaded in 1709 that the Church should return to Rome, but they failed to convince the majority and have since held a rather defensive position in relation to that majority. Their Patriarch alternates his residence between Cairo and Damascus. In modern Lebanon the Greek Catholics are bunched in the middle districts, or *cazas,* of Mount Lebanon Province and in the medium-sized towns.[25] Both the Greek Catholics and the Greek Orthodox have achieved exceptionally high rates of literacy and social mobility. Their upper classes are mainly large merchants, financiers, and bankers. These communities are numerically too small to obtain any of the primary positions under Lebanon's system of political sectarianism; nevertheless, they have come to exercise great power behind the scenes. One well-informed observer has remarked, "Indeed, the making and unmaking of Lebanese statesmen was, certainly before 1958, almost a prerogative of the Greek Orthodox and Greek Catholic upper class." [26]

The most recent group to find refuge in Lebanon, with the exception of the Palestinian Arabs, is the Armenian community. The fourth largest Christian sect (the greater part of it is Orthodox), it is also the least assimilated of all the religious-ethnic groups in Lebanon and is the only community that does not use Arabic in normal conversation. The Armenians were driven through Asia Minor and into Syria during the Turkish massacres in 1895, 1909, and 1922, and in 1929 the Ataturk regime evicted more. In 1938, when the French ceded Syria's Alexandretta province (Hatay) to Turkey, more Armenians fled south toward Lebanon. Many Armenians still regard themselves as foreigners in Lebanon, and many indigenous residents of Lebanon regard them the same way.[27] The language problem and the fresh memory of oppression perpetuate Armenian cohesiveness, but the Armenians' Christianity gives them an extremely important bond with Lebanon's Christian communities, and they have been welcomed by such political groups as the Kataeb, which have a strong interest in maintaining the myth that Lebanon is predominantly Christian. Since 1943 a few seats in Parliament have been reserved for Armenians, and in 1960 one of their deputies was named to a special cabinet position. In the middle 1960s Armenians are demanding regular participation in the cabinet.

Lebanon's three major non-Christian communities are the Sunnite or orthodox Muslims, the Shiite or heterodox Muslims, and the Druzes, an offshoot of the Shiites.[28] The Sunnites constitute the second largest community in the Lebanese Republic, with perhaps 20 per cent of the population. There are reasons, discussed in Chapter 2, for thinking that this estimate is low. In any case, the percentage does not include the considerable number of Sunnite resident aliens who are Palestinian refugees or Syrian laborers. Since Mamluk times, the Sunnites have been dominant in the coastal plain and in the towns of Tyre, Saida, Beirut, and Tripoli. There are also concentrations in the hinterlands of Akkar, the Biqa, and South Lebanon. The mountains, however, have historically been closed to the Sunnites, remaining havens for the Maronites, Druzes, and Shiites. The decision of the French authorities in 1920 to create a state of Greater Lebanon by annexing these largely Sunnite areas to historic Mount Lebanon was galling to the many Sunnites who had enjoyed relatively privileged positions under Ottoman dominion and to those Sunnite Arab nationalists who saw the Arab Revolt betrayed by its Western sponsors. As for the Maronite Christians, as long as their French protectors governed Lebanon, they were content to see their traditional domain extended to ensure an economically viable state.

Lebanon's Sunnites are composed of a small class of large landowners, a professional and commercial bourgeoisie, and a large stratum of peasants and workers. Like orthodox Muslims everywhere, they believe in the supremacy of one God and in His teachings, which were set down by Muhammad, his last and greatest Prophet, and elaborated in the Traditions and Laws of Islam. To the Sunnite the Caliphate, the now defunct legitimizing office of the Islamic community, and the Sultanate, the highest political authority, were always theoretically congruent; to him the polarity between church and state, which so profoundly marks Western political development, was inconceivable. When the Ottoman Empire began to decay rapidly during the reign of Abdel-Hamid II, the Sultan tried deliberately to resuscitate his authority by emphasizing his role as Caliph. Sunnites were thus under spiritual obligation to the political authorities and enjoyed concomitant status as true believers. Nonbelievers were persecuted, and deviant believers —other "people of the Book"—were tolerated but not as equals. Herein lies much of the contemporary friction between Lebanese Christians and Muslims, for after 1920 the status ranks were in effect reversed. Liberation from Ottoman rule placed the Sunnites of the coast under the dominance of the French and their favored clientele, the Maronites. It also destroyed the legitimizing religious tie that had customarily sealed their obedience to authority. At the same time, it separated them from their coreligionists in Syria and beyond. The politics of the independent Republic has revolved to a great extent around the problem of integrating the Sunnites into the political system. Although this problem has been controlled, it has not been solved: Just as the other minorities cherish their autonomous pasts, so many Sunnites feel traditional attachment to a political-religious entity beyond the borders of the little state.

The Shiites and the Druzes together probably outnumber the Sunnites, another circumstance that tempers the Christian-Muslim confrontation in Lebanon. Both groups are heterodox offshoots of orthodox Islam; both have known persecution at the hands of the Sunnites, for example, under the Mamluks at the turn of the fourteenth century. The Shiites parted with orthodox Islam during the seventh century at the time of the struggle between Muawiya (founder of the Ummayad Caliphate at Damascus) and Ali for the succession to Muhammad's divinely ordained position of leadership. Ali was the Prophet's son-in-law, and his supporters were the Shiites. When Ali lost and when his son Hussein was killed at the Battle of Kerbela (681), the dissidents left the fold completely. Since then a number of Shiite communities with varying dogmas have appeared in the Muslim world. Lebanon's Shiites believe that the true succession to Muhammad passed through Ali to a line of eleven other *imams,* or spirit heads, the last of whom disappeared in the ninth century but who is expected to reappear at some time in the future.[29] These Shiites, known as the Metawali, have been described by one French scholar as less puritanical and more emotional in their religious behavior than are the Sunnites, commemorating, for example, the death of Hussein every year with pilgrimages and parades noted for their fervor.[30] In contemporary Lebanon the Shiites appear to be the poorest of all the sects, the least socially mobile, and the least exposed to modernity. They are primarily serfs or indentured farmers in southern Lebanon, a poor agricultural area, and in the northern Biqa. Theirs is possibly the most feudal of the sects, and their leadership—the heads of the major families and clans like the Hamadehs and the Assaads—has been venerated, it is said, with almost religious devotion. As a sect, their lot has been hard since what one scholar calls their "golden age" in the tenth and eleventh centuries—the time at which the Shiite Fatimid Caliphate in Cairo protected the heterodox in Syria.[31] With the decline of the Fatimids, the coming of the Crusaders, and the rise of the orthodox Mamluks and later the Ottomans, the Shiites were largely driven out of Mount Lebanon and reduced to the condition of backwardness from which they have only recently begun to emerge. One of the most interesting political developments in the postwar period has been, as we shall see, the gradual modernization of Shiite leadership, a trend accompanied, of course, by demands for a greater share of power.

Of all the politically relevant sects, the Druze is the most paradoxical. Offspring of the Ismailiyyah, one of the Shiite heterodoxies, the Druzes are described by Philip Hitti as ". . . a religious community that has survived for nine centuries like a fossil." [32] It is an accurate description in many ways, for it is true that the Druzes are extremely closely knit socially, yet at the same time Druzes in modern Lebanon operate an airline serving Bombay, London, and Accra, as well as the entire Middle East; they produce numbers of engineers and doctors; and they support Lebanon's only indigenous socialist party. Whether or not the Druzes are also losing their communal identity—their religion prohibits proselytizing—is a debated point, but the evidence of such identity displayed during the 1958 crisis and in their daily life suggests that it is still very strong. The Druzes believe that the Fatimid Caliph Hakim, who ruled in Egypt between 996 and 1021, was the tenth and most perfect reincarnation of God. This remarkable leader, however, died mysteriously, and his worshipers, mostly Persian in origin, were forced to flee into Syria and the Lebanon. In 1031, the Druze community was closed to outsiders, and its belief and ritual remain somewhat obscure even into the present time. Within the community a distinction is made between the religious elite, the *'uqqāl,* who are privy to the inner secrets of the religion, and the ordinary believers, the *juhhāl,* who are ignorant of these mysteries. The past onslaughts of more powerful communities are reflected in the article of Druze belief known as *taqiyya,* which permits the Druze to profess an alien faith if survival requires it. Several of the Druze areas are still semifeudal in socioeconomic structure, a characteristic also found among the Sunnites and Shiites but to a much lesser extent among the Christians.

Politically, the Druzes reached their peak during the Maan dynasty, which governed in the Chouf area of Mount Lebanon from 1516 until 1697, when the line expired and the Chehab family (then Sunnite) replaced it. Under the great Fakhr al-Din II (1586–1635), the Druzes controlled the area from the Antioch plain to Safad, just below the southern boundary of modern Lebanon, and east to the Syrian desert until the new Ottoman authorities finally put an end to his career. Fakhr al-Din was a tolerant ruler and reopened the Lebanon to European influence: French and Florentine merchants established commercial enterprises, and some Christian missionaries were admitted. But inbreeding, isolation, and the line of lesser Maanids who followed Fakhr al-Din weakened the political power of the Druzes, while the Maronites gained in strength. During the Chehab dynasty (1697–1842), the scales tipped in favor of the Maronites.[33] The Druzes, however, have remained a potent force in the tangled politics of the area, and today the leaders of their rival internal factions play conspicuous roles in nearly every cabinet and assembly, frequently acting as balancer among the larger groups and exercising effective vetos in crises.

The parochialism manifest in Lebanon's family, community, and sectarian structures poses severe environmental adversities for political modernization, yet so far the Republic has narrowly but consistently avoided disaster. That parochialism has not degenerated more often into anarchy or stagnation is essentially the result of political institutions and practices that mesh the various traditional veto groups with one another. This meshing was present in the traditional political system under the Chehab amirs and in the *mutasarrifiyyah* system imposed by foreign interests in the later nineteenth century. It is also present under the Republic, largely because laissez-faire political liberalism is surprisingly congruent with Lebanon's traditional pluralism. In terms of individual and corporate autonomy—values cherished in modern systems that have largely lost them—Lebanese parochialism has desirable consequences. Points of access are numerous, and methods of political recourse that are meaningful to the individual are available. But, in terms of political modernization, which requires centralization, greater governmental intervention, and rationalized procedures, this parochialism poses serious problems. It limits the capacity of the political instrumentalities to induce significant change. As long as there are few elements seeking radical change, the problem is manageable, and the stability produced by Lebanon's neotraditional system has thus far thrown a veil of affluence over the sores of discontent. Whether or not Lebanon's uneven prosperity can alone control the demands for change arising from social mobilization is an open question.

Parochialism also limits the strength of general loyalty toward the country itself. Autonomy may provide a degree of communal security, but by weakening the possibility of authoritative central rule it simultaneously promotes new insecurity. Because the confidence that these communities have in the state is frail, the temptation and need to seek support beyond Lebanon's borders, to the West or to the Arab world, are all the more intense. The legitimacy problem is sustained by this vicious circle, and the cure—local autonomy—only strengthens the malady. As a political culture, Lebanon is a collection of traditional communities bound by the mutual understanding that other communities cannot be trusted. Such a state of affairs may seem grim, but it is assuredly several steps above a Hobbesian state of nature, in which a man is quite certain that all others are his enemies. In Lebanon, at least, the communities can be confident that the other groups, however untrustworthy they may be, have a common stake in the status quo; and the sophisticated Lebanese assume rightly that all important elements know that their counterparts are aware, as they are, that any one can pull down the entire structure. Mutual deterrence and actors with devastating but relatively equal power create an uneasy perpetual truce. Although this situation is better than anarchy, it is still not as good as a consensus founded on positive trust.

EXTERNAL INFLUENCES

From the beginning of recorded history, the Lebanon has been the object of conflicting foreign interests. The Republic that today occupies this crossroads is heir not only to the particularisms of traditional culture but also to the cosmopolitanism resulting from these intrusions. Lebanon as a political entity is, in this rich context, a recent creation: By the most liberal reckoning it dates from the establishment of the Chehab dynasty in 1697 and by a more conservative measure from the Règlement Organique of 1861. The modern state itself, with its critical sectarian composition, goes back only to 1920.[34] The idea of national identity is thin indeed in comparison with the accretion of past loyalties, loyalties confined to specific cliques and communities, often conflicting with one another and incessantly manipulated by outside powers and ideologies. External interventions, whether diplomatic, military, or ideological, have contributed greatly to the fragmentation of political culture in the modern Republic. Historians have fully described these penetrations, and it is necessary here only to mention the most recent ones under two broad categories of origin, Western and Arab.

Lebanon as a Western Preserve

When Amir Bashir II became ruler in 1788, the Lebanon was a subsidiary of the Pashalik of Acre, a unit of the Ottoman Empire, and the Amir was preoccupied for some thirty years in combating interference from its governor, Jazzar Pasha. At the same time, the great European powers were taking a new interest in the eastern Mediterranean. Since the discovery of the Cape route to India in the late fifteenth century, the area had been an economic and strategic backwater. In the post-Congress of Vienna world, however, stimulated by Napoleon's adventure in Egypt and the possibility of a canal at Suez, both British and French interests in the area were reactivated. France had traditionally been the dominant trader with the Levant, and it maintained a religious obligation toward Near Eastern Catholics dating from the Crusades and, according to some, even before.[35] The connection was maintained by Catholic missionaries and traders. Louis XIV declared himself protector of the Maronites after that sect had undergone severe mistreatment first at the hands of Mamluk and then of Ottoman sultans. As the Ottoman Empire began to disintegrate in North Africa and the Balkans during the nineteenth century, France's special relationship with the Maronites assumed political, as well as commercial and religious, significance.

Great Britain too began to take an active part in Levant politics as Ottoman authority declined, particularly in view of the new strategic significance of the area. Alarmed by Napoleon's invasion of Egypt, the English set out to counteract French influence in the eastern Mediterranean. In the Lebanon this intervention meant supporting the rivals of the Francophile Maronite clergy and no-bility.[36] During the reign of Bashir II the British, through their diplomatic agents, began to cultivate the Druze community, after they had failed to win over the Amir himself. The latter, toward the end of his reign, found himself allied with the Maronite lords and the Egyptian conqueror Ibrahim Pasha, both of whom enjoyed French support. Ibrahim, son of Muhammad Ali, the anachronistic modernizer who had broken the reins of Ottoman control, had moved Egyptian troops and administrators into part of Palestine and Syria in order to extend his father's domain and had actually occupied those areas from 1831 to 1840.[37] Great Britain opposed this extension of Egyptian hegemony both because it was supported by France and because it weakened the Ottoman buffer. British agents had little difficulty in winning over the Druze *shaykhs,* who had been harshly treated by Amir Bashir.[38]

Austria and Russia were also competing in the Levant, the former hoping to displace France as protector of the Maronites and the latter seeking to advance its political influence through the Russian Orthodox Church. Russia, indeed, after its emergence as a major force in European politics during the Napoleonic period, presented a serious threat, particularly to the British interest. The Crimean War of 1854–1856, neither the first nor the last of Russia's thrusts toward the Mediterranean, was precipitated by its maneuver to protect Orthodox Christians in the Holy Land from alleged Ottoman oppression.

The Ottoman government, meanwhile, pursued a devious course with respect to the Lebanon. Under the *Tanzimat,* the reform and centralization programs (c. 1826–1827), the Porte tried to reassert its authority over the semiautonomous amirate by convincing the European powers that local rule was impossible. By inciting the Druzes against the Maronite-supported Chehab rulers and refusing to curb sectarian strife, Constantinople helped to bring down the Chehab dynasty in 1842 and to replace it with an ineffectual dual administration known as the "double *qa'imaqamiyyah.*" The northern district of Mount Lebanon was to be governed by a Maronite, the southern by a Druze. Because the distribution of sects did not correspond exactly to the division, however, troubles were only magnified. By 1860, owing partly to this feeble arrangement and partly to growing class unrest among the Maronite peasantry, the Lebanon erupted into the civil strife mentioned earlier, during which the Druzes slaughtered thousands of Maronites. The Turkish forces either refused to help the Christians or, in some cases, actually led them to destruction.

Anarchy in the Lebanon was intolerable to the European powers that had done so much to foment it. The Turks moved in to restore order, the French landed troops to relieve the Christian populace, and in June 1861 the six interested powers (Turkey, France, England, Austria, Russia, and Prussia) signed the Règlement Organique, abolishing feudalism and establishing Lebanon as an autonomous province of the Ottoman Empire. Its governor, or *mutasarrif,* was required to be a non-Lebanese Christian appointed by the Porte but approved by the Powers, and he was to be supported by an administrative council with seats allocated to the major sects. The new province was confined only to the Mountain proper (Mount Lebanon), excluding the Sunnite-dominated coastal strip, Beirut, the Biqa, and the northern plain. Under the *mutasarrifiyyah,* which lasted until World War I, it enjoyed peace, educational development, and prosperity. The divisions that foreign governments had stirred up in the struggle for diplomatic superiority were muffled but not eradicated; World War I and its aftermath rekindled them, particularly those between the British and the French. This particular rivalry ironically contributed to Lebanon's ultimate independence, even as it exploited internal parochialism.

External political complications were multiplied when France's High Commissioner and Commander in Chief in Syria, General Gouraud, established the State of Greater Lebanon on August 30, 1920, by attaching a large Muslim area to Christian Mount Lebanon. The offspring of European diplomatic rivalries and sectarian drives, the new state was born schizophrenic; its Catholics were relieved to find French protection, and its Sunnites were embittered by the betrayal of Arab nationalism. The politicians of the modern Republic have been hard pressed to reconcile the political tensions arising out of its origins in the Sykes-Picot and San Remo agreements, and even after two decades of independence from France the question of Lebanon's political identity remains troublesome. The cleavage between Lebanese who identify with the Arab world and those who identify with the West varies with the divergence of Western and Arab political interests. No understanding of modern Lebanon's political weakness is complete without an appreciation of the seeds of discontent sown in the postwar partition of an Arab world just then embarking on a quest for unity. It would be equally misleading, however, to ignore the forces opposed to the Arabization or Islamization of the Lebanon. Not only were the Catholic Christians of the Mountain simultaneously afraid and contemptuous of the "desert Arabs," but there were also groups of Lebanese notables in Cairo and Paris with highly articulated programs for an independent national Lebanese entity to replace the defunct Ottoman rule.[39] In addition to the traditional parochialisms of family, region, sect, and religion that have complicated the governing of Lebanon, a distinctly political issue had thus arisen by the end of World War I over the kind of political "face" that the area ought to have.

The complex and fascinating story of how France established its Mandate, putting a quick end to the efforts of the Sherifian authorities in Damascus to occupy the Lebanon, cannot be told here; but it must be noted that the Christians, and especially the Maronites, welcomed the French administrators in the expectation that they would provide security, Western cultural development, and eventually independence.[40] Whatever history's verdict about the success of the French occupation may be, these Christian expectations were largely fulfilled, in one way or another, by the end of 1943. The High Commission, in its role as Rousseauian legislator, imposed a parliamentary system modeled roughly after the Basic Laws of the Third Republic; it established a centralized administrative apparatus; it encouraged the development of French Catholic private education; and it undertook a program of road building and water-resource development. With the cooperation of certain Christian notables of Beirut and the Mountain, including such future leaders as Michel Chiha, Emile Edde, Bechara al-Khoury, and Charles Debbass, the High Commission, despite its uneven leadership, managed to integrate into the new system the traditional power structure of a large part of the area.[41] Greater Lebanon was ruled directly by governors appointed by the High Commissioner until 1926. At first, the Governor was provided with an Advisory Council of seventeen representatives of the major sects appointed by the High Commissioner. In 1922 this council was replaced by a Representative Council elected through universal male suffrage. The Representative Council became the Constituent Assembly, which in 1926 wrote the Constitution that, with the important modifications of November 1943, remains in effect today. The Constitution is primarily the work of the Greek Catholic banker and publicist, Michel Chiha, a man whose writings provide the most acute and sophisticated exposition of

Lebanon's political raison d'être.[42] It established a parliamentary republic with two chambers (the Senate was abolished in October 1927), collective and individual responsibility of the ministers, universal and direct suffrage, and the distribution of parliamentary seats along sectarian lines. The Constitution also provided that the Parliament should elect a President, who in turn would choose the head of government and the other ministers.[43] Actually, under the Mandate the Constitution was largely a façade, and Lebanon had two parallel governments: on one hand, the Parliament, President, Prime Minister, and Cabinet stipulated in the Constitution and, on the other, the institutions controlled by the High Commission. The latter consisted of the Services Spéciaux, including the security forces, Bedouin control, and administrative apparatus; the Intérêts Communs, with Syria, including customs administration and concessionary companies; and the Troupes Spéciales du Levant.[44] The Mandatory thus held the real power. In November 1943, however, when the French grip was substantially loosened, the newly independent President began to take over the instruments of power once held by the High Commissioner; and this concentration of power has been perhaps the most important, if the least intended, legacy of the Mandate.

Lebanon in the Arab World

The Maronite clergy, led by the astute Patriarch Elias Butros Hawayek, and the Christian Lebanese patriots of the Alliance Libanaise and other groups were gratified by the creation of Greater Lebanon under French supervision; but the Orthodox Muslims and Arab nationalists inside and outside the territory were profoundly disturbed. Their bitterness was a compound of burgeoning aspirations for Arab unity and independence and of a sense of betrayal at the hands of France and Great Britain, the architects of partition and renewed foreign domination. In their eyes, insult was added to injury when France decided to create a state of Greater Lebanon.

Arab and Muslim antagonism toward the idea of a separate Lebanese state cannot be explained without dwelling briefly on the rise of Arab nationalism in Syria. The political ferment of the modern Arab world has been traced back to the Napoleonic invasion of Egypt in 1798 and the opening of that country to Western influence.[45] The Egyptians, however, failed in their effort to dominate all the Arabs, and it was the cultural awakening in coastal Syria—particularly in the Lebanon—during the latter half of the nineteenth century that spurred a distinctly modern and increasingly secular Arab political consciousness.[46] The implantation of foreign educational institutions is the factor chiefly responsible for this awakening, and as early as 1834 American Protestant and French Catholic missionaries and teachers had initiated a revival of the study of Arab history. A succession of missionary educators like the Presbyterians Eli Smith and Cornelius Van Dyke, the French Lazarist fathers, the Jesuits, and the Russian Orthodox built presses and primary schools. Muslim notables too joined in the revival, establishing the Maqasid Society, which founded schools emphasizing Islamic culture. The Jesuit and American universities, which have so profoundly affected the development of the area, were founded in the 1860s. George Antonius, in his definitive study, has described the political off-shoots of this renaissance: the emergence of such outstanding figures as Nasif Yazeji, Butrus Bustani, Jamal al-Din al-Afghani, and Abdul-Rahman Kawakebi and the growth of secret societies, first Christian separatist groups and later movements to reform Ottoman administration and resist the pan-Turkish movement.[47] Ottoman entry into World War I provided the situation and the Arab Revolt the catalyst for a coherent nationalist movement that, a half-century later, is still shaping the politics of the area. A student of Arab nationalism, Hazem Nuseibeh, has written:

> The living and inspiring history of the Arab Rebellion of 1916 was as worthy a title deed as any to nationhood. No one who lived through that experience or has read its literature can fail to be impressed by the genuineness, the depth, and the idealism of its architects as well as of its rank-and-file adherents. . . . [It] marked a new milestone in the ideological development of Arab nationalism.[48]

The collision of French, English, Zionist, and Arab interests in the aftermath of the fighting has been thoroughly analyzed elsewhere, but it is well to emphasize the strength of the Arab national feeling and not simply the weakness of its political institutions.[49]

The existence of strong Arab nationalist sentiment and resentment at French sponsorship of an "artificial" Greater Lebanon were perfectly apparent to observers on the spot throughout the period 1918–1920, when these critical decisions were being taken. In October 1918, for example, a local observer in Beirut reported:

Since the proclamation, October 1st, 1918, of the Cherifian Government, the Moslem population here have entertained the hope of the constitution of an independent Mohammedan Empire. The Mohammedans, without exception, prefer a purely independent Arabian Government, without any foreign protection or intervention in their affairs.[50]

If foreign protection were inescapable, the observer added, "all the Moslems prefer British protection; they hate France." Furthermore, the Greek Orthodox and the Druzes, harboring their own suspicions of Catholic domination, also preferred the British or the Americans. The King-Crane investigation of summer 1919 recognized the dangers inherent in a solution that flouted nascent Arab national feeling. Of the 1,863 petitions received by the Commission in Syria, 203 (of which 196 were from Lebanon) supported the idea of an independent Greater Lebanon, and 1,062 were against it.[51] It recommended that the Lebanon have considerable local autonomy but only as a constituent part of a large Syrian state, on the grounds that such a state would find tolerance of minorities in its national interest, that a small Christian state outside it would be vulnerable to hostility, and that the better-educated Christians would contribute more fully to the development of the area if they had a stake in it.[52] The King-Crane recommendations, however, were ignored by the diplomats. A few months later, in early March 1920, the Syrian General Congress audaciously proclaimed the complete independence and unity of Syria, including autonomy for old Mount Lebanon. But, at the San Remo Conference of April 19–26, Great Britain and France disclosed their very different plans.

Syria was to be broken up into three separate fractions: Palestine, the Lebanon, and a reduced "Syria" consisting of what was left. [The decisions] gave birth to a new sentiment in the Arab world—that of contempt for the Powers of the West. It was not only the denial of the two cherished goals of independence and unity that provoked the revulsion of feeling, but also, and more profoundly, the breach of faith.[53]

Syrian resistance was feeble, and, at the town of Maisaloun on July 24, French troops and artillery brought Faisal's rule in Syria to an end.[54] France had temporarily defeated the Arab nationalist forces, and the Maronites of Lebanon were relieved, but the tensions remained. Greater Lebanon was regarded by at least a sizable minority of its inhabitants—mostly Sunnites but to a lesser extent Druzes, Shiites, and Greek Orthodox—as a state of dubious legitimacy.[55]

Political life during the two decades of Mandate rule reflected the disaffection of the Sunnites. They refused to participate in the new institutions, which they believed, with some justice, to be weighted against their interests. The revolt of 1925–1927 in Syria and growing tension in Palestine aggravated the anti-Western feelings of Sunnite Arabs throughout the area, including Lebanon. The High Commissioner felt obliged to intervene incessantly in the politics of the new Republic. Twice he suspended the Constitution altogether—from May 4, 1932, to January 1, 1934, and from September 21, 1939, to September 21, 1943.[56] Furthermore, even within the tight circle of officially approved Christian notables a cleavage began to appear between a Francophile faction supported by the Maronite Church and a group seeking genuine independence from the Mandatory as soon as possible. The former was headed by Emile Edde and the latter by Bechara al-Khoury. The Khoury group saw the urgent necessity of integrating Arab nationalist Sunnite notables into the political institutions of the state to preserve its viability once independence was achieved, and it took pains to cultivate the support of these notables and to wean them from rigid insistence that an independent Lebanese entity be merged into a united Syria. The survival of the Lebanese Republic after independence in 1943 is a measure of the achievement of this group of liberal Christians. By the same token, the weakness of a national consensus and the delicate balance of tensions that characterize politics in this era reflect the continuing magnitude of Lebanon's political identity crisis.

Independence and a Pragmatic Accommodation

The events of the late 1930s and early 1940s brought the inhabitants of Lebanon closer together politically than ever before or since. Rising currents of pan-Arabism and Christian Lebanese nationalism found a common foe in the Mandatory Power. The deterioration of France's popularity might have been arrested had the French Parliament ratified the draft Treaty of Amity of 1936; but even that liberalizing measure conceded less than Muslim opinion desired. The capitulation of France in June 1940 made the status of her mandated territories ambiguous and her control tenuous. Lebanon and Syria became a twilight area, competed for by the Vichy government, the British, and the Free French of General de Gaulle. Alarmed by the possibility of German exploitation, Britain and the Free French expelled the Vichy administration in June and July 1941 and promised the people of Syria and Lebanon full independence.[57] This promise, although explicit, proved premature, and for more than two years the area remained under the control of the Free French and the British military mission. The historic rivalry between these two allies, however, was very great, and the local forces demanding independence were not slow to take advantage of it. During the spring and summer of 1943, the elements demanding genuine independence and closer connections with the Arab world gained strength at the expense of the Free French and the Francophile notables, with the obvious encouragement of the British Minister, Major-General Sir Edward Spears. In one case, a French-inspired attempt to enfranchise Lebanese emigrants—mostly Christian—in the reluctantly promised parliamentary election was thwarted by elements enjoying British support: the Muslim Arab leadership and the pro-independence Christian faction.[58] The election itself set the stage for the autumn crisis out of which emerged the independent Republic. Despite French interference, the candidates supporting Bechara al-Khoury gained complete control of the Chamber,[59] and a new era in Lebanese politics began.

Bechara al-Khoury was elected President of the Republic on September 21, 1943. He faced the double problem built into the very structure of Greater Lebanon: internal parochialism and foreign interference, and he faced it in a particularly acute form. The unsettled circumstances of the time had accelerated both the desires of the independence factions and the fears of conservative Christians. Some of the former certainly hoped for eventual political reunification with Syria, whereas others sought simply to throw off the French control; some of the latter wanted to reconstitute an entirely Christian Mount Lebanon under French protection, whereas others sought to maintain a Francophile ruler in Greater Lebanon. Sunnites, Shiites, and Druzes entertained well-founded suspicions that certain Maronite elements wanted to seize the reins from the retiring Délégué-Général, and Maronites suspected, not without reason, that the Sunnite leadership might betray Lebanon's sovereignty and commit the Christians to a feared Islamic domination. It was Khoury's overriding political task to deal with this double problem.

That he did so immediately and decisively is to his credit as a statesman and to the credit of the notables of all sects who joined with him.

The instrument for dealing with the identity problem has come to be known as the National Pact (*al-mithaq al-watani*). Although the National Pact hardly constitutes a solution, it has for two decades been the fundamental institution in the Lebanese political system for coping with the problem. Without this pragmatic accommodation, it is doubtful that the state could have survived as long as it has. The National Pact was an agreement between the new President, a Maronite Christian, and the popular Sunnite Muslim politician Riad Sulh, a pan-Arab nationalist. It stipulated that Lebanon should be completely independent, sovereign, and neutral; that Christians, especially Maronites, should not seek Western protection; and that Muslims, especially Sunnites, should not try to make Lebanon part of a larger Arab Islamic state. Lebanon should have an Arab "face" while retaining a separate identity. The new state should develop a role in the Arab world and cooperate fully with all the other Arab states, especially Syria, providing that they recognize her boundaries. Finally, the government should work to eliminate the sectarian system, which, as Riad Sulh put it, "is an obstacle to national progress, impeding the representation of the national will and poisoning the good relations between diverse elements of the Lebanese population." [60] Nevertheless, the Pact formalized the practice of allocating the top political offices on a sectarian basis, and since then the practice has been accorded the status of a firm tradition.[61] Whereas the amended Constitution of 1926 is the constitution of what Rondot has called the *pays légal,* the National Pact is the constitution of the *pays réel.* The Pact, however, is a remedy for the symptoms of sectarian strife rather than a cure. The bargain between Sunnites and Maronites has proven increasingly difficult to maintain in the domain of foreign relations, and the intention of its authors to eliminate sectarianism has yet to be realized. Proportional representation by sect remains an essential element of the formal system. Nevertheless, the National Pact accomplished the task of recruiting the Muslim notables into the system and excluding extremists, whether Christian, Muslim, pan-Arab, or pro-Western, from the arena of legitimate political behavior. Historic mutual suspicions still lie beneath the surface of politics, but the fact remains that an area of negative consensus has been established by means of the Pact. It has permitted Lebanon to embark gingerly on a process of political modernization.

The National Pact, as outlined by Bechara al-Khoury and Riad Sulh, displeased the Free French, who, despite previous promises of independence, wished to maintain their influential position in the area against the British and hostile local forces. When the new government followed up on its own declaration of independence by unilaterally abrogating the provisions in the Constitution that expressed dependence on the Mandatory, General de Gaulle's Délégué-Général, Jean Helleu, imprisoned the President, the Prime Minister, and all but two members of the Cabinet and installed the Francophile Emile Edde as chief of state.

Public reaction to this *coup de théâtre* was so hostile that General Catroux was sent from Algiers to stabilize the situation. All political forces in the country, with the exception of the extreme Francophile Maronites, denounced the high-handed French action and mobilized in protest. The Maronite Patriarch, Antoun Arida; the Sunnite Grand Mufti of Lebanon, Toufic Khaled; the largely Maronite youth group, the Kataeb; and its Sunnite counterpart, the Najjadeh, stood together in opposition. Notables of all the major communities supported the "resistance government," composed of the two Cabinet members who had eluded arrest. Demonstrations took place in all the major towns, and French Senegalese troops fired on the crowds.[62] General Catroux's mediation and strong Anglo-American pressure led to the reinstatement of the Khoury regime on November 22 amid general popular rejoicing.[63] The November crisis stamped a seal of legitimacy on the National Pact.

By grappling with the problem of national integration in 1943, the Lebanese Republic made it possible subsequently to walk a tightrope, balancing various internal and external pressures and avoiding the chronic danger of chaos and fragmentation. Yet neither political sectarianism nor the National Pact has stimulated a strong civic spirit among the Lebanese people. Indeed, sectarianism is widely regarded among the Lebanese as detrimental to developing national feeling, and the National Pact cannot but represent a second-best arrangement for the numerous extremists on both the "Arab" and the "Western" sides. Unsatisfactory as they may be, however, both institutions have been indispensable to Lebanon's postwar survival and its modest political success. The leitmotiv of politics under the independent Republic has been the struggle to

make these defective institutions work satisfactorily. It is an un-
ending struggle, for the pressures of parochial and external elements
are constantly changing and generally increasing in intensity. The
unevenness of social mobilization among the sects and regions,
described in Chapter 2, exerts strains on the sectarian ratios con-
trived by the men of 1943; the postwar instability of the Arab world,
aggravated by the Palestine problem, has subjected Lebanon to
capricious gales of discontent and intrigue; and the gradual alienation of progressive elements in the Arab world from the West has
made Lebanon's historic position in two worlds more difficult to
maintain. In light of these adversities, the performance of the
Lebanese political system during its first two decades of independence seems more impressive than it otherwise might.

NOTES

[1] "In a country like ours, composed of minorities that are already approximately equal and equally jealous of their rights, where no single element can hope to constitute a dominant majority, where there can be no question of a dictatorial regime—the only possible peace is one arrived at by consent, based on understanding and cooperation, on a state of equilibrium." *Le Jour* (Beirut), November 28, 1941.

[2] Sidney Verba, "Comparative Political Culture," in Lucian Pye and Sidney Verba (eds.), *Political Culture and Political Development* (Princeton: Princeton University Press, 1965), p. 513.

[3] *Ibid.,* p. 525; Verba makes this point at a more general level: "To concentrate only on shared beliefs might lead one to overlook situations where significant political beliefs were held only by certain groups, and where the very fact that these attitudes were not shared by most members of the system was of crucial importance."

[4] Although both elements were present long before this period, the internationalization of Lebanese politics and the modernization of its society on a large scale accompanied the reign of the next-to-last Chehabi amir, Bashir II. For a discussion of this period see William R. Polk, *The Opening of South Lebanon, 1788–1840* (Cambridge, Mass.: Harvard University Press, 1963), especially pp. xv–xx, 213–26. He argues that the Egyptian occupation of the 1830s laid the foundations for the modern age. "It was a decade which cut like a band across the spectrum of Syrian history and began the modern epoch. . . ." (p. 226).

[5] Carleton Coon, *Caravan* (New York: Holt, 1951).

[6] The term "primordial sentiments" is Clifford Geertz's. See "The Integrative Revolution," in C. Geertz (ed.), *Old Societies and New States* (New York: Free Press, 1963), pp. 105–57, especially his analysis of Lebanon, pp. 142–5.

[7] Raphael Patai, "The Middle East as a Culture Area," *Middle East Journal,* 6 (Winter 1952), 1–21.

[8] One of the best descriptions of traditional modes of kinship and conflict resolution is in Victor Ferris Ayoub, *Political Structure of a Middle East Community: A Druze Village of Mount Lebanon* (Unpublished doctoral dissertation, Harvard University, 1955).

[9] Etienne de Vaumas, "La Répartition Confessionnelle au Liban et l'Equilibre de l'Etat Libanais," *Revue de Géographie Alpine,* 43, No. 3 (1955), 511.

[10] Iliya F. Harik, *Political Change in a Traditional Society: A Study of Institutional Conflict in the Iqṭāʿ Political System of Mount Lebanon, 1711–1845* (Unpublished doctoral dissertation, University of Chicago, 1964), chap. 1, p. 63.

[11] Harik (*ibid.,* p. 47) describes the *iqṭāʿ* order during Ottoman times under the local Chehab dynasty: "[A] number of hereditary lords exercised the right to rule and were subject in their relations to a hereditary of the Shihab dynasty." Harik distinguishes between the system of tax farming (*iltizam*), which prevailed generally throughout the areas of the Ottoman Empire that

were firmly controlled by the Sultan's prefects, and the *iqṭā'* system, in which tax-collection functions were more locally controlled, as in Mount Lebanon. See also Polk, *op. cit.,* pp. 32–49, for a detailed description.

[12] The Chehab family ruled in and around Mount Lebanon from 1697 to 1841. The double *qa'imaqamiyyah* (1842–1858) was an administrative solution proposed by Prince Metternich to restore order among sects and classes. It divided the Lebanon into Christian and Druze districts but proved insufficient to end the turmoil. The *mutasarrifiyyah* (1861–1920) was the arrangement, sponsored by the Great Powers, that placed Lebanon under a governor (*mutasarrif*) who was a non-Lebanese Catholic appointed by the Porte and approved by the Powers.

[13] Polk, *op. cit.,* chap. 4. For a discussion of peasant unrest under the double *qa'imaqamiyyah,* see Malcolm H. Kerr, *Lebanon in the Last Years of Feudalism, 1840–1868* (Beirut: American University, 1959), particularly his introduction to a chronicle of the period, pp. 1–31.

[14] Afif I. Tannous, "The Village in the National Life of Lebanon," *Middle East Journal,* 3 (April 1949), 151–64.

[15] Albert Hourani, "Race, Religion, and Nation-State in the Near East," in his collection of papers, *A Vision of History* (Beirut: Khayat's, 1961), pp. 72–3.

[16] Harik, *op. cit., passim,* especially chap. 5 on the political ideology of the Maronites.

[17] See Chapter 2 for a further discussion of demographic trends and problems.

[18] We confine ourselves here to the sectarian groups represented in Parliament. There are also numerous very small sects, mostly Christian. One of the best treatments of the sects in Syria and Lebanon is by one of the foremost scholars of the area, Albert Hourani, *Minorities in the Arab World* (London: Oxford, 1947). See also Hourani's essay, "Race, Religion, and Nation-State in the Near East," in *A Vision of History,* pp. 71–105.

[19] Vaumas, *op. cit.,* p. 515. See also Harik, *op. cit.,* pp. 10–1; Philip K. Hitti, *Lebanon in History* (New York: Macmillan, 1957), pp. 247–52; and Hourani, *Minorities in the Arab World,* p. 65.

[20] Hitti, *op. cit.,* p. 249.

[21] Vaumas, *op. cit.,* p. 517.

[22] Harik, *op. cit.,* p. 27; and Vaumas, *op. cit.,* p. 524.

[23] Kamal Salibi, *The Modern History of Lebanon* (London: Weidenfeld, 1965), p. 106.

[24] Vaumas, *op. cit.,* pp. 526–7; and Hourani, *Syria and Lebanon* (London: Oxford, 1946), p. 124.

[25] Vaumas, *op. cit.,* pp. 529–32.

[26] Salibi, "Lebanon since the Crisis of 1958," *World Today,* 17 (January 1961), 35.

[27] Vaumas, *op. cit.,* pp. 532–5.

[28] Lebanon's small Jewish community lives peacefully in a district of Beirut and observes its religious practices in freedom. The Jews of Lebanon speak Arabic and operate a number of important business establishments. Too few to be represented in formal political institutions, the Jews enjoy good

relations with the Maronite-dominated party, the Kataeb, which publicly guaranteed their security during the Palestine war. Despite the deep enmity that most Lebanese, Christian and Muslim, feel toward Israel, the Lebanese Jewish community has rarely suffered. Some Arab nationalists in Lebanon, however, regard Jewish land purchases and stock-market activity with considerable suspicion.

[29] Hourani, *Syria and Lebanon,* p. 122.

[30] Vaumas, *op. cit.,* pp. 543–8. For one recent description, see Richard Pearse, *Three Years in the Levant* (London: Macmillan, 1949), pp. 234–40.

[31] Salibi, *The Modern History of Lebanon,* pp. xvii–xviii.

[32] Hitti, *Origins of the Druze People and Religion* (New York: Columbia University Press, 1928), p. 27.

[33] On the decline of the Druzes and the rise of the Maronites, see Salibi, *The Modern History of Lebanon,* especially chaps. 1, 5; Harik, *op. cit.,* chap. 5; and Polk, *op. cit.,* chap. 8.

[34] Salibi, *The Modern History of Lebanon,* p. xii. It should be noted, however, that many Christians, and especially the more conservative Maronites, make a point of tracing their origins back to the Phoenicians, in order to score a political point against Sunnite Arab nationalists, who are relative latecomers, and, by implication, aliens.

[35] Godfrey de Bouillon led the Crusader expedition that founded the Kingdom of Jerusalem in 1099, and Raymond de St. Gilles established the County of Tripoli in 1102. There is also a Maronite legend that a grandson of Charlemagne's uncle landed in the Levant and became abbot of the monastery of St. Maron and that he took the name of Yuhanna Maroun, patron saint of the Maronite Church. René Ristelhueber, *Les Traditions Françaises au Liban* (Paris: Alcan, 1925), p. 42–6.

[36] One of the most vivid accounts of the Anglo-French struggle is found in the writings of Colonel Charles Henry Churchill, *Mount Lebanon: A Ten Year's Residence from 1842–1852,* II (London: Saunders, 1853), 275, 315–22.

[37] Polk, *op. cit.,* pp. 83–105, describes the invasion, drawing upon local chronicles and consular reports.

[38] Eugène Poujade, *Le Liban et la Syrie, 1845–1860* (3d ed.; Paris: Lévy, 1867), pp. 19–36, 59. See also J. A. R. Marriott, *The Eastern Question* (4th ed.; Oxford: Clarendon, 1940), pp. 225–44.

[39] See, for example, *Memorandum sur les Aspirations des Libanais* (Cairo: Alliance Libanaise, January 8, 1918) issued by the Alliance Libanaise, a group of expatriate Lebanese founded in November 1909. Originally the group's aim was to secure the continued autonomy of Mount Lebanon within the Ottoman Empire. When Constantinople abrogated the international agreement providing for Mount Lebanon's autonomy and reduced it to an ordinary province during World War I, the Alliance began a campaign to secure the complete independence of an enlarged and economically viable Lebanon, corresponding roughly to the territory of the present Republic, which would have international guarantees. See also the Comité Libanais de Paris, *Compte Rendu de l'Assemblée Constitutive du 24 Janvier 1918*; and the report of E. H. Byrne, *Desires of the Syrians,* October 7, 1918, pp.

68–78. All these documents may be found in the William Yale papers at Yale University. Yale was technical adviser to the King-Crane Commission (The American Section of the International Commission on Mandates in Turkey) in Syria.

[40] The Yale papers provide an informed and detailed account both of the aspirations of the several religious and ethnic minorities and of the actual confrontation among Chukri Pasha Ayoubi, the Sherifian authority in Beirut, the French Rear Admiral Vernet, and the British General Bullfin during the first ten days of October 1918. See also Zeine N. Zeine, *The Struggle for Arab Independence* (Beirut: Khayat's, 1960), pp. 25–41; Harry N. Howard, *The King-Crane Commission* (Beirut: Khayat's, 1963), especially pp. 125–35; and the report of the King-Crane Commission itself in U.S. Department of State, *Foreign Relations of the United States: Paris Peace Conference, 1919,* XII (Washington, D.C.: U.S. Government Printing Office, 1947), 745–863, especially 751–99.

[41] The definitive work in English on the Mandate era is Stephen H. Longrigg, *Syria and Lebanon under French Mandate* (London: Oxford, 1958). A vivid, if jaundiced, narrative in Arabic is Iskandar Riachi, *Qabl wa-ba'd* (Beirut: 1953). Both books are rather unkind to the French. A well-informed French analysis of the era will be found in Pierre Rondot, *Les Institutions Politiques du Liban* (Paris: Imprimerie Nationale, 1947).

[42] Michel Chiha, *Politique Intérieure* (Beirut: Trident, 1964), is a representative selection of the author's editorials in *Le Jour.*

[43] American University of Beirut Department of Political Studies and Public Administration, *The Lebanese Constitution: A Reference Edition in English Translation* (Beirut: Khayat's, 1960).

[44] George Grassmuck and Salibi, *A Manual of Lebanese Administration* (Beirut: American University, 1955), pp. 6–11.

[45] Hazem Zaki Nuseibeh, *The Ideas of Arab Nationalism* (Ithaca: Cornell University Press, 1956), p. 42.

[46] Sati al-Hosri, one of the leading publicists of contemporary Arab nationalism, states that neither the Wahhabite reform movement in Islam, which began in Arabia in the 1820s, nor Muhammad Ali's enlightened despotism in Egypt was directly responsible for this revival. It was, he argues, the Christian missionaries who nurtured the minority that was discontented with Ottoman rule. "C'est au Liban qu'est Née l'Idée Nationaliste," *L'Orient Littéraire* (Beirut), June 9, 1962.

[47] George Antonius, *The Arab Awakening* (London: Hamilton, 1938), especially pp. 35–60, 79–125. For a critical review of Antonius, see George Kirk, "The Arab Awakening Reconsidered," *Middle Eastern Affairs,* 13 (June–July 1952), 162–73. Kirk argues that Arab nationalism was a less popular movement than Antonius suggests. See also Sylvia Haim, *Arab Nationalism: An Anthology* (Berkeley: University of California Press, 1964), pp. 3–72; and Hans Kohn, *Nationalism and Imperialism in the Hither East* (New York: Harcourt, 1932), pp. 179 ff.

[48] Nuseibeh, *op. cit.,* p. 54.

[49] Zeine, *op. cit.,* is one of the best accounts. See also Laurence Evans,

United States Policy and the Partition of Turkey, 1914–1924 (Baltimore: Johns Hopkins Press, 1965).

[50] William Yale, *Notes and Translations Prepared for Me by Local Friends in Beyrouth,* Yale papers.

[51] King-Crane Report, in U.S. Department of State, *op. cit.,* pp. 756–62.

[52] Howard, *op. cit.,* p. 233.

[53] Antonius, *op. cit.,* p. 305.

[54] Zeine, *op. cit.,* pp. 136–88.

[55] As Hourani has put it: "Gradually there grew up an idea of Lebanese nationalism, but so long as the French remained in control the concept was largely artificial. Arab nationalists both inside and outside Lebanon resented its existence as part of the process of dividing and subjecting the Arab world, and the other sects resented the predominance which French support gave to the Maronites." Hourani, "The Decline of the West in the Middle East—I," *International Affairs,* 29 (1953), 37–8.

[56] For some examples of interference, see Riachi, *op. cit., passim.* The *Rapport et Motion du Congrès National Démocrate du Liban,* held at Beirut, November 27, 1938, accuses the High Commissioner of nominating deputies, of interfering in the elections of 1929 and 1934 and of holding the 1937 elections in a reign of terror. It declares that the Commissioner had spent millions of francs to buy off the deputies and had also interfered in the Presidential election of 1936 to ensure Emile Edde's victory. See also Camille Chamoun, *Crise au Moyen-Orient* (Paris: Gallimard, 1963), pp. 83–90; and Longrigg, *op. cit.,* pp. 199–207.

[57] Leaflets dropped over Beirut on June 8, 1941, and signed by General Georges Catroux, proclaimed Lebanon's independence and the end of the Mandate. For the text and his own commentary, see Catroux, *Dans la Bataille de la Méditerranée* (Paris: Julliard, 1949), pp. 137–56. See also Eugénie Elie Abouchdid, *Thirty Years of Lebanon and Syria: 1917–1947* (Beirut: Sader-Rihani, 1948), pp. 83 ff.

[58] General de Gaulle's view of the situation is presented in his *Mémoires de Guerre: l'Unité, 1942–1944* (Paris: Plon, 1956), pp. 238 ff. Spears' position is described in the dispatches of the American Diplomatic Agent and Consul General at Beirut, George Wadsworth, in U.S. Department of State, *Foreign Relations of the United States, 1943,* IV (Washington, D.C.: U.S. Government Printing Office, 1964), especially 976–84.

[59] Wadsworth reported, "Interventions and pressures by French and French-supported Lebanese regional officials continued—even increasing according to Spears—but were in considerable measure effectively blocked by latter's energetic protests and counter measures." *Ibid.,* p. 988, Despatch 266, September 3, 1943.

[60] As the National Pact was never written down as a formal document, there is a certain ambiguity in its precise terms. This ambiguity undoubtedly has contributed to its success as an operational principle. In describing it, I rely principally on President Khoury's inaugural speech to Parliament of September 21, 1943, and the ministerial declaration by Riad Sulh on October 7, 1943. In his memoirs, *Haqā'iq lubnāniyyah* [*Lebanese Truths*], II

(Beirut: Awrāq lubnāniyyah, 1960), 15–6, President Khoury describes his address. Before cheering deputies and visitors, he asserted that Lebanon must cooperate with the Arab countries and emerge from its isolation: "My expression of [this policy] received the complete support [of Parliament] and the session adjourned in an intense atmosphere of enthusiasm." Other public declarations of the National Pact by the President are found in an appendix, pp. 289–99. The text of Riad Sulh's speech is reprinted in *Le Jour,* October 8, 1943.

[61] The agreement that the President should be a Maronite, the Prime Minister a Sunnite, and the Speaker of the Chamber of Deputies a Shiite is perhaps too arbitrary and too recent to be classified as a tradition. Greater Lebanon's first President, Charles Debbass (1926–1934) was Greek Orthodox. Sunnites had no high-level representation at all until the selection of Khaireddine Ahdab as Prime Minister in 1937. Another Sunnite, Shaykh Muhammad al-Jisr of Tripoli, however, had sought the Presidency in 1932. So popular was Jisr that Emile Edde, a prominent and ambitious Maronite, supported him, thinking that he would defeat Edde's rival, Bechara al-Khoury. The French High Commissioner, Henri Ponsot, believed that a Muslim president would not serve France's interest, even though Jisr had cooperated with the French, and he suspended the Constitution to prevent Jisr's election. It was only in 1943 that a Shiite became President of the Chamber. Rondot, *op. cit.,* pp. 15–6; Chamoun, *op. cit.,* p. 84; Ahmad Haidar, *Al-dawlah al-lubnāniyyah* [*The Lebanese State*] (Beirut: Nijmeh, 1954).

[62] Wadsworth reports that Amir Majid Arslan asked "How can you expect me to control the Druzes?" The Maronite Patriarch called the French move a *coup de folie.* The Mufti asked, "Are we slaves?" Habib Abuchahla, a Greek Orthodox notable and one of the two cabinet members at large, protested, along with Arslan, France's "illegal and brutal acts" and the "violation of our independence and constitution and of principles for which the Allies are fighting." U.S. Department of State, *Foreign Relations of the United States, 1943,* IV, 1013–9, Despatch 311, November 11, 1943.

[63] For a day-by-day account of these events, see Abouchdid, *op. cit.,* pp. 133–71. See also *Le Jour,* November 25, 1943, for a résumé (during the crisis the newspapers had been shut down). Also see Catroux, *op. cit.,* pp. 400–28; De Gaulle, *op. cit.,* pp. 239–44; and Longrigg, *op cit.,* pp. 328–33. Longrigg comments: "A bitter blow to French prestige had been sustained. It had been invited by her weakness, her disproportionate pretensions, and a particular act of gross impolicy, and there was to be, this time, not even a façade of recovery from it. . . ." (p. 333)

CHAPTER · 2

Social Mobilization in Lebanon

Lebanese citizens are no longer surprised to hear that Lebanon is a society in movement. Movement is evident in the demand for telephone lines, the rate of construction of luxury apartments, the growth of shantytowns around Beirut, and, not least, the awesome traffic jams that clog Beirut's narrow streets and the approaches to the city. Per capita income has risen from $362 in 1958 to $449 in 1963. The booming tourist industry pours foreign currencies not only into Beirut but also into the surrounding mountain resorts. Outside Greater Beirut and in the enclaves of poverty inside it, this kind of movement is greatly diminished. Although the transistor radio is ubiquitous, the other signs of modernization are less noticeable: Education, avenues of physical and social mobility, steady employment, and health services are not readily available outside the core area. Just as some regions and sectors are more favored than others, so are various aspects of modernization occurring at a faster rate than others. For example, urbanization is outrunning industrialization; exposure to mass media is outrunning formal education; and the supply of secondary and university graduates is exceeding the demand for their services. Though the socioeconomic changes in Lebanon are occurring rapidly, they are also occurring unevenly throughout the society. How is this situation relevant to the political system?

This question is one of the most intriguing in comparative politics.[1] One of the most illuminating approaches is that of Karl W. Deutsch, who has conceived of modernization as a process of social mobilization. Social mobilization is

. . . an overall process of change, which happens to substantial parts of the population in countries which are moving from traditional to modern ways of life. . . . It . . . brackets together a number of more specific processes of change, such as changes of residence, or occupation, of social setting, of face-to-face contacts, of associates, of institutions, roles and ways of acting, of experiences and expectations, and finally of personal memories, habits and needs, including the need for new patterns of group affiliation and new images of personal identity. . . . Social mobilization can be defined therefore, as the process in which major clusters of old social, economic, and psychological commitments are eroded or broken and people become available for new patterns of socialization and behavior.[2]

According to Deutsch, the political consequences of rapid social mobilization may include the following: The politically relevant stratum will expand, the potential level of political tensions will increase, politics will be more oriented toward welfare, the government share of the national economy will increase, administration will be improved, the political elite will be broadened, political participation by the people will increase, and there will be a shift away from parochialism and internationalism toward nationalism. Finally, social mobilization "may tend to strain or destroy the unity of states whose population is already divided into several groups with different languages, cultures or basic ways of life."[3] Lebanon, as we have seen, is a divided country; the question of social mobilization therefore is particularly relevant for an understanding of its politics. In order to discover how social mobilization affects Lebanon's distinctive political life, it is necessary to examine the trends more intensively. Three dimensions of social mobilization seem particularly relevant to our inquiry: demographic trends, economic trends, and exposure to modernity.

DEMOGRAPHIC TRENDS

Compared with India or the United Arab Republic, Lebanon does not seem to have a population problem, at least not one relevant to politics; however, Lebanon's high rate of population increase, its increasing density, and its rapid urbanization *are* changing the political environment. These trends in fact underlie the transformation that has created two Lebanons: the highly mobilized Lebanon consisting of Beirut and Mount Lebanon Provinces and the Lebanon that includes the provinces of North Lebanon, South Lebanon, and the Biqa—an area just beginning to feel the effects of social mobilization (see Map 2).

In describing this demographic shift it is necessary to say a word about Lebanon's statistical problem. There has not been a general census since 1932, and the last year for which reasonably reliable data is available is 1943, the year the British 7th Army carried out a survey based on food-ration cards. Although various departments of the government have made regular estimates, based on rates calculated for the 1932–1943 period and from municipality rolls, these estimates cannot be regarded as highly accurate.[4] This statistical delinquency reflects the precariousness of the myth of sectarian balance upon which Lebanon's political system rests. This myth, it will be recalled, sanctions the allocation of political positions on the assumption that Christians outnumber Muslims by approximately six to five. If today a census should reveal that non-Christians are in a majority—and there are good reasons for thinking that it would —the existing movement to change or abolish the sectarian proportions in the Parliament and administration might develop greater momentum. The mere anticipation of such increased pressure, it is feared, would be sufficient to excite sectarian anxiety. Because social mobilization seems to accentuate rather than smother certain unpleasant historical memories, notables and groups with an interest in preserving the status quo have sought to soft-pedal the question of a census; and only a few groups outside the establishment—like the Najjadeh, an Islamic party—have called openly for a census. The heavily Maronite Kataeb (Phalanges Libanaises) has already agreed to a census, but only if Lebanese emigrants—numbering over a million and largely Christian—are counted along with resident citizens of Lebanon and non-Lebanese residents (mostly Muslim) are excluded from the census. Many Lebanese regard the official attitude toward a census as hypocritical, detrimental to national development, and possibly dangerous in the long run; others, however, are more concerned about short-run stability and are content to maintain the status quo.

There is some basis in fact for thinking that Muslims are increasing in number faster than Christians. Kingsley Davis studied the more reliable statistics for Palestine, assuming they would reflect demographic patterns also found in Lebanon, and he found that the rate of increase of Palestinian Muslims was 28.6 per 1,000 whereas that of Christians was only 19.5.[5] Although the Muslims' death rate

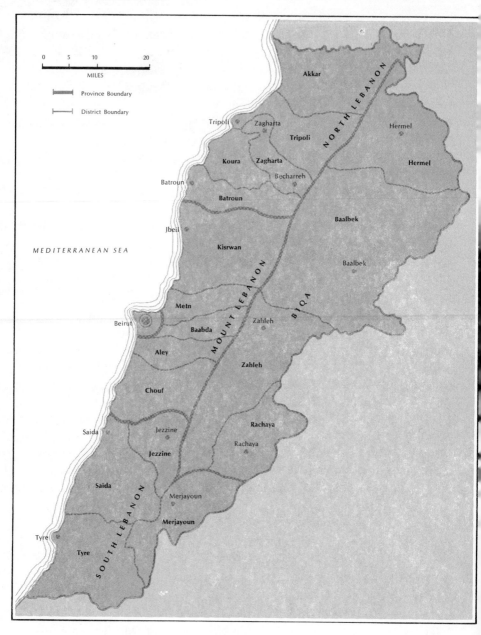

MAP 2

Provinces and Main Towns of Lebanon

After Etienne de Vaumas, "La Répartition Confessionelle au Liban et l'Equilibre de l'Etat Libanais," *Revue de Géographie Alpine,* 43 (1955), 511–603.

was higher than the Christians', the Muslims' birth rate was a great deal higher. Similar evidence has been reported by David Yaukey. He found little difference between rural Christians and rural Muslims, but educated and uneducated urban Muslims showed fertility rates of 5.56 and 7.35, respectively, whereas the corresponding figures for urban Christians were 3.44 and 4.14. Christians in general have made the transition to the limited family model more readily than have Muslims.[6]

Lebanon, with an area of 10,400 square kilometers, is roughly four-fifths the size of Connecticut. In 1932, 756,000 people lived there, and the population density was 72 per square kilometer. In 1943, the population was 1,022,000 and the density was 101; the annual rate of increase of Lebanese residents had been around 2.6 per cent.[7] For subsequent years there is less agreement. Figures released by the Census Directorate in 1963 recorded a 4.24 per cent annual increase between 1951, when the population was 1,416,000, and 1961, when it was 2,150,526; these figures, however, include overseas Lebanese who opted for Lebanese nationality under the Lausanne Treaty. The Doxiadis Associates of Athens made a study in 1957 under the auspices of the U.S. Operations Mission and arrived at a rate of 2.8 per cent for the early 1950s.[8] Another research mission, the French Institut International de Recherches et de Formation en Vue de Développement (IRFED), which was invited to Lebanon by President Fuad Chehab and which will be discussed in detail in Chapter 8, arrived at an estimated annual population increase of 2.3 per cent, but this figure seems too low.[9] The most persuasive estimate has come from the Lebanese Ministry of Planning. It calculates that the losses from emigration were nearly covered by the influx of Lebanese from Egypt and other countries and that urbanization is probably reducing the birth rate as it does in other countries. The Ministry therefore contends that the annual rate for the 1945–1962 period remained at 2.6 per cent and that it will slow down in the years to come.[10]

Three special factors, however, operate against this tendency. Formerly, emigration siphoned off some of the surplus population, but in the post-World War II period this safety valve began to close, largely as a result of tighter immigration and business restrictions levied by newly independent African states. Until World War I, emigration was great, and an estimated 7,500 Lebanese left annually between 1900 and 1914; the outflow reached another peak of 8,000 in 1923. As other countries began to restrict immigration, however, it fell to about 1,000 per year. During World War II, emigration stopped almost entirely, and since then it has averaged around 3,000 annually. In the period 1951–1959, the annual average was 2,850. In 1960, the rate of emigration had declined to 2,700.[11] Because the restrictive policies of African and Latin American governments have diminished opportunities for Lebanese emigrants, the rate of emigration seems to have stabilized at this low level, even though the basic motivations for emigration—a limited domestic market, a weak industrial sector, and a high degree of rural unemployment—remain.

The second factor aggravating the demographic problem is the high rate of population increase (an estimated 3.5 per cent) among the Palestinian refugees who live in Lebanese camps. According to United Nations Relief and Works Agency for Palestine Refugees (U.N.R.W.A.) figures there were more than 106,000 refugees living in sixteen camps throughout the country in 1960, out of a total of 137,000 on the rolls.[12] For the refugees the birth rate is higher and the death rate lower than for the population in general. Although the refugees do supply cheap labor, they inevitably add to the social problems of Beirut, Saida, and Tyre and compete with Lebanese for the insufficient number of jobs. Given their experience of past injustice—the origins of which are outside Lebanon—is it surprising that the refugees are politically volatile?

The third factor that may retard the expected decline in population rate is the level of public health. Although they generally get enough to eat, Lebanese citizens, particularly those living in rural areas, are subject to a variety of diseases and deficiencies.[13] The Minister of Public Health estimated in 1961 that the infant mortality rate per 1,000 live births was 120, about five times the American rate, whereas in rural areas an earlier (1953) study found a rate of 244. Tuberculosis, typhoid, and paratyphoid fever rank highest among a number of communicable diseases. It is probable, however, that the level of public health is rising and will rise considerably in the future. The emergence of Beirut as a first-class medical center, the propensity of young Lebanese to go into medicine, and the growth of government health services suggest that the rate of infant and general mortality will continue to fall rapidly.[14] In this mostly Catholic and Muslim country, where fertility is encouraged by both religious belief and traditional culture, this may well be a trend to reckon with.

By 1963 there were at least 2,005,000 people living in Lebanon and the population density was at least 193 per square kilometer.[15] The population and its density had almost doubled in twenty years of independence, and 70 per cent of the population is now under thirty-five years of age. Even if urbanization should gradually reduce the rate of population increase, Davis' prediction in 1956 seems valid:

> Our estimated natural increase . . . is not only high itself but it derives from an extremely high birth rate and a rather high death rate. Everything we know about contemporary population trends indicates that such a death rate will probably be brought down rapidly in a modernizing country such as Lebanon. It can easily be reduced to half in a few years. If this should happen there is no particular ground for expecting the birth rate to drop correspondingly. So we have to conclude that Lebanon is due for very rapid population growth in the next few decades unless some catastrophe intervenes.[16]

Not only is the gross population of Lebanon rapidly increasing, but also there is a marked internal migration to urban areas. Beirut and, to a lesser extent, Tripoli have been population magnets; and the Beirut–Mount Lebanon area has experienced a rate of population growth greater than the rest of the country. In 1922 Beirut was a charming little port town of 140,000 inhabitants;[17] in 1963 the Greater Beirut area embraced about 800,000 people, 40 per cent of Lebanon's entire population. Lebanon's second city, Tripoli, numbered 30,000 in 1914 and 180,000 in 1946.[18] In thirty years the municipality of Bourj-Hammoud has mushroomed from a suburb of 40,000 people on the northern edge of Beirut to Lebanon's third largest town—it has 125,000 people and some of the worst living conditions in the Beirut area.[19] The rate of change is dramatic. Whereas the total population increased by 89 per cent between 1943 and 1963, the population of towns of more than 20,000 people increased by 146 per cent. Approximately 28.7 per cent of the Lebanese lived in towns of more than 20,000 inhabitants in 1943, but in 1963 the percentage was 37.4. If the definition of urbanization is loosened to include everybody living in agglomerations of 4,000 or over—which seems reasonable given Lebanon's degree of modernization and communications exposure—the country was about 56 per cent urbanized in the early 1960s.[20] Of the 1,119,000 Lebanese living in towns of 4,000 or more, 74 per cent live in the Beirut–Mount Lebanon area.

A comparison of the density figures of the five provinces in 1955

and 1963 reveals the full extent of the population pressure (see
Table 3). Both the population levels and the rates of change in
Beirut and Mount Lebanon provinces are higher than in the outly-
ing areas. Nevertheless, two of the three outlying provinces are in-

TABLE 3

POPULATION DENSITY BY PROVINCE, 1955 AND 1963

PERSONS PER SQUARE KILOMETER

Province	1955	1963	Percentage Increase
Mount Lebanon	187	340	84.5
Beirut	18,090	23,034	27.3
South Lebanon	112	137	22.3
North Lebanon	159	191	20.1
Biqa	47	47	0.0

Figures for 1955 from U.S. Operations Mission in Lebanon, *Economic Data
for the Ekistic Programme of Lebanon* (Beirut: Doxiadis, 1957); figure for
1963 from Republic of Lebanon Ministry of Planning, *Besoins et Possibilités
de Développement du Liban,* I (Beirut: 1960–1961), 45–54.

creasing in density, despite the demographic shift to the cities. According to the IRFED mission, physical mobility is very high in
the Beirut–Mount Lebanon area and much lower in North Lebanon,
South Lebanon, and the Biqa.[21] The 1943 census estimated that
14.2 per cent of the persons born and living in Mount Lebanon
since 1932 had moved to Beirut, whereas only 3.5 per cent of
those living in the Biqa had moved there. South Lebanon's physical
mobility was 6.2 per cent whereas North Lebanon's was only 2.2
per cent.[22] A study of thirteen villages in the Biqa found that nine-
tenths of the villagers lived in the same village from birth to death
and that nearly all those who moved to the village were from other
Biqa villages. This lack of mobility was found over three generations.[23] Lebanon is thus afflicted with both urban and rural over-
crowding.

What kinds of political stress do these trends place on Lebanon's
political system? First, the concentration of people in a region of
great modernity, where exposure to mass communications, political
appeal, and political organization is great, is enlarging the politically
relevant population. Second, the demographic trends raise a host of
administrative problems, ranging from sewage disposal to traffic
regulation and slum control. There is, in particular, an acute shortage

of low-income housing. An architect and city planner acquainted with these problems summarized the matter this way:

> One wonders what Shelley, Dickens, or Bellamy would think of the bedlam that is Beirut—mid-twentieth century! . . . Too many factors have collaborated in the past ten to fifteen years, to dim the bright prospects that the future of Beirut once promised. These factors are: caprice; speculation; lack of a civic and governmental participation in the growth of Beirut; international and regional politics and dynamics; prosperity and oil. The rapid interplay of these factors . . . made Beirut both the *enviable* city of the Middle East, while at the same time these same factors have made it the most precariously-disposed, for its future urban-regional posture is not very bright.[24]

Third, urbanization appears to fortify, rather than diminish, Lebanese parochialism and transnational feelings. There is reason to think that the poorer-class individuals and families experiencing these demographic changes have not lost their traditional orientation but, on the contrary, have carried into the core region their traditional affiliations and attitudes.[25] This tendency may reduce the relevance of the concept of anomic, floating masses that preoccupies many sociologists. Insofar as it perpetuates, even fortifies, sectarian and family particularism as well as pan-Arab longings, however, it hinders development of common Lebanese loyalties and public spirit. In the sprawl of Greater Beirut, sectarian, class, and political communities cluster together in an uneasy, twentieth-century mosaic. Just as the famous "melting pot" has proved to be more myth than fact in New York City,[26] so the crucible of Beirut does not appear to be molding less particularistic Lebanese citizens. On the contrary, because political life in the city is corrupt and the formal political institutions in such an environment appear irrelevant to political realities, the experience of urbanization may even increase primordial loyalties.

ECONOMIC TRENDS

The Lebanese economy has undergone spectacular development since World War II. Lebanon appears glutted with material wealth, in relation both to what it enjoyed before and to what its Arab neighbors now enjoy. In this light it is easy to ascribe Lebanon's relative political success to prosperity. Marxists and non-Marxists alike have made convincing presentations of this argument. Members of Lebanon's Community Party, for example, point out that Lebanon is a capitalist anachronism, in which a fat middle class rules and enough surplus trickles down to the workers and peasants to tranquilize their revolutionary spirit. Outstanding Lebanese capitalists use the same argument to account for what they consider to be the country's economic and political success.

Statistical indicators provide a rough idea of Lebanon's material transformation. For example, one of the indicators used to chart basic development is production of electric energy; Lebanon's production has more than doubled between 1959 and 1962.[27] National income has advanced strongly since independence, allaying a widespread fear among many Lebanese that the little state could not become self-sustaining, much less grow. Even after the breakup of the customs union with Syria in March 1950, which greatly augmented this fear, national income increased annually at almost 6.5 per cent. Discounting a 3 per cent increase in the price level, the net rate of increase was between 5 and 6 per cent. The Doxiadis Associates' survey of 1957 plotted this data against the population rate and estimated an annual increase in per capita income of about 3 per cent.[28] Estimates for the late 1950s have been a bit lower. The IRFED group suggested that the annual increase in national income in 1959 was about 4.4 per cent and that the per capita income increase was about 2.1 per cent. Official statistics for subsequent years show that this rate has in fact been maintained: For the 1961–1964 period the annual rate of increase remained at 4.4 per cent.[29] Lebanese Gross National Product in 1963 was approximately $725 million, compared with $520 million in 1953. Per capita income, which was placed at $235 in 1950 and $310 in 1956, was well over $400 in 1963.[30]

Other indicators show why Lebanon today seems to exude prosperity. Imports have increased markedly, rising from $144 million in 1953 to $358 million in 1962. About 55 per cent of the imports come from the United States and Western Europe and include automobiles, electrical machinery and appliances, and all manner of luxury goods. It is no exaggeration to say that almost anything for sale anywhere can be bought in Beirut. If in this enormous propensity to consume Beirut is the equal of any world capital, it also generates a huge and increasing trade deficit: $119 million in 1953 and $229 million in 1962. A deficit this size naturally worries many people, particularly in light of Lebanon's weak agricultural and industrial sectors, but the surprising fact is that Lebanon has managed to expand its "invisible exports"—especially its financial and tourist services—to soak up the trade deficit. American foreign aid from 1952 to 1962, amounting to some $88.3 million, helped in this respect, but the development—if not overdevelopment—of the trade and service sectors has been much more important. These sectors were earning together some $200 million annually in the mid-1960s. Tourism especially has become a major source of income; the number of tourists and summer vacationers has risen from 179,000 in 1955 to more than 600,500 in 1965.[31] Tourism reportedly brings in about $40 million a year to help offset the unfavorable trade balance. Since 1950 Lebanon has also derived important revenues from oil transit and refinery fees.

By far the most important factor in Lebanon's postwar economic development is its emergence as a major center of finance. Lebanon's growth as a financial center has been spectacular indeed: Before 1951 there were only five banks in Beirut; in 1966 there were ninety-three. Lebanese prosperity relies on a pool of capital fed to a large extent by the inflow of funds from the Arabian oil-producing states, as well as by the remittances from emigrants to their families. The oil money has been attracted to Lebanon by favorable interest rates, by a banking-secrecy law modeled after the one in Switzerland, by the perceived remoteness and complexity of Western money markets, and by the relative stability of Lebanon's political situation. During the 1961 crisis between Iraq and Kuwait, an estimated $100 million flowed into Beirut banks; and Syrian capitalists are said to have smuggled out vast amounts to Beirut when the Baath regime took power. Profiting thus from the political difficulties of its neighbors, the Lebanese financial situation gives every appearance of health: The Lebanese pound enjoys 86 per cent gold coverage; foreign exchange holdings have risen between 1955 and 1965 from $86.5 million to $236 million; and the money supply has increased from over $80 million in 1954 to nearly $180 million in 1964. The number of American companies has risen from 147 in 1961 to 264 in 1965, a sign of Western confidence.

These indicators of prosperity are impressive, but they are also deceptive because they mask conditions that impose constant and perhaps growing strains on the country's delicate political processes. Lebanon's traditional political stability has bestowed the gift of prosperity, but the maldistribution and possible future diminution of prosperity challenges that stability. Three types of strain are par-

ticularly noticeable. First, Lebanon's dependence on outside investment is enormous; perhaps in no other country are financial services such a large percentage of the gross national product. Yet these
capital inflows can be easily and suddenly diminished by changes in
the world financial situation, by Arab-world politics, or even by
personal whims. The crisis in Beirut's huge Intra Bank in 1966
made this danger apparent to all. The leftist and anti-Western
tendencies in Arab-world politics exert pressure on Lebanon's allegedly parasitic and artificial prosperity. Lebanon enjoys a prosperity
that is, at best, uncertain.

A second set of strains is imposed by the uneven distribution of
prosperity. This unevenness is not readily apparent in Beirut itself.
The manifestations of the capital inflow appear everywhere around
Beirut and its suburbs; the most impressive indications are, perhaps,
the forest of high-rise luxury apartment buildings. The proliferation
of such buildings, monuments of millionaires, has nearly transformed
Beirut from a romantic town of graceful arches and red roofs to
another jet-age metropolis—a collection of flashy buildings unrelated
to the people or the terrain. Outside the capital proper, however, it
is not difficult to see where the prosperity stops: The Beirut slums
or the depressed areas in South Lebanon are vivid reminders. Less
obvious but no less important is the lack of economic infrastructure
(small factories, low-income housing projects, markets outside
Beirut) that could have been developed with more socially conscious investment behavior.

It is possible to obtain a rough picture of Lebanon's uneven prosperity from some recent economic studies. The Doxiadis Associates'
study of 1957 estimated that 3 per cent of the work force, about
14,000 men, earns $3,300 or more annually; 51 per cent earns
$500 or less.[32] The United Nations Food and Agriculture Organiza-
tion (F.A.O.) study of 1959 suggested that per capita income in
the low-income groups may be only about $147, compared with a
national average of about $327.[33] The IRFED study of 1960–1961
reported that half the work force is engaged in agriculture, yet only
15.8 per cent of the Gross National Product goes to the agricultural
sector.[34] The ratio of percentage of national product and percentage
of work force in agriculture is therefore 0.324. At the other extreme
are the people employed in the finance sector; they constitute only
0.44 per cent of the work force but account for 6 per cent of the
Gross National Product—a ratio of 13,623.[35]

Although the over-all income distribution of Lebanon is hardly as unequal as that prevailing, say, in Colombia, it does not approach the more equitable Western levels, as Table 4, derived from the *IRFED Report,* indicates. According to IRFED, half the population may be classified as "destitute" or "poor" and half as "average" or better. The half that is "destitute" and "poor" accounts for only 18 per cent of the Lebanese G.N.P.

TABLE 4

INCOME DISTRIBUTION, 1959

Category	Percentage of Population	Level of Family Income (L£)
"Destitute"	9	1,200 and below (0-$400)
"Poor"	40	1,200-2,500 ($400-$830)
"Average"	30	2,500-5,000 ($830-$1,660)
"Well off"	14	5000-15,000 ($1,660-$5,000)
"Rich"	4	15,000 and above

Republic of Lebanon Ministry of Planning, *Besoins et Possibilités de Développement du Liban,* I (Beirut: 1960–1961), 93.

The regional variations in income distribution are also striking. IRFED carried out two field studies in Lebanon, one in the rural areas and one in the major towns; its object was to compare the level of sociological, psychological, cultural, and economic development in all parts of Lebanon. The country was divided into regions, zones, and subzones, each with its main town, or "polar" locality, and each subzone was scored in terms of eleven to fourteen indicators of development.[36] The various zones were then classified according to degree of development as shown by the mean of their over-all scores. The figures are not based entirely on "hard" data. They might more accurately be regarded as standardized impressions. They are good enough, however, to permit rough comparisons.

The findings from the IRFED study indicate that the Central region (which includes the Beirut suburbs and Mount Lebanon, as well as the capital) ranks dramatically higher than the other regions on the IRFED scale of development. Not a single polar locality in this area is completely undeveloped, and only 5 per cent are underdeveloped by the IRFED criteria. By contrast, 46 per cent of the polar localities of the Northern region, 30 per cent of those in the Southern region, and 35 per cent of those in the Eastern region (Biqa) fall into the two lowest categories. (The Northern, Southern, and Eastern regions of the IRFED study correspond closely but not exactly with the provinces of North Lebanon, South Lebanon, and the Biqa respectively. The Central region comprises, again approximately, the Beirut and Mount Lebanon provinces together.)[37] Furthermore, the IRFED study makes it possible to specify in what areas of development the regions are strong and weak. We find, for example, that the Central region scores high on certain categories: health levels, school facilities, domestic situation, neighborhood conditions, housing, family situation, educational situation and psychology, and domestic facilities. It has low scores, however, in various subzones, in the categories of leisure and cultural activities and health facilities. The Northern, Southern, and Eastern regions all have fairly high scores with respect to the educational situation and psychology and domestic facilities, but they do very poorly with respect to leisure and cultural activities, health facilities, and economic and technical capacity.[38]

IRFED's analysis of the four regional urban centers—Beirut, Tripoli, Saida, and Zahleh—reveals that Beirut is, on the average, the most developed of the four towns, followed in descending order by Zahleh, Tripoli, and Saida.[39] In domestic facilities and situation, housing, and leisure activities, Beirut city does very well; in neighborhood life and diverse services it does very poorly; and its health, urban, educational, and cultural levels are generally acceptable. Tripoli and Saida, on the other hand, do not rank in the top group in any respect and are lowest with respect to domestic situation, neighborhood life, and educational facilities, among others.

Although they are deficient in several areas of development, all the principal towns of Lebanon are greatly superior to their rural surroundings. By IRFED's criteria, every urban center offers a better standard of living than does its surrounding area. This finding helps explain the lure of the cities for Lebanon's rural inhabitants and thus the accelerating rural-urban migration.

A third set of strains accompanies Lebanon's extraordinary economic development. Lebanon faces an unemployment problem because it has a fast-growing, youthful population, a rapid rate of urban migration, a relatively stagnant industrial and agricultural sector, and the tendency among many *hommes d'affaires* to opt for short-run gains in their business investments at the expense of long-run benefits. The job shortage is apparent at all levels, among university graduates as well as among the uneducated. Ironically, even though Lebanon is deficient in administrative skills, liberal-arts graduates do not find government jobs easily available because of the lack of positions, a situation aggravated by the allocation of posts according to sectarian considerations. Increased mechanization in agriculture has reduced the number of jobs that used to exist in labor-intensive cultivation of Lebanon's limited soil. Investment in industrial enterprises does not create enough additional employment for the approximately 11,000 young men—a conservative estimate[40] —entering the work force annually. To discover the magnitude of these strains it is necessary to look a bit more closely at Lebanon's demographic trends and its economic performance.

Projections of future unemployment figures are not reassuring. In fact, experts within the Lebanese government suggest that in 1980 one man out of every three in the active population will be without work. Because of the inadequacy of available quantitative data, any forecasts must be unusually tentative, but the implications are too important to ignore. These government experts predict, on the basis of a continued 2.6 per cent annual increase in population, that the active work force, which in 1959 was estimated at 450,000,[41] will have risen in 1980 to 915,000 (the maximum hypothesis) or 870,000 (the minimum hypothesis). The government experts predict that the percentage of the active population unemployed will be about one third—34 per cent or 33 per cent.[42] Few would argue that the projected size of the active population is too large—if anything, it is conservative. The projected growth rate of new employment, however, is less acceptable. The government forecast was made by analyzing the growth of the three main sectors: agricultural, industrial, and service. The analysis contends that the agricultural sector is likely to lose 40,000 to 50,000 jobs by 1980 because the possibility of cultivating new lands is limited by nature and because technology is reducing the labor-intensive sector of Lebanese agriculture.[43]

It is more difficult to forecast employment trends in the industrial sector. The absolute gains have been clear—industrial investment did increase 15 per cent between 1960 and 1964, and its total value exceeded $275 million in 1964. The evidence suggests, however, a certain stagnation. The industrial sector's share of G.N.P. has shown no significant increase since 1950; it has remained about 12 or 13 per cent, an unusually low figure for such a highly urbanized country. The level of new investment in industry has also not been particularly striking: In 1950, new investment was valued at 23 million Lebanese pounds (L£) or 16 per cent of the value of all industry, whereas in 1963 it was valued at L£22.7

TABLE 5

RECENT TRENDS IN THE INDUSTRIAL SECTOR

	1958	1959	1960	1961	1962	1963	1964
Number of workers	21,814	39,033	50,403	59,523	60,867	63,091	61,716
Number of factories	3,200	3,302	4,559	5,901	6,271	6,647	6,854
Capital invested (millions L£)	212.3	434.6	578.0	640.8	691.3	805.7	827.5
Value added *		222.3	143.4	62.8	50.5	114.4	21.8

* 1958 was a year of political crisis, which greatly curtailed economic activity.

Le Commerce du Levant, March 5, 1966, p. 11.

million, or 2.5 per cent of total industrial value[44] (see Table 5). The ratio of new industrial investment to additional Gross National Product between 1950 and 1957 was 2.5, compared with 10.7 in real estate and buildings.[45] Based on the predicted growth trends in the three sectors, one projection, which seems optimistic in light of recent trends, foresees an increase of about 20,000 new jobs every five years. By 1980, therefore, there might be 60,000 new jobs in industry, or about 4,000 a year, if that rate can be maintained. Whether or not this projection will prove accurate depends partly on the development of sufficiently attractive local and foreign markets for Lebanese goods: processed food, furnishings, textiles, cement, aluminum, and light manufactures. The increase in new jobs also depends on whether or not the level of imports will remain stable. We have already noted that imports cut very deeply into the relatively rich Greater Beirut market. Here is a political issue that has been with the Lebanese since independence: To what extent should foreign trade be regulated to encourage domestic manufacture and employment? Assuming that industry *can* continue to open up some 4,000 jobs a year, the over-all employment picture is still dark. By 1980 agriculture will have lost between 40,000 and 50,000 jobs, and industry will have picked up 60,000 jobs, which means (calculating from the 1960 figures of 220,000 agricultural jobs and 90,000 industrial jobs) that these two sectors will supply some 330,000 jobs for an active population of between 870,000 and 915,000. Can the service sector make up the difference?

The best educated guess is that it cannot. Although the service sector is elastic and buoyant with the remarkable tourism development and although it permits the Lebanese to exercise their full resourcefulness, it cannot be expected to provide more than 127,000 new jobs by 1980 if its development continues at the same pace as in the early 1960s. Even if the pace were to remain constant, this good performance would not prevent considerable unemployment. The Arab-Israeli war of June 1967, which drastically cut into Lebanon's tourist-transit trade to the holy places, showed how vulnerable the service sector is to the chronic turbulence of the Middle East and cast doubts on whether or not the earlier growth rate could be maintained, much less increased.

If these trends in the creation of new jobs are reasonably correct, the only way to avoid widespread unemployment and its consequences is to advance the whole rate of economic growth and to give new investment more socially useful functions. Lebanon is getting richer, but investment in the private sector has not helped sufficiently to spread the prosperity. The public sector has been left this task by default.

The achievement of higher standards of living has imposed strains as well as gains. The economic gains make Lebanon the envy of its neighbors and help ameliorate the problems raised by the demographic trends discussed earlier. If prosperity in general seems to lubricate the frictions of a growing and highly fragmented society, however, the uneven distribution of its benefits aggravates tensions as well. Uneven distribution among regions, classes, and sectors raises a host of problems that challenge the toughest political institutions. Regional disparities in living standards weaken national unity, impose great burdens on both the developed and the undeveloped areas, and promote dissatisfaction with the functioning of the Lebanese political system at many levels. Disparities in income distribution by class, though not as great as in many underdeveloped countries, are highly visible in Lebanon. The overdevelopment of the finance, commerce, and service sectors is made at the expense of the agricultural and industrial sectors, thus making Lebanon vulnerable to numerous economic and political stresses.

EXPOSURE TO MODERNITY

It may seem out of place to speak of "exposure to modernity" in a book about Lebanon. The very name connotes cosmopolitanism, sophistication, and the meeting of world cultures. To analyze recent political adaptation to modernity it is not necessary to pinpoint the beginnings of Lebanese contacts with the outside world because the attempt would involve a recitation of the whole history of the Lebanon.[46] Lebanon's exposure to the modern world, that is, the world of industrial revolution, begins with its occupation by Muhammad Ali in the years 1831–1840.[47] In the 1830s American Protestant and French Jesuit missionaries and educators established schools and printing presses to initiate what George Antonius has called the "Arab awakening," the effects of which are still being felt.[48] The French influence has been very great, supported by France's historic "special relationship" with Levantine Catholics; in fact, the Université de St. Joseph, established in 1875, has exerted the dominant educational influence among Lebanon's ruling elite, Christian and non-Christian. Lebanon's other great center of higher learning, the

American University of Beirut, founded in 1866, has diffused liberal ideas not only in Lebanon but also throughout the Arab world. Furthermore, in the nineteenth century it was common for the wealthy to educate their children abroad. The Muslims sent their sons to Constantinople, where they absorbed the culture of an advanced, cosmopolitan city. The Catholics educated their sons in the universities of Italy and France. Finally, the letters and visits of Lebanese who had emigrated to North and South America were of great importance in exposing the people of Lebanon to Western ways. To the Lebanese upper classes, therefore, exposure to the techniques and culture of the West is nothing new.

The lower classes had to wait until World War II for their exposure to the modern world. During the French Mandate, there was some selective exposure. The Mandate authorities encouraged private religious schools, which discriminated in favor of the Christians, and built roads. These policies placed some additional Lebanese in contact with modernity, but in general they were not the poorer ones. World War II, however, brought the British and with them a vast inflow of money. The tales of spectacular profiteering and the Horatio Alger stories of the time are part of the folklore of modern Lebanon. From the peasant who found a job as chauffeur with the British 7th Army to the *homme d'affaires* who made a fortune selling tank barricades, nearly everybody benefited. The boom has never really ended. Twenty years after the expulsion of the Vichy regime, the inhabitant of Beirut, rich or poor, can hardly avoid the ultramodern world around him. Deafened by the jet airliners landing at the nearby international airport and by the horns of 35,000 new automobiles in a chronic traffic jam, he may retreat several evenings a week to the movies and for 35 cents view the latest American, Egyptian, English, French, Indian, Italian, and Russian films. He can also stay home and watch television: American Westerns and crime programs on one of the local, privately owned channels or the television offerings from Cairo.

In order to appreciate the magnitude of exposure in the postwar period it is helpful to observe a few quantitative indicators. They may be subdivided into three categories: internal communications, mass communications, and education.

Even such a crude indicator as domestic mail per capita[49] reveals the rapidity of the transformation in internal communications: In 1948 there were 2.8 letters per capita; in 1963 the figure had risen to 8.5, an increase of about 207 per cent. Foreign mail (sent and received) per capita increased 195 per cent during the same period. There were 23.6 telephones per 1,000 people in 1955 and 47.3 per 1,000 in 1963. During the Chehab regime (1958–1964), the number of telephones more than doubled. If we look at automobiles as an indicator of internal communications, we see that in 1948 there were some 8,100 passenger vehicles in Lebanon or about 6.7 per 1,000 people; in 1963 the number was up to 73,300, or 36.4 automobiles per 1,000.

The growth of exposure to modernity through mass communications has been even more impressive. The average Lebanese citizen is probably as aware of national and international affairs as his counterpart in the United States, because the mass media are so readily available. The radio carries a variety of messages beyond the Greater Beirut area, and the dial covers a full spectrum of sources: Cairo, Amman, Jerusalem, Moscow, Washington, London, Peking, and Damascus. The Beirut radio network broadcasts locally in Arabic and French and to a lesser extent in English and Armenian. Whatever his physical immobility, the most provincial Biqa villager is exposed to points of view not easily available even to readers of *The New York Times*. There is little doubt that Lebanon has been virtually saturated with radios since the advent of the transistor. A sample survey by the Association Libanaise des Sciences Politiques (A.L.S.P.) in 1963 put the number of radios at 500,000. Assuming four listeners per set, the population has been theoretically blanketed. Fifteen years earlier there were perhaps one-tenth as many radios.[50] The A.L.S.P. suggests that radios are ubiquitous in all regions and among all socioeconomic groups. South Lebanon has slightly fewer radios than do the other provinces, but even there more than three-fourths of the people have access to radio; farmers fall behind other occupational groups, but a good two-thirds are nevertheless exposed. Most people prefer music and news to other types of programs, and two-thirds of the sample (mostly white-collar employees, university graduates, and merchants) reported that they listen to foreign stations to obtain different points of view.[51] It is certain that the proportion of "non-listeners" described by Lerner in his study of modernization in the Middle East has greatly dwindled since 1951 and with it the proportion of "non-empathetic Traditionals" has also declined.[52]

Lebanon is sometimes called "a nation of journalists." Certainly the Lebanese have been the journalists of the Arab world and have established presses wherever there was a colony of Lebanese emigrants. The first paper in Arabic to appear in any Arab territory was founded by Khalil al-Khoury at Beirut in 1858. In 1911 Lebanon's first press association was founded, headed by Khalil Sarkis, and the Lebanese Press Syndicate obtained governmental sanction in 1921.[53] Despite Ottoman and French restrictions, around 256 newspapers and 141 magazines had been founded by 1927, although most of them were short-lived. After World War II the press continued to develop although the state continued to interfere. One need only look at the statistics of recent years (see Table 6)

TABLE 6

NEWSPAPERS AND PERIODICALS BY LANGUAGE, 1962

Dailies		*Weeklies* (*nonpolitical*)		*Weeklies* (*political*)		*Periodicals* (*once or twice monthly*)	
Arabic	43	Arabic	88	Arabic	44	Arabic	80
French	4	French	10	French	2	French	6
English	2	Armenian	5	English	1	English	1
Armenian	4		—	Armenian	2	Armenian	12
Total	53	Total	103	Total	49	Total	99

Grand Total 304

Lebanese Press Syndicate, *List of Registered Publications*. Beirut: 1962.

to agree that Lebanon is a journalistically overdeveloped country. In the United States thoughtful citizens worry about the disappearance of the daily newspaper; in 1965 a Lebanese journalist (who writes for at least four publications herself) remarked that the country has too many daily newspapers. It is all very well to have a diversity of points of view, she argued, but how can cohesive public opinion exist without some common agreement on what is important and what is true?

In 1950, there were forty-five dailies and an estimated circulation of 80 copies per 1,000 people, and, by 1957, the circulation was 100 copies per 1,000 people.[54] By 1963, according to the A.L.S.P., general circulation was around 200,000, or 120 copies per 1,000.[55] "Eighty-five per cent of the Beirutis and 77 per cent of the Lebanese in general read the papers frequently," the A.L.S.P. reported.[56] Per capita consumption of newsprint has risen from 0.9 kilograms in 1951 to 3.9 kilograms in 1964.[57]

A word should be said about the movies and Lebanon's newest

mass medium, television. Both media are heavily concentrated in the Greater Beirut area, perhaps even more than are the other components of "exposure." In the absence of a survey of Lebanese film-going habits, one must rely on impressions and some rough statistics to judge the impact of the cinema. Impressions suggest strongly that Beirut may be the movie-going capital of the world. Many people, especially in the middle-income groups, attend twice or more a week, lured by the convenience, the wide choice of films, the comfortable surroundings, and the very low price. The success of the movies in Lebanon is amply borne out by the impressive increase in both the number of theaters and in their seating capacity. According to the United Nations Educational, Scientific and Cultural Organization (UNESCO), Lebanese per capita film attendance in 1951 was 5; in 1962 it was 22.5, the second highest in the world.[58] The number of movie theaters has increased from 48 to 170. Lebanese parents and social critics worry about the possible effects of this sort of exposure. Although there is no indication that movie going has significantly weakened the family or increased juvenile delinquency, it has contributed to a certain alienation among college youth and younger Lebanese in general.[59] The growth of television, although it is much more recent, seems to be equally rapid. In 1959 there were just over 6,000 television sets in the country and, if we may assume five viewers per set, an audience of some 30,000. Four years later, the number of television sets had risen to about 100,000, which suggests that perhaps 25 per cent of the population is exposed to the programing that Beirut's two private companies and Cairo television offer.[60] The greatest bulk of the sets is found in the Greater Beirut area, and the most avid spectators are young: It has been estimated that 80 per cent of the persons under twenty who have access to a set watch television every night, whereas somewhat less than one-fourth of the adult population does so. The same study suggests three findings about the effects of television on family life. First, businessmen, white-collar employees, and bureaucrats are the groups most frequently experiencing a "change in habits" (except in South Lebanon); second, the population of the province of Mount Lebanon, which has a high living standard and proximity to the television transmitters, has the highest proportion of viewers who find that television is changing their habits; and, third, Beirut, in contrast, has the lowest proportion of viewers in this category, reflecting—the study observes—the many distractions available to the Beiruti.[61]

Education as a form of exposure to modernity has particular political relevance because it crucially affects the extent and substance of political participation. Certainly this is true in Lebanon, and the high educational level in Mount Lebanon and Beirut undoubtedly contributes to the sophistication evident in the political behavior of the middle- and upper-income groups. Equally important, however, is the uneven distribution of educational opportunity. The educationally deprived areas—rural and urban—have long been controlled by political bosses. As the people in these areas become more educated, and, as the number of educated people in general grows, the stresses on traditional political arrangements are increasing. Because education is a means of politicization in Lebanon both its expansion and its substance deserve examination.

The literacy level is one basic indicator of education spread. Lebanon has a degree of literacy equal to those in politically modernized countries like Italy, Cuba, Yugoslavia, and the Philippines. Officials in the Ministry of National Education estimate that in 1965 more than 80 per cent of the entire population could read, write, and figure. This figure may be compared with UNESCO's estimate of between 45 and 50 per cent literate in 1950.[62] About 60 per cent of the literate population has command of two languages; about 25 per cent has command of three. The level of literacy alone, however, is misleading for political analysis. In the first place, illiteracy is significantly higher in rural Lebanon than in the core area; illiteracy accentuates the historic divisions in the political culture. One study, based on a survey of twenty-one villages, found an adult illiteracy level of 38 per cent in 1957.[63] Another states that nearly half the adults over twenty years of age living in the rural areas have had only two or three years of elementary education, and their literacy is consequently weak.[64] Mount Lebanon, with its history of missionary education, is thought to have the highest literacy level in the five provinces; it is followed at some distance by North Lebanon, South Lebanon, and the Biqa. For Beirut, estimates vary between about 70 and 90 per cent literacy. Bilingual literacy, too, is concentrated in the Beirut–Mount Lebanon area: The formative influences of French, as a vehicle of Western culture, are decidedly weaker in the rural zones. The core area thus contrasts sharply with rural Lebanon on the basis of one of the key variables in modernization. This imbalance, however, should not obscure a trend of long-run political significance: The deprived area

is now making the transition to general literacy that the core area
began to experience a century ago.

Because the literacy level also varies sharply according to religion, it further emphasizes historical divisions. The village study
mentioned previously reports that Christians are more generally
literate than are Muslims, primarily because Christians predominate in private schools and the government schools are weak (see
Table 7). Table 7 shows the decline in illiteracy among the youth

TABLE 7

RURAL ILLITERACY RATES

PERCENTAGE OF ILLITERACY

	Men	Women	Boys	Girls
Christians	23	45	22	29
Muslims	39	69	28	33

Selim Abou, *Le Bilinguisme Arabe-Français au Liban* (Paris: Presses Universitaires de France, 1962), p. 111.

and the attendant lessening of differences in illiteracy among the
sects as well as between the sexes. The political effects of these
trends are only beginning to be felt; in the next generation they
may transform the character of Lebanese politics.

Let us look at primary and secondary education in detail. In
the school year 1944–1945, there were 150,362 elementary and
secondary students in public and private schools; in 1963–1964,
the number of students was 371,239, an increase of 147 per cent.
During the same period, the school-age population increased by
only 85 per cent. The percentage of the school-age population actually attending school in 1944–1945 was thus 35.1 whereas nineteen years later it was 46.9 per cent.[65] The rate of expansion has
increased markedly since 1959. In the fourteen years between 1945
and 1959 the percentage of school-age population in school increased by only 4.6 percentage points, from 35.1 per cent to 39.7
per cent. In the next five years, however, the percentage increased
7.2 percentage points. Both educational levels and progress under
the Mandate were much less impressive. In 1932, for example,
there were about 100,000 primary- and secondary-school students
out of a school-age population of approximately 317,000, a percentage of 31.7.[66] By 1943 the number of students had increased

approximately 30 per cent, and the school-age population had increased 32 per cent, a feeble performance compared with the postindependence developments.

The educational explosion affects all levels. In 1950, the number of Lebanese in primary school was 115 per 1,000 inhabitants of the country; in 1963 the proportion had risen to 160 per 1,000. There were twenty secondary-school students per 1,000 population in 1950 and thirty-one per 1,000 in 1963;[67] and the number of university students increased from 6,822 in 1959 to 15,978 in 1963.[68]

These figures show that the demand for education, traditionally high among the Lebanese, has resulted in an ever-increasing proportion of educated people. The literacy statistics bear this conclusion out: Whereas 39 per cent of Lebanese aged sixty-one or above are literate, 74 per cent of the 21–30 age group and 84 per cent of the 6–20 age group are literate.[69] The demand for education has strained both public and private resources and has put a very high price on private education in the middle 1960s. Increasing the number of educated men and women also implies finding jobs for them once they have received their certificates.

It would be misleading to assume that the educational boom has affected all parts of Lebanon equally. The IRFED mission estimated that, in 1959, the percentage of students to province population was 18.8 per cent in Beirut and 17.4 per cent in Mount Lebanon, whereas North Lebanon registered only 16.3 per cent, the Biqa 13.5 per cent, and South Lebanon 13.2 per cent.[70] All three outlying provinces fell below the national average of 16.4 per cent. The disparity is heightened by the fact that Mount Lebanon and Beirut are served primarily by private schools, which are considered to be of higher quality than the government schools, whereas the rural districts, especially South Lebanon and the Biqa, must rely heavily on the government for the relatively little education available. On still another indicator of social mobilization, Mount Lebanon and Beirut are ahead of the districts added by France in 1920.

We may conclude this discussion of exposure trends by calling attention to their speed and their unevenness. Increasing exposure to modernity is enlarging the politically conscious population. The Lebanese political system, in the past a field of action for only a small part of the population, faces the task of integrating a newly politicized population. The unevenness of exposure in general makes such integration a formidable task. Radio, which carries many kinds of political messages, reaches virtually all areas of Lebanon. Education, which is intended to foster Lebanese citizenship, does not. The concentration of internal communications in the Beirut–Mount Lebanon area divides that region from its neighboring provinces and accentuates historical separateness.

SUMMARY

A brief recapitulation of the trends in Lebanon's social mobilization may be helpful at this point. Table 8 provides an idea of the magnitude and rapidity of these changes.

TABLE 8

SUMMARY OF SOCIAL-MOBILIZATION TRENDS

	Year	*Data*	*Year*	*Data*
Demographic trends				
Population (millions)	1943	1.02	1963	2.00
Persons per sq. km.	1943	101	1963	193
Percentage of persons in cities of 20,000 and over	1943	28.7	1963	37.4
Economic trends				
Energy consumption per capita (kgs. of metric tons of coal equivalent)	1960	520	1964	689
Electricity (millions of kw. hours produced)	1959	267	1962	551
Per capita income	1959	$362	1963	$449
Number of banks	1951	5	1966	93
Exposure trends				
Telephones per 1,000	1948	10.8	1963	47.3
Passenger vehicles per 1,000	1948	6.7	1963	36.4
Number of radio listeners (in thousands)	1948	200	1963	2,000
Newsprint consumption per capita (kgs.)	1951	0.9	1964	3.9
Primary school students per 1,000	1950	115	1963	160
Secondary school students per 1,000	1950	20	1963	31
University students per 1,000	1950	2.4	1963	8.2

The demographic movements, insofar as they are creating an urban proletariat, are no doubt establishing a base for future industrialization, but they are also accelerating the growth of Greater Beirut and increasing its burden of social, administrative, and political problems. Meanwhile, talented manpower leaves the outlying areas for the cities at the same time that rural needs and expectations increase. Economic development is occurring, but its unevenness may be offsetting its politically soothing effects with increased tension and division. Greater exposure to modernity may be promoting tolerance, cooperation, and a civic spirit among some people, but among the well-educated this increased exposure adds to discontent and unemployment. Exposure produces mass sophis-

TABLE 9

SOCIAL MOBILIZATION BY REGION

Indicator	Beirut	Mount Lebanon	North Lebanon	South Lebanon	Biqa
Persons per square kilometer	23,034	340	191	137	47
IRFED development scores		2.22 *		1.70	1.75	1.92
Per capita income, 1957 †	$803	$205	$200	$151	$206
Percentage of radio owners	85	85	85	78	91
Percentage of television owners	39	35	27	28	18
Newspaper consumption (percentage of total circulation)	70 *			30 §	
Percentage of readers interested in internal politics **	68	63	53	45	49
Percentage of students in population	18.8	17.4	16.3	13.5	13.2

* Figure is for Beirut and Mount Lebanon combined.
† United States, Operations Missions in Lebanon, *Economic Data for the Ekistic Programme of Lebanon* (Beirut: Doxiadis, 1957), pp. 23–7.
§ Figure is for North Lebanon, South Lebanon, and Biqa combined.
** Association Libanaise des Sciences Politiques, 3ème Congrès de Science Politique, *Presse, Radio, Télévision et Opinion Publique* (Beirut: May 1963), p. 13 (mimeo).

tication, and in Lebanon, for better or worse, this sophistication presents an implicit challenge to the substantive and procedural aspects of Lebanese politics. The unevenness in Lebanese social mobilization is summarized in Table 9.

Finally, it is useful to ask how Lebanon compares with other Arab states on certain indices of social mobilization. Table 10

TABLE 10

COMPARISON OF SOCIAL MOBILIZATION IN LEBANON
AND FIVE ARAB STATES

Indicator	Lebanon	Syria	Jordan	Iraq	U.A.R.	Saudi Arabia
Population, annual rate of increase (1964)	2.6	3.2	3.1	1.7	2.7	1.7
Persons per square kilometer (1963–1964)	193	28	21	16	812 *	3
Percentage of population in cities 100,000 and over (1952–1958)	33.2	28.9	8.1	14.5	22.2	9.5 †
Energy consumption per capita (1964)	689	351	261	666	321	320
Daily calories (1957–1962)	2,550	2,330	2,050	n.a.	2,690	n.a.
Inhabitants per physician (1960)	1,100	4,600	5,800	5,600	2,600	13,000
Gross national product per capita (1957)	$362	$173	$129	$156	$142	$170
Newspaper circulation per 1,000 (1965)	120	21	11	12	15	3
Primary school students per 1,000 (1959)	93	85	102	80	92	12

* Density to cultivated land.
† Percentage in cities larger than 20,000.
  Statistical Yearbook: 1965 (New York: United Nations, 1966); and *Demographic Yearbook: 1960* (New York: United Nations, 1960). G.N.P. data are from Bruce M. Russett *et al., World Handbook of Political and Social Indicators* (New Haven: Yale University Press, 1964). Education data are from *Middle East Forum,* 36, No. 6 (1961), 11. Figures for Lebanon are corrected where necessary.

shows that Lebanon is substantially ahead of some of its neighbors. This kind of unevenness is also important. If the Arab world is considered as a unit—and it is by a great many Arabs—Lebanon's share of the area's modernization resources is disproportionately large. In an underdeveloped area Lebanon is a highly developed enclave. Lebanon is, however, bound to the other Arab states by cultural, economic, and political ties, and as a part of the Arab world it is obliged to justify and defend its relative attainments. Inevitably these attainments stimulate envy, bitterness, and political tension between Lebanon and its neighbors, especially Syria. This tension places still another load on the Lebanese system.

NOTES

[1] The following works are relevant to the present chapter. Daniel Lerner, *The Passing of Traditional Society* (New York: Free Press, 1958); Leonard Binder, *Iran* (Berkeley: University of California Press, 1961); Gabriel Almond and James Coleman, *The Politics of Developing Areas* (Princeton: Princeton University Press, 1960); and Manfred Halpern, *The Politics of Social Change in the Near East and North Africa* (Princeton: Princeton University Press, 1963).

[2] Karl W. Deutsch, "Social Mobilization and Political Development," *American Political Science Review,* 55, No. 3 (1961), 493–4.

[3] *Ibid.,* p. 501.

[4] This discussion relies heavily on information from the Lebanese Ministry of Planning.

[5] Kingsley Davis, "Population Analysis," in *The Republic of Lebanon* (New Haven: Human Relations Area Files, 1956), pp. 54–80.

[6] David Yaukey, *Fertility Differences in a Modernizing Country* (Princeton: Princeton University Press, 1961), pp. 79, 81.

[7] The figures are from the Ministry of Planning. The total figure for 1932 is 793,000. But 37,000 of those counted had emigrated between 1924 and 1932, although they had opted for Lebanese citizenship under the terms of the Lausanne agreement. The total figure for 1943 is 1,060,000, but it includes 38,000 foreigners. The increase rate is calculated from the reduced figures for each year, but the density figure for 1943 is based upon total resident population, Lebanese and non-Lebanese, as are subsequent density figures.

[8] U.S. Operations Mission in Lebanon, *Economic Data for the Ekistic Programme of Lebanon* (Beirut: Doxiadis, 1957), hereafter cited as *Ekistic Survey.*

[9] Republic of Lebanon Ministry of Planning, *Besoins et Possibilités de Développement du Liban,* I (Beirut: 1960–1961), 46. This report is the work of the Institut International de Recherches et de Formation en vue de Développement and is cited hereafter as *IRFED Report.*

[10] Yaukey, *op. cit.,* p. 77, shows that Lebanon fits the European pattern of demographic transition; the total fertility rate of educated city dwellers is lowest, the fertility of uneducated city dwellers is higher, and the fertility of uneducated village dwellers is highest. For the near future, "among Christians one would expect (1) a further decrease in the already small socio-economic fertility differences in the city and, accordingly, (2) an increase in the difference between uneducated city dwellers and uneducated isolated villagers. Among the Muslims, one would expect (1) a continued decrease in the fertility of both educated and uneducated city dwellers and, accordingly, (2) an increase in the fertility differences between uneducated city dwellers and uneducated isolated villagers, then finally (3) a decrease in the socio-economic fertility differences in the city. In the more distant future, one might expect the villages as well to start the transition to the limited family model. But what to expect ultimately of city fertility is not suggested

by demographic transition theory. After all city classes have brought fertility under voluntary control, then fertility will reflect the choices of the partners at the time, just as it does at present in urban United States." Yaukey, *op. cit.,* pp. 82–3.

[11] *IRFED Report,* I, 49.

[12] United Nations Relief and Works Agency for Palestine Refugees, *Activities in Lebanon* (Beirut: United Nations, April 1, 1961), p. 1.

[13] Republic of Lebanon, *Nutrition Survey: A Report by the Inter-departmental Committee on Nutrition for National Defense* (Beirut: 1961), pp. 1–16. The specialists from the Lebanese government and the U.S. Department of Defense who prepared this report judged the average caloric intake of 2,300 "adequate."

[14] Between 1951 and 1961 the budget of the Ministry of Public Health increased by 152 per cent, or from L£3.5 (approximately $1.16) to L£6.4 (approximately $2.15) per capita for Lebanese citizens. *IRFED Report,* I, 339.

[15] Figures submitted by the Lebanese government to the United Nations for 1965 reported a total population estimate of 2,280,000 and a density of 219 per square kilometer—a sharp upward revision of earlier estimates. United Nations, *Statistical Yearbook: 1965* (New York: United Nations, 1966).

[16] Davis, *op. cit.,* p. 70.

[17] Said Chéhabe ed-Dine, *Géographie Humaine de Beyrouth* (Beirut: Calfat, 1960).

[18] John Gulick, "Old Values and New Institutions in a Lebanese City," *Human Organization,* 24 (Spring 1965), 50.

[19] Figures are from the Ministry of Social Affairs and Labor.

[20] Calculated from Ministry of Planning information and figures given in the *IRFED Report.*

[21] IRFED, *Le Liban Face à son Développement: Etudes et Documents* (Beirut: IRFED, 1963), Appendix R.

[22] *Ekistic Survey,* tables on migration to Beirut. North Lebanon's lack of mobility is probably exaggerated, because migration to Tripoli was not examined in this study.

[23] Charles W. Churchill, "Village Life in the Central Beqa Valley of Lebanon," *Middle East Economic Papers: 1959* (Beirut: American University Economic Research Institute, 1959), p. 7. Churchill concluded, "If anything, the youngest generation is less mobile than its elders."

[24] Saba G. Shiber, "A Critical Glance at Greater Beirut," in Shiber (ed.), *Urban Form and Aesthetics* (Kuwait, 1961), pp. 88–9 (mimeo.).

[25] Gulick has commented on this apparent coexistence of new and old ways in his studies of a small Lebanese village and a large town, Tripoli. Discussing the latter, he writes, "So far, anthropological findings indicate that urbanization per se does not necessarily destroy traditional cultures." Gulick, *op. cit.,* p. 52. See also Gulick, *Social Structure and Culture Change in a Lebanese Village* (New York: Wenner-Gren, 1955).

[26] Nathan Glazer and Daniel P. Moynihan, *Beyond the Melting Pot* (Cambridge, Mass.: Massachusetts Institute of Technology Press, 1963).

[27] The number of kilowatt hours produced in 1959 was 267 million; in 1962 it was 551 million. United Nations, *Statistical Yearbook: 1964* (New York: United Nations, 1965). Per capita consumption of energy (measured in kilograms of metric tons of coal equivalent) was 520 in 1960 and 645 in 1963.

[28] *Ekistic Survey,* p. 22. Doxiadis Associates used figures calculated by the Economic Research Institute of the American University of Beirut.

[29] Republic of Lebanon, Ministry of Finance, 1965.

[30] Using the 1963 estimate of the Lebanese gross national product made by the U.S. Department of Commerce and the population estimates made by the Lebanese Ministry of Planning for the same year, the per capita income of Lebanese citizens can be estimated at $449, whereas the per capita income of inhabitants of Lebanon is estimated at $361. See *International Commerce,* February 1, 1965, p. 8. It should be noted that the U.S. Department of Commerce estimate is conservative; another reputable American source puts the gross national product at $770 million. The 1950 and 1956 per capita estimates are from Professor A. Y. Badre, "The National Income of Lebanon," *Middle East Economic Papers: 1956* (Beirut: American University Economic Research Institute, 1956).

[31] *Le Commerce du Levant,* March 5, 1966, p. 17.

[32] *Ekistic Survey,* pp. 30–2.

[33] Food and Agriculture Organization of the United Nations Mediterranean Development Project, *Lebanon: Country Report* (Rome: United Nations, 1959), pp. 11–4.

[34] *IRFED Report,* I, 57, 81. Agricultural workers make up 49 per cent of the permanent active work force and 55 per cent of the permanent and temporary work force. The IRFED investigators thought the Doxiadis experts had underestimated the percentage of workers in agriculture and industry. The disparities in income distribution reported by Doxiadis may thus also have been understated. *Preliminary Assessment of Manpower Resources and Requirements in Lebanon* (Beirut: American University of Beirut Economic Research Institute, 1960).

[35] *IRFED Report,* I, 87.

[36] For a complete explanation of the methodology see *IRFED Report,* II, 19–50. For a clearer, if less detailed, exposition, see *Le Liban Face à son Développement,* pp. 13–21.

[37] *IRFED Report,* II, 31–50.

[38] IRFED, *Le Liban Face à son Développement,* p. 158.

[39] *Ibid.,* p. 166; *IRFED Report,* II, 92.

[40] Marwan Iskandar, *Social Security for Lebanon* (Beirut: Dār al-ṭalī'ah, 1962), p. 33.

[41] They were the permanently employed; there are also some 130,000 seasonal workers, mostly in agriculture. See *IRFED Report,* I, 57.

[42] These calculations are based on the assumptions that by 1980 Lebanon will have eliminated about 60 per cent of the foreign laborers (mainly Syrians) who presently do menial and hard labor and that these jobs will be filled by Lebanese. Otherwise, 38 per cent of the Lebanese active work force would be unemployed by 1980.

[43] Even assuming that irrigated land will double from 111,195 acres in 1965 to 222,390 acres in 1980 and that the remaining cultivatable land (580,685 acres) is exploited for dry farming—this total is the maximum cultivation possible—the agricultural sector will still support only 140,000 workers in 1980, assuming that technology allows only one man per approximately 2.5 acres of irrigated land and one man per 12.3 acres of dry farmland. If that were the case, then the agricultural sector would actually lose 80,000 jobs by 1980. The Lebanese experts do not believe this many jobs will actually be lost because new developments in marine and forest agriculture will open some new jobs.

[44] *IRFED Report,* II, 380, 378. Industry's share of new investment in 1950 was 13.5 per cent; in 1961 it was 12.2 per cent. *Le Commerce du Levant,* March 5, 1966.

[45] *IRFED Report,* II, 389.

[46] See Philip K. Hitti, *Lebanon in History: From Earliest Times to the Present* (New York: Macmillan, 1957).

[47] How the rationalistic policies of that strangely modern ruler were imposed upon the Lebanon's particularistic culture has been discussed in William R. Polk, *The Opening of South Lebanon, 1788–1840* (Cambridge, Mass.: Harvard University Press, 1963).

[48] George Antonius, *The Arab Awakening* (London: Hamilton, 1938), chaps. 3, 5; and Kamal Salibi, *The Modern History of Lebanon* (London: Weidenfeld, 1965), pp. 120–48.

[49] All figures for internal communications are drawn from United Nations, *Statistical Yearbook: 1960* (New York: United Nations, 1961); and United Nations, *Statistical Yearbook: 1964.*

[50] Association Libanaise des Sciences Politiques, *Presse, Radio, Télévision, et Opinion Publique* (Beirut: May 1963), p. 26 (mimeo.), hereafter cited as *A.L.S.P. Study.*

[51] *Ibid.,* pp. 29, 30. These findings are consistent with those of a survey made in 1950–1951 for the United States government, which attributed the apparent effectiveness of the B.B.C. in part to the credibility of its news programs and the strong emphasis on good music in its programing. This survey suggested that the Voice of America would be more effective if it would strengthen its signal, free its news reporting from obvious propaganda, and present more local news and Arabic music. Bureau of Applied Social Research (B.A.S.R.), *The Radio Audience of Lebanon* (New York: 1951) (multigraph).

[52] Lerner, *op. cit.,* pp. 174–204, reanalyzed the 1951 B.A.S.R. data and showed that Lebanon even in 1951 was "not ridden by traditionalist fears that public awareness of internal social problems must inevitably undermine the entire structure of authority" but did face formidable problems related to sectarian fears, economic progress, and Arab nationalism.

[53] Conversations with Lebanese Press Syndicate sources.

[54] United Nations, *Statistical Yearbook: 1960.*

[55] *A.L.S.P. Study,* p. 6. *Cf.* Selim Abou, *Le Bilinguisme Arabe-Français au Liban* (Paris: Presses Universitaires, 1962), pp. 125–6. A figure reported in United Nations, *Statistical Yearbook: 1961,* gives Lebanon 153 daily newspaper

copies per 1,000 in 1960. The discrepancy probably results from using a smaller population base (Lebanese citizens rather than inhabitants).

[56] *A.L.S.P. Study,* p. 35.

[57] United Nations Educational, Social and Cultural Organization, *World Communications: 1964* (Paris: UNESCO, 1965).

[58] Hong Kong ranked first. *Ibid.*

[59] See, for example, two novels by young Lebanese writers, both girls, one Druze and the other Shiite, one American educated and the other French educated, which both have alienation as their theme. Rima Alamuddin, *Spring to Summer* (Beirut: Khayat's, 1963); Leila Baalbaki, *Anā aḥyā* [*I Live*] (Beirut: Dār majalat al-shi'r, 1963). A number of lectures and magazine articles have dealt with the problems of Lebanese youth. See, for example, "Crise de Jeunesse Libanaise," *Cénacle Libanais* (Beirut), 1958.

[60] Figures are from *A.L.S.P. Study,* pp. 17 ff.; and from United Nations, *Statistical Yearbook: 1964.*

[61] *A.L.S.P. Study,* pp. 19–20.

[62] UNESCO, *Basic Facts and Figures: 1960* (Paris: UNESCO, 1961).

[63] Abou, *op. cit.,* p. 92. This estimate is based on a survey of 7,908 inhabitants of twenty-one villages. It must be noted that seventeen of the twenty-one villages are located within old Mount Lebanon, and thus the figures probably understate the extent of rural illiteracy by underrepresenting the areas outside historic Western influence.

[64] *L'Orient,* September 22, 1966.

[65] If the base population is restricted to Lebanese citizens, as opposed to inhabitants, the percentage of the school-age group attending school in 1963–1964 was 48.4. Figures for 1944–1945 are drawn from Mohammed Majzoub, *Le Liban et l'Orient Arabe, 1943–1965* (unpublished doctoral dissertation, University of Aix-en-Provence, 1956), p. 50. The school-age population estimate is drawn from the 1944 population distribution by age calculated by J. Gholl, *L'Evolution Démographique Libanaise,* Travaux du Semaine d'Etudes Economiques et Financières, No. 1 (Beirut: 1957–1958), and the 1959 distribution was calculated by the IRFED mission. See *IRFED Report,* I, 48. The 1963–1964 enrollment figures are from the Ministry of National Education.

[66] R. D. Matthews and Matta Akrawi, *Education in the Arab Countries of the Near East* (Washington, D.C.: American Council on Education, 1949), p. 422.

[67] The 1950 figures are taken from data presented at a UNESCO Conference on Education in Beirut, February 1960. *Middle East Forum,* 36 (June 1960), 11. The 1959 and 1963 data come from the Ministry of Education. Secondary-school students are those who have the certificat and are aiming for either the brevet or baccalauréat degrees.

[68] *IRFED Report,* I, 63; United Nations, *Statistical Yearbook: 1965.*

[69] Abou, *op. cit.,* p. 96.

[70] *IRFED Report,* I, 65.

CHAPTER · 3

Lebanon's Political Dilemma

The Lebanese Republic faces a continuing dilemma because it is confronted with problems of national integration and social mobilization. Integration requires the maintenance of an intricate balance among competing interests, parochial and foreign. Social mobilization imposes additional burdens on the entire political system: new power groups, new policy demands, new administrative loads. These two conditions are mutually reinforcing, and thus their politically dysfunctional effects are amplified. Parochialism is an obstacle to the even spread of social mobilization, and social mobilization magnifies rather than obliterates the divisions in the political culture. A political dilemma is the result: The institutional means for coping with a fragmented political culture are antagonistic to the development of a system strong enough to handle the multiple challenges posed by social mobilization. Lebanon currently manages its complex identity difficulties through the institutionalization of traditional pluralism.

Chapter 2 has suggested that the mechanisms involved in the Lebanese solution are as fragile as they are sophisticated. In Lebanon, a modicum of security from historic divisions has been bought at the expense of political modernization. Balance takes precedence over the institutional flexibility and dynamism that a society in rapid transition requires for security, social justice, and national development. The Lebanese political apparatus is ill equipped to carry out tasks of regulation, adjudication, and development, and these tasks are beyond the capacity of even the most resourceful individuals and special interests. It is not a complete exaggeration to state that the basic structures and functions in this system are mismatched: The executive branch is more important for the representation it gives to parochial elements through the sectarian allocation of administrative posts than for its policy-making activities, whereas the legislature is more effective in promoting special interests through its influence over routine administration than in representing the public interest.

Lebanese politics in the postwar era is essentially a struggle with this dilemma. Efforts to concentrate more power in the presidency are challenged and corrupted by the parochial leaders, who fear that their influence over it could thereby decline, but the resulting tendency to *immobilisme* is consistently and repeatedly challenged by the chronic administrative crises and the demands of the newly politicized for power and policies attuned to contemporary needs and values. A decade of revolution in the Arab world and the deeper scars of the 1958 crisis (fears of what it might have become, for example) have made confessional and class tensions more apparent in the middle 1960s than they were during the Khoury regime. The overdevelopment of the Greater Beirut area has cast a shadow over the lesser progress made in the outer regions. Political ferment in the eastern Arab world, which shows no signs of abating, shakes the entire Lebanese political system. Population increase and urban migration are more rapid than the expansion of the industrial and agricultural sectors. As the pressures for jobs mount, the economic situation of the resident Palestinians and Syrians becomes increasingly precarious. The perceived accuracy of the established sectarian proportions dwindles with time, eroded by the faster population increase among non-Christians. Furthermore, the ordinary people in Lebanon are more politically critical, more knowledgeable, more and more politically active in the middle 1960s than they were two decades earlier. This growing sector of potential power aggravates the problem of institutionalizing mass participation. Modes of conflict resolution that were adequate for a thin stratum of notables in the early postindependence era are no longer appropriate. There is a pressing need to institutionalize political participation by the growing untraditional, skilled strata, which are deprived of power yet impatient to exercise it, and by the increasingly politicized common people.

This chapter discusses some of the more serious manifestations of the dilemma of reconciling social mobilization and national integration and attempts to show where the political system is particularly vulnerable. It examines, first, the political loads imposed by the historic integration problem and some of the political responses. Second, it analyzes some of the political consequences of social mobilization. Finally, it analyzes Lebanon's two major crises, in which the gravity of the dilemma is most clearly evident.

THE STRAIN OF INTEGRATION

Although traditional pluralism has contributed to the liberal and democratic aspects of Lebanese politics, it also remains the greatest threat to the political system. The veneer of integration, founded on convenience rather than conviction, is constantly challenged by friction caused by sectarian suspicions and external pressures.

Sectarian Suspicions

It seems unlikely that sectarian suspicions can be eliminated in the foreseeable future both because they are rooted firmly in the traditional culture of Lebanon—dating at least from the double *qa'im-maqamiyyah*—and because uneven social mobilization and economic development have sharpened rather than blunted them. The relevant questions for the short and middle run, therefore, are whether or not the system will be able to cope with the tensions that will inevitably produce a certain amount of open strife and whether or not there are any realistic options for improving its ability to cope with them.

During the Mandate the major political concern was antagonism between Christians and non-Christians. This antagonism proved both useful and inconvenient to the French, useful in that it facilitated their policy of divide and rule but inconvenient because of resulting Muslim resentment. After independence, during the Presidency of Bechara al-Khoury, Lebanon enjoyed relatively peaceful sectarian relations, but there was a recrudescence of tension in 1953 and 1954. In March 1953, for example, the Hay'at al-Watania, an organization of Sunnite notables, led a movement to gain a greater share of administrative appointments for Sunnites. An Islamic congress convened to press more radical demands. Although it was repudiated by some of the prominent Sunnite and Shiite notables, it alarmed the Christian leaders, who issued a declaration that they would never accept physical modification of the country. The crisis abated when the Kataeb (mostly Maronite) called an interconfessional congress and the Nida al-Qawmi group (mostly Sunnite) appealed for an end to sectarian rivalry.[1] In July and August of the following year a more serious incident occurred. A pamphlet that spoke irreverently of Islam appeared under the name of a former student, Georges Chakar, following the publication of an anti-Maronite pamphlet called "Muslim Lebanon Today." Sectarian feeling was so sensitive that a protest strike took place, followed the next day by violent demonstrations in which fifty-five people were hurt. Although Chakar was in jail at the time and the pamphlet had apparently been written in 1947, tensions did not ease. President Camille Chamoun, in a national address, warned that mixing religion and politics would mean the end of an independent Lebanon. Prominent Sunnites like Hussein Oueini attempted to mediate the affair; and the Grand Mufti of Lebanon, Shaykh Muhammad Alaya, called for unity. Finally order was restored, and Chakar was sentenced forthwith.[2]

The insurrection of summer 1958, discussed at greater length later in this chapter, disrupted political, social, and economic life but did not degenerate into a confessional struggle until well after a political settlement had been reached. At that point, however, and for a full month afterward, there was a rash of incidents with distinctly sectarian overtones. Although most of them may have been matters of personal vengeance and isolated aggression, they were sufficient to remind Christians and Muslims of their mutual fears of persecution.[3]

Sectarianism remains a critical problem in the 1960s. In March 1965, West Germany gave Israel diplomatic recognition. High-school and university students in many parts of Lebanon participated in the wave of demonstrations protesting this event. In Tripoli a Christian private school was attacked and its superior injured by a crowd of Sunnite youths, apparently because they believed that the school authorities had forbidden the students to demonstrate. The incident touched off protest rallies in Christian schools and further violence, including a dynamite explosion. Sixty arrests were made, several people were injured, and at least one was killed.[4] A year later a teacher at the American University of Beirut was hurriedly deported when an extremist Muslim newspaper charged that some writings of St. Thomas Aquinas that were considered derogatory toward Islam had been distributed in a course.[5] It is significant that such incidents involve newly politicized elements, especially students, and are not restricted to the older, presumably more parochial, generation. These incidents are hardly indicative of diminishing sectarian tensions. Indeed, many knowledgeable Lebanese interviewed in the early 1960s felt that these tensions were increasing.

In assessing Lebanon's ability to cope with the sectarian problem, it is necessary to recall the argument about the sources of sectarian feeling advanced in Chapter 1 and to analyze the system's defense mechanisms in terms of that framework. Chapter 1 suggested that both doctrinaire Christians and doctrinaire Muslims feel superior to and threatened by each other. Because the demographic proportions are so close neither side has an unchallengeable claim to dominance; therefore, there are continuing pressures for adjusting the distribution of power as manifested in administrative appointments, the allocation of public-works funds, and ultimately the National Pact itself. In earlier days sectarian suspicions were kept down by a number of factors that have become less important with time. The physical separation of different communities previously permitted a sufficient degree of peaceful coexistence. In modern Lebanon—in the mobilized Beirut and Tripoli areas, where Christians and non-Christians rub shoulders—this separation is much reduced. The spread of education and exposure to mass media has created a stratum of people deeply involved in the Lebanese identity crisis; they are educated enough to see the problem but not sophisticated enough to live with it easily. The old notables, when they ruled virtually unchallenged, were well equipped to control sectarian problems through traditional channels; and the establishment was itself largely untroubled by sectarian disputes. Since 1950, however, the newer strata have forced themselves upon the political scene, and the role of the establishment has declined relatively. Whereas most of the new groups profess secularism there is not one that commands purely nonsectarian loyalty. Even the army is vulnerable to sectarian paralysis at those moments of crises in which national unity is so precious. As social mobilization forces the state increasingly to intervene in ordinary life, it also subjects it to growing sectarian strains.

The Republic is vulnerable to these strains but not entirely helpless. It possesses several instruments for dealing with sectarian explosions. Foremost among these are the procedures for institutionalizing sectarianism itself. The most prominent architect of these procedures was the banker, Michel Chiha. His analysis illustrates the Lebanese talent for making virtues of necessities.

Le confessionnalisme au Liban . . . est la garantie d'une représentation politique et sociale équitable pour des minorités confessionnelles associées . . . [il] est avant tout un facteur d'ordre et de paix. . . . Le Liban est fait de minorités confessionnelles associées. Ces minorités se présentent sous l'étiquette confessionnelle parce que le Liban a toujours été le refuge de la liberté de conscience. Cela a été possible à cause de la situation géographique du Liban, pays de montagne où il a toujours été possible de se défendre, et pays maritime d'où il a toujours été facile de prendre la mer. . . . Malgré beaucoup d'erreurs et d'abus, c'est le confessionnalisme qui a enseigné au Liban la tolérance. . . . L'équilibre libanais à base confessionnelle n'est pas un équilibre arbitraire. Ce n'est nullement le préjugé qui l'a fait; c'est la nécessité de reconnaître des particularités qui vont aussi loin que celles des partis politiques entre eux. Avec le temps, ces différences peuvent s'atténuer et lentement disparaître. Actuellement, la raison d'être du Liban est justement dans l'équilibre confessionnel qui le caractérise et qui se manifeste d'abord sur le plan du Pouvoir législatif.[6]

Chiha's analysis, written in 1954, is sophisticated, but the turbulent events since then cast doubt on the efficacy of his remedy for sectarianism and on the likelihood of an early disappearance of sectarian feeling. The major notables of all sects who mediate potential confessional disputes through traditional means are just as important as are the formal arrangements. Sectarian crises are still settled largely through the intervention of the traditional notables, each of whom can calm excited feelings by personal access to his clientele. As long as the old notables as a group exercise dominant control and continue to act in a united manner to check sectarian explosions, Lebanon weathers the storms. New mechanisms may soon be necessary, however, because increasing political participation is eroding the power and effectiveness of the old notables.

The government also uses its police power to prevent the spread of writings that might stir up sectarian feelings. The law contains severe penalties for those who engage in activities of this sort: Censorship can be heavy, and hardly a month goes by without an official announcement that a certain pamphlet or book has been suppressed. Since 1958, the internal security and military forces have kept a sharp vigil against such threats, but this vigilance has not reduced appreciably the number of breaches that actually occur. On the contrary, the Beirut and Tripoli areas nurture political-protest movements of all kinds, including highly fanatic sectarian groups like the Muslim Brotherhood and the Islamic Liberation Party and antireligious groupings like the Syrian National Party (known generally by its French name, Parti Populaire Syrien, or P.P.S.).

Finally, the government can enact policies of "social justice" that have at least the potential for reducing the inequities that promote sectarian strife. The Lebanese state has only recently begun to explore the possibility of redistributive measures to reduce the imbalances that history and the social-mobilization process have produced. Among Christians and Muslims the question of social justice is inextricably bound up with the question of relative political power. If it were simply a matter of raising the economic level of an oppressed minority, the state might act directly to improve the condition of the deprived group. Christians and non-Christians, however, exist in nearly equal proportions, and, although most Muslims seem to be poorer than most Christians, each religious group has its indigent and its wealthy. The state lacks the resources, the skills, and the will to equalize the various communities. Even if it could accomplish this formidable task, it is still not clear that sectarian tensions would be substantially reduced. The issue among the sects is not exclusively economic or social. Clashes also occur over differences in belief, and the sects are profoundly concerned about the possibility that their rivals may gain political power at their expense. This does not mean, however, that social and economic policy is irrelevant to sectarian conflict. Well-reasoned policy can be instrumental in showing the state's impartiality among the sects. Many Muslims think that Christians exploit the state at the expense of non-Christians, and many Christians believe that the Muslims are encroaching on Christian prerogatives in the hope of seizing complete power. In recent years the state has made a number of gestures to strengthen its reputation of sectarian neutrality and to show that all sects have a share in political rule. Few Lebanese, however, think that the state has reached an acceptable degree of impartiality, and some feel that the state ought to be "more than equal" in benefiting the needy.

External Pressures

Lebanon is bordered on the west by the Mediterranean and the fleets of the United States and the Soviet Union, in the south by its enemy, Israel, and in the north and east by Syria—a jealous brother. It is committed to friendship with the United Arab Republic (Egypt), the most powerful Arab state, and with the Christian powers of the West, especially the United States and France. Maintaining a balance among these more powerful entities presents chronic and delicate problems for the Lebanese. The necessity for equilibrium has been discussed in Chapter 1; in this section, we shall show Lebanon's difficulties in preserving this equilibrium in the turmoil of Arab and world politics since independence.

If Lebanon's external relations were merely a matter of diplomacy, there would be no unusual problems, but they are much more, for all the Republic's interested neighbors exert substantial influence in the domestic political process. Lebanon is not the only state whose internal and external situations are closely interwoven, but it is one of the few in which many of the most powerful actors in domestic politics live outside its borders. The boundaries of the Lebanese political system are as porous as the boundaries of its territory.

Each of the interested foreign states has cultivated certain Lebanese leaders and communities with sentimental, educational, religious, or simply monetary inducements. The precariousness of Lebanese institutional arrangements promotes such special foreign relationships. Shiites who fear Gamal Abdel Nasser or Syrian socialism find it difficult not to accept Saudi Arabian money or propaganda. To a pious Maronite or a graduate of the Jesuit university, Lebanon's "special relationship" with France is not an empty phrase. A British subsidy is a legitimate and necessary weapon for the editor who fears Lebanon is falling under Soviet-Egyptian control. The United States has been known to bestow substantial favors on anticommunist leaders. Arab nationalists rely heavily upon Cairo for sustenance. In Lebanon foreign embassies are frequently the functional equivalent and substitute for political parties, financing parliamentary candidates, pressuring policy makers, and influencing public opinion through the press.

Outside powers use various inducements to further their interests inside Lebanon, but they also use formidable sanctions to alter the domestic balance. If the American 6th Fleet is not in the immediate vicinity, it can be called quickly; its massive presence during its semiannual calls at Beirut is a visible reminder of American power. To some Lebanese it is a symbol of outside protection; to many others it represents the threat of neoimperialism.

Foreign powers also exert compelling leverage through their financial and trade policies. Neighboring Arab states account for about two-thirds of Lebanon's exports and two-thirds of its capital inflow. It is very easy for a Syrian regime to punish Lebanon by closing the frontiers or impeding truck traffic. Iraq and the U.A.R. occasionally bar Lebanese fruits or threaten Lebanese business interests in their countries.

The collapse of Beirut's Intra Bank in 1966 illustrates Lebanese vulnerability. When a tight money market and the enmity of rival banking factions inside Lebanon threatened to undermine Intra's overextended position, a number of external interests that the Lebanese normally neutralize through the intricate balancing process suddenly saw an opportunity for advancement. The United Arab Republic and its wealthy clients within Lebanon supposedly saw a chance to weaken a bank that finances important newspapers hostile to Egypt. According to another report, the British were irked when Middle East Airlines, in which Intra Bank held a controlling interest, chose to buy American rather than British airliners; they therefore persuaded Kuwaiti investors to transfer their sizable accounts from Intra to British banks. French and Soviet interests, which had common antipathy for the pro-American management of the Bank, undermined Intra holdings in Paris. Then the Saudi Arabians seized the occasion to embarrass a Lebanese government that they perceived as more sympathetic to President Abdel Nasser than to King Faisal. The withdrawal of the big Saudi Arabian oil accounts precipitated a run on the bank.[7] In the resolution of the Intra crisis a year later, Lebanon characteristically was dependent upon foreign assistance—the good offices of the United States government and American financiers. With an economy so heavily weighted toward services, financial and otherwise, Lebanon finds itself extremely vulnerable to foreign manipulation and to external crises.

Foreign interests also intervene in local affairs through propaganda. Chapter 2 showed that nearly all Lebanese are exposed to the radio. Those with a predisposition toward pan-Arabism in one form or another are particularly receptive to the voices of Cairo and Damascus. When President Nasser speaks on a hot July evening, thousands of radios in Beirut carry his voice; should he have critical words for a Lebanese politician or government, there will be immediate repercussions. During the crises of the 1950s the radio was used to incite disorder and rebellion, and it was all the more effective because of the volatile and unorganized condition of mass political opinion in Lebanon.

Fated by its strategic location to be the object of many conflicting foreign influences, the Republic of Lebanon finds itself buffeted by Great Power and Arab-world politics. Indeed, as Chapter 1 suggested, independence itself was partially the result of long-standing rivalries in the Middle East between Great Britain and France. The Franco-British rivalry continued to affect the country's factional political process throughout the regime of Bechara al-Khoury (1943–1952). Britain, which had made every effort in 1943 to ensure that the French protégé, Emile Edde, would not be given the Presidency, exerted a similar though more discreet influence to hasten the downfall of Bechara al-Khoury nine years later. Khoury, although he had benefited from the British presence in 1943, was resolutely opposed to the plans of the British client, King Abdallah, in Jordan to establish under his aegis a unified state in the Fertile Crescent; and he had thrown his weight with the Egyptian–Saudi Arabian faction in Arab-world politics. Camille Chamoun, a friend of the British, the Hashemites, and the Turks succeeded Khoury as President. As the American-Soviet rivalry developed in earnest, Chamoun and his chief ministers also became useful to the United States. Chamoun's regime ended in chaos partly because he made too many commitments to the West and thus lost control of the Lebanese whose loyalties were directed toward, and by, the United Arab Republic. Although the Americans

were instrumental in persuading General Fuad Chehab to take the Presidency in 1958, Chehab's rule facilitated a resurgence of French influence. The Soviet Union, although it is at a disadvantage owing to the sizable American presence during the 1950s, nevertheless labors resolutely and with increasing success to assert itself, using the instrumentalities of the Orthodox Church, the Communist Party, finance and business operations, and cultural programs. Since World War II Lebanese stability has been increasingly endangered by the rivalry between the American and Soviet superpowers. The very preponderance of American influence during the 1950s contributed to the strain, because it gave credibility to the accusations of the Left that Lebanon was an American puppet. In light of the widely heralded "thaw" in the Cold War in the early 1960s, it seems paradoxical that this rivalry exerts even greater strains in Lebanon than it did previously. Whatever rapprochements may have been reached between the United States and the Soviet Union in other domains, the Great Power struggle in the Middle East reached a new intensity as a consequence of the Arab-Israeli war of June 1967. The Soviet Union crowned its years of piecemeal erosion of the Western position with a spectacular diplomatic and political victory, by supporting the Arab states, "conservative" and "radical" alike. Under these circumstances the American presence has made Lebanon's already delicate position in the Arab world even more awkward than before.

When the Arab world shows signs of political unity, Lebanese policy makers fear that there will be a concerted effort to deprive

FIGURE 2. *Foreign Policy. Left to Right: King Faisal of Saudi Arabia, the Lebanese Foreign Minister, President Nasser of the United Arab Republic, President Charles Helou of Lebanon.*

Lebanon of its autonomy and its liberal economic system. Yet, when there is discord among the Arab states, competing factions pressure Lebanon to choose sides. The rise of pan-Arabism, which followed the Egyptian-Soviet arms agreement and culminated in the Egyptian-Syrian union, set in motion forces within Lebanon that nearly reduced the state to its pre-1920 boundaries: There was little doubt of the strong affinity of Lebanese Sunnites for Arab unity in a physical sense. Several years later, however, when the drive for unity had become less intense, Lebanon's position was scarcely more enviable. The division of the Arab world into a "progressive," socialist, and pro-Soviet faction and a "conservative," free-enterprise, and pro-Western faction found the Lebanese government torn between the powerful advocates of each faction, just as during the period before the Suez crisis it had been torn by the Egyptian-Iraqi rivalry. In both cases Lebanese Catholics suspected Lebanese Muslims of harboring radical and subversive ambitions, and the Sunnites regarded the Christians as puppets of the United States and England and enemies of the struggle for Arab independence.

In addition to its embroilment in Great Power and Arab-world rivalries, Lebanon has troubles with two neighbors, Israel and Syria. Lebanon and Israel have been in a technical state of war since 1948, and their common frontier is officially closed. Although this border is Israel's most peaceful one, that fact should not obscure the dangers in the situation for Lebanon. Indeed, the lack of conflict along this border raises the suspicion among Arabs, both inside and outside Lebanon, that the state is not sincere in its opposition to Israel. Israelis themselves like to imagine that Lebanon is secretly benevolent toward them. The Lebanese people, however, both Muslim and Christian, believe Israel is an illegitimate state and fear its power. Beirut may well have prospered from trade and transportation routes that have been diverted from Palestine, but the South of Lebanon is blighted economically by the sealed border. Thousands of embittered Palestinian refugees wait to return to their homes and have no particular affection for their host government. Every flare-up in the Arab-Israeli conflict strains the Lebanese political processes because it draws attention to Lebanon's relative military weakness. When Israel diverted Jordan River waters, for example, Syria proposed that Lebanon permit Syrian troops inside its territory to protect the Arab counterdiversion installations. Lebanon's reluctance to consent was embarrassing because it indicated that some Lebanese thought there was more to fear from Syria than from Israel. When Palestinian commandos were using Lebanese territory as a base for raids into Israel in the early 1960s, the government faced another dilemma: To suppress the commandos meant incurring the anger of Arabs inside and outside Lebanon who believed that raids were morally and politically justified; not to suppress them invited Israeli retaliation.

Lebanon experienced an acute domestic crisis during the Arab-Israeli war of 1967 as the result of its prudent failure to join the hostilities. The army's commander, General Emile Bustani, a Maronite Christian, refused to commit his small force to a cause that he believed would certainly be lost and instead positioned sizable detachments around Beirut and Tripoli to control the demonstrations and riots protesting his decision not to aid Syria, Jordan, and the U.A.R. In addition, General Bustani's decision put him directly at odds with Prime Minister Rashid Karami, a Sunnite Muslim from Tripoli, who insisted that the army fight Israel. This confrontation, like those between Lebanon's civilian and military leadership in the 1952 and 1958 crises, resulted in the military's temporary seizure of power and a new erosion of confidence in the capability of Lebanon's political institutions. Although Israel's ferocious and successful blitzkrieg of Lebanon's more powerful sister states mitigated short-run discontent with the army's nonbelligerence, it appears to have aggravated Lebanon's problem of maintaining a domestically acceptable balance in its relationships with the other Arab states and with the Great Powers. Furthermore, it revealed Lebanon's utter vulnerability. Taunted by the Israelis during the war for military impotence and threatened afterward by ominous Israeli comment about the Litani River (which rises and flows in Lebanon but which is at one point only about three miles from the Israeli border), the Lebanese were divided over the proper course to follow and began to question the efficacy of their political institutions and policies. Ought Lebanon to continue to seek security through weakness, by offering no threat to Israel and relying upon American or United Nations protection in case Israel should encroach anyway? Israeli and American behavior in the 1967 war cast doubts upon the wisdom of this stance, and many Lebanese considered such a policy dishonorable as well. On the other hand, a more active policy of self-defense and cooperation with the other Arab states incurred the risk of alienating American support; courting Soviet influence, with possibly dangerous consequences; providing the Israelis with a pretext for aggression, and inviting the interference of other Arab states like socialist Syria in Lebanon's sovereign affairs.

Lebanese relations with Syria are also a chronic foreign-policy worry. The barriers between Syria and Lebanon are relatively recent. Syrian Arabs still resent the manner in which France parceled out Syrian territory to create Greater Lebanon in 1920. Again Lebanese parochialism shows its paradoxical affinity for supranational loyalties: Many families have members on both sides of the ill-defined border. These patterns of supranational loyalty were sharply revealed during Lebanon's 1958 crisis when the insurgents made full use of their Syrian relationships to control virtually all the border territories. Sunnites in Tripoli were well supplied by their Syrian kin, and Syrian Druzes furnished their Lebanese cousins with the necessary arms by moving freely across the frontiers. Even in normal times, however, there is a basic conflict between Syria and Lebanon: Their economic systems clash. When independence was achieved, Lebanese notables decided that their state should pursue policies to promote free trade and to develop the service sector. Syrian politicians, notably Khaled al-Azm, resolved that their state should develop its industrial potential, a policy that required protectionist and autarchic measures. These basic differences in economic orientation led to the termination of the customs union in 1950 and to subsequent periodic conflicts. As Lebanon's major trading partner, as its gateway to other Eastern markets, and as its major supplier of wheat, Syria is too important to be ignored. Yet, despite the obvious importance of Syria, there is no formal diplomatic representation between the two states, for, in addition to the reason of economic separatism, Syrian governments paradoxically have held that such representation would sanction the "artificial" barriers between the two sister states. The problem of Syrian-Lebanese relations is complicated by Syria's political turmoil and radical tendencies, which have steadily widened the ideological gap between the two.

Although foreign intervention in Lebanese internal affairs has serious implications for Lebanese independence and sovereignty, the crucial and unique threat posed by the foreign situation is that of internal disintegration. So intimately bound together are domestic and foreign politics that a major factor in the choice of a Lebanese prime minister is his current position in the context of the regional situation. Lebanon has had only one major prime

minister since 1954—Sami Sulh—who was not touted as a warm
friend of President Nasser; it is quite normal in a Lebanese government crisis for potential prime ministerial candidates to pay osten-
tatious visits to Cairo. Such dependence on external sources of
support generates suspicions in conservative Christian quarters.
Christian suspicion, however, is matched by Muslim displeasure
at the proximity of the United States fleet and the activities of
Western embassies. The essential foreign-policy problem is to keep
these suspicions in rough balance. Those aspects of the National
Pact that deal strictly with foreign relations remain the best possible means for keeping the balance, but they can deal only with
independent external conditions. Lebanon, small and weak, its
policy options limited by the necessity to maintain the delicate
internal balance, is virtually powerless to affect those conditions
substantially. As such, it is fated to remain forever a dependent
variable in the area's international politics, with its only bargaining
power a credible threat to destroy itself.

Socioeconomic Tensions

If the probability of revolution, or serious unrest, is inversely
associated with the "continuous, unimpeded opportunity to satisfy
new needs, new hopes, new expectations," [8] then it is possible in
a very crude manner to assess the politically relevant socioeconomic
tensions in contemporary Lebanon. First, however, it is necessary
to make some conservative assumptions about the growing politically conscious stratum of the Lebanese population, its expectations, and the extent to which these expectations are fulfilled in
modern Lebanon.

Who are the socially mobilized, politically conscious, potential
political activists in Lebanon today? Assuming a resident population
of 2 million in the early 1960s, it is possible to make some numerical estimates of the politically relevant subpopulations. First,
we shall exclude all but the critical age group, that is, the 40 per
cent of the population between twelve and thirty-five, some 800,000
people. This move excludes at once most of the ruling establishment.
It also makes the exaggerated but convenient assumption that the
population over thirty-five is politically inert. We then subdivide
this stratum into the educated and uneducated. The education statistics report that some 385,000 of this group are currently enrolled
at some level of education—primary, secondary, or university.
We will exclude primary-school students, for the moment, and

narrow the field to include the 60,000 secondary-school and 12,000 university students enrolled at a given time. These 72,000 are the primary pool of persons who can be mobilized for political action: They are literate, educated, exposed, and sophisticated. They are concentrated in the Greater Beirut area. Every year, about 2,000 receive university diplomas. Approximately 10,000 receive secondary-school diplomas; of these latter about 4,000 may go on to the university, and 6,000 will enter the labor force, leaving 8,000 secondary and university students who terminate their education every year. Let us further assume that one-fourth of these 8,000 terminal-degree receivers are women and will become politically inert after graduation; that leaves around 6,000 male degree holders passing into the "real world" every year. Assuming that they enter it, on the average, at age twenty; that the trend is constant over time (when actually it is increasing); and that they remain potential political activists until they are thirty-five, then at any given time the politically critical educated population is around 90,000, a total of 6,000 activists added in each of fifteen years. Their expectations include a desire for nonmanual jobs with some prestige and the opportunity for advancement. They have idealistic and politically utopian values. To what extent does Lebanon satisfy their expectations? To what extent will it satisfy them in the future?

The politically critical group experiences considerable difficulty in fitting reality to expectation in contemporary Lebanon. The difficulty is immediately apparent for those who hold only a secondary-school degree or a B.A. degree in liberal arts—the lower stratum of the politically critical group. They may work as clerks, as salesmen, or as employees in banks and commercial establishments. Jobs for them are scarce and the pay far too low to support the desired style of life in the city. There is plenty of time to dream. It is this subgroup that supplies the cadres of Lebanon's more radical political movements: the Arab Nationalist Movement (A.N.M.), the Parti Populaire Syrien (P.P.S.), the Progressive Socialist Party (P.S.P.), the Baath Party, and the Communist Party.[9] The young men with medical and engineering degrees fare somewhat better than the liberal-arts or secondary-school graduates, but their professional fields are also crowded. There is obvious competition among doctors in the Beirut area, even though the hinterlands are understaffed; and new engineers may have difficulty establishing themselves in Lebanon. For these groups emigration is a feasible alternative, and Lebanon is losing increasing numbers of skilled personnel to the United States and the oil principalities. Doctors, for example, are urged to specialize in hopes of filling new research niches, only to find themselves excluded by other specialists who finished sooner. The higher political and bureaucratic positions are filled largely by men with law degrees from French universities; but supply is beginning to outstrip the demand for these positions as well.

If the supply of secondary-school and university students were to remain at its 1963–1964 level for the next fifteen years, then the educated stratum might be absorbed in a rapidly expanding services sector. According to the Ministry of Planning, some 130,000–150,000 jobs could open up in that fifteen-year period for only 90,000 new educated men. Such a calculation, however, does not take into account the considerable expansion of both the public and private school systems, and the strong pressure from Lebanese parents to expand them even more. In the five-year period 1959–1960 to 1963–1964, the number of students in secondary school alone increased by nearly 45 per cent. If subsequent five-year periods should show similar growth, then by 1972 the supply of educated men would have already exceeded the quota of new jobs through 1980. This calculation does not even assume an increase in university graduates. Although projections of this sort are crude, the image of job insufficiency is very clear, and the expectations of a substantial section of the educated group may be disappointed. The educated face the prospect of either emigrating or settling for menial service jobs, for which there will be additional competition from unskilled, or manual, workers. The competition for the service jobs, therefore, may be even more intense than for the prestige occupations.

The sector of the population between twelve and thirty-five that is not in secondary schools or the university in the early 1960s numbers around 638,000, of whom half (319,000) are male. Less than half this group has been exposed to some primary education, but all of it has been exposed to radio programing. If the sex distribution within this age group is even, we may estimate that around 13,900 boys enter it every year, assuming for the sake of analysis that the population-increase rate is zero. We may also assume that these young men are poor and likely to remain so, and that they are relatively more numerous in the "other Lebanon," rural North Lebanon, South Lebanon, and the Biqa. What are their expectations, and how are they politically relevant?

The primary concerns of this "uneducated" group are making

a living and raising a family. In the middle 1960s, their unskilled and semiskilled labor is absorbed by the agricultural sector (approximately 220,000 work in agriculture) and the industrial sector (where about 87,000 work). There is also an indeterminate number engaged in minor services.[10] In all likelihood, it will become increasingly difficult for the men in this sector to realize their simple ambitions, given the present pattern of economic development in Lebanon. The basic reasons for this unhappy prognosis have been discussed in Chapter 2. According to the Lebanese Planning Ministry, the number of jobs in the agricultural sector will shrink considerably, despite the development of new lands, whereas the rate of job creation in the industrial sector will be insufficient to support a growing unskilled labor force. Despite sharp job expansion in the period after the 1958 crisis, the trend in Lebanese industrial development in recent years does not augur a bright future for this sector.

In the postcrisis recovery period (1958–1963) under President Fuad Chehab, the number of jobs tripled, but it will be necessary to quadruple the number of jobs by 1980 in order to absorb the predicted potential industrial work force.[11] The industrial sector thus ought to increase to 275,000 jobs. Government officials predict, however, that, under the best of circumstances, there will be only 150,000 industrial jobs by 1980. One out of every three workers may be unemployed by that time, and a heavy proportion of them will be in the politically critical age group. For workers in this category emigration is only a remote possibility. Even if Syria should greatly expand its industrial capacity by that time, the 60,000 or more Syrian laborers currently employed in Lebanon presumably will fill the new openings there. Furthermore, as future Lebanese regimes pursue development policies the prospect of inflation will arise. This will weigh heavily on the poor, because the economic pressure for higher prices is likely to exceed the pressure for higher wages and because new capital investment continues to be heavily directed into areas of meager social usefulness. The grimness of this projection will doubtless be offset to some extent through traditional channels, as it is today: Families will continue to look out for their own; there will always be room for another tiny grocery or an extra pair of hands; expanding tourism may provide some new openings for the unskilled. The traditional solutions, however, cannot begin to satisfy the expectations of the expanding sector of the young and unskilled, and there is every indication that the problem will become more serious in the future.

Two Crises

Lebanon's political dilemma is the product of environmental adversity generated by parochial tendencies, foreign activities, and social mobilization. Behind the façade of stability and the ritual maneuvers of the cliques is the constant possibility that matters will get out of hand. Twice during the first two decades of independence matters have in fact gotten out of hand. The over-loaded current, in Trotsky's analogy, burned out the safety switches. An examination of the crises of 1952 and 1958 will permit an intuitive judgment as to the seriousness of Lebanon's dilemma.

The 1952 Crisis

According to the Lebanese Constitution, the President is to be elected by at least a two-thirds vote of a popularly elected Parliament to an unrenewable term of six years.[12] In 1947 Lebanon had its first opportunity to try out these procedures without the overt interference of Western diplomatic missions. Many believed that the 1947 parliamentary elections had been rigged by the Khoury regime, and these suspicions were reinforced a year later when the President used his clear parliamentary majority to suspend the nonrenewal clause in his particular case in order to present himself for re-election. Khoury's re-election was denounced by many notables, some because their ambitions had been damaged and others because they were concerned about the harm done to the country's institutions.[13] The Constitution had been easily circumvented by the ruling clique. The opposition had not been given a fair opportunity to compete with the Khoury machine. The devices for institutionalizing opposition had failed. This institutional failure dealt a blow to hopes that Lebanon would develop workable democratic processes. It persuaded the notables opposing Khoury that they would have to apply extraordinary pressures in order to break his power. By exploiting the well-founded stories of administrative corruption, the opposition notables, who had never succeeded in banding together successfully, began to mobilize a mass following. In 1949 the Committee of National Liberation was created.[14] The opposition grew until by 1952 it included Kamal Jumblat's new

Progressive Socialist Party, important regional notables and presidential aspirants, newspaper editors, the remnants of the Parti Populaire Syrien, the National Bloc, the Najjadeh (the Sunnite youth group), the Ghassanides (the Greek Orthodox youth organization, later disbanded), the Hay'at al-Watania (the organization of Sunnite notables), and the Kataeb (the Maronite youth organization).

By spring and summer of 1952 the domestic situation had deteriorated. There were controversies over nationalizing the electricity company and changing the personal-status legislation. The cost of living index in Beirut was up eight points over 1950, and the wholesale price index had risen twenty-one points.[15] According to Prime Minister Sami Sulh there were about 50,000 unemployed.[16] These unfavorable background conditions set the stage for Khoury's fall. The leaders of the Socialist National Front (S.N.F.) that had been elected from Mount Lebanon in the 1951 elections staged a series of demonstrations, rallies, and strikes.[17] They culminated in a huge rally on August 27 at the town of Deir al-Qamar in the Chouf, an area in which Camille Chamoun and Kamal Jumblat were traditionally strong.[18] The opposition's success in mobilizing the people contrasted with the Khoury machine's inability to keep control. Well suited for playing caucus politics with the notables, it was ill equipped to rally popular support in any organized manner. Its weakness was compounded by the loss of the popular Riad Sulh, who had supplied its strongest link to the Sunnite masses. Shutting down opposition newspapers only strengthened the regime's enemies.[19] Reports of scandals in the Beirut municipality and the Ministry of National Economy, a purge of the gendarmes, a boycott of electricity tax payments followed by power shutdowns, strikes by newspapers and taxi drivers all added to the snowballing movement. A belated effort by the regime to launch a major reform program failed to cool down the crisis. Then, early in September, Prime Minister Sami Sulh's cabinet began to disintegrate, and the Prime Minister, who was at odds with a faction within Khoury's following, administered the *coup de grâce* by delivering in Parliament an emotional but highly explicit indictment of the regime's corruption. He then dramatically left the Chamber.[20] Successive efforts by President Khoury to form a cabinet between September 9 and September 18 failed; the notables, particularly the Sunnites, would not cooperate. The fact that Khoury still held a strong parliamentary majority meant little. The significant political struggle had moved outside the Chamber of Deputies. Meanwhile, the screws were being tightened by the opposition, which had called an effective general strike. It might seem strange that at this critical juncture, the President did not call upon the army to preserve order. It seems, however, that General Fuad Chehab, the Commander, was unwilling to interfere in politics.[21] On September 17, President Khoury had several conversations with General Chehab concerning the attitudes of the opposition and the state of public safety during the strike. The General reported that he was apprehensive about the situation, that he expected trouble, and that the army would act to preserve peace only if all else failed. At this moment the President suddenly could see "a bloody movie" with many Lebanese dead. He handed General Chehab two decrees, one of which appointed Chehab Prime Minister. After a fruitless attempt to designate a civilian prime minister from among the Sunnite notables and thus to restore the normal situation, Khoury told General Chehab that he was leaving the Presidency to avoid bloodshed. The enigmatic General replied, "You might think, Your Excellency, that I have not performed my duty completely in such a situation; I am sorry for the result." [22] General Chehab served as acting head of state and head of government until Parliament elected a new President, Camille Chamoun, on September 24.

The 1952 crisis shows that the Lebanese system, although it was adequate for routine politics, was unequal to a basic dilemma of power: It had failed to provide strong leadership and it had failed to institutionalize a responsible opposition. This incapacity was visible on three levels. First, the parliamentary and the presidential electoral processes lacked legitimacy because formal channels were obstructed by clique politics. Second, the executive apparatus could not cope with the demands for vigorous, effective policies to deal with mounting national problems. Corruption and inefficiency flourished, and legitimacy was further eroded. Third, both the regime and the opposition failed to manage the popular forces that were drawn into the struggle. The regime had neglected to develop organized popular support and was outmaneuvered by the erratic activities of a motley opposition. The opposition was able to mobilize crowds and call a strike, but it could not organize the people for persistent rational activity. Kamal Jumblat later wrote that the Socialist National Front had never intended to overthrow the regime but only to reform it. Lacking an organized party mechanism, the S.N.F. was unable to control the forces it had unleashed.[23]

Although the process of executive succession failed its first test in the 1948–1952 period, this failure was quickly repaired with a minimum of damage, but the causes of the failure remained. Six years later the crisis was far more serious, because the external and internal strains had increased.

The 1958 Crisis

A crisis that erupts into civil war and leaves 2,000 to 4,000 casualties does not indicate great strength in a political system.[24] Such an eruption does, however, imply that the forces converging on the system are both strong and collectively dysfunctional.[25] In 1958, one of the major stresses was the uncertainty arising from President Chamoun's refusal to promise publicly that he would not induce Parliament to amend the Constitution and re-elect him for another term. His attempts to reduce the influence of several important rural bosses clearly conveyed the impression that he would try to do what his predecessor had done a decade earlier. The opposition had been demanding that he remove the succession issue from politics since March 1957, but at the end of that year the President's determination to retain freedom of decision was evident in the following statement:

> J'ai mes raisons. Je ferai connaître mon point de vue en temps opportun. Ce sera en mai, juin ou juillet. . . . Je comprends très bien les soucis que peut vous inspirer l'éventualité d'une révision de la Constitution. Je suis moi-même à principe, contre la révision. Cependant, il est un point sur lequel je ne veux laisser subsister aucune ambiguité: si, au moment voulu, je ne suis pas assuré de trouver un successeur qui assure la continuité de ma politique, je le déclare d'ores et déjà, je reconsiderai ma position.[26]

During winter and spring of 1958—a period that Fahim Qubain has aptly designated as the "slide into anarchy"—the crisis developed a momentum of its own and the original dispute receded in importance. Indeed, the most disorderly and bloody events took place after President Chamoun, in June 1958, finally made it clear that he would not seek renewal of his term.[27]

President Chamoun entered office a popular figure—attractive, intelligent, friendly to Christians and non-Christians alike. His popularity, however, was not enough to prevent other leaders from maneuvering him into a minority position. Lacking a firm institutional base and the political finesse demanded of Lebanese politicians, he was especially vulnerable to pressures. Yet even with these resources, President Chamoun would have been lucky to avoid the crisis. He had the misfortune to rule during a difficult period. Sectarian feelings were high. Arab regional politics were in turmoil. The American-Soviet rivalry was acute. New political elements were emerging, challenging traditional political values. The issues involved in the crisis were not easily susceptible to compromise. Of the many issues involved three stand out as the most troublesome: foreign orientation, socioeconomic-group alignments, and sectarian hostility.

During the Suez crisis of 1956 President Chamoun's lukewarm support for Cairo aroused visible discontent among Lebanese Sunnites and Arab nationalists at all levels. His foreign minister did not hide an undiplomatic enthusiasm for things Western and accepted all too eagerly the helping hand of the American "Eisenhower Doctrine." Such acceptance was sufficient evidence for the opposition that the neutrality provision of the National Pact had been violated, and it eroded the little that remained of the regime's legitimacy. On the eve of the crisis a journalist of the moderate wing of the opposition summarized the foreign factor as follows: "Un nouveau crédo politique est proposé depuis huit mois, aux Libanais: Si vous n'êtes pas chamounien, c'est que vous êtes un traitre et un syro-bolchevik." [28] From the point of view of the regime, winning the struggle over foreign orientation was a matter of political survival. Cairo radio, the Egyptian Embassy in Beirut, the pro-Nasser Lebanese press, the radical groups, and the notables unfriendly to Chamoun were working actively to liberate Lebanon from his regime. Chamoun obviously did not consider his own overthrow a negotiable issue, and, because the insurgents were assisted by Syria and Egypt, he began to solicit further support from the West. Because both sides solicited foreign help, the Lebanese crisis was internationalized. Lebanese domestic politics was a function of the post-Suez ferment in the Arab world, and Lebanon became an object of Cold War rivalry. When proceedings before the League of Arab States failed to reduce tensions, the United Nations Security Council debated a Lebanese complaint against the United Arab Republic, and a United Nations Observer Group was dispatched to look into the case. There is no doubt whatever that anti-Western elements in the Syrian region of the United Arab Republic assisted the insurgents to a tangible degree, but the full significance of this participation remains a matter of controversy.[29]

The Lebanese crisis took a new turn on July 14, when a revolution destroyed the Hashemite monarchy in Iraq, seat of the Baghdad Pact. It was a stunning blow for Western interests. Jubilant Arab nationalists foresaw the imminent collapse of the pro-Western regimes of Jordan and Lebanon as well and considered the revolution a giant step toward unity. Alarmed at the possibility of Soviet gains in this turbulent situation, the West reacted in a historically familiar manner. The next day 15,000 American troops landed on Lebanese soil, supported by the 40,000 men and seventy ships of the American 6th Fleet, and the British dropped paratroopers in Jordan. Because of this substantial military commitment, President Eisenhower's special emissary, Robert Murphy, was able to give a certain weight to the mediation of a group of Lebanese notables calling themselves the Third Force. A compromise was arranged on the basis of the formula "no victor—no vanquished," and General Chehab was prevailed upon to become the new President.

The breakdown of Lebanon's internal balance prompted overt interference by the United Arab Republic, the United States, and the United Nations because the interests of all three were very much involved in its internal affairs. The claims of Arab nationalism and traditional relationships with Syrians made the U.A.R. and the Lebanese insurgents parties to the struggle to rid the Arab world of an alien regime. The Americans were cast in the historic role of the West; they found themselves suddenly committed to protecting the non-Muslim communities that had been too open in expressing their affinity for the West. The Cold War perspective, however, probably was a more compelling reason for United States military participation. Because the Great Powers had once again been drawn into intervention in Lebanon, the United Nations could not ignore events there, for they threatened world peace.

The 1958 crisis illustrates Lebanon's persistent problems of parochialism and foreign entanglement. It also shows that the complex effects of social mobilization make the stability of the formal political structures more and more precarious. The progressive intellectuals among the 1958 insurgents assert that the crisis was rooted in class hostility and believe that the basic cleavage was between the poor, both urban and rural, and the upper bourgeoisie of Beirut and Mount Lebanon. There is substance to this argument. A glance at the map of areas held by loyalists and insurgents (see Map 3) shows that the loyalists were defending the developed area of Lebanon against the poor regions controlled by the insurgents. An examination of the cost-of-living index at Beirut reveals that prior to the 1958 crisis there was an increase rate even greater than the increase that preceded the 1952 crisis. From 1950 to 1951 the index rose by thirty-six points; from 1955 to 1957 it rose seventy-five points.[30] The index is a crude but significant measure of economic difficulties to which the poor are especially vulnerable.

An examination of the forces on each side and their policy positions, however, suggests that the divisions were more complicated than simple economic-class hostility. There were rich bankers and landlords in the leadership of both the loyalists and the insurgents; and relatively progressive elements confronted each other across the barricades. Each side had an important measure of support from both the urban and the rural poor, and the religious cleavage was much more important at this level than among the middle and upper classes. President Chamoun's loyalist backing consisted of the more conservative notables of Christian Mount Lebanon, elements of the business, commerce, and finance community that had benefited from his economic encouragement of these sectors. To the moderate intellectuals and professionals he appeared more modern, cosmopolitan, and dynamic than did the typical deputy or establishment politician, even though some questioned the rationality of his public-works projects. At ribbon cuttings, inaugurations, meetings, and commencements the President and his wife were familiar figures, and both were known for their patronage of the arts and numerous charities. All these activities strengthened the President's position with many people in the educated middle class and hindered the efforts of the insurgents to label him as a reactionary who was solely interested in private aggrandizement. President Chamoun's organized support at the popular level was weak, however, because his regional allies lacked local followings big enough to compete successfully with the traditional leaders. By the time the crisis broke into the open—on May 8, after the murder of an anti-Chamoun Christian journalist—the President could count on the forces of the two best-organized political parties, the P.P.S. and the Kataeb (the former Maronite youth group, which had become a party in 1952), the latter reluctantly. The insurgents, on the other hand, were led by the rural feudal chiefs whom President Chamoun had been making persistent attempts to destroy as a political force. Leaders like Sabri Hamadeh, Ahmad al-Assaad, Saeb Salam, Rashid Karami, and Kamal Jumblat, however progressive they might be personally, never-

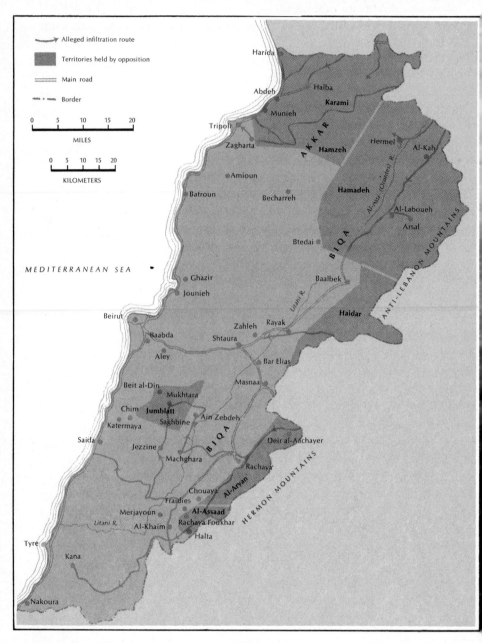

MAP 3

Insurgent Areas in the 1958 Crisis

After United Nations Observation Group in Lebanon, *Report* (New York: Security Council document S/4040, 1958), Annex C.

theless represented a political order founded on traditional obligations and structures. Their united opposition to President Chamoun
was motivated to a considerable extent by his efforts to undermine
their power. On the surface, then, the 1958 crisis is typical of conflict during the political modernization process in general, in the
sense that it pits a "progressive" head of state who has important
urban middle-class support against the conservative old-style bosses.

To describe the situation in these terms, however, is to overlook
the peculiarities of the 1958 socioeconomic alignment. President
Chamoun was hardly in the same category as the socialist and
nationalist leaders common in the new states. Indeed, the President
was cast in quite the opposite role—a lackey of foreign interests and
high finance, a man bent on establishing personal rule rather than
social justice. Of all the charges leveled by the insurgents against
the President that of "puppet dictator" was uttered with the greatest
fervor.[31] Nor did the insurgents fit the usual image of feudal reac-
tionaries, although many attempts have been made to give them that
label. Although some of the rural chieftains could hardly be called
progressive, other leaders, like Jumblat, Nassim Majdalani, Henri
Pharaon, and Salam did represent at least an enlightened liberalism.
Furthermore, the insurgents had strong backing from decidedly radical elements in the youthful, educated middle class. Arab nationalists,
the Baath, a broad stratum of the professionals and intellectuals, the
Najjadeh, the communists (to a minor extent), and university and
high-school students in many areas all gave the insurgency a
progressive and reformist—if not revolutionary—character. Conventional explanations of class conflict thus are not sufficient to
explain the presidential transition crisis of 1958: Class and economic interests were divided internally by other overriding loyalties.

It would be a mistake, however, to write off this crisis simply as
an inflated quarrel among the establishment politicians. Although
the demands of the opposition and the Third Force were focused
primarily on purely political questions—the control and use of
power—two new factors had also intervened to impose significant
strains on the old mechanisms. First, a set of policy grievances had
arisen to set rural against urban interests. The rural-urban split had
been aggravated by the Chamoun regime's deviation from the National Pact in the realm of foreign policy and its relative neglect of
the hinterland in domestic affairs. Most of the rural areas were
non-Christian, poor, and pro-U.A.R. Second, new interests and
tendencies within the educated middle class had not become inte-

grated into the political system, which meant in effect that a new stream of unorganized power had spilled over the traditional channels, fed by rising discontents. The system was thus doubly paralyzed by the rural-urban split and lack of middle-class participation.

Both sides in the 1958 crisis vied for the support of the newly politicized but unorganized people in the younger educated middle class. President Chamoun's success in obtaining their support was limited to the P.P.S., the Kataeb, some student groups and professionals, and white-collar employees. If he had been able to organize a rationalized, liberal presidential party, he might have been able to achieve his objective of naming a successor who would carry on his policies.[32] The insurgents also were able to mobilize only a segment of the younger middle class, but they were on the whole more successful than the loyalists. If they had succeeded fully, the 1958 crisis might have become a revolution. The insurgents had two powerful drawing cards in addition to their strong traditional support: Arab nationalism and social reform. Each of the major insurgent leaders could claim the friendship of President Nasser and his Syrian colleagues, and this association gave each a stronger position than that of President Chamoun, whose earlier service to Arab nationalism was dismissed as opportunistic. The insurgents depicted President Chamoun as a tool of the enemies of Arab nationalism; they thus attracted not only Arab students but also Arabs of the non-Maronite lower middle, peasant, and working classes. The social reform appeal was articulated most clearly by Kamal Jumblat in his various demands to the regime but was also emphasized by the Arab nationalist and Baathist contingents.[33] The fact that the insurgents—composed as they were of both the most traditional and the most progressive elements—had such a split personality doubtless made many public-spirited and educated citizens skeptical of their reformist intentions. Some important army officers, for example, seem to have questioned the insurgents' sincerity. Because the newly politicized stratum was inchoate both sides suffered: The regime was denied the capacity to withstand a serious attack on its structure, whereas the opposition lacked the means to carry out its objectives. The results were civil war, extensive foreign intervention, and finally, sectarian strife.

It is remarkable that overt sectarian conflict did not break out sooner. Although the general situation had been deteriorating for nearly two years and open fighting had gone on for nearly four months, it was only late in September that the violence took on a distinct sectarian coloration. This is not to say, however, that the political expression of sectarianism was not an issue from the beginning of the crisis. Since the days of President Khoury the non-Christian sects had complained of their underrepresentation in the institutions of formal power. One of the main points of the insurgents was justice and equality in the allocation of jobs and privileges by sect. This meant a fifty-fifty distribution of important posts between Christians and non-Christians and an increase in the power of the Sunnite Prime Minister at the expense of the Maronite President.[34] It was only when the "no victor—no vanquished" solution appeared to go too far in meeting non-Christian demands that the Kataeb, which had hoped in vain for an international guarantee of the Lebanese entity, took to the barricades.[35]

That sectarian tensions could be so long contained, delayed, and muted resulted from the fact that membership in the insurgent group and in the loyalist group cut across sectarian lines. Several of the most important leaders of the insurgent opposition and the Third Force were Christian: The Maronite Patriarch himself opposed the President and did much to destroy his reputation as a savior of the Christians. Hamid Frangieh and René Moawad (Maronites) were also rivals of the President. Nassim Majdalani (Greek Orthodox) was the key Christian insurgent leader in Beirut. Henri Pharaon (Greek Catholic) and Charles Helou (Maronite) led the Third Force, whose manifestos opposing renewal of Chamoun's term warned that the degradation of the Constitution constituted the gravest possible threat to national unity—that is, to the harmony between Christians and non-Christians.[36] On the loyalist side there were important non-Christians, including, most prominently, President Chamoun's Prime Minister, Sami Sulh. There were also a number of non-Christian loyalists within the government, who had been brought in by the President to replace the old leaders whom he was seeking to destroy. These included Sunnites like Fawzi al-Hoss, Jamil Mikkawi, and Khalil Hibri; Shiites like Kazem Khalil and Rida Wahid; and Druzes like Kahtan Hamadeh. These men, however, were eventually branded turncoats to their sects as the crisis grew hotter. This change was evident when the Muslim Superior Council held an *iftār* (the first meal after sunset during the fast of Ramadān), attended by some 200 notables, to honor the Sunnite chiefs of the insurgent National Front; Prime Minister Sami Sulh was not invited.[37]

Despite these important cross-sectarian affiliations, there was not the slightest doubt that the insurgents were mostly non-Christian and the loyalists mostly Christian. As civil disorder continued, the veneer of etiquette and tolerance wore away. Even after the main issue had been settled and the insurgents had endorsed General Chehab as the new President, a wave of petty sectarian incidents broke out. The kidnapping of a Kataeb journalist in the autumn precipitated a Christian "counterrevolution" against the "no victor— no vanquished" settlement, which in the opinion of many pro-Chamoun Christians had in fact given the insurgents control of the country. As a result of the new violence, President Chehab appointed a new four-man emergency cabinet that fortunately was able to restore general stability within a year, and sectarian feelings were reduced to their former level, just beneath the surface of ordinary political life.

The crisis of 1958 came about in part because the Maronite President, by trying to strengthen his own powers, seemed to reduce the power of the Sunnite Prime Minister's office and the influence of non-Christians in general. It was hardly accidental that the President tried to reduce Muslim and Arab-nationalist influence at a time when both regional and internal trends were driving non-Christians to seek a relatively greater role. Lebanon's political dilemma is reflected in the 1958 crisis: The same forces that drive the President to expand his power drive his rivals to expand theirs. Institutionalized sectarianism is Lebanon's substitute for positive consensus, but at the same time it is a great barrier to Lebanon's political modernization. The parochial divisions in Lebanon's political culture retard the development of legitimacy and dynamic policy making. They also make the state highly vulnerable to foreign manipulation. Social mobilization makes more people more competent politically, but it also drastically transforms the standards of political performance in a system whose primary function is adjustment, not action. Continuing turbulence in the Middle East, among the Arab states themselves and between Arabs and Israelis, imposes additional stresses on Lebanon, dividing its people—Muslim and Christian—over the ideologies of Arab nationalism and socialism, over relations with the Great Powers, and over policies for national security and development. As the necessity for political modernization increases, it is reasonably certain that further crises of the kind described here may be expected.

NOTES

[1] *L'Orient*, March 14–20, 1953.

[2] *The Arab World* (Beirut), August 2–9, 1954; *L'Orient*, July 30–August 5, 1954; Jean-Pierre Alem, *Le Liban* (Paris: Presses Universitaires, 1963), p. 81.

[3] For a description of the "counterrevolution" of September–October, 1958, see Fahim I. Qubain, *Crisis in Lebanon* (Washington: Middle East Institute, 1962), pp. 156–61.

[4] *L'Orient*, March 20–21, 1965.

[5] *al-Nahār* (Beirut), March 19, 21, 1966.

[6] "Sectarianism in Lebanon . . . is the guarantee of equitable political and social representation for the associated minorities . . . [it] is above all a force for order and peace. . . . Lebanon is composed of sectarian minorities. These minorities appear under the sectarian label because Lebanon has always been a refuge for freedom of conscience. Its role as a haven has been possible because of Lebanon's geographical situation—in a mountainous land where it has always been possible to defend oneself and in a maritime land from which it has always been easy to take to the sea. . . . In spite of many errors and abuses, it is sectarianism that has taught tolerance to the Lebanese. . . . The Lebanese equilibrium, based on sectarianism, is not an arbitrary equilibrium. It is by no means prejudice that has created it, but the necessity for recognizing the parochialisms that cover as broad a range as do those among political parties. With time, these differences may blur and slowly disappear. Actually the purpose of Lebanon's existence lies precisely in the sectarianism that characterizes it and manifests itself first in the arrangement of legislative power." Michel Chiha, *Politique Intérieure* (Beirut: Trident, 1964), pp. 303–6.

[7] *The Economist*, October 22, 1966, pp. 394–5; *Time*, November 25, 1966, p. 116.

[8] James C. Davies, "Toward a Theory of Revolution," *American Sociological Review*, 27 (February 1962), 17.

[9] For example, the Kataeb reported that the mean age of its members was twenty-four years. Lucien George and Toufic Mokdessi, *Les Partis Libanais en 1959* (Beirut: L'Orient-al-Jaryda, 1959), p. 36. The mean age of civilians arrested in the 1962 attempted coup (instigated by the Syrian National Party) was thirty-two years. Arab nationalist and Baathist leaders reported in interviews that their principal recruits were young and educated. Several of the second-echelon leaders of the Progressive Socialist Party are American University graduates who are now employed in foreign companies in Beirut. See Chapter 5.

[10] Estimates from Lebanese Ministry of General Planning for 1964.

[11] Ministry of General Planning figures, 1964.

[12] The Lebanese Constitution, Article 49.

[13] A good example of the latter is Michel Chiha, a guiding spirit in the writing of the Constitution, who was related by marriage to President Khoury and who supported him during the 1947 election. See his *Le Jour* editorial of April 13, 1948, "Sur la Révision de la Constitution," reprinted in Chiha, *op. cit.*, pp. 148–53.

[14] See the Committee of National Liberation manifesto in *L'Orient,* August 12, 1949.

[15] Republic of Lebanon, *Bulletin Statistique Trimestrial* (1959); Republic of Lebanon Ministry of Planning, *Besoins et Possibilités de Développement du Liban,* I (Beirut: 1960–1961), p. 84, hereafter cited as *IRFED Report.*

[16] *L'Orient,* April 23, 1952.

[17] Bechara al-Khoury, *Haqā'iq lubnāniyyah* [*Lebanese Truths*], III (Beirut: Awrāq lubnāniyyah, 1961), 442 ff., and Sami Sulh, *Mudakkirāt* [*Memoirs*] (Beirut: Maktabat al-fiqr al-'arabī, 1960), p. 215, note that they were aware of the deterioration but could not command the power and influence to check it. See also George Britt, "Lebanon's Popular Revolution," *Middle East Journal,* 7 (Winter 1953), 1–17.

[18] The rally reportedly was attended by some 30,000 people. Alem, *op. cit.,* p. 77.

[19] Khoury, *op. cit.,* III, 449, claims that his previous leniency in the face of insults to the Presidency had been interpreted as a sign of weakness rather than of tolerance and that suspensions of opposition newspapers were necessary to preserve the dignity of the state. The suspensions had been prompted by an article in Kamal Jumblat's newspaper headlined, "He was put there by foreigners; let the people remove him."

[20] For the text, see Republic of Lebanon, *al-Jarīdah al-rasmiyyah* [*The Official Gazette*] *1951–1952* (Beirut: 1952), pp. 2505–10 (*The Official Gazette* contains the proceedings of the Chamber of Deputies). See also Sulh, *op. cit.,* pp. 222–7. "Rule is divided between the Serail [Prime Minister's Office] and the [Presidential] palace," Sulh told the deputies. He also charged that unnamed elements in the palace had fought against him when he tried to make laws against gambling, hashish growing, and smuggling goods into Israel and when he attempted to pass a regulation requiring the newly rich to disclose the sources of their incomes. Some people, he continued, had tried to use the state to further their own greed.

[21] Three months earlier President Khoury had offered General Chehab the Presidency. At a meeting held some time between June 15 and 20, Khoury told Chehab of his disgust at the pettiness, disloyalty, and greed that were poisoning the political atmosphere. The President said that he would like to retire while he still had the power to choose a worthy successor—Chehab. The General politely refused. Khoury, *op. cit.,* III, 451.

[22] *Ibid.,* p. 479.

[23] Kamal Jumblat, *Ḥaqīqat 'an al-thawrat al-lubnāniyyah* [*The Truth about the Lebanese Revolution*] (Beirut: Dār al-nashr al-'arabiyyah, 1959), p. 23.

[24] Casualty estimates vary a great deal. An army officer declared in an interview in 1963 that about 4,000 were killed and wounded. "A correspondent lately in Beirut," writing in *The World Today,* 15 (April 4, 1959), 136, said that the number of fatalities was perhaps 2,000. Emile Bustani, an active participant, stated that 3,000 had died, of whom 1,000 were Syrians. Emile Bustani, *March Arabesque* (London: Hale, 1961), p. 86.

[25] The most detailed account of the 1958 crisis in English is Qubain, *op. cit.* See also a critical review of this book by Nabih Faris in *Middle East Forum,* 38 (January 1, 1962), 32; Charles Thayer, *Diplomat* (New York:

Harper, 1959), chaps. 1, 2; Richard I. Miller, *Dag Hammarskjöld and Crisis Diplomacy* (New York: Pyramid, 1961), chaps. 6, 7; and Leila M. T. Meo, *Lebanon: Improbable Nation* (Bloomington: Indiana University Press, 1965), chaps. 7, 9. A knowledgeable and succinct description appears in Alem, *op. cit.*, pp. 87–96. See also Alem's article, "Troubles Insurrectionnels au Liban," *Orient* (Paris), June 1958, pp. 37–47; and, in the same issue, Pierre Rondot, "Quelques Réflexions sur les Structures du Liban," pp. 23–6. See also Kamal Salibi, "Lebanon Since the Crisis of 1958," *The World Today*, January 1961, pp. 32–42; the reports from the representative of the American Universities Field Staff in Beirut, C. F. Gallagher before, during, and after the crisis, and Desmond Stewart, *Turmoil in Beirut* (London: Wingate, 1959). For a review of writing in Arabic on the subject, see Malcolm H. Kerr, "Lebanese Views on the 1958 Crisis," *Middle East Journal*, 15 (Spring 1961), 211–7. Important writings by participants include Jumblat, *op. cit.*; Henri Pharaon's essays in his *Au Service du Liban et de Son Unité* (Beirut: Le Jour, 1959); Camille Chamoun, *Crise au Moyen-Orient* (Paris: Gallimard, 1963); Sulh, *op. cit.*; and Robert Murphy, *Diplomat Among Warriors* (Garden City, N.Y.: Doubleday, 1964).

26 "I have my reasons. I shall make known my point of view at an appropriate time. That will be in May, June, or July. . . . I understand very well the anxiety that the possibility of revising the Constitution arouses in you. I am myself against the revision in principle. There is, however, one point on which I wish to leave no doubt: If, when the proper time comes, I am not assured of finding a successor who will guarantee the continuation of my policies, I declare here and now that I shall reconsider my position." *L'Orient,* December 31, 1957.

27 *L'Orient,* June 5, 1958. *Cf.* Prime Minister Sami Sulh's statement of May 27: "Je dois dire en toute sincérité que le Président de la République ne m'a jamais entretenu de son désir de renouveler son mandat. Ni le Chef de l'Etat, ni le Gouvernement, n'ont inscrit cette affaire dans leur programme. En outre, le Gouvernement n'a entrepris aucune démarche dans ce sens et ne présentera jamais à la Chambre un projet d'amendement de la Constitution." ["I must say in all sincerity that the President of the Republic has never mentioned to me any desire to extend his stay in power. Neither the Chief of State nor the Government has included such an item in its future plans. Besides, the Government has taken no steps in that direction and will never present to the Chamber a proposal for amending the Constitution to permit such an extension."] *L'Orient,* May 28, 1958.

28 "A new article of political faith was presented to the Lebanese eight months ago: If you are not a Chamounian, then you are a traitor and a Syro-Bolshevik." Georges Naccache, "A l'Heure de Mme. Afaf," *L'Orient,* January 17, 1958.

29 One may obtain a rough idea of the extent of U.A.R. interference by examining the following sources: United Nations Security Council, *Official Records* (New York: United Nations, 1958), Meeting 825, June 11, 1958; and the Swedish resolution creating a United Nations Observation Group in Lebanon, Resolution S/4023. The five reports submitted by UNOGIL between July 3 and November 17, 1958, are found in United Nations Security

Council documents S/4040, S/4069, S/4085, S/4100, and S/4114. The observer group lacked sufficient personnel and access to the borders during the critical period. See also the debates in the Security Council of June 6 (Meeting 823) and June 10 (Meeting 824) on the Lebanese complaint (S/40007) and of July 21 (Meeting 835) on the question of Syrian subversion. See also *The New York Times* for the period, especially "Unsifted U.S. Intelligence Reports of Syrian Complicity," July 17, 1958, p. 9. The memoirs of such leading participants as Camille Chamoun, *op. cit.*, and Kamal Jumblat, *op. cit.*, are also illuminating. The insurgent leaders interviewed freely admitted that they had received aid of various sorts, although they emphasized that the crisis was essentially an internal matter. See Qubain, *op. cit.*, pp. 133–53, for a detailed account of the quantity and the source of the aid.

[30] *IRFED Report,* I, 84.

[31] This point is evident in the insurgents' "14 points," which formed the basis for the formal termination of the rebellion at the end of July 1958. Eleven of these points are directed specifically at limiting the President's personal power and policy options. The manifesto is a kind of latter-day Magna Charta. The text was printed in *L'Orient* and *The Arab World* of July 30, 1958.

[32] After his term expired, President Chamoun tried to form such a party, but his National Liberal Party, like several other parties in Lebanon, is hard to distinguish from a traditional client following. See Chapter 4.

[33] For example, in a declaration on the eve of the Presidential election, Jumblat made a set of demands independent of the fourteen points of the insurgents. He asked that two portfolios (one of them the Ministry of the Interior) be set aside for socialist ministers exclusively and called for an independent development board, national health insurance, and financial reforms like the creation of a central bank. *Arab World Opinion,* July 29, 1958.

[34] Point number eleven of the fourteen points submitted by the insurgents on the eve of the Presidential election. See *The Arab World* and *L'Orient,* July 30, 1958; and *Beirut al-Massa,* July 29, 1958.

[35] Concerning the insurgents' manifesto the Kataeb stated in its newspaper: "There was nothing constructive or social in these demands. They are primarily political demands emanating from an inferiority complex and hatred. . . . You should read these . . . demands and laugh. . . . We refused to believe that such a terrorist movement where crime abounded could really be regarded as a 'revolution' or as an expression of the will of the people." *al-'Amal,* July 31, 1958, quoted in *The Arab World,* August 1, 1958.

[36] See, for example, the text of the Third Force Press Conference in *L'Orient,* January 18, 1958: "L'anarchie a envahi les services publiques; les fonctionnaires ont été mobilisés et les ressources de l'Etat ont été mises à contribution au profit des militants de la réconduction. Dans toutes les colonnes des journaux, rebondit tous les matins la cascade des scandales où sont impliquées les plus hautes personnalités. . . ."

["Anarchy has invaded the public services; state officials have been mobilized, and the resources of the State have been diverted to private profits for militant supporters of the President's continuation in power. Every morning, in the columns of every newspaper, there rebound the cascading scandals in which even the highest leaders are implicated."] See also the Resolutions of the Interconfessional Congress, signed by eighty-two dignitaries (of whom half were Christian), meeting at the house of Henri Pharaon on March 27, 1958, in *L'Orient,* March 28, 1958. The Congress called for a return to the principles of the National Pact.

[37] *L'Orient.* April 18, 1958. The American Ambassador held his own *iftār* and invited seventeen pro-Western Muslim notables, including the Prime Minister.

PART TWO
Actors

CHAPTER · 4

The Establishment and Its Politics

Foreign visitors to Lebanon are inevitably told about the Belgian economist and statesman Dr. Paul Van Zeeland, who was commissioned to advise the Lebanese government about the economy. After careful study he is supposed to have declared, "I don't know what it is you are doing, but whatever it is, keep it up." [1] If it is hard to explain Lebanon's prosperity, it is even harder to explain its political viability. The divisive forces of parochialism, external meddling, and uneven social change create a genuine political dilemma for the young Republic, yet somehow its political system keeps going, avoiding disaster and confounding the pessimists. Only once, during the insurgency of summer 1958, has the machine completely collapsed, and even then it was restored quite successfully; few other newly independent states have fared as well. A political system that performs even moderately well under such adverse conditions is worthy of further study.

How does the political system in Lebanon function and what are its prospects for breaking out of the dilemma outlined in the preceding chapters? This and the following chapters attempt to answer these questions. These chapters will examine the adjustments and innovations of the traditional elite and the modern counterelite, the broadening scope of political life, and the development of the executive powers and responsibilities that political modernization requires. In all these areas Lebanese ingenuity is readily apparent. It is easy for a political scientist to admire the techniques of bargaining and coordination that maintain domestic tranquillity; but, ingenious as these techniques may be, they are inadequate to surmount the basic dilemma. Without strong institutions Lebanon must count upon extraordinary good luck.

Power in Lebanon is monopolized by an establishment of clerics, semifeudal political bosses, bankers, businessmen, and lawyers. The members of the establishment come from fewer than fifty prominent families. The establishment derives its influence partly from these traditional affiliations and partly from economic success, and Lebanese politics today is still essentially the competition among its members to advance their various parochial interests—sectarian prerogatives, commercial privileges, and pork-barrel benefits. Increasingly, however, politics is beginning to revolve around a new competition between this establishment as a whole and the outsiders—the more recently politicized strata excluded from significant participation in the formal political system.

The most striking aspect of the Lebanese establishment is its lack of modern political organizations. The personalities and groups to be described here are highly sophisticated but parochially organized. In general, the prevailing political organization in the establishment is the personal clique. The influential landlords, lawyers, and businessmen of Lebanese politics operate through such informal groupings. The Constitutional Bloc and National Bloc discussed here are important examples. There are, however, more elaborate organizations in the establishment. For example, religious leaders utilize their sectarian organizations in politics: This practice is particularly notable within the Christian communities. Two establishment groups have developed a degree of specialized political organization that is especially noteworthy, although both remain essentially sectarian in character and are dominated by personalities whose influence is rooted in parochial rather than in modern affiliations. They are the Armenian Tashnaq Party and the Kataeb, a basically Maronite organization.

The establishment, although it is composed largely of particularistic leaders, is definitely capable of political adaptation and innovation, but probably not as much as Lebanese conditions seem to require. Extensive interviews with a large number of notables reveal that there is a shared doctrine of sophisticated pragmatism in the establishment that makes possible significant, though circumscribed, flexibility in political behavior. There is a common understanding of the limits that Lebanese particularism places on political choice and a sensitivity to political currents both in Lebanon and in the Arab world. This sensitivity within the establishment explains perhaps the development of a mildly progressive philosophy among some notables since the end of the 1940s. This chapter describes the several elements that the establishment comprises and analyzes its changing factional patterns.

THE MEMBERS

Clerics

As long as Lebanon has had significant minority groups, men of religion have performed political functions as leaders of their communities in a hostile environment. Under Mamluk and Ottoman rule, the Christian sects especially developed a solidarity and a suspicion of outsiders that remains evident in Mount Lebanon today. The clergy embodies and perpetuates these attitudes. Sixty years before France established the state of Greater Lebanon, the Maronite Patriarch Boulus Masaad was a major instigator of civil strife that led to the great massacre of Christians. Indeed, the Patriarch was a general and a conspirator, as well as a religious leader.[2] At the end of World War I, with the withdrawal of the ruling Sunnite Turks in prospect, the heads of the religious minorities—especially the Maronite and Greek Orthodox—lost no time in trying to protect and enlarge their influence. The inquiries of the King-Crane Commission show clearly that the primary political groups at that time were religious in character and that the primary political question was the distribution of power among them.[3] The political role of the Maronite Patriarch Elias Butros Hawayek in creating a Christian-dominated Greater Lebanon (exemplified by his meeting with Georges Clemenceau) was more important than that of all the politicians of the area.[4]

Once installed, the Mandate authorities secured their position by soliciting the support of the clerics, and the clerics also found the close relationship with the authorities advantageous.[5] During the Mandate the religious leaders found their privileged position compromised by rising demands for independence, but, though their influence was challenged, their activity hardly decreased. Stephen Longrigg comments on the "fulminations" of the Patriarch Antoun Arida in the last days of the Mandate and characterizes his policy as pro-Zionist and anticommunist and, above all, as devoted to his own community.[6] Gabriel Puaux, a Protestant and the last High Commissioner before the Vichy regime, has left a vivid description of the "panthéon syrien," in which he catalogues each of the sectarian leaders with whom he had to deal as High Commissioner.[7] Puaux comments wryly on Patriarch Arida's taste for temporal power and his readiness to interfere in administrative activities[8] and on the efforts of the Greek Orthodox leaders to use his (Puaux's) support to heal schisms in the Church. Puaux contrasts Arida's persistent political manipulation with the dignified conduct of the Mufti Toufic Khaled and the mystical activity of the Shiites. For the French Mandate authorities, calming mutual fears among these sects was the chief problem of governing, whereas each religious head felt that his essential duty was to maintain the security of his flock and, if possible, to obtain a more equitable place for it in Lebanon.

After independence the clerics still played an impressive role in Lebanese politics, although they had competition from strong secular powers. The unusually corrupt parliamentary elections in 1947 were strongly opposed by various religious dignitaries, including the Maronite Patriarch, the Greek Orthodox Archbishop of Beirut, and the Grand Mufti of Lebanon, as well as important Shiites, Druzes, and Catholics.[9] The religious leaders, though generally disagreeing among themselves, showed solid unity in 1952 against the Lebanese lawyers' syndicate's strike. The lawyers struck for three months in protest of a law that limited their rights to practice and also enhanced the power of religious courts in matters of personal status. The strike failed, indicating that the religious leaders would not tolerate a diminution of their traditional powers and that the state was unable to force change in that direction.[10] In the 1958 crisis clericalism was still a significant factor. The Maronite Patriarch, Monsignor Butros-Boulus Meouchy, was probably the strongest of President Camille Chamoun's opponents in Lebanon; certainly Monsignor Meouchy was outspoken in his criticism.[11] The non-Christian religious leaders also played an important role. It will be recalled that President Chamoun's regime suffered a serious blow when the Mufti pointedly neglected to invite any government officials to a Muslim *iftār,* violating the usual courtesy. There is today no sign that the men of religion are about to retire from the political arena.[12] Indeed, as long as sectarian suspicions remain, they can hardly avoid taking political roles.

A closer examination of the role of the Maronite Patriarch reveals the nature of his political involvement. Monsignor Meouchy is not at all apologetic about engaging in politics, for it is the tradition that the Maronite Patriarch, as the shepherd, protects and counsels his flock. A man of strong character, the Patriarch looks down upon the Lebanese political scene from his mountain residence at Bkerke with benign tolerance and tells the visitor that Lebanon is a family and that, like all families, it has its little squabbles. In practical politics his attitude is less detached. He speaks as bluntly as any other politician and makes it clear that he is a partisan in the continuing struggle to maintain equilibrium. The Patriarch does not strike out at Muslim politicians or notables as much as he does at other Christian leaders. Indeed, he has devoted considerable energy to opposing two Presidents of the Republic, Camille Chamoun and Fuad Chehab. There is ample precedent for such opposition: His predecessor fought a continuing battle with the Khoury regime, perhaps because he resented the intrusion of a Maronite secular leader into the relationship between shepherd and flock. It is suggested that personal differences led to Patriarch Meouchy's break with President Chamoun, principally because the President did not take kindly to clerical advice. During the 1958 crisis, however, the Patriarch justified his opposition by arguing that President Chamoun was leading the Christians toward disaster by jeopardizing their position in the Arab world. He worked vigorously to erode the conservative Christian support that President Chamoun relied on increasingly in his struggle with the rural bosses, the progressives, and President Nasser. President Chamoun's activities were increasing sectarian divisions within Lebanon, but, during the crisis, there was more amity between the Patriarch and the non-Christian communities than ever before or since. His stand, however, cost him the support of many conservative Maronites.[13] Some well-informed observers believe that Patriarch Meouchy had his eye on the Presidency in 1958 and that this ambition was the reason he worked so diligently against any movement for the renewal of President Chamoun's term. General Chehab was scarcely installed as President when the Patriarch and ex-President Chamoun were reconciled. The Patriarch also turned against Chehab immediately after the first signs of military intrusions into the political sphere began to appear. Patriarch Meouchy's view of President Nasser's role in the 1958 crisis changed from praise of the Egyptian President's benevolent neutrality to castigation of Nasser's blatant interference, to which Lebanon had luckily avoided succumbing. On the eve of the expiration of President Chehab's term in 1964, the Patriarch again made his stand against renewal clearly known and was reported to be lunching with ex-President Chamoun. The issues between the Patriarch and President Chehab were (in the Patriarch's view) Lebanese subservience to the policy of the United Arab Republic and the interference of Lebanese army officers in political affairs.

The Patriarch's influence derives from his exalted religious position in a culture in which religion and politics are inseparable. His most important instrument of influence is the priestly hierarchy, which serves not only as a means for disseminating his authoritative views but also as an effective intelligence service. He views Lebanon as essentially a Christian country and believes that his duty is to keep it that way. The Patriarch feels that the best way of keeping this status quo is to assert and constantly reassert the role of the Maronites and of the Patriarchy in the delicate balance of power. It appears that the Patriarch does not believe that the balance is self-regulating: Only by positive action can the interests of his community be preserved. The future is uncertain because so much hinges on the behavior of a few people—the President, for instance, may not always be the wisest member of the Maronite community—and on forces outside the country. Social policy is clearly the Patriarch's secondary concern, apparently because he believes that, if the sectarian balance is maintained, social policy will take care of itself. The Patriarch also interprets foreign policy through the screen of sectarian requirements, which dictate that the Church must skillfully counter any trends that threaten the Christian predominance. For example, when Egypt and Syria were united and exerting pressure on Lebanese Muslims in 1958, it was the wisest policy to show flexible acquiescence, within limits, rather than rigid opposition; but, when there was an opportunity to play one neighbor off against another—Syria against Egypt, in 1961, for example—the Church was quick to exploit it. At the same time, lines to the West and opposition to communism have always been maintained.

Landlords

Great landlords are another category in the establishment's membership. These men have inherited sufficient lands to provide them with substantial income, which frees them for other pursuits, and to create local clienteles of tenant and yeoman farmers, laborers, and neighbors, which have considerable political utility. These landholders are generally found in North Lebanon, South Lebanon, and the Biqa, where vestiges of economic feudalism remain, and they typically sublet property to lesser families and peasants. In 1953, for example, Joseph Skaf owned an estimated 5,000 fertile acres in the Biqa; the heads of the Khalil, Osseiran, Zein, and Assaad families held about 3,700 acres apiece in South Lebanon (as well as five seats in Parliament); and in the Akkar plain in North Lebanon Abboud Abdel Razzak and his sons probably owned about 5,000 acres.[14] Under the Ottoman administration many of these prominent landed families had cooperated with Constantinople and in return had been allowed to manage affairs and to settle conflicts in their localities. When Greater Lebanon was created, the French found it necessary to acquire allies among these great families in order to check the Arab nationalist movement in Syria. The gravitation of Sunnite and nationalist landowners toward Damascus made the task of recruiting notables more difficult in the outer regions of Greater Lebanon than in the Mountain. Nevertheless, France succeeded in winning support in Tripoli from the respected Mufti Shaykh Muhammad al-Jisr. In the Biqa two important Shiite families, the Haidars and the Hamadehs, each split their allegiance between Beirut and Damascus, and, in southern Mount Lebanon, the French struck up an agreement with the Jumblat family, leaders of one of the two rival Druze factions and traditionally clients of the British.[15] In South Lebanon Hussein Zein (Shiite), a notable of Nabatieh, was drawn into the ruling circle of Greater Lebanon, as were members of the important families of Osseiran and Chehab.

Independence from France brought to an end the isolation of Sunnite landowners from the established institutions. The rapprochement was symbolized by Riad Sulh, the principal Lebanese Arab nationalist, who became Prime Minister in the first government. Just as nineteenth-century Lebanon was run by a gallery of landed notables, so is the independent Lebanese Republic governed by the descendants of these leaders: in North Lebanon Karamis, Miraabis, Muqaddams, and Jisrs (Sunnite), Frangiehs and Moawads (Maronite), and Ghusns (Greek Orthodox); in the Biqa Hamadehs and Haidars (Shiite) and Skafs (Greek Catholic); in South Lebanon Assaads, Osseirans, and Zeins (Shiite) and Sulhs (Sunnite). In Mount Lebanon the great personalities of the "age of independence" bore the same names as nineteenth-century aristocrats: Chehab, Jumblat, Khazen, Karam, Abi-lamaa, Arslan.

The feudal gentlemen of the past had personalities strong enough to induce considerable respect, if not affection, from their clienteles. Today, with increasing modernization, the descendants of these men perhaps lack the magnetism, strength, and ruthlessness of Bashir II,[16] but postwar Lebanon still has its share of colorful landed political bosses, and they play a decisive part in present-day affairs. A glance at some of these leaders in action will illustrate their style of politics. Richard Pearse, a British agent, arrived in Tripoli in 1944 and wrote:

> Just before my arrival at Tripoli the Prime Minister, a native of the town, had been shot up in his car close to his home by the gunmen of one of his rivals. The Prime Minister, Abdul [Hamid] Karami, was pro-British; his assailant . . . pro-French. Political passion was also the cause of trouble between various guests. Politically speaking, Tripoli was not exactly a dull place. Political murder, gangsterism and racketeering were as common as they were in Chicago in the late twenties.[17]

Another boss, Ahmad al-Assaad (Shiite), held extensive lands around Taybeh in South Lebanon and wielded great influence because he could project his own local power throughout South Lebanon and indeed through the whole country under the electoral system of the "grand list." [18] At the height of his influence, in 1948, he was more powerful in South Lebanon than his friend the President of the Republic. The Lebanese journalist Kesrouan Labaki was hardly exaggerating when he wrote that Assaad and Sabri Hamadeh, the Shiite leader of the Baalbek-Hermel area, actually ruled Lebanon: Assaad was the political boss of South Lebanon, Hamadeh was the political boss of the Biqa, and Assaad was the father-in-law of Hamadeh. Assaad, idol of the Shiites of Jebel Amal, was also master of the Greek Orthodox of Merjayoun and the Sunnites in Saida by virtue of his eminence in the region. Hamadeh controlled the Greek Catholics in Zahleh. When these two combined with Majid Arslan, the Druze leader of Chouiefat, who also controlled the Maronites in Jbeil, they could control Parliament.[19]

Landlord dominence has declined somewhat since the early years of independence; nevertheless, it remains a major force. Following the forced resignation of President Bechara al-Khoury in September 1952, Assaad's alliance with the national government was broken, and a new electoral law did away with the grand list, reducing Assaad's power, but he was still a man to reckon with. On March 9, 1954, Prime Minister Abdallah Yafi, in the course of a typically warm parliamentary debate, told Assaad's son Kamel (the only successful member of the Assaad ticket in the 1953 elections) that he and his father had ruined the country. The next day father and son mobilized a crowd of 1,000 partisans that marched to Parliament demanding an apology. One person was killed in the ensuing riot. Although Assaad never received his apology, neither was he called to account for the disturbances.[20] In their own local domains, the landlords are still virtually supreme, acknowledging no party, and they are still able to hold the state itself at bay, as the 1958 crisis dramatically illustrated. As late as 1960, Sabri Hamadeh, one of the most important landlords of the Baalbek-Hermel area, is reported to have shot an officer when he refused to allow Hamadeh's friends to enter the polling place with him. Not only did Hamadeh escape censure, but he was also elected Speaker of the Parliament shortly afterward.[21]

Saeb Salam is an atypical member of the land-owning elite in the sense that he lives in Beirut. Perhaps he is also more sophisticated than others of his class, but in a number of other respects he is representative. In his district he is a figure who commands deference, loyalty, and protection. When Saeb Salam campaigns in Mousseitbeh, he does not need to dwell at length on programs or positions: Everybody knows all about him and what he will do for them. They know that the Salams (Sunnites) are an old political family, that Saeb's father was an important enemy of the Turks, and that Saeb played a major role in the agitation for Lebanese independence as head of the Muslim Congress. They know he resisted Chamoun in 1958 and can see the bullet holes in the mirror in his house. They may not know that he studied at the American University of Beirut and the London School of Economics, but they recognize his trademarks—the cigar and the carnation. Every weekday the outer parlor of Salam's elegant old house is filled with people in trouble wanting help, and they will be unhappy unless they see Salam personally. Salam can and does help in many ways. He settles private quarrels and intercedes with the municipality for constituents. Like the American city boss in an earlier time, Salam distributes money occasionally to the slum dwellers in his area who need medical treatment, and, in the tradition of many an American philanthropist, he contributes time, money, and influence to the Maqasid Islamic Education Society. Like most Lebanese Muslim leaders he professes admiration for Nasser and displays on his mantelpiece a signed photograph of the Egyptian leader.

No Lebanese leader understands the factional process better than Salam. On more than one occasion he has successfully thrown his weight against the Sunnite mainstream in order, he says, to blur the sectarian aspect of various struggles. In the presidential election of 1964, for example, he would not endorse a renewal of General Chehab's mandate and thus placed himself on the side of the conservative Christians in an issue that had begun to take on a sectarian coloration. It would be naïve to suppose that this aim was his sole motivation, but concern for balance was at least one factor in his decision. Salam, in fact, has produced an elaborate analysis of the Lebanese problem in an address before the Lebanese Cénacle, a society of prominent intellectuals, entitled "One Lebanon, Not Two." [22] Sectarianism is not the only problem that Salam considers relevant to Lebanese politics. In Salam's opinion, politics in Lebanon—and in most other countries—is guided by the big merchants and financiers. He believes that this rich class is more exploitative in Lebanon than elsewhere, however; the financiers keep only enough capital in the country to sustain their flow of income and salt away the surplus in Europe. Therefore, this "blood sucking" is worse than the high finance in the United States or Britain because there the capitalists confine their greed within the limits imposed by the national interest. In Lebanon, if something should go wrong, the financier can simply leave on the next plane. Coming from a man regularly accused by the radical Left of being a prime example of such a politician, Salam's expressed views are unusually candid. Salam believes that politics under such circumstances tends to reflect this exploitative, tomorrow-we-may-die spirit, and that there is, at worst, an atmosphere of "every man for himself." In Salam's view, only very rich countries can afford such political anarchism, and Lebanon, although it is relatively prosperous, finds itself increasingly burdened with such public problems as slums. Salam thinks that, if anything, the political process is less adequate in the 1960s than it was twenty years earlier or during the Mandate. Today, in Salam's view, individual services to constituents are a much more important key to political success than before, and politicians are more inclined to use their government posts to recover whatever they paid out to capture them. Lebanon needs structural political reform, he argues: "Enlightened" notables are not enough. At the elite level it is possible to form coalitions across religious and regional lines—for example, Salam, Kamel al-Assaad (Shiite, South Lebanon), Sleiman Frangieh (Maronite, North Lebanon), Joseph Skaf (Greek

Catholic, the Biqa), and Nassim Majdalani (Greek Orthodox, Beirut) can form a parliamentary grouping—but at the mass level, Salam feels, each of these leaders is limited to his sect and neighborhood because he is indelibly labeled in the public mind as a Sunnite leader, a Biqa landowner, and so on. In Lebanon there is no left-right spectrum, he argues, only Christian-Muslim. Prisoners of circumstance, the notables who are liberally inclined can only do what they can for their own people and try to keep the system evenly balanced.

The clerics and feudal bosses can be distinguished from other elements of the political elite by their traditional following, their parochial outlook, and their strong character. These characteristics have given them enormous influence within their respective geographical, social, and sectarian domains. Political relations among these leaders, which reflect this local autonomy, are analogous to the relations among small states in a multipolar international system. The tacit operating principle of the Lebanese system is that none of the actors can be removed or seriously challenged. They therefore form alliances that might remind the diplomatic historian of Renaissance Italy, and they deal with one another on the basis of sovereign equality. Bargaining is the primary process for peaceful political relations. French imperial interests and Wilsonian liberalism converged upon Lebanon in the wake of the disintegrating Ottoman Empire; and the institutions of parliamentary democracy established by General Gouraud and his colleagues not only harmonized with the prevailing political elements but also served French policy through the exploitation of parochial divisions. The political elite, however, began to expand even before the ink was dry on the declaration that created Greater Lebanon.

Lawyers and Businessmen

When the French seized authority in 1918, they found clerics and landlords already playing significant roles in the political process, but they also discovered a source of potential political assistance among the notables of business and legal background. The administrative needs of the French helped to recruit these notables for positions of power. Indeed, even independent Lebanon's founding fathers—the nuclei of the Constitutional Bloc (Destour) and the National Bloc, which later became the main rival political groups—were drawn into politics by the High Commission.[23] Sometimes it was not clear whether these new recruits were the tools of

the French or vice versa; the relationship was more likely one of
mutual exploitation.[24] In any event, by recruiting prominent bankers and lawyers into their civil service, the Mandate authorities
took an important step toward preparing Greater Lebanon for self-
government and added a modernizing element to the local political
elite. This element differed from the clerics and landlords in its
cosmopolitan outlook and its European culture. The lawyers and
businessmen had studied philosophic and economic liberalism,
whereas the traditional leaders in general had no abstract philosophy
of government. The new cosmopolitan elite—illuminated by personalities like Michel Chiha, Emile Edde, Bechara al-Khoury, and
Camille Chamoun—was committed to the development of Greater
Lebanon as a viable and independent state with modern political
institutions. At that time, modern political institutions meant liberal
parliamentary democracy. Viability meant, at the minimum, a
condition of peaceful coexistence among the sectarian and other
factions. As Michel Chiha has put it, "Le Liban, au fond, est une
belle et noble tentative de cohabitation paisible des religions, des
traditions, des races. C'est une tentative naturelle que l'histoire pro-
pose comme un témoignage plus décisif encore que celui de la
Suisse au coeur de l'Europe." [25]

The 1930s were years of political ferment in Lebanon and the
rest of the Arab world. The activist spirit of the times was manifested in new political organizations. It was a time of radical ex-
perimentation in which communist, pan-Syrian, pan-Arab, pan-
Islamic, and militant Christian nationalist movements began to
challenge French control of the Lebanon. Many of these radical
movements were outlawed and persecuted.[26] At the same time,
within the French-sponsored elite, the lawyers and businessmen
were organizing to bring about Lebanese independence. Among
the moderate Sunnites a group of notables headed by Kazem Sulh,
called the Nida al-Qawmi (National Appeal), set forth a doctrine
embodying the principles of what was to become the National
Pact.[27] Groups like the National Democratic Congress agitated
against the Mandate. The High Commission itself contributed
to the elaboration of groups by assisting factions favorable to the
French interest, like the Party of Lebanese Unity, headed by
the nephew of the Maronite Patriarch. The major actors within
the establishment, however, were Emile Edde and Bechara al-
Khoury and their respective followings, the National Bloc and the
Constitutional Bloc (Destour).

The National Bloc and the Constitutional Bloc were the organizational manifestations of the rivalry between Emile Edde and Bechara al-Khoury. Edde and Khoury were both Maronites, both owed their positions of influence to the Mandate, both spoke fluent French and Arabic, and both held law degrees from French universities. Khoury, in fact, had begun his law practice in Edde's office. Edde, who was brought back to Beirut on a French warship in 1919, immediately became one of the leading politicians, but the Mandate authorities shrewdly elevated Khoury into the administration to balance him.[28] The rivalry that developed between these two gave the French a strong position as balancer; this role was evident, for example, in their manipulation of the presidential election in 1936, which Edde, the favorite of the French, won. The basic rivalry between these two men also molded the political framework of Mount Lebanon for the first decade after independence.

Edde, who is remembered as an inflexible, short-tempered, volatile personality, was culturally Francophile and, like most of the Maronite elite, well aware of France's historical role as the protector of that sect. Edde's circle was limited to the exclusively French-speaking commercial and financial society of Beirut. By contrast, Khoury used his position in the Interior Department to cultivate a wide circle of acquaintances among the non-Christian notables of the outlying areas. The rivalry between these two men, visible since 1926, crystallized after 1929 when they began the campaigns for the Presidency that eventually ended with the French suspending the Constitution. A combination of personal ambition and programmatic goals led each to form caucuses and to espouse different views on the issue of national independence. Edde pledged the National Bloc to maintaining France's special relationship with Lebanon even after independence, a view that was in harmony with the Mandate policy. Khoury's Constitutional Bloc advocated restoration of the Constitution after its suspension in 1932.[29] Against the background of increasing nationalism and sectarian problems in Syria and Lebanon, Khoury's group became increasingly identified with the anti-French and radical independence currents.

The Constitutional Bloc, in alliance with key rural leaders, carried the 1943 elections, overcoming the Francophile opposition. Khoury was elected President of the Republic and promptly eliminated all the constitutional provisions requiring or implying submission to France. In the ensuing crisis Khoury's wide popular support and British diplomatic pressure prevented the French from removing the President and his government from office and restoring Edde. By the end of 1943, several factors, notably the Anglo-French rivalry, had consolidated each of the two blocs to such an extent that they were the poles of elite conflict for the next nine years. They continue to be powerful factors in Lebanese politics today, supported by factions within the banking and commercial community, though in a multipolar arena they are no longer as important as they were.[30]

What kind of politicians are these bankers and lawyers? Two examples will suggest some answers. The banker, publicist, and political mediator Henri Pharaon (Greek Catholic) "retired" from politics after the Khoury regime, but he remains active in the 1960s as one of the most prominent Christian leaders, even though he is past seventy. Pharaon has long represented Lebanon's community of high finance. Once the leader of a formidable, multisectarian coalition embracing notables of North Lebanon, the Biqa, and Beirut, a broker between the Khoury machine and its enemies, and in 1958 a leader of the Third Force, Pharaon is the epitome of the wealthy, cultivated, and liberal Beirut politician. His view of Lebanon reflects the thinking of Michel Chiha, his friend and brother-in-law. He expressed it concisely in a eulogy to the late Habib Abuchahla, an old companion and rival, in 1957: ". . . [N]ous sommes, du fait de notre diversité même, voués à une politique de tolérance et de liberté, à l'intérieur, et à une politique d'équilibre et de sagesse, à l'extérieur, qui sont les conditions de notre sauvegarde et de notre progrès."[31] To Pharaon political life in Lebanon is something more positive and valuable than a state of truce between rival communities. He believes that there is a common interest that will be served as long as the notables can get along with one another and realize that the boundaries of acceptable behavior given in the National Pact may only be exceeded at great risk. In Pharaon's view, serving this common interest is the primary goal of politics and requires constant attention. He believes that the common interest is never more endangered than in the period approaching a presidential election. According to Pharaon, no modern Lebanese president, despite his public protestations to the contrary, has been willing to give up power as the Constitution requires, and this reluctance in the cases of Khoury and Chamoun has led to chronic conflict, which only the most resourceful mediation by disinterested notables and out-

side powers can bridge. In comparison to these chronic constitutional problems, internal reforms and development are far
down the scale of Pharaon's political priorities. The governmental
corruption of bribes and favors is infinitely preferable to military
interference in government and administration. No amount of
social reform is worth this price, particularly if it disturbs the free-
enterprise economy. Another of Pharaon's priorities is a foreign
policy that maintains absolute sovereignty, a requirement that cannot be taken for granted in a country as tiny as Lebanon, situated
in a turbulent environment. Pharaon believes that one of his greatest services to Lebanon was his intervention during the period between the signing of the Alexandria Protocol and the promulgation of the Arab League Pact. His efforts resulted in the closing of
a loophole in the Protocol clause that required individual state
policy to fall within the collective approval of the Arab League.[32]
Had the Protocol clause been written into the League Pact, Lebanon would have faced the dilemma of choosing between violating
the spirit of the National Pact by making an open-ended commitment to the Arab League or declining to join the League at all,
which would have been disastrous.[33] In this case, as in 1957–1958,
Lebanon's international position was nearly compromised by her
well-meaning but misguided Western friends, England and the
United States. Pharaon thus also makes the classic balance-of-
power argument; and, although he is an enlightened liberal and
humanist, he prefers *laissez faire* to the policy planning and initiative of Western polities because in Lebanon these methods inevitably threaten the classic equilibrium. The delicacy of the situation imposes a politics of inactivity; maintaining the balance alone
requires the full attention of the politicians. Pharaon's view is lofty
and far removed from the vulgarities of daily politics, yet it is realistic insofar as it properly identifies the traditional conditions of
political stability. Whether or not it sufficiently recognizes other
conditions of stability, like those posited by the radical left, is
another matter.

The Armenian deputy Khatchik Babikian is a successful lawyer.
He is especially interesting because he represents the least integrated
of all the major religious communities and—with the possible exception of the Druzes—the most tightly knit. Perhaps this exclusive-
ness explains why Armenian leaders prefer to remain relatively in-
conspicuous politically. If this factor, as well as the fact that the
bulk of the community came to Lebanon relatively late (1920s),

leads to a certain distance from other Christians as well as Muslims, it is all the more reason for the Armenians to support staunchly but quietly the sectarian status quo. As Christians Lebanon's 100,000 Armenians cannot avoid being a factor in the sectarian equation, and their dominant party, the Tashnaq, maintains a close liaison with the conservative Lebanese Kataeb (see p. 142). Babikian represents Tashnaq views in the Chamber of Deputies, but he is not a member of the party itself. Strictly an Armenian party, the Tashnaq is probably the best organized and most disciplined political group in Lebanon, and it dominated the politics of the sect long before independence.[34] In modern Lebanon an Armenian cannot win without Tashnaq support. Even so, the opposition of the Henchaq Party since 1956 has been fierce, and Armenian politics have been marked by violence and coercion. Mr. Babikian was drawn into Armenian politics in 1956 during a crisis in the community over an attempt by the Soviet branch of the Armenian Gregorian Church to disestablish the Lebanese Catholics of Armenian descent. The struggle immediately took on political overtones because the Armenian community throughout the world is divided between those who diligently oppose the Sovietization of Armenia (in Lebanon, they are the Tashnaq "rightists") and those who recognize the Soviet hegemony in Armenia and who support socialist programs (in Lebanon, the Henchaq "leftists").[35] Babikian, who had studied in Italy and Cyprus and who is one of the few Armenians fluent in Arabic, was prevailed upon to be a Tashnaq candidate in 1957. He felt it would be bad for Armenians in Lebanon to be suspected of domination by a foreign church. He won and was re-elected twice.

Babikian's function as a community leader determines his behavior as a national politician. As a new constituent minority, Armenians support the state because it gave them refuge. In Babikian's view, the security of his community depends directly on the security of the regime. The logic of this position explains why Babikian supported the Chamoun regime,[36] until it was clear that it was doomed, and then became an enthusiastic supporter of the new regime of General Chehab. In the aftermath of the 1958 crisis, the Chehab regime was eager to recruit as many members of the Christian community as possible in order to isolate the hard core of opposition centered around ex-President Chamoun and Raymond Edde, son of former President Emile Edde. The regime's interests coincided with those of the Armenians, and Babikian became the first Armenian to hold a cabinet post.[37] Babikian and the other three Armenians again went along with the majority in 1964 and supported the parliamentary resolution asking President Chehab to serve a second term.

Babikian's view of the Lebanese situation is comprehensive and sophisticated. Representing an influential but vulnerable community, he is compelled by the logic of the Lebanese situation to support balance in the political system. He goes further than others, however, when he suggests that a true security and a genuine rule of law can only come about when the apparatus of the state has the capability to be a strong, impartial umpire in internal disputes and to enact social reform. The Armenian community could be badly hurt by prolonged civil disorders; thus this Armenian notable believes that working for general social improvements best serves the parochial interests of his sect. Not only do the Armenians themselves stand to gain directly, for some of them inhabit the worst slums of Beirut, but they also benefit from state policies that reduce the misery in non-Christian communities, insofar as such policies promote general social and sectarian stability. This enlightened self-interest does not exist in some other segments of the Christian communities. In foreign policy Babikian is obliged to be as circumspect as Lebanon itself. Like most Christians he is unswerving in his support of an independent Lebanon, and as an Armenian of the right wing, he opposes Soviet communism because he believes that it has oppressed Armenian nationalism and that its economic philosophy is unsound. These beliefs drive him dangerously close to the West, in a country where the West no longer enjoys a reputation for justice and rectitude. In order to avoid this impression, the Armenian lawyer balances his opposition to Arab unity (until each state "puts its own house in order") by his approval of the social and economic reforms in the United Arab Republic (Egypt). His role is that of the liberal honest broker in Lebanon's factional politics.

At the dawn of independence, the establishment was an amalgam of parochial clerics and landlords, with their faithful clienteles, and the sophisticated notables with law degrees and extensive financial and social ties with Europe. The substance of normal Lebanese politics since independence has been the rivalries within this elite. The Constitutional Bloc and the National Bloc (to a lesser extent) lent a degree of coordination to this amalgam and structured the rivalries in a crude way in terms of a national politics.

The independence platform of the Constitutional Bloc imposed enough cohesion on the fragmented power elite to carry the state through its critical first four years.[38]

The Kataeb

With one possible exception, the establishment has no parties in the Western sense, lacking as it does secular, broadly based organizations and doctrine. Even the well-organized Tashnaq is fundamentally parochial. The one establishment group that most closely approaches a Western party is the Kataeb, or the Phalanges Libanaises. The Kataeb belongs in the establishment because it is unambiguously committed to maintenance of the Lebanese entity. In spite of its Maronite origins and interests, it might be called a "party" because its programs are specific, and its organization highly differentiated. In both programs and organization the Kataeb has sought to broaden its original sectarian coloration.

By 1936 the pan-Syrian and pan-Arab movements were so highly developed that, to many Maronite Christians, they threatened to break Lebanon apart after independence. Many Maronites feared that Lebanon might be drawn toward a Fertile Crescent scheme by Hashemite and British interests or toward an Arab national federation by an awakening Sunnite population, and they doubted that the delicate machinery of the establishment could control either tendency. On November 21, 1936, four Christians (three of them Maronites) founded the Kataeb.[39] Its mission was to preserve and strengthen the Lebanese political entity against these strains. The Kataeb took as its motto "Lebanon first," although many Muslims think this motto would more accurately read "Maronite Christians first." [40] It is the only clearly successful modern mass organization in the establishment.

Although the Kataeb's goals are as conservative as those of the National Bloc or Constitutional Bloc (Destour), its means are hardly as traditional. A product of the radical ferment of the 1930s, it borrows heavily from the style of the European parties of that era: salutes, uniforms, strict discipline, physical fitness, paramilitary training. Dissatisfaction with the Mandate was a common meeting ground for all tendencies, and the Kataeb—then officially a youth group—was in the forefront of the resisters. On the first anniversary of the founding of the Kataeb, 600 members demonstrated in downtown Beirut, and, when the authorities tried to disperse them, a number of people, including the Kataeb's leader,

Pierre Gemayel, were wounded. This incident strengthened the movement and helped to generate a mystique around Gemayel. The events of 1943 established the Kataeb as a significant political force. When the French arrested the Khoury-Riad Sulh government, the Kataeb and Najjadeh (a Muslim youth group), along with other groups, organized the strike described earlier. This strike and other popular activities in support of the imprisoned ministers were important in bringing about their release.[41]

In the years following independence the Kataeb has perfected its organization. It has established relations with Lebanon's feeble labor movement. By 1947 the Kataeb had 40,000 members and offices in all sections of the country, with the central organization under the command of Gemayel. In 1949, a year of domestic unrest, the government thwarted the Kataeb's attempt to become a political party. At the same time, however, it seems to have used the Kataeb in its struggle against the Syrian National Party (P.P.S.), which tried to foment a rebellion in the same year. The Kataeb finally became an officially recognized party in 1952. In the 1952 crisis the Kataeb took to the streets along with the other groups to force the resignation of the President. Throughout the tense period leading up to the 1958 civil war the Kataeb maintained a vigilant stance.

During the crisis of summer 1958 the Kataeb aligned itself reluctantly with the forces of President Camille Chamoun, even though it meant fighting on the same side as its old enemy, the P.P.S. The common bond was a belief that the insurgents were an instrument of President Nasser, the enemy of both Lebanese independence, championed by the Kataeb, and the Greater Syria scheme, championed by the P.P.S. To the Kataeb at that time, a greater Syria was less a threat to Lebanon than was Nasser's Arab unity. During most of the crisis the Kataeb's role was minor in a military sense, but in the "22 journées glorieuses de la contre-révolution," from September 24 to October 15, the Kataeb, inflamed at the kidnapping of one of its journalists, spearheaded the drive to revise the American-sponsored settlement that, to the Kataeb, had excessively benefited the pro-Nasser insurgents. The "counter-revolution" differed from the previous stages of the crisis in that it bore distinct signs of religious hatreds, and the Kataeb became involved in situations that revived its reputation as the protector of Christians above all. The political results of the unrest were the fall of Rashid Karami's three-week-old cabinet, which had been heavily weighted with insurgents, and the creation of a four-man emergency cabinet including Pierre Gemayel himself. With this appointment, the Kataeb for the first time achieved a first-rank position in the hierarchy of formal power and held it throughout the regime of General Chehab. It held six seats in the ninety-nine-man Parliament of 1960—more than any other single group—and its chief was the Minister of Public Works. With its daily newspaper and its monthly serious journal, with its many clubhouses and cedar-tree emblems displayed in mountain villages, the Kataeb is the only group within the establishment that can claim to be a modern political party.

The Kataeb, however, has not yet achieved the status of a truly national, nonsectarian organization. If it had, the level of political institutionalization in Lebanon would be higher than it is. The Kataeb has been speaking in mildly progressive terms since independence. It has expounded a strong social welfare program, and it contributed to drafting the Labor Code of 1946, one of the few significant pieces of social legislation ever passed in Lebanon. At the same time it has fought all efforts to weaken Lebanon's economic liberalism. The Kataeb has supported the rural development program and social reform studies of the Chehab regime. It has shown interest in resource development.[42] If Kataeb declarations may be taken at face value, they are unquestionably nonsectarian in intent. "Lebanon shall be neither church nor a mosque," Pierre Gemayel has said.[43] The party points with some pride to the fact that it has some 2,000 Shiite members in South Lebanon and that it has run strong parliamentary races in South Lebanon, North Lebanon, and the Biqa.[44] These characteristics give it more of an appearance of a national party than do the other establishment organizations.

These tendencies toward broad national orientation must be evaluated, however, in the context of the core concerns of the Kataeb. The primary concern is maintaining the Lebanese equilibrium. To Kataeb leaders this concern means preventing any moves that would lead to shifts in the ratio of Christians to non-Christians in high political positions. A constant theme of Kataeb activity is keeping Lebanese emigrants in close touch with the homeland. The Kataeb has helped to organize the emigrants, who are mostly Christian, in behalf of an independent and prosperous Lebanese entity and has always insisted that if a new census is taken the overseas Lebanese must be counted. Lebanese citizens are permitted to hold dual citizenship, but they cannot vote or hold office in Lebanon, much to the regret of the Kataeb. The Kataeb's position neatly counters the demands of non-Christian elements for a new distribution of power based on the religious breakdown of the resident population or for the granting of citizenship to the large numbers of Arab immigrants (mostly Muslim) from Syria and Iraq. To the Kataeb, political sectarianism is very evil but very necessary. There are also limits to the Kataeb's desire for social reform. To counter demands from non-Christian socialists for significant income-redistribution policies, Pierre Gemayel has suggested that, because Christians pay about 80 per cent of the taxes (his figure), they are theoretically entitled to 80 per cent of the services. Although the Kataeb does not advocate strict adherence to such an allocation, Gemayel's statement is a reminder of how the party views social progress. Within this framework there is nevertheless unquestionably a realization that the stability of the Lebanese entity depends increasingly on "social justice" as well as a "free economic system."

The deeper purposes of the party are evident in its paramilitary organization. This elaborate organization is hierarchical and is governed by democratic centralism; once the central council has decided on a program, the party regional and sectional organizations implement it without question.[45] Kataeb sections are mobilized to carry out propaganda functions, to assist with electoral campaigns, and, if necessary, to fight. A high party official states that the military discipline, uniforms, parades, and training are the main reasons for the party's success as an organization. The paramilitary aspect probably has even more to it, for, as one unusually fanatical Kataeb member pointed out in reference to the 1958 crisis, the party was the only organized form of Christian resistance. The Kataeb leaders believe that none of the other Christian leaders are strong enough or astute enough to provide the kind of deterrence to the non-Christian movements that may threaten; indeed, some of their harshest criticism has been directed at Camille Chamoun, Raymond Edde, and the Maronite Patriarch. Opinions differ as to the effectiveness of the Kataeb "policemen" in 1958, but it is generally agreed that they brought coercive pressure to bear against the pro-Nasser insurgents. During the "22 journées glorieuses" Kataeb section members carried out kidnappings and murders in Beirut with a ferocity at least equal to that of the insurgents, and in South Lebanon they claim that they held off a 6,000-man Syrian force with their 1,000 riflemen.[46]

At the same time they work diligently and sincerely to promote Lebanese nationalism, the Kataeb is thus also a guardian of Christian interests, and it makes little secret of its coercive power even though it continues to press for social development. As long as "Lebanon first" continues to be interpreted by Muslims as "Christians first," however, the Kataeb will not become an integrating national party.

The Establishment in the 1960s

After two decades of independence the notables who govern Lebanon command a political system that is still most responsive to considerations of family, sect, and wealth, but it is by no means as isolated as that description suggests. Since the early 1950s organizations within the establishment have proliferated. The Hay'at al-Watania (National Committee), which is composed of Sunnite businessmen and lawyers, has applied pressure for a sectarian allocation of positions more favorable to Muslims. Former President Camille Chamoun has organized the National Liberal Party (N.L.P.), which is largely composed of his friends and clients,[47] and some of the younger notables like Kamel al-Assaad and Rashid Karami have tried, though with little apparent success, to establish organizations distinct from their traditional power base. The Kataeb, which began as a militant Christian youth group, has left the streets and entered the establishment. The notables of business, commerce, and finance have developed interest groups. They have also cultivated journalistic outlets that compensate significantly for the lack of party organizations. The proprietors of the major establishment papers, like *al-Nahār, al-Ḥayāt, L'Orient,* and *al-Ṣafā,* expose the elite to sophisticated conservatism and force it to confront the issues of the day. The establishment's traditional foundations continue to provide many points of access for individuals. Every head of a major family, every parliamentary deputy, and every notable with influence has important direct contacts with his local circle of relatives and friends. Such contacts keep members of the elite in touch with popular feelings.

The establishment is also remarkably homogeneous and well integrated, compared with the general population. One need only follow the social columns, the marriage announcements, and the inexhaustible stream of society photographs that appear weekly in the

Revue du Liban to be convinced that the contacts among the elite are numerous and usually harmonious. Beirut's huge diplomatic community only multiplies the necessities and opportunities for intra-elite contact, and more than one ambassador has complained of the arduous "night shift." Not only do the notables and their entourages meet constantly, but they also share the same backgrounds; they have been educated in Europe and have been exposed to the sophistication of a most cosmopolitan environment. A university professor can call up his friend in the General Security Department and ask a favor; the special adviser to the President is well acquainted with the high official in the Finance Ministry; the deputy from Byblos lunches with his journalist friends at the private beach of the St. Georges hotel; a notable from Zagharta invites twenty-five fellow notables from all over the country for an outdoor banquet; a distinguished banker assembles seventy-five distinguished men, each of whom he knows well, and issues an important policy declaration. In the higher realms of the establishment cohesion is limited neither by sectarian nor—under most circumstances—partisan cleavages. Even the ubiquitous personal rivalries are normally muffled in the establishment ambiance.

Behind the ambiance is a tacit understanding of Lebanon's insecurity. Notables whose political orientations are diametrically opposed share an awareness of the fragility of the Lebanese political situation and of the new social and international forces that challenge it. At the popular level, it is hard to observe any positive Lebanese consensus, but within the establishment there is most definitely a common code of political conduct. This code does not resemble that of the Marquis of Queensberry, and it certainly does not prohibit, or inhibit, rivalries. Conflict at the personal level is expected and widely tolerated. Personal rivalries occasionally lead to physical violence, but it is rare indeed that any member of the establishment exploits confessional suspicions or latent hatreds for political advantage. The rare exceptions, of course, like the 1958 crisis, can be disastrous. In general, however, the establishment consensus has quite successfully limited the behavior even of notables whose personal commitment to the National Pact is questionable.

These, then, are the elements of the Lebanese establishment: religious dignitaries, great families, bankers, lawyers, and businessmen. Together they constitute a fragmented amalgam of special interests. How do they operate politically?

CHANGING FACTIONAL PATTERNS

Factionalism is the dominant characteristic of Lebanese establishment politics. Lebanese commentators often describe their factionalism as an endless game of musical chairs, in which notables compete incessantly for power and prestige. Because factional loyalties are so impermanent, they provide for a widespread sharing of power within the establishment. The fluidity of factional loyalties also presents some obvious drawbacks to political system performance. The evils catalogued in *The Federalist,* Number 10, are all too familiar to the Lebanese citizen:

> A zeal for different opinions concerning religion, concerning government, and many other points, as well of speculation as of practice; an attachment to different leaders ambitiously contending for pre-eminence and power; or to persons of other descriptions whose fortunes have been interesting to the human passions, have, in turn, divided mankind into parties, inflamed them with mutual animosity, and rendered them much more disposed to vex and oppress each other than to co-operate for their common good.

Whatever faction the Lebanese citizen sides with, he will, in reflective moments, agree that the public interest is poorly served. An examination of factional patterns over time will afford a clearer idea of their advantages and drawbacks.

The Khoury Regime (1943–1952)

The Khoury regime manipulated factions to maintain itself in power, but factionalism also encouraged the corruption, inefficiency, and authoritarian measures that led to its downfall in 1952. Indeed, corruption associated with the 1947 elections generated a public cynicism toward politicians and institutions alike that remained long after the regime had disappeared.

Bechara al-Khoury, the master builder of the Republic, used factionalism to solidify the forces that had won independence into a political machine. He created a national machine made up of bosses who could control the whole country through traditional affiliations. The shabby climax of the Khoury regime has tended to diminish the magnitude of this accomplishment. Without a firm power base, it is doubtful that Lebanon could have survived the first years of its formal independence. Those years were marked by the need to remove the French (the last French soldiers were not recalled until the end of 1946), to solve the food shortage and hard-currency problems, to establish Lebanon's independent existence before the United Nations and the Arab states, and above all to maintain sectarian peace and political control.

A study of the electoral lists in the 1943, 1947, and 1951 elections shows that Khoury molded his alliance of regional bosses and Beirut businessmen by establishing alliances with a few key notables: Riad Sulh, Henri Pharaon, Majid Arslan, Ahmad al-Assaad. These political brokers in turn harnessed their own diverse clienteles to the regime and gave it sufficient strength, through manipulation of patronage and electoral lists, to keep the opposition notables divided. This process was particularly clear in the three outlying regions. In the Biqa, the machine was headed by Henri Pharaon, the Beirut banker, and Sabri Hamadeh, a member of the area's dominant Shiite family, who were comrades in arms in the struggle with the French. It won virtually without opposition in 1947 and 1951. Pharaon's influence, however, extended far beyond the Biqa. In Beirut, he wielded considerable influence through his ties with Christian banking circles. In North Lebanon, he was a close friend of the political boss of Tripoli, Abdel-Hamid Karami, who later became one of the important opposition leaders under the Khoury regime. Pharaon's mediating talent kept this important leader within the regime fold until 1947, but by that time Pharaon himself was beginning to back off from an increasingly corrupt Destour (Constitutional Bloc).

Khoury, however, sought continually to broaden his base of support among the notables, shrewdly realizing that dependence on just one or two would quickly bring all the others into a superior coalition against him. The President controlled an overwhelming power bloc in North Lebanon, including not only Abdel-Hamid Karami but also members of the other great families of the area— the al-Ali, Abboud, Frangieh, Muqaddam, and Jisr families. When Abdel-Hamid Karami ultimately defected, the regime still had a strong position. In this region, as in the others, Khoury exploited family rivalries to the regime's advantage. In South Lebanon, Ahmad al-Assaad was the pre-eminent Shiite. Assaad had cooperated with Beirut under the French and continued to do so under Khoury. South Lebanon also provided the electoral base for Riad Sulh, Lebanon's foremost Arab nationalist and cosigner of the

National Pact. Riad Sulh held the bulk of the Sunnites in his charismatic sway. Riad Sulh, however, was not popular with the Sunnite leaders of Beirut, who held tight control over their districts through a highly organized system of neighborhood strong men. The regime as a whole was not fond of the Sunnite leaders in Beirut either. Once independence had been achieved, it consistently sought outside Beirut for Sunnite leaders to fill the post of Prime Minister. In Beirut, the regime derived its support instead from mostly non-Maronite Christian trade and finance groups. The Armenian community provided faithful support, as it always does for the regime in power, whereas the Greek Orthodox elite, represented by Habib Abuchahla, supplied funds and influence. The regime found Mount Lebanon the most difficult area to control because the proliferation of independent groupings was so great. Among the Druzes Khoury maintained a firm alliance with Amir Majid Arslan, another leader of the independence movement, whose leadership over the Yazbaki Druzes was particularly useful because Kamal Jumblat, the leader of the other Druze faction, proved to be too much for the regime to handle. In the nineteenth century the Jumblat family had favored the British; under the Mandate, Kamal's mother, Sitt Nazira Jumblat, was a formidable ally of the French. Kamal had thus been brought up in an atmosphere favorable to the party of Emile Edde, the rival of Bechara al-Khoury, but, like most of the other notables, joined Khoury's group in order to struggle for independence. Once independence was achieved, however, Kamal Jumblat began to raise trouble for the regime as a reformer; instead of being silenced with the ministerial portfolios of National Economy and Agriculture in 1946, he turned upon the regime, attacking it for its numerous faults. Among the Christians of Mount Lebanon the regime found its most consistently strong opposition. Emile Edde and his colleagues in the National Bloc worked diligently to undermine the regime's support among the Maronites and were aided in their efforts by the Patriarch himself and numerous lesser clerics. Still, the President's family was eminent, and it was related through marriage and finance to powerful notables of the Greek Catholic community like Philippe Taqla, Michel Chiha, and Henri Pharaon.

Scarcely had the French released the government from the Rachaya prison on November 22, 1943, when Khoury's grand coalition began to crumble. In South Lebanon the single campaign list of Khoury supporters in 1943, comprised of Ahmad al-Assaad,

Adel Osseiran, Yussef Salem, and Kazem Khalil, among others, had collapsed by the time of the next election in 1947, when the last three organized their own list and put up a close but losing struggle. Riad Sulh was the Sunnite candidate on both lists. In Mount Lebanon there were two "official" lists, owing to the growing rivalries within the old Constitutional Bloc. On one list were five incumbent ministers, all of them popular in their own right and all necessary for the stability of the machine. But two of the five —Kamal Jumblat and Camille Chamoun—had ambitions of their own. After they had obtained a place on the "official" list for Mount Lebanon, they insisted that the President's brother, Shaykh Selim al-Khoury—the President's hatchet man of unsavory reputation—be dropped from the list along with a number of other old Destourians. The President agreed, reluctantly (he writes), and Shaykh Selim was forced to organize his own list in semiopposition. Of this "neo-Destour" list, only Shaykh Selim and one other candidate won.[48] President Khoury wrote that he regretted the maneuver; and well he might have, for after the election Jumblat and Chamoun charged him with corruption and seriously began to engineer his downfall.

The opposition National Bloc list polled 20 per cent of the vote. In Beirut the government successfully thwarted a rising current of opposition by assembling a list headed by three top Sunnite leaders, Abdallah Yafi, Sami Sulh, and Hussein Oueini. It won with 88 per cent of the vote, but the easy victory only fed the fires of discontent, and the losers—backed by an influential segment of the press—denounced the government's steamroller tactics. The defection of Abdel-Hamid Karami in Tripoli weakened the regime's position there, but it minimized its losses by building a coalition of other great families, including rivals of Karami; and this coalition polled approximately 95.7 per cent of the vote. Only in the Biqa was the old Khoury coalition unopposed, but even there a quarrel between Henri Pharaon and Sabri Hamadeh, in which the latter briefly joined with another wealthy Greek Catholic, Joseph Skaf, threatened to raise difficulties until President Khoury arranged to run Joseph Skaf from South Lebanon.[49]

Despite growing problems within his coalition, President Khoury's choices won without exception, and he had no difficulty whatever persuading Parliament to amend the National Pact and then to vote him a second term the following year. The Khoury regime actually was undermined by its erstwhile stalwarts and not by the formal opposition. This was certainly clear by 1951. The preceding years had been hard: The wartime boom had petered out, the customs union with Syria had collapsed, the Palestine tragedy had loaded the government with human as well as political burdens, and the abortive P.P.S. rebellion of 1949, which received initial support from the new Syrian government of Colonel Husni Zaim, had shaken the country's security. A highly articulate opposition had arisen: The agitation of youth groups and new political parties had effectively disintegrated the postindependence consensus. The regime had reacted by closing down newspapers and banning political activity by the youth groups. The Khoury machine tried to recoup its fortunes by increasing the number of seats in Parliament from fifty-five to seventy-seven and by isolating the opposition, which was strongest in Mount Lebanon, through redistricting. The elections in the rural provinces showed less change than in Beirut and Mount Lebanon. There was, however, a tendency toward increased competition. In North Lebanon, the old single district was now three, and in two of the new districts there was a bifactional struggle. Rashid Karami's list in Tripoli won with two-thirds of the total vote; the al-Ali list beat the Abboud list in Akkar by a similar margin. A trifactional feudal struggle took place in Christian Zagharta-Batroun. South Lebanon experienced another struggle between the Assaad and the Osseiran machines, and in the Biqa, a Pharaon-backed Hamadeh list won over a list headed by Joseph Skaf but by a much narrower margin than in its previous victories.

In Beirut, the "grand list" organized by Henri Pharaon, which included stalwarts like Habib Abuchahla, Moses Derkaloustian (the perennial Armenian Tashnaq representative); Amine Beyham, of a distinguished Sunnite family; Charles Helou, who was close to the Catholic "aristocracy"; and Pharaon's relative Moussa de Freige won easily over an opposition headed by Muhieddine Nsouli. The Pharaon list received two-thirds of the total vote. The situation, however, was not as secure as the victory might indicate. The leading Sunnites on the grand list—Sami Sulh, Saeb Salam, and Abdallah Yafi—operated from invulnerable power positions and, as indicated earlier, had reason to be unhappy with a regime that had given Riad Sulh the prime ministership in four successive governments lasting three years altogether. There were other ominous signs: Nassim Majdalani ran ahead of the next-highest opposition candidate by about 3,700 votes and nearly unseated Abuchahla for the Greek Orthodox seat. Majdalani, though a banker, was also affiliated with the rising opposition. The communist leader, Mustafa Ariss, polled 5,500 votes, which was far behind the 12,000 votes that the lowest Sunnite winners polled but enough to show real strength.

In Mount Lebanon, 1951 found the Khoury supporters weaker than they had ever been, holding about fifteen of the twenty-three seats in the three districts of Metn, Chouf, and Kisrwan. Their share of the total vote in each district was 45.5, 48.7, and 51.8 respectively. In Metn, they carried only five of a nine-man list and were unable to prevent the election of Pierre Edde, a son of Khoury's deceased rival, in a runoff election.[50] The loss in the Chouf was to prove ultimately fatal. Out of nine seats the Destour list won only four, and the opposing list headed by Kamal Jumblat polled 49.6 per cent of the vote, winning the remaining five seats. The Jumblat group was called the Socialist National Front (S.N.F.), although its primary unifying doctrine was not socialism but governmental reform. Its five winning members were Kamal Jumblat; Camille Chamoun; Emile Bustani, a self-made millionaire contractor; Ghassan Tueni, a young Orthodox, Harvard-educated editor, who enjoyed the support of the P.P.S.; and Anwar Khatib, a jurist and intellectual ally of Jumblat. In September 1952, in the wake of the Egyptian revolution and despite some last-minute reform proposals from President Khoury, the S.N.F. spearheaded the opposition movement that forced the President to resign.

The night President Khoury gave up his mandate (it had two years to run) nearly sixty members of the seventy-seven-man Parliament came to his house in Aley in a futile gesture of support.[51] Clearly, the Parliament was not representative of forces in the country, and the government was incapable of governing even though its legal mandate was unquestionable. A handful of opposition deputies had rallied a collection of interests, new and old, legal and illegal, and brought down a regime with a short general strike. The factional situation had permitted the regime to consolidate both itself and the state at the cost of excluding a great many elements and failing to provide a framework for legitimate opposition activity.

The Chamoun Regime (1952–1958)

President Camille Chamoun is not remembered for his progressive or reformist ideas, perhaps because of his position in the 1958 crisis; yet he attempted to make important structural innovations, particularly in curbing the powers of the rural political bosses. Instead of exploiting traditional pluralism as had his predecessor, President Chamoun sought to undermine it. During the Khoury regime factional divisions were relatively simple and shallow; under the Chamoun presidency, they became chaotic and deep. Both Khoury and Chamoun shared the same basic interest—consolidating and expanding the power of the President—but the circumstances under which Chamoun came to power forced him to adopt more radical measures. Chamoun was propelled to power by a temporary coalition of establishment forces, impatient with their long exclusion from power, and forces outside the establishment that had been mobilized by a band of reformist middle-class intellectuals. The 1952 crisis marks the first time that these outside forces had significantly penetrated the traditional system, and the resulting factional disequilibrium left the new President in an awkward position. He had inherited the enmity of the important notables who had worked with the deposed President. The traditionalists in his own coalition wanted to compete with him for power and spoils rather than to support him; and the radicals of the Socialist National Front, encouraged and perhaps surprised at having drawn blood so easily, sought to implement sweeping reform programs. Furthermore, there was an external problem that soon multiplied his local difficulties: the convergence of radical Arab nationalism and Cold War pressures upon Lebanon. It is hardly surprising, therefore, that Chamoun set out immediately to strengthen his power by intervening in the electoral process.

The 1952 election law was aimed at breaking the power of rural feudal elements. In the 1953 elections, the rural areas (North Lebanon, South Lebanon, and the Biqa) showed a higher degree of competition, largely because they were no longer simple districts: North Lebanon now consisted of eight districts, South Lebanon seven, and the Biqa four. The landlords as a group remained firmly entrenched. In North Lebanon five of the seven winners in single-member contests received 59 per cent of the total vote or less, but the faces were still the same and dominated by the Sunnite leader of Tripoli, Rashid Karami, and the Maronite from Zagharta, Hamid Frangieh. In Akkar the family feud between Sleiman al-Ali and Muhammad Abboud resulted in the assassination of the latter during the campaign.[52] In Tripoli city Rashid Karami narrowly defeated a "popular" candidate, Muhammad Hamzeh, and in Tripoli district a pro-Soviet leftist, Hashem Husseini, was elected. In Zagharta and Batroun the local bosses, Frangieh and Jean Harb, won seats. The

Greek Orthodox seat in Koura went to its leading family, the Ghusns, but the nearest rival was the P.P.S. leader Abdallah Saadeh. The big families continued to rule the South, but the scope of Ahmad al-Assaad's power was greatly curbed, permitting representation from the Osseiran and Khalil families for the first time in a decade. Although al-Assaad had his son Kamel elected from Merjayoun, the father for the first time faced a serious rival in Ali Bazzi, then a member of a moderate Arab nationalist party, Nida al-Qawmi, in Bint Jbeil. In the Biqa Sabri Hamadeh survived the fall of the Destour by a bare 757 votes, and other notables who had been poorly treated by the Destour, like Georges Hraoui and Joseph Skaf, did well.

The new President was able, however, to weaken both his tradition-based and his progressive opponents in Mount Lebanon and Beirut. In Mount Lebanon, the National Bloc did better than it ever had since 1943 by seating Raymond Edde, Pierre Edde, and Georges Akl, and notables friendly to the National Bloc such as Clovis al-Khazen, Gabriel Murr, Maurice Zouein. On the other hand, the old Destourians like Wadih Naim, Bahige Takieddine, Georges Karam, Edmond Noun, and Louis Ziadeh, were defeated; only Emile Lahoud and Majid Arslan, now independent in name as well as in fact, were returned from the original Constitutional Bloc caucus.

What happened to the new elements that had formed a coalition in the Chouf two years earlier? They had already begun to splinter. Once the objective of bringing down one President had been achieved, Kamal Jumblat soon found himself at odds with Khoury's successor. President Chamoun would not support Jumblat's proposals for land reform and nationalization of businesses. Furthermore, the nonsocialist reformists who had formed the old S.N.F., Ghassan Tueni and Emile Bustani, were not interested in further changing the political structure. Jumblat was put on the defensive when the new President called for new elections. Because of the redistricting, he squeaked through with a margin of only 613 votes,[53] and his Progressive Socialist Party (P.S.P.) colleague Anwar Khatib lost to the list of Emile Bustani. In Beirut another old member of the S.N.F., Ghassan Tueni, barely edged out Nassim Majdalani, Jumblat's associate in the anti-West, neutralist P.S.P. Tueni, who at the time was still associated with the P.P.S. (Parti Populaire Syrien, the party that advocated a Greater Syria) was running with the former President of Lebanon and a staunch independent, Alfred

Naccache; and Majdalani was running with a member of the Kataeb, which had a pro-Western, Maronite, nonsocialist posture.[54] Such mixed tickets indicated the irrationalities of the 1953 election. The various elements of the opposition to President Khoury—Jumblat, P.S.P., S.N.F., P.P.S., National Bloc, Sunnite leaders, Kataeb—were too particularistic to band together in a strong national party, although there were a few attempts.[55] President Chamoun had failed to build a positive, rationalized presidential party, but he had succeeded in dividing his opponents.

By 1957 international politics had provided the domestic political scene with an organization that local initiatives had failed to give. Lebanon's political life was becoming polarized between supporters and opponents of President Chamoun and his increasingly close relationship with the United States. The crises of 1956 and 1957 in Egypt, Jordan, and Syria had magnified the sectarian problem as well: Strong support of President Nasser among Sunnite Muslims made Christians, especially the Maronites, apprehensive. President Chamoun had also made a number of enemies since 1952, particularly among some important non-Christian notables, whose political power Chamoun had sought to curb in his electoral reform and his administrative appointments. The elections of 1957 partly reflected this polarization. Following in his predecessor's footsteps, President Chamoun enlarged the parliamentary membership by twenty-one seats and proceeded by all the means at his disposal to fill all the seats with his supporters. The situation in North Lebanon and the Biqa remained relatively stable: The regime could not unseat notables as well established as Rashid Karami, Hamid Frangieh, and Sabri Hamadeh. It did, however, go to unusual lengths to ensure that Foreign Minister Charles Malik run virtually unopposed for the Greek Orthodox seat in Koura. In other areas, however, key leaders of the opposition to Chamoun were defeated. In Beirut Saeb Salam and Abdallah Yafi, who had resigned in protest against the regime's handling of the Suez crisis, were defeated by Chamoun-backed newcomers. The regime list, headed by Sami Sulh, received only 51 per cent of the vote, but that was sufficient because the remainder of the vote was split between the Salam-Yafi list (40.5 per cent) and miscellaneous individuals. In the Chouf Kamal Jumblat lost to a regime-sponsored newcomer and charged that his traditional area had been gerrymandered by a regime working hand in glove with American imperialists.[56]

Personal rivalries as well as foreign policy undoubtedly contributed to Jumblat's defeat, but, whatever the causes, the result was to force Jumblat to resort to extralegal politics. Even the "Seigneur of Taybeh," Ahmad al-Assaad, lost to a lesser rival, Kazem Khalil. His only consolation was that his son Kamel narrowly edged out a regime candidate in Merjayoun. Of Beirut's eleven deputies, ten were allies or clients of President Chamoun, and eighteen of the twenty Mount Lebanon deputies supported him. The opposition to Chamoun was stronger in the traditional and rural areas: In the Biqa four of ten elected were opposition candidates; in South Lebanon five of eleven; and in North Lebanon six of fourteen. A full year before the civil war the geographic lines of the conflict were thus reasonably clear in the geographical origins of the minuscule opposition in Parliament, just as the political lines were already drawn. The regime held the core Beirut–Mount Lebanon area—with certain prominent exceptions—whereas real power in the outlying regions remained in the hands of the traditional leaders.

Any evaluation of factionalism during the Chamoun regime must take account of the deepening rift between Arab nationalists and Lebanese independents; between the prosperous and the backward areas; and between Maronites and Sunnites. Equally important, however, is the narrow political struggle between a President trying to enhance his effective power and rural notables trying to maintain their political influence. President Chamoun used factionalism vigorously to divide his enemies and to build a superficially strong support base. At the same time, however, factionalism prevented him from recruiting enough new sources of support. President Chamoun badly needed a strong party, but all he had was a bickering, divided, and relatively weak coalition. In the case of the important opposition leaders, the President's refusal to play the factional game drove them to insurrection because the numerical balance in the Chamber did not reflect the intensity of the opposition. From early 1957 the opposition notables regarded the electoral and parliamentary institutions as illegitimate, and the President did not possess a sufficiently positive backing of his own to make a convincing case that they were wrong. On the surface the institutions seemed to be functioning normally: The President had a substantial majority and a vocal opposition group remained in Parliament.

The Chehab Regime (*1958–1964*)

General Fuad Chehab, whose low regard for politicians is well known, made it clear that traditional factionalism must not stand in the way of executive action. He found, however, that factionalism is inevitable in a polity that is fragmented and lacking in rationalized structures. After he reached this conclusion, he tried to circumvent the old pluralism and begin anew by building up his own power base (see Chapter 8). In this effort, General Chehab had certain advantages. Not only did nearly everybody consider him a savior from the horrors of 1958, but he also had the support of many of the newer intelligentsia in the professions and the military.

Instead of fighting the old factions, General Chehab left them alone, perhaps on the assumption that they were less harmful when visible. The 1960 Parliament (with an increased total of ninety-nine seats) was somewhat more broadly representative than its predecessors. It included nearly all the factions that had been fighting two years earlier. The Kataeb list was propelled to victory in Beirut's all-Christian first district by what one journalist called the "implacable efficiency" of its machine, and it won with more than two-thirds of the total vote. The list of the National Bloc, headed by Pierre Edde, could not hope to match this kind of organization because it had never been organized as a cadre party. In the election of 1964, the Kataeb list ran unopposed in the same district. Saeb Salam and Nassim Majdalani, along with other stalwarts of the one-time insurgents, won in the classic traditional style in the nearly all-Sunnite third district. In Beirut's second district, an interesting struggle brought victory to a list of radicals headed by Adnan Hakim, chief of the Najjadeh, the Sunnite pan-Islamic party. Mohsen Slim, a well-known Shiite liberal, and Farid Jibran, representing Jumblat's P.S.P., won on the same list. This combination swamped a group from the older generation, including Rashid Beydoun, Moussa de Freige, and Takieddine Sulh. Sami Sulh, his power broken by the outcome of the 1958 crisis, ran alone and received only half as many votes as the winning Sunnite, Adnan Hakim. If this election indicated a breakthrough to the left, the returns four years later showed that sectarian insecurities and personal charm were still effective in Beirut's second district: Hakim was narrowly edged out by "Papa" Sami Sulh, whose votes were mostly delivered by the Christians in the district, and Beydoun, another old establishment figure, beat Slim. Of the 1960 winning trio, only Jibran survived, and his survival was attributed to the fact that his association with Jumblat delivered the Druze vote.

In Mount Lebanon, too, both the loyalists and the insurgents of 1958 won in 1960. On the old loyalist side there was evidence of more cooperation among groups than there had been. In Baabda, for example, a list made up of members of the National Bloc, the Kataeb, and Camille Chamoun's new party, the National Liberals, did well against the newly resuscitated Constitutional Bloc (now called the "Constitutional Union Bloc"). In Metn former President Chamoun and a member of his list won, as did three members of the opposing list; all leaned to the old loyalist side. In Chouf the Jumblat-P.S.P. list won six of eight seats, whereas of the opposing list supported by President Chamoun only the redoubtable Emile Bustani and a Sunnite, Qablan Qablan, survived. In Aley it was, as always, Amir Majid's list that triumphed, carrying with it Khalil al-Khoury, a son of former President Khoury, who was the nominal head of the Constitutional Union Bloc; but this time the opposition vote was divided between a P.S.P. list and a collection of strong independents. In 1964 a reshuffling of this opposition was still not enough to disturb the Amir's position. In Kisrwan and Jbeil, the almost exclusively Maronite districts, men allied or friendly with the National Bloc beat lists affiliated with the Destour in 1960, perpetuating the most constant cleavage in Lebanese politics. Four years later Raymond Edde, the head of the National Bloc, was, to the surprise of many, defeated in his home territory of Jbeil: The defeat resulted in part from a shift in the family alliances of the region, but there was also the familiar specter of interference from the regime, this time in military dress. Following the death of Edde's opponent in 1965 a special election was held in which Edde regained his seat, but not without confronting a group of traditional enemies and, behind the scenes, agents of the army security forces. The latter had never forgiven Edde's outspoken attacks on the army for its alleged interference in politics after 1958.

In the rural provinces too, nearly everyone who had any influence found a place in the biggest Lebanese Parliament ever, but there were certainly fewer Chamounians in 1960 than before. Maarouf Saad, virtual ruler of Saida during the 1958 disturbances, won again from that town. Elsewhere in South Lebanon the influence of Ahmad al-Assaad was restored almost to its former brilliance. It was marred only by the defeat of his son Kamel at the hands of an Arab nationalist, Ali Bazzi. Bazzi, it might be added, had been Interior

Minister before the election. When the elder Assaad died, however, his son completed his term and won again in 1964 to extend even further the family's influence. The same leaders continued to represent North Lebanon: Rashid Karami, Sleiman al-Ali, Sleiman Frangieh, Fuad Ghusn, Philippe Boulos, Jean Harb, and René Moawad. The style of campaigning was typically rough. Certainly the most notable regional event in the 1960 election was the very strong performance of a member of the Baath Party, Abdul-Majid Rifahi, whose 14,000 votes came within 800 votes of the lowest man on Rashid Karami's list. In the Biqa Joseph Skaf's list defeated the list of his Phalangist cousin in Zahleh, and the Jumblatist Druze, Chebli al-Aryan, won in Rachaya. In the Baalbek-Hermel district a trend toward tribal multifactionalism developed in connection with an observed decline in the traditional feudal spirit. The power of Sabri Hamadeh, the old boss of the Hermel, a member of every national legislative body since 1925 and a member of the brief resistance movement of 1943, was weakening. In 1953 he had carried his reduced district in Hermel by a mere 757 votes, a far cry from 1947 when he received 29,500 and was unopposed, or even 1951, when his list won with a comfortable margin of nearly 6,000. His margin in 1957 (just over 4,000 votes) was better, but it was based less on his feudal position than on his membership in the opposition to President Chamoun. In 1960 his margin again fell to about 1,300, and his position was challenged by a new crop of Shiite notables with both tribal support and new faces.[57] In 1964 Hamadeh was the only Shiite of his list who won in a battle contested among four strong lists.

The members of the 1960 Parliament represented some fourteen parties and groupings (by most generous count).[58] There were the cliques of the traditional leaders: Sabri Hamadeh, Joseph Skaf, Sleiman Frangieh, Sleiman al-Ali, Rashid Karami, Ahmad al-Assaad, and Majid Arslan. There were the caucuses: the National Bloc (six deputies); the Constitutional Union Party, the former Destour (six deputies), and the Sunnite Hay'at al-Watania (one deputy). Among the more or less organized political parties, the Kataeb had six members, Jumblat's Progressive Socialist Party had ten (counting its list allies), President Chamoun's National Liberals had six, the Armenian Tashnaq had four, and the Najjadeh had one. In general outlines the 1964 Parliament was the same, although the Najjadeh and Hay'at al-Watania representation had disappeared, and representation of the Kataeb and National Bloc had diminished. If anything, the traditional organizational forms were reasserting their strong dominance on the parliamentary scene. The only significant change was the defeat of the two most prominent Christian leaders, Raymond Edde and Camille Chamoun, under somewhat suspicious circumstances. These defeats may well have been decisive factors in preventing the renewal of General Chehab's mandate in the summer of 1964.

The old factionalism had been renewed after the anarchy of the 1958 crisis: To all outward appearances the game of musical chairs was being played in much the same manner as it had been played during the two previous regimes. Although General Chehab found much to criticize in the process, he undoubtedly realized its value in the management of Lebanon's parochial tensions. Instead of attempting to abolish the game altogether, he thus appeared to encourage it in order to restore political normality and confidence. Not only were more factions represented in the Chehab Parliaments, but also the major leaders of all tolerated tendencies were included in the enlarged Cabinets.

There was, however, an important difference in the factional politics of the establishment after 1958. Factionalism was no longer the exclusive process by which power was allocated. Although he seemed to tolerate the old politics and even to encourage it, President Chehab was also trying to develop processes that would sustain the reforms of the state that he felt were necessary for Lebanon's future stability. This attempt is described in Chapter 8. Many establishment politicians, both Christian and Muslim, complained that the Chehab regime had tried to deprive them of influence and to reduce factional politics to a hollow ritual at the same time that the important state decisions were actually being made by a group of military men and technocrats. Their complaint was well grounded. Establishment factionalism, however, is deeply rooted in the Lebanese political culture; and events after the end of the Chehab regime in 1964 revived it, with all its virtues and defects, as the predominant decision-making process.

The Lebanese establishment shows considerable capabilities in the management of traditional types of conflict, and it has developed the ability to regulate its own internal rivalries. It has performed less adequately, however, in dealing with the chronic and increasing stresses arising from forces outside its scope of influence. These stresses support a counterelite whose orientations and perspectives challenge the Lebanese system. Chapter 5 discusses these "outsiders."

NOTES

[1] Perhaps the story is apocryphal. Doctor Van Zeeland did advise the government to develop the productive sectors in order to avoid excessive reliance on the vagaries of commerce. *L'Orient,* April 25, 1947.

[2] Malcolm H. Kerr, *Lebanon in the Last Years of Feudalism* (Beirut: American University, 1959), pp. 22–5.

[3] U.S. Department of State, *Foreign Relations of the United States: Paris Peace Conference, 1919,* XII (Washington, D.C.: U.S. Government Printing Office, 1947), 745–863, especially 759–60, 774–7, 848–63. See also Harry N. Howard, *The King-Crane Commission* (Beirut: Khayat's, 1963), pp. 125–35; and the William Yale papers, Yale University Library, New Haven.

[4] Zeine N. Zeine, *The Struggle for Arab Independence* (Beirut: Khayat's, 1960), pp. 37–8, 143–5, 263–4.

[5] General Georges Catroux, *Deux Missions en Moyen-Orient, 1919–1922* (Paris: Plon, 1958), pp. 68–83; Iskandar Riachi, *Qabl wa-ba'd [Before and After]* (Beirut: Maktabat al-'arfān, 1953), pp. 44–6; and Riachi, *Ru'usā' lubnān kama araftuhum [Presidents of Lebanon as I Knew Them]* (Beirut: Maktabat al-tijārah, 1961), pp. 24–5.

[6] Stephen Longrigg, *Syria and Lebanon under French Mandate* (London: Oxford, 1958), p. 252. For other discussions of clerical interference, see Bahige Tabbarah, *Les Forces Politiques Actuelles au Liban* (Unpublished doctoral dissertation, University of Grenoble, 1956), pp. 94–6; and Pierre Rondot, *Les Institutions Politiques du Liban* (Paris: Imprimerie Nationale, 1947), pp. 107–10.

[7] Gabriel Puaux, *Deux Années au Levant: 1939–1940* (Paris: Hachette, 1952), pp. 80–111.

[8] *Ibid.,* pp. 84–5, 88.

[9] *The Black Book of the Lebanese Elections of May 25, 1947* (New York: Phoenicia, 1947), prepared by the opposition National Bloc (Emile Edde's group).

[10] When the cabinet refused to present to Parliament a bill prepared by the Lawyers' Council that would have instituted a personal-status code common to all sects, the lawyers struck. *L'Orient,* February 5, 1952, noted that the lawyers had appealed to the cabinet for action and not to the Parliament, indicating the latter's relative unimportance. It also noted that the cabinet was reluctant to stop the strike because nine of its ten members were lawyers. Later, when a compromise was proposed that would have given people a choice of religious or nonreligious court jurisdiction in legal matters not strictly related to dogma, the religious leaders called a general strike that closed down the markets. In present-day Lebanon the religious courts retain their authority in matters of personal status and dogma.

[11] For example, he told a reporter from *al-Jarīda*: "Le présent Régime doit partir, car il a échoué, tant sur le plan extérieur, que sur le plan intérieur. . . ."

["The present regime must go, for it has failed; this failure is as clear in foreign affairs as in domestic matters."] *L'Orient,* April 20, 1958. See also Chapter 7.

[12] During the 1964 elections, for example, the Maronite Patriarch issued a declaration attacking the Chehab regime for flagrant violation of fair procedures.

[13] For a discussion of the Patriarch's activities, see Fahim I. Qubain, *Crisis in Lebanon* (Washington: Middle East Institute, 1961), pp. 50, 83, 87.

[14] Figures quoted by Tabbarah, *op. cit.,* pp. 153–60.

[15] Riachi, *Qabl wa-ba'd,* pp. 22–3.

[16] Bashir II, the famous and next to last ruling Chehab amir (1788–1840), survived three attempts by Jazzar Pasha of Acre to remove him and consolidated his power by destroying the influence of all but one of the important Druze shaykhs. At the same time he meted out stern justice and built impressive public works. His portrait, on view at the mountain palace he built at Beiteddine, conveys his character perfectly. See Kamal Salibi, *The Modern History of Lebanon* (London: Weidenfeld, 1965), pp. 18–23. For a discussion of modern feudal notables, see Arnold Hottinger, "Zu'amā' and Parties in the Lebanese Crisis of 1958," *Middle East Journal,* 15 (1961), 127–40; and Hottinger, "Zu'amā' in Historical Perspective," in Leonard Binder (ed.), *Politics in Lebanon* (New York: Wiley, 1966), pp. 85–105.

[17] Richard Pearse, *Three Years in the Levant* (London: Macmillan, 1949), p. 61.

[18] The "grand list" system divided the country into five electoral districts, which corresponded to the province (*muhafaza*) boundaries and enabled the most influential families to extend their immediate influence at the expense of lesser families, thus allowing a small oligarchy to control Parliament. The grand list was used in the 1943 and 1947 elections. For a discussion of competitive patterns over time see Chapter 6.

[19] Kesrouan Labaki, "Sous le Signe du Féodal," *L'Orient,* June 1, 1948.

[20] For an account, see *The Arab World,* March 10, 1954.

[21] Kerr, "The 1960 Lebanese Parliamentary Elections," *Middle Eastern Affairs,* 11, No. 9 (1960), 270.

[22] Saeb Salam, *Lubnān waḥidun lā lubnānān* (Beirut: Cénacle Libanaise, 1961). For a later general statement see his interview with Charles Aste in *Magazine,* June 26, 1965, p. 11.

[23] Bechara al-Khoury, *Ḥaqā'iq lubnāniyyah* [*Lebanese Truths*], I (Beirut: Awrāq lubnāniyyah, 1961), 94–103; Riachi, *Qabl wa-ba'd,* pp. 42, 47–9.

[24] Riachi, *Qabl wa-ba'd,* pp. 36–7.

[25] "Lebanon is basically a beautiful and noble experiment in peaceful cohabitation of religions, of traditions, of races. It is a natural experiment, which history offers as a still more decisive demonstration than that of Switzerland in the heart of Europe." Michel Chiha, "Vérites Libanaises," in *Politique Intérieure* (Beirut: Trident, 1964), p. 250.

[26] Albert Hourani, *Syria and Lebanon* (London: Oxford, 1946), pp. 196–8.

[27] Kazem Sulh, *Le Problème du Rattachment et de la Séparation au Liban* (Beirut: 1936). Sulh opted for a separate and independent Lebanon by dissenting from the "Congress of the Coast," an assembly of Syrian Muslim notables that met in Beirut in March 1936 to petition France to leave Syria (including Lebanon) independent and unified. The party helped to consolidate Muslim support for independent Lebanon under the auspices of Sulh

and his brother Takieddine. Mohammed Majzoub, *Le Liban et l'Orient Arabe, 1943–1956* (Aix-en-Provence: Pensée Universitaire, 1956), pp. 106–7.

[28] Riachi, *Qabl wa-ba'd,* p. 49; Salibi, *op. cit.,* pp. 171–6.

[29] Camille Chamoun, one of the original Destourians, broke with Khoury in 1948, when the latter had the Constitution amended and his term renewed. Chamoun implies in his memoirs, *Crise au Moyen-Orient* (Paris: Gallimard, 1963), p. 88, that Khoury was not the founder of the Destour. Chamoun writes that the party was originated by a three-man delegation that included Michel Zaccour, Shaykh Farid al-Khazen, and Chamoun himself and that had presented a list of grievances to the High Commissioner Martel following the 1934 elections. This group was then enlarged to include Amir Majid Arslan, Hamid Frangieh, Sabri Hamadeh, and Selim Taqla. Khoury waited six weeks before joining it. The three-man delegation, however, had met at Khoury's house before seeing the High Commissioner.

[30] The issues of *Le Jour* (published by the banker Michel Chiha, a friend and, in some instances, a relative of men in the Destour) for August 3, 10, and 18, 1943, give reports of pre-election rallies of the Constitutional Bloc in Mount Lebanon that indicate the spontaneous, loosely organized, and popular nature of the Destour at the moment of its greatest solidarity. At one rally nearly 15,000 persons from all over Lebanon reportedly listened enthusiastically to speeches from the notables who were members of the Destour: Wadih Naim (Maronite lawyer), Amir Majid Arslan (Druze landlord), Louis Ziadeh (Maronite lawyer), Camille Chamoun (Maronite lawyer), Abdallah Hajj (Shiite *rentier*), Dr. Aziz Aoun (Maronite), Bahige Takieddine (Druze lawyer), Emile Lahoud (Maronite lawyer), Dr. Elias Khoury (Maronite). In addition, the Destourians formed the core of a broader independence movement that included important leaders like Saeb Salam and Riad Sulh and lawyer-bankers like Henri Pharaon, Habib Abuchahla, and Selim Taqla. On the other hand, the National Bloc of Emile Edde was largely confined to Mount Lebanon, although it was loosely connected through the Maronite Church with notables in North Lebanon and Beirut. The following notables of Mount Lebanon were associated with Edde: Amin Saad, Georges Akl, Toufic Rizk, Ahmad Husseini (Shiite), Georges Zouein, Kesrouan al-Khazen, Wadih Ashkar, Gabriel Murr, Roukoz Abunader, Georges Yazbek, Abdul-Ghani al-Khatib (Sunnite), Kamal Jumblat (Druze; he was a member of the National Bloc until the November crisis, when he broke with the caucus), Jamil Talhouk (Druze), and Amine Nakhleh. In socioeconomic and cultural background, these notables were hardly distinguishable from their opposite numbers in the Destour.

[31] ". . . [W]e are, because of our very diversity, devoted internally to a politics of toleration and liberty and abroad to a policy of equilibrium and wisdom, which are the conditions of our defense and of our progress." Henri Pharaon, *Au Service du Liban* (Beirut: Le Jour, 1959), p. 63.

[32] Article I, paragraph 3 of the Alexandria Protocol of October 7, 1944, states: "The decisions of the Council will be binding on those who have accepted them except in cases where a disagreement arises between two member states of the League in which case the two parties shall refer their dispute to the Council for solution. In this case the decision of the Council will be binding." The Covenant of the Arab League of March 22, 1945,

states in Article VII, "Decisions of the Council by unanimous assent shall be obligatory on all the states participant in the League. Decisions of the League by majority [vote] shall be obligatory on those who accept them." Muhammad Khalil (ed.), *The Arab States and the Arab League,* II (Beirut: Khayat's, 1962), 53–61.

[33] The Protocol was entered into by Riad Sulh, the "cosigner" of the National Pact, a fact that suggests that he had not entirely shed his Arab nationalist commitment upon assuming office in Lebanon. See Pharaon's article "From the Protocol of Alexandria to the Establishment of the League of Arab States," *Tayār wa-telegrāf* (Beirut), February 15–16, 1965.

[34] The Tashnaq and the Henchaq both antedate the establishment of Greater Lebanon: The Tashnaq was established in Tiflis in 1890, and the Henchaq in Geneva in 1887. The Armenian parties have disciplined memberships and paramilitary capabilities. Total membership of the Tashnaq in 1964 was estimated to be 2,000, whereas the Henchaq claimed to have 5,000 members. Michael W. Suleiman, *Political Parties in Lebanon* (Ithaca: Cornell University Press, 1967), pp. 222–3.

[35] There is also a middle group of the Liberal Democratic Party (the Ramgavar Azagadan) that would like to see Armenia freed but sees no immediate prospects that this liberation will occur and works instead to preserve Armenian culture wherever Armenian communities have been established.

[36] Babikian voted with the Sami Sulh government in the confidence votes of January 30 and March 27, 1958.

[37] Babikian was Minister of State in charge of administrative reform in the Saeb Salam government of August 1960–May 1961. He had been chosen for this task, he says, partly because there were few Armenians in the bureaucracy and he would thus be considered relatively neutral.

[38] This program consisted of the following points: first, defense of Lebanese sovereignty and independence; second, support for the Allies in the cause of democracy; third, tolerance for all beliefs and individual rights; fourth, establishment of treaties, to reflect good and brotherly relations with neighboring states without impairing Lebanese sovereignty; fifth, political harmony, peace, and progress and the appeasement of passions in a just manner; sixth, on the administrative level, maintenance of order and equal rights for all citizens; seventh, on the moral, social, and cultural level, improvement of family life and education, the right to work, and protection of the young and old; eighth, on the economic and financial level, development of the national resources—agriculture, commerce, industry, tourism, winter sports, and so on—and fiscal justice; ninth, improvement of the future of youth; tenth, development of better contacts with Lebanese overseas. *Le Jour,* August 14, 1943.

[39] The men were Pierre Gemayel, who has remained its chief for twenty years; Chafic Nassif, a lawyer who left the party and became a follower of President Chamoun in the 1950s; Georges Naccache, the publisher of *L'Orient,* who has been a supporter and friendly critic of the party from the beginning; and Charles Helou, the future President, who was also associated with the Destourians and Greek Catholic circles.

[40] Statements of the party's position may be found in the following of its

publications: *Declaration* (Beirut, 1956), which contains, among other things, a speech by Pierre Gemayel that he delivered in August 1954; *National Unity* (Beirut, n.d.), the proceedings of a press conference given by Pierre Gemayel.

[41] For eyewitness accounts, see Eugénie Elie Abouchdid, *Thirty Years of Lebanon and Syria: 1917–1947* (Beirut: Sader-Rihani, 1948), pp. 133–71; see also "Pierre Gemayel dans la Petite Histoire," *Action Proche-Orient* (Beirut: 1961), pp. 43–7; and Les Phalanges Libanaises, *25 Ans au Service du Liban* (Beirut: 1961).

[42] See, for example, Maurice Gemayel, *Le Planification Intégrale des Eaux Libanaises* (Beirut: St. Paul, 1951).

[43] Phalanges Libanaises, *op. cit.,* p. 19.

[44] Out of a reported membership of 50,000 in 1959. Lucien George and Toufic Mokdessi, *Les Partis Libanais en 1959* (Beirut: Editions l'Orient-al-Jaryda, 1959), pp. 35, 41. See also Nicola Ziadeh, "The Lebanese Elections, 1960," *Middle East Journal,* 14 (Autumn 1960), 370. In 1965 a party official said that there were now 10,000 Shiite members and a total membership of 68,000.

[45] A Kataeb party official went to some length to distinguish between Kataeb democratic centralism and communist democratic centralism. In the Kataeb, he said, members at all levels discuss issues before the central council takes a decision. The results of these discussions are transmitted from the sections—the basic units consisting of fifty to one hundred members each—through two intermediate levels to the central council.

[46] My interview with a Kataeb leader, May 24, 1962, and with a former Kataeb member, May 8, 1962.

[47] In an interview on August 11, 1965, President Chamoun claimed that the N.L.P. was far more than a caucus of notables, because it had between 17,000 and 18,000 registered members, but he also stated that the party is not well organized.

[48] Bechara al-Khoury, *Haqā'iq lubnāniyyah,* II, 40–1. Camille Chamoun in his memoirs, *op. cit.,* pp. 198–9, writes that he insisted that President Khoury remove the allegedly corrupt *éminence grise* and purify his entourage but that the President took the suggestion as a personal insult.

[49] Khoury, *op. cit.,* III, 34–6.

[50] His opponent, however, was not a Destourian: Pierre Gemayel of the Kataeb was defeated by Edde, although the Kataeb was at the time under theoretical suspension by the government.

[51] Khoury, *op. cit.,* III, 472.

[52] On his deathbed, Abboud accused his rival of having arranged his murder, and a later investigation implicated Ali in the crime. Ali, who had also been under attack for his part in wheat-purchase scandals, went to prison for two years. This legal difficulty did not noticeably impair his political career; he was returned to Parliament in 1960 and held a cabinet post.

[53] Emile Bustani later claimed that, although he had broken with Jumblat, he had still helped him in 1953 and was responsible for supplying the votes that enabled him to beat his opponent, the ex-Destourian, Bahige Takied-

dine. See Bustani's declaration of June, 1957, *Reasons for the Failure of Kamal Jumblat in the General Elections* (in Arabic), American University of Beirut Library.

[54] For a commentary on the Beirut elections, see Richard H. Nolte, "Lebanese Elections," American Universities Field Staff Letter, July 13, 1953.

[55] Kamal Jumblat had almost merged his following with the Syrian National Party in 1949, but doctrinal and leadership differences and then the abortive P.P.S. coup of that year had prevented it. In 1951 there was discussion of a merger between Jumblat's P.S.P. and the Kataeb. George and Mokdessi, *op. cit.,* p. 14.

[56] In a postelection press conference, Jumblat complained that President Chamoun, the gendarmerie, and certain officials had engineered his defeat. *L'Orient,* June 19, 1957. As Jumblat's former ally, Emile Bustani, *op. cit.,* tells it, Jumblat promoted the cause of Bustani's own electoral rival in a neighboring district at the same time he exploited Bustani's reputation by attaching Anwar Khatib, the P.S.P. vice-president, to Bustani's coattails. Bustani was not to be used so brazenly. He insisted that Khatib quit the P.S.P. and toured Jumblat's district, urging his friends to elect Jumblat's rival, which they did.

[57] A reporter in *L'Orient,* July 4, 1960, remarked: "Sans doute, il ne faut pas croire que Baalbek et le Hermel se soient métamorphosés. Le Bey y reste le Bey. Mais il est incontestable qu'un très fort courant anti-féodal se dessine dans la région."

["Doubtless, one cannot assume that Baalbek and Hermel have altogether changed. The Bey is still the Bey. But it is unarguable that a very strong antifeudal current is taking shape in the area."]

[58] *L'Orient,* July 4, 1960.

CHAPTER · 5

The Radical Outsiders

The Lebanese establishment described in the preceding chapter must now contend with a radical counterelite composed of assorted cliques, movements, and parties representing both the right and the left. Although this counterelite is rarely organized for concerted action, its members share some important characteristics. They are all hostile, or at least lack commitment, to the Lebanese entity as it now exists. To the establishment they appear as real or potential fifth columnists. Their programs stress sweeping reform and range from advocacy of Islamic theocracy to proletarian democracy; their various doctrines share an orientation to total commitment, in contradistinction to the prevailing pragmatic and instrumental tenor of establishment politics. Prominent in this counterelite are Syrian nationalists, Muslim nationalists, communists, Lebanese socialists, and Arab nationalists of Nasserist or Baathist persuasion.

The names of the counterelite groups alone suggest that these outsiders should generate tensions in the Lebanese system, and indeed they do. Although it is true that each explicitly and perhaps sincerely professes allegiance to the Republic, such protestations cannot obscure the inherently revolutionary implications of their basic objectives. It is therefore not surprising that the establishment has worked to exclude them from participation in power. Exclusion from the formal system appears to aggravate rather than to reduce this danger. The political effect of these outsiders, however, is not entirely dysfunctional. They are the most important deterrents to stagnation in the political system. Although they play only a small role in the formal institutions, their influence is widely felt. The outsiders force the establishment to recognize the existence of demands for

168

nationalism and social justice. Recognition is an important first step toward political innovation; unfortunately it is not a substitute for implementation.

The radical outsiders come from a growing, newly politicized stratum in the middle class. They fall materially somewhat below the socioeconomic level of the successful lawyers and businessmen who are the liberal element in the establishment. At present their groups exist in a kind of political limbo—several are illegal but not persecuted—turning out their newspapers full of dreams and grievances, meeting in coffeehouses and stuffy offices, attracting students, teachers, technicians, clerks, white-collar employees, and small-time lawyers to discuss, organize, and plot. Lebanese parochialism, however, remains a formidable obstacle to political organization, a fact that representatives of all the major political tendencies among the outsiders readily admit. Matters are further complicated by the transnational perspectives of most of the outsiders. Lebanon still fulfills its historic function as a refuge for persecuted minorities, and the political conflicts of the Arab world are thus played out, almost bigger than life, on this tiny stage. In this sense, Lebanon is indeed a barometer of inter-Arab relations. The integration of the outsiders is thus at once most crucial for Lebanese stability and most difficult to achieve.

Bizarre is perhaps the best word to describe radical politics in Lebanon. The organizations that have developed outside the formal arena include an astonishing range of attitudes, behavior, and philosophies. To talk with brilliant young recruits of the Syrian National Party—the party that has made two serious attempts to overthrow the regime—is to confront thwarted idealism twisted into a doctrine of total escape. The Progressive Socialists are simultaneously mystics and pacifists. The various Sunnite theocrats preach rule by the Koran. The Arab nationalists, in their several forms, simultaneously exalt the past glories of Arab civilization and claim to be the vanguard of modernity. Within the establishment the range of attitudes runs from liberal conservatism to conservative liberalism. Outside the establishment there are no limits; indeed, there is not even a satisfactory spectrum along which to arrange the different organizations. What they do have in common, however, is radicalism, illegitimacy (in terms of the present political system), and isolation from the formal political institutions. They embody the new tendencies and dreams of the excluded but expanding political stratum.

Since the creation of Greater Lebanon in 1920 there has been a rapid proliferation of radical organizations, just as there has been increasing differentiation of groups within the establishment. The first series of new radical organizations was created during the 1930s, at the same time that such establishment groups as the Destour and the National Bloc began to develop. Of the several associations, committees, and congresses active during that period, three organizations remain significant today: the Syrian National Party (P.P.S.), the Najjadeh, and the Communist Party. Under the Mandate they all were suppressed at various times. Each developed a conspiratorial style, some degree of mass following, elaborate hierarchy of command, strong discipline and dedication to an almost totalitarian ideology. The P.P.S. and Najjadeh organizations placed heavy emphasis on physical prowess and paramilitary training, the Communists upon secret organization. Since independence all these groups have undergone organizational changes and have continued to suffer from official displeasure and some popular suspicion, but they have not lost their political significance.

In the postindependence period, and particularly in the period since the Palestine War, a new group of organizations has appeared on the Lebanese scene, differing from the earlier ones in form and philosophy but sharing the characteristics of radicalism, nonlegitimacy, and isolation. The newer groups—of which the most important are the Arab nationalist movement, the Baath, and the Progressive Socialist Party—do not share the fascistic style and the militia organization of the first mass organizations. Unlike the first-generation outsiders their ideologies favor Arab unity, Arab nationalism, Arab socialism, and democracy. Indeed, postwar equalitarian populism has affected the older groups too: There has been a tendency toward social democracy observable in the P.P.S., partly for tactical reasons. The Communists have made the ideological adjustment most easily. New or old, however, the important radical organizations cannot commit themselves fully to accepting the legitimacy of the Lebanese political system. Whether their orientation is pan-Syrian, pan-Islamic, pan-Arab, or Communist and no matter how loudly they proclaim Lebanon's "special status," the ambiguity of loyalties among the radicals has hindered the emergence of an effective or a responsible opposition, except within the constrictive limits imposed by establishment rivalries.

THE RADICAL RIGHT

In the topsy-turvy politics of Lebanon the terms "right" and "left" are perhaps too simple to be appropriate. Nevertheless, they may be helpful for distinguishing between those groups whose orientation is essentially romantic and those that at least profess a scientific basis. Even this crude distinction is open to objection in the case of the P.P.S., which has a certain attraction for "modern" types, and the Arab nationalists, whose instrumental programs are clothed in primordial appeals. The participants themselves make such distinctions, however, so this classification may have some utility.

The Syrian National Party (P.P.S.)

The Syrian National Party (Parti Populaire Syrien), later named the Socialist National Party, is a semisecret, pseudofascist, paramilitary cadre party. It was founded by Antoun Saadeh, a thirty-year-old Greek Orthodox teacher and former émigré (to Brazil), in the years 1932 to 1934.[1] Saadeh, remembered as a charismatic personality, founded his organization on eight fundamental principles: First, Syria is for the Syrians, and the Syrians are a complete nation. Second, the Syrian cause is an autonomous national cause. Third, the Syrian cause is the cause of the nation and homeland. Fourth, the Syrian nation is the ethnic unity of the Syrian people, a unity dating back to prehistoric times. Fifth, the Syrian country is geographically distinct, extending from the Taurus Range to the Suez Canal, including the Sinai Peninsula and the Gulf of Aqaba, and from the Syrian Sea (*sic*) in the west to the desert in the east up to its junction with the Tigris.[2] Sixth, the Syrian nation is one society and community. Seventh, the Syrian national movement seeks its inspiration in the talents and genius of the Syrian nation in history. Eighth, Syria's interests are above all other interests.[3]

The Syrian spirit, according to the P.P.S., is to be elevated by adherence to the ideals of Truth, Justice, Love, Beauty, Power, and Order. The party defines the Syrian personality as "a new racial compound. This process started with the peoples of the neolithic age which preceded the Canaanites in settling this land, to the Canaanites themselves, to the Amorites, Hittites, and Aramaics, to the Greeks, Romans, and Arabs. Thus we see that the principle of

Syrian nationhood is not based on race or blood unity, but rather on the natural social unity of a racial compound." [4] It seems, therefore, that P.P.S. nationalism is based partially on racial pride but more heavily on a common social and cultural heritage. Its similarity to German fascism is greater in terms of organization than of philosophy.[5] The party's policy positions include the separation of church and state, the removal of sectarian barriers, and the non-interference of the clergy in politics. This last belief, if nothing else, is enough to challenge the fundamental political formula of Lebanon and accounts in some measure for the failure of the P.P.S. to attract general support. The Syrian Nationalist Party's implacable opposition to communism and Zionism, as threats to the Syrian nation, has drawn Lebanese intellectuals and professionals who otherwise might not have been attracted. In recent times, since Antoun Saadeh's death by firing squad in 1949, a faction representing socioeconomic reform has generally dominated the party; there has also been talk of finding ways to attain a "normal balance" of income distribution and a guarantee for the rights of labor. This talk marks an extension of the ideas of state capitalism originally put forth by Antoun Saadeh. A central issue in the trials after the party's unsuccessful coups in 1949 and 1961 was whether social reform or the absorption of Lebanon into a greater Syrian state was its dominant motive. The leader of the *Putsch* of 1961 fervently declared that the party had adopted a position of respect toward Lebanese sovereignty.[6]

By 1935 the P.P.S. numbered about 1,000 members. Outspokenly antisectarian, the membership was predominantly from the minorities—principally the Greek Orthodox and Protestant groups, though there were also Druzes and Shiites. Opposed at that time both to the Lebanese entity and to Muslim or Arab nationalism, the party was understandably less popular with the two major sects, Sunnite and Maronite. Saadeh's doctrine and organization provided an outlet for the growing number of politically conscious young men who could not accept French-Maronite paternalism or the alternative radical ideologies. The P.P.S. was remarkably tenacious, considering the adversities it suffered. Dissolved in 1937, it was again legalized in 1944 when the local leadership came to terms with the authorities over Lebanon's status while Saadeh was still in Argentina. When Saadeh returned in 1947, however, he vitiated this rapprochement and expelled a number of important subleaders. In the following months, during the Palestine crisis and the subsequent upheavals, the P.P.S. strengthened its armed militia, aided in Syria by the new revolutionary government of Husni Zaim. The Lebanese government of Riad Sulh, who had no sympathy for an anti-Arab nationalist doctrine, saw a substantial threat to its security developing and therefore, it is said, precipitated a bloody clash between the P.P.S. and the Kataeb in the Jummaizeh quarter of Beirut. Taking the incident as a pretext, the government arrested 250 members, dissolved the party again, made more arrests, and declared that it had evidence implicating the P.P.S. in antinational activities, in particular, collaboration with the Zionists.[7] Saadeh escaped to Syria and organized some P.P.S. commando raids into Lebanese territory during the following days. Then, on the night of July 7, Antoun Saadeh was captured, tried, and executed before a firing squad.[8]

Saadeh's martyrdom weakened the P.P.S. but did not destroy it. In Syria the pro-Egyptian, anti-British Colonel Zaim was assassinated barely a month later in a coup reportedly supported by Iraq, Jordan, and Britain; but the P.P.S. continued to operate there, as in the other Fertile Crescent countries, until the socialists emerged. In Lebanon the party regrouped, finding sympathy among notables hostile to the Khoury-Riad Sulh regime. Kamal Jumblat and Camille Chamoun condemned the government for its summary execution of Saadeh, and they joined with Ghassan Tueni—a former P.P.S. member and an active sympathizer of the party—to form the nucleus of the anti-Destour opposition. The National Bloc, which had long-standing grievances against Khoury, was also associated with the general opposition. It was outside the Parliament, and indeed outside Lebanon, however, that the P.P.S. made its most effective move: On July 16, 1951, a P.P.S. agent assassinated Riad Sulh at the Amman airport. It was an act of personal revenge and a blow at the Arab nationalism that Riad Sulh had championed since the Peace Conference. The murder also weakened the regime of Bechara al-Khoury by depriving it of the essential Sunnite Muslim support that Riad Sulh had mobilized. Now leadership of the Sunnites was parceled out among less charismatic and more parochial notables, most of whom had nursed grudges against the regime for a long time. After the election of Camille Chamoun to the Presidency the P.P.S. enjoyed increasing governmental tolerance, even at the expense of Lebanon's relations with Syria and Egypt after 1954. When the militant wing of the P.P.S. assassinated the Syrian Baathist Chief of Staff, Colonel Adnan Malki, in 1955, the wrath of Baathists, Nasserists, and the military forced the P.P.S. leaders to take refuge in Lebanon. Two years later, when the Nasserist-socialist movement began to gain ground in Lebanon, President Chamoun's government had at hand a formidable paramilitary instrument with which to combat the insurgents. Party officials estimated that in 1958–1959 the P.P.S. numbered 25,000 active members in Lebanon and 3,500 overseas.[9]

Although at the end of the Chamoun regime the party was legal and had a man in Parliament, the P.P.S. found the going tougher under the regime of General Chehab, which was weighted in favor of the insurgents—old Destourians, young officers, socialists, Arab nationalists, and Muslim notables. On December 31, 1961, the party, by then in cooperation with a dissident clique of junior army officers and encouraged by the secession of Syria from the United Arab Republic three months earlier, struck again with its customary audacity and nearly achieved a successful *Putsch*. There was strong suspicion that the coup had been financed partly by Jordan and Britain as part of a plan to encourage an anti-Nasser federation of Syria, Iraq, Jordan, and Lebanon.[10] The head of the party, however, declared at the trial that the plot was motivated solely by Lebanon's interior malaise. Abdallah Saadeh said:

> Les causes du putsch relèvent de la politique intérieure uniquement. Elles ne s'inspirent pas, contrairement à ce que dit l'acte d'accusation, d'une idée étrangère au Liban. Notre but était d'opérer une réforme et une renaissance sociale modérées de gauche, d'instituer la justice sociale et la démocratie authentique, de relever le niveau de vie dans toutes les régions du pays. Nous voulions délivrer le pauvre de la misère, du besoin et de la maladie.[11]

The grievances of Captain Fuad Awad, leader of the dissident officers, were more specific. He complained that the army had remained indifferent to the massive influx of smuggled arms from Syria in 1957 and 1958, and he objected to the pro-Nasser tendencies of some officers and men. He felt that the American-sponsored solution to the 1958 crisis had given the insurgents an undeserved victory. The dissatisfied officers also objected to alleged intervention by the army's Deuxième Bureau in certain election campaigns.[12] Had the plot succeeded it is likely that the civil war of 1958 would have broken out anew, for the plotters could claim dedicated support from only a few areas.[13] The coup failed by a narrow margin, and the regime hunted down suspects with an efficiency that surprised everybody and dismayed many. The P.P.S. again went underground to begin anew.

The Najjadeh

The Najjadeh ("Helpers") is the most prominent of several Islamic political groups in modern Lebanon. Others include the Islamic Liberation Party and the Muslim Group. The journalist Muhieddine Nsouli founded the Najjadeh as a youth group in 1936, at the same time that the Maronite youth leader Pierre Gemayel was forming the Kataeb. Like the P.P.S. and the Kataeb the Najjadeh has a paramilitary aspect, but it has a smaller and less tightly managed organization than the other two have. The Mandate authorities dissolved the Najjadeh in 1937, but it functioned underground until independence in 1943. During the events of November 1943, the Najjadeh joined forces with the Kataeb and other anti-French elements to carry out the general strike that ultimately led to the liberation of the government. Though the Najjadeh and the Kataeb soon parted company, each claims the initiative and the credit for having won independence. The postindependence years were good ones for the Najjadeh. In 1944 Riad Sulh publicly praised its 13,000 members, calling them his partisans, and there were signs of genuine cooperation with the Maronites who largely made up the membership of the Kataeb.[14]

Five years later, however, as the domestic situation deteriorated, Riad Sulh dissolved the organization, along with all youth groups that were involved in politics, because he felt that such involvement was incompatible with the dignity of the state and the army. In 1953, after the death of Riad Sulh and the fall of Bechara al-Khoury, the Najjadeh returned with a new leader and a new organization. The new leader was Adnan Hakim, proprietor of an optical store in Beirut and a flamboyant stump speaker. This time the Najjadeh was officially recognized as a political party, and as such it sought to build electoral strength in the Sunnite areas not only in Beirut but also outside it. In the 1958 crisis the Najjadeh was dissolved again for its antiregime operations, but during the insurgency a bitter dispute developed between the party and the insurgent chief of Beirut, Saeb Salam, who shut down its radio transmitter. It reappeared in 1959, and it had about 10,000 members by its own estimate. In 1960 Adnan Hakim's ticket won an upset victory in Beirut, defeating, among others, the moderate Arab nationalist, Takieddine Sulh. It hoped to pick up six seats in the 1964 election from Beirut and the Biqa but only managed to lose the single seat it had won four years earlier.

The chief theoretician of the Najjadeh, Ramadan Lawand, who is a former member of the Arab nationalist Nida al-Qawmi, is in his own way as utopian as the ideologists of the Syrian Nationalist Party. He feels that the goal of the Najjadeh is the resurrection of Arab-Islamic culture. In the Lebanese context this view represents an extreme—if not subversive—position, and the Najjadeh official freely admits as much. Lebanon, he notes, has a split cultural personality: Part of it is Westernized, and part of it is not. This situation is unsatisfactory because the Westernized elements control the country and deprive the Eastern elements of the chance to pursue their cultural destiny. The Western tradition is based upon Greek and Roman rationality, with a thin overlay of Oriental Christianity. Islam, on the other hand, is a total way of life for the Easterner. It cannot be "Occidentalized" by Western universities like the American University of Beirut. Lawand concedes that the unified Arab-Islamic state of the future will borrow freely from the "uncontaminated" aspects of Western culture, its administrative and bureaucratic techniques, for example. In the Najjadeh conception, this new state will not be an Islamic Republic like Pakistan, because it will instead downgrade the formalistic and doctrinaire aspects of Islam in favor of promoting Islamic culture in general. The unified Arab-Islamic state envisaged by the Najjadeh will not be achieved in the near future, Lawand admits. Western political influence in Lebanon is still very great, and Lebanese Muslims are still too divided and underprivileged to act decisively. Najjadeh leaders are nevertheless confident that the state will become a reality someday because they believe that all nations have destinies to fulfill. They hope that within fifty years the Arabs will have beaten back all "contaminated" incursions of Western culture. According to the Najjadeh's view, Lebanon presumably would be a region within the new state, and its Christians would be accorded the status of a special community similar to their position during the rule of the caliphs. It is not surprising that Lebanese Christians are uneasy when they consider what their future would be like in the kind of state envisaged by the Najjadeh.

In 1943 the Najjadeh supported the independence movement and the National Pact principally as expedients to get rid of the French. When the new state and the Pact clearly became instruments for perpetuating the dominance of Christians, the Najjadeh withdrew its support. Not that the Najjadeh is openly subversive, for, although it makes such contentions on a broad level, it also operates within the general rules of the game—but clearly outside the establishment. Because it insists on a new census, the Najjadeh is reviled by establishment Christians and non-Christians alike. When it denounces the sectarian system as it operates in Lebanon, it is denounced for exploiting sectarian tensions. Adnan Hakim dismisses such charges and claims that the Najjadeh is nothing more than a mirror of the people, a statement that mixes disingenuousness with a kernel of truth.[15]

The Najjadeh, like all the radical groups, also supports large-scale social reform like the 1962 social-security legislation.[16] It has supported President Chehab because of his intentions to improve the livelihood of the rural provinces, which are mostly Muslim, and it has supported President Nasser as a constructive Muslim-Arab reformer. Its greatest scorn has been reserved for the big politicians of all sects, especially the Sunnite politicians, whom it calls "compromisers" and treats with the bitter contempt reserved for brothers who betray a cause. Lebanon has only two kinds of politicians, the Najjadeh rightly argues; compromisers and extremists. The Najjadeh is proud to belong to the latter category.

The limited success of the Najjadeh is owing largely to the populist and antiestablishment feeling among Sunnite Muslims, but support for the Najjadeh is hardly a good indicator of the strength of that feeling because there are rival groups competing for these sentiments. The Najjadeh, which espouses policies that locate it on the fringes of secular Arab nationalism, has been crowded out of this competition. At the mass level it can appeal only to memories and religious feeling, and at the elite level it spins out romantic and utopian theory; at neither level is there the program or organization that can guide institutionalized political behavior.

The Najjadeh Party is only one of several Muslim political groups. Some of the others, like the "Worshippers of the Compassionate" ('Ubād al-rahmān) and its more aggressive offshoot, the Muslim Group (al-Jamā'ah al-islamiyyah), are so poorly organized that their political activities have been generally tolerated. Lebanon's Muslim Brothers (al-Ikhwān al-muslimīn) have suffered from similar organizational problems and also from their opposition to secular Arab nationalism. The Muslim Brotherhood originated in Egypt, and its adherents have not forgotten how President Nasser crushed it there in 1954. Organizational weakness and opposition to Nasser have hindered the Brotherhood's development in Lebanon; it too has thus been generally tolerated.[17] Another Muslim organization, the Liberation Party, enjoys no such tolerance, however, because it is more politically extreme than any of the others. The Liberation Party, founded in Jerusalem in the early 1950s, apparently began operating in Lebanon in 1959. The Lebanese government lost no time in trying to suppress it for its hostile intentions toward Christians and capitalists. The party's doctrine would allow Christians no political participation in the unified Islamic state, and it would forbid capitalist companies, usury, or monopoly. Even gambling would be forbidden. Education would be "Islamicized" for all. Needless to say, a doctrine of this nature is not acceptable to the Lebanese establishment, Christian or Muslim. Yet a Liberation Party candidate, although under arrest, was able to win 400 votes in Beirut in the 1964 legislative elections.[18]

The Islamic groups, even the ostensibly religious ones, remain potentially capable of rousing Muslim masses by working through the religious organizations. In a crisis like the alleged defamation of the Prophet in an American University of Beirut classroom in 1966, the mosques serve as effective rallying points and the Muslim groups become formidable political agitators.

THE RADICAL LEFT

The Lebanese establishment views any proposal that infringes upon the untrammeled freedom of the wealthy citizen as both radical and leftist. Whether the proposal is for traffic lights or for a central bank, the characteristic response will be the same: a spirited struggle against "socialist regimentation." It is therefore not surprising that there has been virtually no representation in the institutions of the Lebanese Republic for political positions left of center since the Republic was created.

Euphoric conservatives, however, tend to neglect certain trends in Lebanon's political environment that make the relative absence of the left in formal politics a matter of concern. There has been an active underground left within Lebanon since the early days of the Mandate, and there is a labor force that is small but relatively sophisticated. Both have been systematically excluded from power. Outside Lebanon, the continuing revolution in the Arab world has allied socialism with progressive Arab nationalism and brought pressure to bear on Lebanon's delicate political system.

There has been a development on the left in Lebanese politics, as the following pages attempt to show. If it gives rise to concern, however, the concern should not be that the development is taking place, but rather that it has been so inadequate.

The Communist Party

It is fashionable in certain establishment circles of the 1960s to make fun of the bourgeois background of the members of Lebanon's Communist Party. They are usually portrayed as eccentric lawyers. Nothing seems quite so incongruous as a Communist party in a country where the doctrine of the free economy is hardly less well accepted than is sectarianism itself. The Lebanese Communist Party seems to have been even less successful than all the other radical organizations, whose performances are hardly impressive standards of success. Other radical groups have at least occasionally been represented in Parliament. Arab nationalists and, in recent years, even Baathists have drawn more substantial followings than have the Lebanese Communists. The Americanization of Lebanon after 1952 has made it increasingly difficult for Communists to break into the establishment, and the post-Cold War fragmentation of the world communist bloc has divided the movement in Lebanon too. Despite the adversities that have befallen them, Lebanon's Communists are patiently optimistic that the political situation will change in their favor, and, as Chapter 3 suggests, there are reasons for their optimism.

Communists have been active in Lebanon since the Paris peace settlement. In 1925 a Lebanese People's Party was established under the supervision of Yussef Yazbek, in association with, but distinct from, the stronger Palestinian communist movement. The Lebanese People's Party and the Armenian group that shortly joined it were interested primarily in alleviating the conditions of labor and in establishing strong unions.[19] In 1930 the brilliant Khaled Bakdash, a Syrian Kurd, assumed leadership of the party, which became the Communist Party of Syria and Lebanon, and in the following decade the party underwent "consolidation and concentrated ideological indoctrination" and enjoyed rare official toleration during the Popular Front regime in France.[20] From 1939 to 1942 the Communist Party was again suppressed, but it re-emerged to run three candidates in the 1943 election, all of whom lost. The party was still on the way up, however, and in December 1943 it convened a congress in Beirut at which Khaled Bakdash defined the party's national orientation and support for the newly independent states of Syria and Lebanon.[21]

The party declared its support for the national regime because the regime was trying to wrest control of the Syrian-Lebanese Common Interests Administration (the government department that regulated the customs and joint public services of the two states) and certain companies from the French and to complete the national liberation. It spelled out the advantages of free democratic institutions for Lebanon, emphasized minority rights, and—most interestingly—de-emphasized the socialist character of communism, citing Stalin's words on the necessity for cooperation between the workers and the bourgeoisie against the imperialists. It limited its economic recommendations to improving administrative efficiency, spreading basic education, raising the country's economic level through the development of commerce, improving agriculture, encouraging tourism, struggling against unemployment and poverty, protecting the workers through labor legislation, improving the situation of the peasant, and making the tax burden more equitable.[22] It also approved of closer relations between Lebanon and the Arab countries, especially Syria, and dismissed Christian claims that Lebanon does not have a strictly Arab face and Christian fears that cooperation would lead to annexation.[23]

The Communist Party was thus generally in line with the over-all policies of Riad Sulh and Bechara al-Khoury. The party, now divided again—officially at least—into Lebanese and Syrian branches, did rather well in the 1947 elections, with two candidates running in Mount Lebanon and one each in North Lebanon and Beirut.[24] Later, in the general unrest that began to trouble the Khoury regime, the Communist Party was forced to go underground, where it has remained officially ever since.[25] Despite this inconvenience, however, six known Communists ran for Parliament in 1951, and one ran in 1953, even though there was a warrant out for his arrest at the time. One of the two Communists to run in the 1957 elections received 276 votes to Charles Malik's 10,302. The other, Antoine Tabet, head of the communist-sympathizing "Partisans of Peace" movement, did better in Beirut with 11,000 votes, but he was some 5,400 votes behind the lowest winner there. Under the Chehab regime, Communist electoral strength declined even further; there were no candidates in 1960, and the four who ran in 1964 did worse than Communist Party candidates usually do.

The year 1959 was particularly bad for the party in Lebanon and throughout the Arab world. President Nasser turned against it and pre-empted its major areas of appeal with his own brand of socialism. The Lebanese and Syrian branches moved even farther apart from each other. The Baath (the noncommunist, pan-Arab socialist party) was driven into Lebanon and began to compete with the Lebanese Communists for the support of poor workers and peasants in Tripoli, Nabatieh, and Baalbek. The political logic of this situation in North Lebanon influenced the Communists to oppose the Baath by supporting the Rashid Karami ticket in 1960 and 1964; and one of the Karami's co-listers, Hashem Husseini, is known to sympathize with the party's social welfare and anti-imperialist positions.

The party has developed factional problems in the 1960s. There is, as in the past, an orthodox group aligned with Moscow, headed by Yussef Helou, Nakhleh Moutran, Georges Hawi, and others. It publishes a daily newspaper, *al-Nida,* and a weekly, *al-Akhbar.* This group represents the mainstream of the Lebanese movement, and it is a direct descendant of the original labor-oriented communists of the Lebanese People's Party. There is also a splinter group headed by an old-time Greek Orthodox lawyer, Hassib Nimr, who wishes to reshape the party along Italian lines and to free the party from the guidance of Moscow. Although the splinter group is generally pro-Moscow, it also tries to deal with Peking. Finally, a pro-Peking social-revolutionary faction has also emerged. Little is known about its strength and membership, but it is thought that this group is subsidized through the Embassy of Communist China in Damascus. Because it depends on Chinese Communist funds and guidance, the goals of this group are understandably less moderate. Political observers guess that membership in all factions of the Communist Party combined probably came to about 4,000 members in 1965, about half the estimated membership in 1959. It is also generally agreed that the bulk of the membership comes from the middle class. The greatest number of lower-class communists are probably not members of the party at all but rather belong to the Federation of Labor Unions, an illegal combination of the unions of the carpenters; printers; builders; cooks; hotel, restaurant, and coffeeshop workers; painters; and shoemakers. These seven unions include some 3,000–4,000 workers and are affiliated with the communist-backed World Federation of Trade Unions.[26]

Although recent history does not seem to have been very kind to the Lebanese Communists, they do not give the appearance of being discouraged. Leaders of the old Moscow group and the Italian-style splinter are in basic agreement that the social situation in Lebanon is becoming increasingly ripe for an awakening of political consciousness among the poor workers and farmers. A writer for *al-Nida* declared in an interview that the political system in the 1960s is more vulnerable to communist attacks than ever before. He suggested that, as only 4 per cent of the population benefits from the "free economy," there is a great deal of potential opposition waiting to be organized. He also believed that most Lebanese workers and farmers are disgusted with the situation. Confronted with the apparent disarray of the Communist Party apparatus, a member of the dissident group conceded that post-World War II commercial development and enlargement of the middle class had delayed the class struggle, but he felt that the setback was only temporary. During 1965 the Communist Party was engaged in trying to promote the class struggle by collaborating in a coalition socialist front with the stronger radical groups in the country, like Kamal Jumblat's new Free Labor Front, and by incessantly attacking all things imperialist—from the Vietnam war to a proposed American-Lebanese investment-guarantees treaty.

The persistent optimism of the Communists in free-enterprise Lebanon seems unwarranted in the short run, but their middle-run and long-run prospects are very different matters. Under normal circumstances the urban and rural proletariat seems to prefer primordial affiliations to modern ones, but such loyalties result in political weakness that becomes less tolerable with every economic or political crisis. One veteran Western observer of the labor scene sees no linear trend toward increasingly serious strikes, but he thinks that Lebanon's chronic labor unrest is politically dangerous, particularly the waves of trouble that occur about every four years. Another student of Lebanese labor, however, has suggested that there is a discernible rising trend of industrial conflict.[27] This observer has also discovered that the employers win the greater part of the conflicts, a fact that at once underlines labor's discontent and its organizational weakness. If Lebanon's Communists could overcome their own organizational weakness, they could probably develop a powerful following.

Socialists and Arab Nationalists

After the corrupt elections of 1947, Riad Sulh predicted the development of loyal, legitimate, and modern parties in the four years following the elections as a consequence of his pledge to abolish the system of sectarian political representation.[28] Sulh, like many Lebanese, believed that sectarianism was the chief barrier to political modernity. Sulh was never able to redeem his pledge because agents of the P.P.S. murdered him, and a Western-style party system failed to materialize. Instead, three new radical movements burst into importance.

Whereas the preindependence period was favorable to the development of parties with totalitarian appeals, the 1940s produced organizations with an emphasis on equalitarianism and social reform. The domestic corruption of the Khoury regime stimulated their growth. The Progressive Socialist Party, the Arab nationalist movement, and the Baath had a focus quite different from that of the preindependence movements. Men in the new groups had little first-hand experience of the Ottoman period, the early Arab national struggle, or World War I and its Peace Settlement. They were children of the Mandate to whom Lebanese independence, World War II, the successes of the communist movement, and the Palestine struggle were landmark events. Social reform, social justice, and Socialism came to occupy a place in the forefront of their thinking, along with a demand for Arab unity or cooperation. The major problem thus remained: to integrate the new organizations into the old, carefully balanced, formal institutions.

Kamal Jumblat and the Progressive Socialist Party (P.S.P.)

Lebanon's brightest hope for an indigenous party of the left, integrated both across sectarian lines and into the formal political system, has rested for years with Kamal Jumblat and his Progressive Socialist Party. Unfortunately, the hope has faded in the 1960s. Nevertheless, Jumblat and his party remain highly significant in Lebanese politics, although the content of the P.S.P.'s ideology, a mixture of French socialism, Indian pacifism, and Lebanese Druze traditionalism, might seem strange to foreign observers.

Kamal Jumblat is a feudal socialist. As chieftain of one of the two traditional factions of the Lebanese Druze sect, he distributed some of his lands among his tenant farmers in 1948 as a gesture toward the socialism that he advocates. He has extended his own influence in Lebanese affairs far beyond the scope that might be allotted to the leader of a small and reclusive sect by championing every important radical movement that has appeared on the Lebanese scene. He is probably more responsible than any other politician for the rise of an indigenous left-wing reform spirit in Lebanese politics. At the same time his personal behavior constitutes the greatest single limitation on the institutionalization of that spirit. If Kamal Jumblat is idealism incarnate, his political behavior is erratically pragmatic.

Kamal Jumblat lives in the family palace, a splendid old structure with delicate arches and high ceilings perched on the rugged hills of the Chouf. Jumblat's mother is remembered throughout Lebanon as one of the most astute and influential politicians of the Mandate era (through her close association with the French).[29] Young Jumblat received his early education at the French Lazarist College and, according to some, was converted to Catholicism at that time. He studied social philosophy at the Sorbonne from 1943 to 1947 and took a law degree from the Jesuit Université de St. Joseph in Beirut in 1942. Elected at age twenty-six to the 1943 Parliament as a supporter of the French-backed Emile Edde, Jumblat embarked on his eventful political career.

Scarcely had he been elected when the independence crisis with France broke out; it caused him to disown his affiliation with Emile Edde. Appalled at the fast-growing corruption in the Khoury regime, he used his appointment to the Cabinet (as Minister of National Economy) in 1946 to galvanize the opposition. At the time when the P.P.S. was making its postwar comeback, Jumblat considered joining forces with it. Instead, he formed his own Progressive Socialist Party. In 1951 his Socialist National Front, which included representatives of other groups opposing the Khoury regime, won four seats from the area of his traditional following, and a year later it engineered the President's resignation. In 1953 he lashed out at United States imperialism in the Middle East, and it was reported that he had negotiated an alliance with the Kataeb. He quarreled with his former ally Chamoun and worked as part of the insurgent group in 1958. Although he supported the mildly progressive regime of General Chehab, he quarreled with a Prime Minister, Saeb Salam, and tried diligently to build up a broad socialist front, including the leftist labor unions, the Communist Party, and the Arab nationalists.

Jumblat's tendency to wander all over the radical side of the political spectrum belies a basic consistency in his political perspective. Jumblat is an idealist searching for harmony and purity in human affairs. The ironies of fate have placed him in a chaotic situation. At the age of ten or twelve, Jumblat had a prophetic vision of a new world. Gradually the outline of the future became clearer: Brotherhood, solidarity, and equality would replace disorder and egoism. Jumblat was determined to struggle for harmony and morality in Lebanese life and to destroy a politics based on constantly shifting private interests.[30] Jumblat's description of the current Lebanese political scene is one of Hobbesian anarchy: A Parliament full of smugglers and thieves is surrounded by corrupt bureaucrats and selfish politicians, and imperialist embassies plot ceaselessly against the true interests of the country. In his vision of Lebanese politics there is no rule of law, and the only order is the result of a stand-off among rival interests. Although he puts it more pungently, his interpretation is similar to the imagery of struggle, insecurity, and delicate balance that so many other notables hold.

That Jumblat has been an unusually disruptive force in Lebanese politics is by no means accidental; his avowed purpose has been to clear away the imperfect old system for the newer, more just, and more orderly one.

> J'estime d'ailleurs personellement que l'Asie—cette terre du Christ, de Mahomet, de Confucius et de Bouddha—a quelque chose d'originel à donner au monde, quelque chose autre qu'un matérialisme bourgeois ou dialectique, une dictature de race, de continent ou de classe, autre chose aussi qu'une formule de simple compromis qui est un leurre, une injustice perpétuée et une honte. C'est une conception d'harmonie sociale et humaine totale qu'il s'agit de réaliser.[31]

It is necessary to expose the decay in present Lebanese society if a better society is to be created, Jumblat states. It is also necessary to make some compromises with the decadent social milieu if anything effective is to be done to transform it. These reasons allow Jumblat to call himself a "practical idealist" and to justify his rather startling political switches. Although he concedes that his Progressive Socialist Party has not yet fulfilled his expectations, Jumblat hopes that he has managed to inculcate the Lebanese people with new ideals and to generate a concern for the public interest, which has always been lacking in Lebanon. A desire to stimulate public concern explains why Jumblat speaks frequently about strengthening the traditional family life at the same time that he urges sweeping educational reforms that will develop the mentality of the people. The same goal explains his attacks on the decadence of Beirut—its youth, its night clubs, its easy atmosphere—and his need to set a personal example of asceticism by practicing yoga.

To Jumblat, nationalism in the narrow nineteenth-century conception cannot achieve the social ideal, but modern Arab nationalism, which has a humanistic aspect, can bring about such a state. Since about 1956, he has become an advocate of a humanistic Arab nationalism, as opposed to "selfish" Lebanese or Syrian nationalism, as long as it does not conflict with his ideals in international affairs: nonalignment, an international moral force, and an organized Third World that can mediate between the great power blocs. The place of the political entity Lebanon in this order is not entirely clear, but there is reason to think that Jumblat does not value it very highly. Jumblat's ideal Lebanon is nonpolitical and radically different from the present-day Republic.

Why is Jumblat important? In his peculiar way he has forced the establishment to consider ideas that most of its members find alien or utopian. The more sophisticated politicians openly ridicule his inconsistencies, but he is still the only authentically Lebanese reformer. He is also Lebanese in his eclecticism. He borrows unabashedly from East and West alike to create a philosophy for reconciling Lebanon's cultural and political schizophrenia. In his own words, he has a dual personality, representing simultaneously the antagonistic forces of tradition and modernity, of old values and new techniques. It cannot be said that Jumblat is entirely successful in trying to harmonize these forces; and in pursuing his goals he has acted too often arbitrarily and unpredictably in his efforts to secure a loyal following. He too is afflicted with an inability to organize politically.

In the first years of the Progressive Socialist Party the progressive side of its philosophy attracted a number of outstanding young political activists because it was the only alternative to establishment politics that did not involve the dangers of fascism, personality cults, or sectarianism. At the same time, because its leader was one of the indispensable traditional leaders by virtue of his chieftainship of an important Druze community, it had the kind of access to Lebanese institutions that no other radical organization has enjoyed. It was no wonder that the P.S.P., during its first six years, was the best hope for the new elite. More than any other party it seemed to have the potentiality for joining the old and the new in Lebanese politics.

Founded in 1949 after negotiations between Kamal Jumblat and the P.P.S. had failed, the P.S.P. and several less permanent organizations emerged out of the growing opposition to the Khoury regime. The P.S.P. attracted disaffected young professionals from all sects. The establishment opposition press welcomed the new party as a healthy addition to the political scene, a modern institutionalized base for the landed notable Jumblat, who had already done a great deal of good in combating the administrative excesses in the Khoury machine.

A former high official in the party believes that the P.S.P. attained its greatest strength, 18,000 card-carrying and dues-paying members, in 1953. Membership fell rapidly, however, as the gulf between Jumblat and the new President Camille Chamoun, erstwhile allies, widened over the extent of domestic reforms. Primarily because of pressures from the regime, membership had dropped by 1957 to between 10,000 and 12,000. [32] In 1959 party officials reported a membership of 10,000, but a less biased estimate made in 1962 placed membership at between 4,000 and 6,000, of whom a great many do not pay dues.[33] The majority of the party rank and file is Druze, a fact reflected in election returns, which show that the party's strength is primarily in the Chouf, the zone of Jumblat's traditional influence. P.S.P. candidates also win a seat or two from the Biqa and Beirut, but in both cases the victors are either Druze or supported by a Druze voting bloc.[34] It is not easy to tell whether those listed on Jumblat's ticket are party colleagues in the most formal sense or just traditional clients. A much more serious attrition of the party's intellectual cadre has paralleled the decline in general membership. Five important intellectuals left the party in 1956 as the result of Jumblat's relative reluctance to commit the party wholeheartedly to the Arab nationalist struggle, despite his previous public support for the Arab effort in Palestine and his frequent denunciations of Western imperialism.[35]

After the 1958 crisis another power in the party, Nassim Majdalani, who had been with the P.S.P. since 1951, resigned as a vice-president (Jumblat never accepted the letter of resignation) because Jumblat wanted to import "outside models" of socialism that Majdalani felt were ill suited to the peculiarities of Lebanon. Majdalani says that Jumblat also sought to short-circuit the democratic mechanisms within the party and eventually began to dictate to the party's political bureau, whose decisions the president of the party is supposed to execute.[36] The party, which in 1951 held a promise of success because it was well organized and not yet cursed with sectarianism, had originally led Majdalani to leave the Greek Orthodox Ghassanides organizations that he had founded in 1943 for the purpose of strengthening the Christian commitment to Arab nationalism.

Although the P.S.P. excels in the formulation of ideology, it has stumbled in organization. In its peak years—the early 1950s—its 18,000 members were mobilized by 220 committees throughout the country, of which 14 operated in Beirut. Members were carefully recruited, and they had to take affiliate status before they could become full members. The rank and file were organized in sections that had between ten and fifty members each, linked through intermediate committees to the party's national assembly, which in theory elected the policy council and the party president. During the 1958 crisis the party was still strong enough to organize supply lines from the insurgents outside Beirut to their colleagues inside the city. When the Christian rank and file (mostly Greek Orthodox) followed its leaders out of the party after 1958, the meager replacements were mostly Druze, and soon the party's national assembly was more than 90 per cent Druze.

Even though Kamal Jumblat strongly supported the relatively progressive programs of the Chehab regime, the more favorable official climate has not been enough to revive the party's organizational strength.[37] During the Chehab regime, the party was both in the government and in opposition to that government at the same time, a situation that did not make the most of the less adverse official climate. Perhaps only in Lebanon is such a paradoxical situation normal. In any event, when the P.S.P. tries to extend its influence among the labor unions the security forces openly harass its labor candidates. This harassment occurred even when Jumblat was Interior Minister. A party official readily admitted that the state of the party in the 1960s is not what it used to be or what it ought to be, for it has offices only in Beirut, Tripoli, Batroun, Aley, and a few other towns; he blamed the party's troubles entirely on governmental blackmail and intimidation.

Cynics sometimes say that the Progressive Socialist Party is not progressive, not socialist, and not a party. There is some truth in such exaggerations. Whatever successes the party has enjoyed are due less to its espousal of progressive socialism than to its calls for moral reform. The element of humanistic idealism in the party's stance comes from Kamal Jumblat himself, who, as has been suggested, is a man of ascetic vision, mysticism, and ambiguity. In the broadest perspective the P.S.P. stands for a new democracy. One may ask what "new democracy" is. Its economic component may be summed up in the slogan "Bread and labor in justice and liberty," which means realizing the fundamental principle, "From each according to his abilities, to each according to his needs." [38] Its social component rests upon the definition by Henri Bergson: a community of voluntary obedience to an elite of innately superior intelligence and virtue.[39] The chief characteristic of this social order is what Jumblat calls the democratic principle *par excellence:* basic equality of rights and obligations. The political component of the party's beliefs involves the creation of institutions for the realization of the essential harmony of man in society and nature: "La Démocratie politique est une entreprise de la Raison appliquée aux relations qui peuvent surgir dans la Société entre l'homme et l'homme . . . la Démocratie est donc une oeuvre de sapiens, de science, c.à.d. de Sagesse." [40] To achieve this new order in Lebanon, the P.S.P. advocates programs for the full development of man, the enrichment of family life in a society beyond the class struggle, the elevation of intellectual life, improvement of public health and sanitation, and a planned economy with equitable distribution of income. It calls for the adoption of a bill of rights as a prologue to the Lebanese Constitution, for electoral and administrative reforms, and for the abolition of political sectarianism.[41]

In theory, the foreign-policy position of the P.S.P. is consistent with that of the National Pact. Kamal Jumblat says that the rule of friendship with both the Arabs and the West but alignment with neither that the Khoury regime followed was as sound as Khoury's domestic administration was weak.[42] The party supports world peace, the United Nations Charter and Declaration, and the idea of a nonaligned Third Force that gained currency after the 1955 Bandung Conference.[43] In practice, however, the P.S.P. has moved increasingly away from the kind of lofty disdain that condemns all imperialism and nationalism. The persistent American attempts "to organize the defense of the area" and the emergence of progressive nationalist leaders after the Suez crisis of 1956 have made international neutrality an untenable policy for a party of strong moral convictions. For the Progressive Socialist Party, however, morality resides not with Washington but with the other side. The locus of political morality has moved ever farther east since Suez: By 1965, it was in Peking.

The P.S.P. in the middle 1960s is, as its founder has said, more a pressure group than a political party[44]—a reasonable assessment. As a party it has failed as a device for achieving power through institutionalized procedures, as have all Lebanese parties with the partial exception of the Kataeb. But there is no doubt that the party —even through its mistakes—has influenced the generation of Lebanese politicians who will hold responsible positions in the 1970s.

The New Arab Nationalists

It is important to distinguish between new and old Arab nationalists in Lebanon. There is hardly a Sunnite politician in the establishment who does not claim to be an Arab nationalist of some kind, but these are mostly the old Arab nationalists, oriented toward the primary aims of achieving independence and establishing liberal constitutional regimes. Several members of the Sulh family are among the most prominent Arab nationalists of the old generation. Other Beirut Sunnite notables who derive considerable popularity for their support of Arab nationalism are Saeb Salam and Abdallah Yafi. In North Lebanon the late Abdel-Hamid Karami and his son Rashid laid claims to represent Arab nationalism. In addition, a number of Christian, Shiite, and Druze notables profess Arab nationalism.

The younger generation of non-Maronite Lebanese Arabs, however, believe that these old Arab nationalists have left a bequest of political failure and corruption. The young nationalists blame the old generation because complete Arab unity has not yet been achieved. In an age of socialism the older generation is merely liberal, and, although the elders may have recognized the existence of new demands, the new generation is not convinced for a moment that the Lebanese equivalent of the Christmas turkey constitutes the proper kind of social-welfare program. By far the heaviest liability for the old generation, however, is the loss of Palestine. Fairly or unfairly, the nationalist notables who were the mature leaders of the 1930s and 1940s are saddled with this burden, and it has clouded the

reputation of more than one of them. In Lebanon the conflict between generations is important because Lebanon has not yet joined
the ranks of the "liberated" Arab states. This claim is the young
nationalist way of saying that Lebanon is still under the control of
an establishment composed of non-Arab nationalists, anti-Arab nationalists, and old-generation Arab nationalists.

The metamorphosis of Arab nationalism may be easily observed
in the case of one of Lebanon's most important Sunnite families.
Members of the Sulh family, originally from Turkey, have represented nearly every shade of Arab nationalism in Lebanon. The most
famous Sulh of the older generation was Riad, who exercised great
influence with Lebanese Sunnites and supported the Arab cause
with distinction. To the end he remained an exponent of Arab unity
and tried his best to strengthen Lebanon's ties with the Arab world.[45]
Sami Sulh, a cousin, rose to prominence on the eve of independence
and developed a devoted local following on the basis of his "common touch" and individual services. Looking back on the evolution
—such as it is—of Lebanese politics, Sami Sulh regrets somewhat
that contemporary politics are complicated with ideologies and programs and that it is no longer enough for a man simply to serve his
individual constituents well and to give people enough to eat.[46]
Nevertheless, Sami Sulh has never changed his style, and he has
served both Bechara al-Khoury and Camille Chamoun. As Prime
Minister under Chamoun, Sami Sulh suffered the wrath of Sunnite
Arab nationalists, including two assassination attempts, and was accused of selling out to the United States. As a classical parochial
politician, Sami Sulh stands at the extreme right of the Sulh family's
political spectrum. Squarely in the middle are Kazem and Takieddine
Sulh, founders and mainstays of the Nida al-Qawmi (National Appeal), a group of liberal Arab-nationalist notables. This group was
active until the early 1950s, and it had an important role in integrating the Sunnites into Lebanese political life; but the revolutionary
changes that began to be felt in 1954 swept the Nida al-Qawmi
outside the mainstream of Lebanese politics. The Sulhs made the mistake of supporting the agreements that led to the Baghdad Pact
(even though they had opposed the American Middle East defense
plans of 1951). They failed to appreciate the fact that the new Arab
nationalism was anti-Western.[47] The obsolescence of the National
Appeal was apparent by 1957.[48] Looking back on the history of the
group, Takieddine Sulh finds that the youth no longer see anything
interesting in the National Appeal because they are hotheaded and

extremist, searching for more sweeping and more disciplined ideologies and groups.[49] The moderate Sulhs still play an important political role, but they have clearly lost their hold on the Sunnites. In recent years both Kazem and Takieddine have run for their Parliamentary seats in the Biqa, profiting from the Christian votes in Zahleh. The younger generation in the Sulh family has responded directly to the changes that have occurred in the Arab-nationalist movement. A nephew of Kazem and Takieddine, Munah Sulh, has become active in the new Arab nationalism and expresses ideas resembling those of the Baath.[50]

The Arab Nationalist Movement (A.N.M.)

It is obvious that the new generation Arab nationalists find their position in contemporary Lebanese politics somewhat ambiguous. Like the other radical mass organizations, the Arab nationalists and their fraternal rival the Baath implicitly and sometimes explicitly question the desirability of the Lebanese entity in its present form. At the tactical level, of course, the new Arab nationalists, like the other radical groups, place Lebanon in a "special category." They then go on to attack directly the conditions of this special status—sectarianism and traditionalism.

The Arab Nationalist Movement has taken many forms. Originally —immediately after the Palestine war—the movement was entirely clandestine. It was also opposed to the doctrinaire ideologies of the other radical groups and thus rejected any elaborate philosophies.[51] At that time it advocated Arab unity specifically for the sake of liberating Palestine and developing the Arab nation, and its approach was pragmatic. The subsequent years have shown that the process of achieving Arab unity is far from simple and that pragmatism and moral feeling are insufficient means to achieve it. The Arab Nationalist Movement thus has been and still is searching for an effective ideology.[52] It has begun to create not one but a coalition of organizations. In the middle 1960s the Arab nationalists' activities are both visible and clandestine, and, though the real leaders of the movement are not popularly known, its spokesmen are. The movement speaks through its own daily newspaper and weekly magazine. The movement mobilizes students and professionals through clubs like the Arab Culture Club and al-Urwa al-Wuthka, which has headquarters near the American University of Beirut. Following the riots at the university in 1954, which protested the formation of the Baghdad Pact, al-Urwa al-Wuthka was shut down, but it reopened in

1962 a few blocks away from the campus. There is also a highly articulate circle of professors, newspapermen, civil servants, and other professionals that discusses, analyzes, and charts the direction of the movement in general but avoids direct participation in Lebanese politics under normal circumstances.

At the popular level the shape of the Arab Nationalist Movement in Lebanon cannot be charted precisely. One crude indicator is the number of portraits of President Nasser; these are readily visible in the Basta quarter of Beirut and in the predominantly Sunnite coastal towns from Tyre to Tripoli. Organization in these areas is kept relatively loose in order to avoid alarming the Lebanese authorities and also to avoid complete destruction should its uneasy truce with those authorities be broken. It is probable that the most highly differentiated Arab nationalist groups are in South Lebanon. Tyre, for example, is supposed to have a dues-paying membership and a policy-making branch. In Saida the local political machinery has been controlled since 1957 by Maarouf Saad, a burly ex-police officer. Educated at the American school in Sidon, Saad fought in Palestine in 1936, became a protégé of the old nationalist Riad Sulh, taught athletics at the Maqasid (Sunnite religious) school in Saida, and became a follower of President Nasser in 1955, after the Soviet arms deal. Capitalizing on the anger that Lebanon's acceptance of the Eisenhower Doctrine had aroused among the voters, Saad defeated the government candidate in 1957 (in a none-too-gentle campaign) and became a deputy, one of the few "men of the people" to enter the Chamber. Arab nationalists are also found in the large Palestinian refugee camps around Tyre, Saida, and Beirut, and the government intelligence services are instructed to keep them under close surveillance.

In Tripoli and Beirut pro-Nasser Arab nationalists have, independently of the wishes of Sunnite notables, organized massive demonstrations like the riots of 1965, which denounced the West German decision to recognize Israel and the President of Tunisia for his advocacy of containment rather than outright destruction of Israel as a political entity.[53] In Beirut the membership is said to be mainly middle-class intellectuals, who pay dues ranging from 2 to 40 per cent of their incomes. One source close to the A.N.M. has said that the Arab nationalists, although they can mobilize considerable pressure in a crisis, are no more powerful than any other political party in Lebanon.

The philosophy of the Arab Nationalist Movement in Lebanon is as diffuse and ambiguous as its organization. In the years since the Palestine war the goal of unity and retribution has remained the core belief, but this goal has raised many subsidiary questions that have yet to be answered satisfactorily. Such questions include, for example, union from above or below? socialism before unity or after it? federation or unitary state? a unified Islamic state or a secular state? For Arab nationalists in general, time has shown these problems to be difficult, but for Arab nationalists in Lebanon they are even more serious. The Lebanese entity and its present political institutions are incompatible with the purer ideas of Arab unity, and any organization that works to establish new institutions is regarded as potentially subversive by those who want to protect the present entity and institutions. The older generation of Arab nationalists solved the same dilemma that the new generation now faces by accepting the National Pact as a sufficient compromise. The context of the middle 1960s, however, is not the context of the late 1930s, and the National Pact is no longer regarded as the reasonable victory for Muslims that it seemed to be in an earlier period. This change of attitude is increasingly evident today. For example, conservative Christians who opposed the National Pact in 1943 because it granted too much to the Muslims defended it in 1958 as a last line of defense for Christian prerogatives.[54]

Today the spokesmen for the Arab Nationalist Movement speak in general terms of "unity, freedom, and socialism" for an Arab nation that extends in theory from Morocco to Kuwait. They also insist that the Arab Nationalist Movement will never try to impose these three goals on any people that does not wish it. Because a sizable proportion of the Lebanese population clearly does not share these three goals, the Arab nationalists regard their task as one of changing this opinion by peaceful means. They interpret their function as education and persuasion and thus wish to be regarded today as a pressure group rather than as a party that aims to obtain control of the institutions of state. In an interview with the moderate, Christian-owned newspaper, *L'Orient,* an Arab nationalist leader put his position this way: "Au Liban, nous cherchons à présent à propager notre doctrine; jusqu'au jour où la majorité des Libanais croiront en l'idée du Nationalisme Arabe. Alors seulement commencera notre véritable action, que nous entreprendrons par toutes les voies democratiques." [55]

It will be difficult for Lebanese to determine when that day comes, of course. There is still no general agreement on what would constitute a majority of the population. Furthermore, the fact that the political system operates by concurrent rather than absolute majority raises the difficult problem of what form unity would take. Certain Lebanese Arab nationalists interviewed in 1965 argued that the correct form of Arab unity at this stage is not a unitary state, but a loose federation in which individual states could if they wished retain their distinctive form—for example, monarchy—but give up sovereignty in foreign and economic policy. Although such an arrangement might not leave many prerogatives for the member states beyond routine administration, it would at least be an attempt to square the policy of the National Pact with Arab unity and to avoid a direct collision with Lebanese sovereignty. The Kataeb and conservative Christian notables are not persuaded by such a formulation, but there is still considerable political advantage in preserving the appearance of support for the Lebanese political entity.

Arab nationalists deliberately sidestep these awkward questions about unity, but they do not hesitate to exert their influence in matters of government policy. In fact, they do constitute an effective pressure group. Unlike the Kataeb they are not formally represented within the establishment institutions, but like the Kataeb—and to a greater extent—they exert influence in the form of an implicit threat of violence and subversion. They exert more positive influence through establishment notables who share—genuinely or for political convenience—the basic emotional orientation of the Arab nationalists.

The new Arab nationalists are quite specific in their recommendations for Lebanon's domestic and foreign policies once the latent difficulties surrounding the unity problem are dismissed. Lebanon, they concede willingly enough, is a land of the free economy, but they feel that this economy is nothing to be proud of. A considerable amount of the movement's intellectual energy is spent in an attempt to devise and propagate a socialism that would be appropriate for Lebanon.[56] Like the Communist Party, the P.S.P., the Baath, and many articulate but unaffiliated new men of the left, the Arab nationalists believe that Lebanon has a false prosperity and an artificial economy. As one Arab nationalist put it, Lebanon—a country in which the real power lies predominantly with the bankers—feeds on the troubles of the oil-producing lands, drawing off their capital, which is then put to socially unproductive uses. Instead of relying upon foreign investment in land, buildings, and services for an uncertain and maldistributed prosperity, Lebanon ought to have a

planned, rational economy in which the condition of the very poor
—some 40 per cent of the population, according to criteria of the
Institut Internationale de Recherches et de Formation en Vue de
Développement (IRFED)—is alleviated through public policy. The
Lebanese government should interfere with the free economy in order
to direct the flow of capital toward more productive purposes. Banks
should be nationalized; speculation and borrowing beyond one's
means should be curbed; interest rates should be controlled; a
bigger long-range development program should be undertaken. Instead of merely providing mild tax incentives for new business, government should actively subsidize light manufacture and modernize
agriculture. The Arab nationalists, however, state that land redistribution is not necessary or generally desirable in Lebanon. Tariff
policy, they believe, should be used to ease foreign competition with
actual and potential local manufactures and not simply to protect
certain companies in which high officials may have a special interest.
They feel that a national health plan should replace the alleged
collusion between the Ministry of Health and pharmaceutical companies. Of course, the Arab nationalists also subscribe to the
ubiquitous demand for curbing government corruption.

Arab nationalist leaders have exerted consistent pressure to bring
Lebanon into closer relations with an Arab world dominated by
the United Arab Republic (Egypt). As far back as 1943 Riad Sulh,
as the foremost Lebanese Arab nationalist, made an alliance with
Bechara al-Khoury because Khoury championed a policy emphasizing Lebanon's basic Arab interests. In the two critical years
after independence the Khoury coalition was seriously strained by
conflict between the more militant nationalists, including Riad Sulh,
who sought to commit Lebanon to a common Arab policy under the
Alexandria Protocol, and liberal Christians who wanted friendship
but not domination. The Palestine war of 1948–1949 transformed
the Arab Nationalist Movement in Lebanon and everywhere else
into a movement marked by bitterness and disillusionment, despite
its positive emphasis on national development. The Khoury regime
initially survived the Palestine disaster, but the discontent it aroused
probably contributed to the President's rapid decline in popularity.
His successor, Camille Chamoun, vigorously criticized Khoury's
handling of the Palestine affair.[57] Chamoun's honeymoon with the
new Arab nationalists was abruptly terminated, however, when
the Cold War became significant in Middle Eastern politics and
pan-Arabism arose in Egypt after 1954. Chamoun himself has

vividly described how the Nasserite Arab nationalists succeeded in arousing large areas of the countryside against him.[58]

After Chamoun's fall in 1958, however, the A.N.M. helped to influence the Chehab regime's shift toward policies of greater friendship with Egypt, participation in the Arab High Command, and close cooperation with the "liberated" states. Intellectuals in the movement praised the regime for having pursued the best possible course, given Lebanon's schizophrenic foreign policy problem. Short of the basic dilemma that the goal of Arab unity presents, the Arab nationalists have thus proven to be a potent foreign-policy pressure group.

The Baath

Although the Baath (the Arab Socialist Renaissance Party) shares with the Arab Nationalist Movement a slogan, "unity, freedom, and socialism" and a firm position on Palestine, there is a considerable distance between these two currents of the new Arab nationalism. The Baath existed in Syria as early as 1942, but it is relatively new to Lebanon, where it developed out of the ferment of 1952. The Baath disdained any immediate interest in Lebanese internal affairs because its primary concern was developing a total and organic unity in the Arab world, but it could not avoid competing for supporters among the other radical left groups. Armed with an appealing ideology, it has lured away important elements from the A.N.M., the Communists, and the P.S.P. Many young A.N.M. members have decided that their own movement is too primitive in a philosophic sense to command loyalty and dedicated service. It is difficult, they find, to adhere slavishly to a cult of the personality of President Nasser, particularly when the pressures of his domestic and international problems cause him to veer and maneuver in the revolutionary struggle. Baathist theory, which is articulated primarily in the writings of Michel Aflaq, appears to supply a complete justification for Arab unity and an explanation of the total context in which the rebirth of the once-great Arab nation must take place.[59] To Baathists it is clear that the rebirth will come about only as the result of a truly revolutionary event and that the substance of the new society is far more important than the form. Unity for the sake of unity is a shallow slogan that can produce incorrect prescriptions for action. Socialism and secularism, however, are indispensable, for through these concepts alone can the genius and essential morality of the Arab nation be realized.[60]

The certainty and comprehensiveness of Baath ideology exerts a strong pull on members of the Arab Nationalist Movement in all countries, not only for the intrinsic merits it may have but also because Arab nationalism in general needs a strong, binding, and specific operational code.[61] The Baath claims that it represents genuine Arab nationalism and criticizes the Lebanese Arab Nationalist Movement for its essentially reactionary character and for its lack of a coherent ideology. The Baathists believe that it is not enough simply to seek revenge for the loss of Palestine; there must also be a positive doctrine. Lacking such a doctrine, the other Arab nationalists are propelled into adventurism for the sake of hollow unity. Even the socialism of the Nasserites—which Baathists claim was borrowed from them—is imperfectly understood and executed. To the Baathists true socialism is not the "state capitalism" of Nasser's Egypt but an arrangement under which the state controls only production and the workers in the factories make their own decisions and even set their own salaries.

Members of Kamal Jumblat's Progressive Socialist Party have also been vulnerable to the lure of the Baath. It will be recalled that the P.S.P. lost important members of its own elite to the Baath in 1956 because the P.S.P. had been insufficiently loyal to the Arab cause during the Suez crisis and because Jumblat himself was too autocratic and eccentric to be a real socialist leader.[62] The Baath has even gained converts from the Communists, whose ideology is far more tested and substantial. Since the 1958 crisis, when the Baath first came to prominence on a mass level in Lebanon, it has moved into areas that the Communists had long controlled through their influence in certain labor unions. The Baath has made inroads into Communist strongholds among the port workers in Tripoli and the tobacco workers around Nabatieh.

Although there is deep rivalry within the radical left in the middle 1960s, the Baath shares with the Arab nationalists, the socialists, and the communists the same attitude toward Lebanon. In the words of a leading Lebanese Baathist, the party wants to create a "receptive atmosphere" toward the true Arab unity.[63] The Baathists believe that unity and socialism can never be achieved by coercing an important sector of the population that is not prepared for them, and it is clear that most Lebanese Christians still equate Arab nationalism with Islam. The Lebanese problem is compounded by the fact that its political conflicts are "artificial," complicated by sectarianism and traditional particularism. They do not involve the "real" issue, which to the Baathists is the relationship between the dispossessed and the exploiters. With a few exceptions, the middle and upper classes are politically inert, unwilling to tamper with the status quo. Despite these difficulties, the party rejects any notion of a "special status" for Lebanon in an Arab union; and, because Lebanon's present status—sectarian and capitalist—is clearly unsatisfactory, one can only conclude that sooner or later the party will have to persuade the Lebanese that revolution is desirable. Such persuasion appears to be a formidable task, but Baath theoreticians think it is within their capacities. In their analysis of the political forces at work in Lebanon they agree in general with the other radical groups. They believe that a great deal more political consciousness exists in the deprived lower classes than in the middle classes and that it is eroding the particularism that has thus far delayed political progress. According to the Baath, the lower classes—workers and many peasants in the outlying areas—are not directly represented by the establishment, but they are ready for political mobilization.

The guarded optimism of Baathist analysis is supported by the growth pattern of the radical organizations in general but not by the development of the Baath itself. Not until the post-Suez troubles did the party begin to move beyond its elite constituency in Lebanon and to acquire a mass following. A Baathist from Tripoli, Dr. Abdel-Majid Rifahi, polled about 7,000 votes in the 1957 elections. During the crisis of summer 1958, the Baath played a prominent role in North Lebanon and—as mentioned earlier—began to branch out into Baalbek, Saida, Tyre, Nabatieh, and Bint Jbeil. Its much stronger showing in 1960 was, as one Baathist put it, "inflated" because in the spring of 1960 the ordinary voter still thought that the Baath supported President Nasser. The breach between Nasser and the Baath over the Syrian region, then a part of Nasser's U.A.R., widened enormously after the coups and countercoups in Syria and Iraq, and in 1964 the party did not even run a candidate. By 1965 the party was down to its "natural" size, which is estimated by one non-Baathist observer at about 3,000 members. It is, however, a more important political force than that figure indicates. For one thing, the membership is well organized. The Baath has three stages of membership: the supporter, the trained member, and the active member. Because the party is under surveillance and arrests are frequently made, however, general party meetings are impossible. Furthermore, the Baath in Lebanon is only one branch of the International Baath Party. As long as the Baath is a popular force elsewhere in the Arab world, the Lebanese authorities must treat its Lebanese organization with circumspection.

ORGANIZING THE LEFT

There is a clear need to organize new radical forces in a manner that will give them positive political effectiveness but will minimize— if possible—their destructive characteristics. This need is more than the collective self-interest of the new left; it also concerns the maintenance of the Republic itself. But the problems of organization are enormous. Not only is there a problem in uniting the left tendencies into a responsible and coherent organization, but there is also a need to develop a role for the increasing number of politically concerned but unorganized individuals. As we have seen, no single radical group has succeeded in monopolizing all the potential sources of opposition. Nor have the persistent attempts to establish a unified opposition coalition front yet managed to produce a permanent popular and effective opposition. While he was Interior Minister in 1962–1963, Kamal Jumblat, the most persistent worker for a unified opposition, tried for the third time since 1949 to establish a socialist front by granting a license to an organization called the Labor Liberation Front. Jumblat's first two attempts—the Socialist National Front of 1951–1952 and the National Front of 1957–1958—were directed toward ousting the President and had been composed of coalitions of notables. The Labor Liberation Front, however, was an attempt to organize the left on a mass basis under the aegis of Jumblat and his Progressive Socialist Party. The front used the mass drawing power of the A.N.M. and the ideological support, for whatever it was worth, of the Communists. As its name implied, the front sought to give the labor movement a politically active role, using the illegal federation of seven Communist-dominated unions as a core organization. Dismissed by the establishment as just another of Jumblat's eccentricities and attacked by the Baath as a plot designed to isolate its own position, the Labor Liberation Front also provoked the opposition of the orthodox labor movement, which wished labor to remain strictly nonpolitical. In mid-1965 there was a prolonged debate within the leftist press over the conditions for cooperation among groups that had recently been openly attacking or privately ridiculing each other. Jumblat and the Arab nationalists, whose followings constituted the main mass strength of this new front, demanded that the Communists admit their error in opposing Nasser and the Egyptian-Syrian union in 1958 and accept a policy of "self-criticism" in the front.[64]

Both the Moscow-oriented Communists and the Arab Nationalists were disturbed by Jumblat's warm pronouncements in favor of Peking, and the Arab Nationalists were also displeased by his relatively late and qualified espousal of nationalism. Despite these suspicions, however, there was a core of agreement concerning the exploitation of workers and peasants at the hands of businessmen whose enlightenment, the front claimed, is more verbal than real. In 1965 the leftists were attempting to consolidate their unity through concerted attacks on American policy, whether in Vietnam or in Lebanon.[65] They staged a mass meeting in a Beirut movie theater to protest, among other things, a proposed treaty under which the United States government would guarantee United States capital investments in Lebanon.[66] Kamal Jumblat also sponsored rallies in several mountain villages badly affected by lack of markets for their apples and used each occasion to call for more vigorous research, production, and marketing efforts by the government.[67]

Nobody can be sure whether or not this effort at organizing the left will eventually succeed in altering the balance of forces in the establishment. The nationalists and socialists complain about objective conditions that are by no means imaginary. Nevertheless, their road is hard. As long as there is growing prosperity in the middle and upper levels, many new professionals will be diverted from political involvement, particularly involvement with radicals. The new doctor is interested in setting up a clinic in Beirut; the new engineer in getting work with an American firm; the new intellectual in pursuing his graduate studies abroad. They have no wish to become mired in the *immobilisme* of local politics. One highly educated, socially conscious Druze—an admirer of Kamal Jumblat— said that, although Jumblat is a good man, his socialism is capricious and inappropriate to Lebanon, and his associates of the left are a mixture of scoundrels and opportunists. He would vote in the parliamentary district against a candidate whom he considered particularly corrupt, but he felt that it is impossible to do more because real power is confined to the small circle that shares control of the administrative apparatus. The only kind of pressure outsiders can bring to bear is coercive, through demonstrations or the threat of demonstrations; and this kind of activity cannot be undertaken lightly.

Another problem for the left is recruiting those people who are willing to act individually but unwilling to establish or participate in a political organization. One man, for example, who has an American Ph.D. degree, believed that in 1965 there were no serious, rational, open reform movements. Although highly critical of the failure of the administration to tap the talent necessary to undertake the broader responsibilities of the times, he complained that he has no organized means of access to the powers that might consider his recommendations. As a Sunnite he would never join the Kataeb, even if the Kataeb were an effective vehicle for progressive reform; as a nonsocialist and an anticommunist, he would not care to associate with the Jumblat group. The only realistic hope for the moderate progressives, he suggested, would be the appearance of an outstanding man in the Presidency, because a strong executive could independently influence the Parliament and notables and would have the capability of acting progressively.

In short, although Lebanon is developing an increasingly articulate left and although this left may become well organized, there is one gap between the left and the organs of responsible power and another between the parties of radical coloration and the moderate progressive opposition opinion.

NOTES

[1] Mohammed Majzoub, *Le Liban et l'Orient Arabe; 1943–1956* (Aix-en-Provence: La Pensée Universitaire, 1956), pp. 94–5, gives 1934 as the date. A little book, *The Principles and Aims of the Syrian National Party, Interpreted by the Leader* (U.S.A.: Fast Printing Service, 1943), states, however, that the principles were first articulated in 1932 and published in newspapers in 1935 and in various books in 1936, 1939, and 1943. A study by Nadim K. Makdisi, "The Syrian National Party: A Case Study of the First Inroads of National Socialism in the Arab World" (Unpublished doctoral dissertation, American University, Washington, D.C., 1959), p. 16, states that the party was officially founded on November 16, 1932, and that it was not until November 21, 1934, that Saadeh wrote his basic doctrines.

[2] In later declarations, Cyprus and Kuwait were added to the Syrian nation.

[3] *Principles and Aims,* pp. 1–11.

[4] *Ibid.,* p. 5.

[5] There seems to have been no connection between the P.P.S. and the German Nazi Party itself, though Michael W. Suleiman, *Political Parties in Lebanon* (Ithaca: Cornell University Press, 1967), p. 94, reports that Antoun Saadeh had allegedly visited Nazi leaders in Berlin in 1938. The German Nazis did, however, try to establish themselves in the Levant during the 1930s. A small group, which was linked to an active Nazi Party in Haifa, appeared in Beirut late in 1933. The Beirut branch was founded by an itinerant Nazi agent, who was the principal of the royal public school at Kabul. There were six members in Beirut, led by an ex-officer of the German Imperial Navy. The Nazis supported Arab, not Syrian, nationalism. H. D. Schmidt, "The Nazi Party in Palestine and the Levant, 1932–1939," *International Affairs,* 27 (October 1954), 460–9.

[6] Testimony of Abdallah Saadeh, *L'Orient,* June 20, 1962, p. 9.

[7] *Le Jour,* June 10–22, 1949. See also Eugénie Elie Abouchdid, *Thirty Years of Lebanon and Syria: 1917–1947* (Beirut: Sader-Rihani, 1948), pp. 77–8; Bahige B. Tabbarah, *Les Forces Politiques Actuelles au Liban* (Unpublished doctoral dissertation, University of Grenoble, 1956), pp. 267–8; and Suleiman, *op. cit.,* pp. 96–7.

[8] *Le Jour,* July 9, 1947. The Zaim regime delivered Saadeh to the Lebanese authorities in apparent betrayal of the bargain struck earlier between the head of the P.P.S. and the Syrian dictator. Patrick Seale, *The Struggle for Syria* (London: Oxford, 1965), pp. 69–71.

[9] Lucien George and Toufic Mokdessi, *Les Partis Libanais en 1959* (Beirut: L'Orient-al-Jaryda, 1959), p. 53. See also Majzoub, *op. cit.,* pp. 94–100; Makdisi, *op. cit., passim;* and Tabbarah, *op. cit.,* pp. 265–75.

[10] Testimony of Muhammad Baalbaki at the *Putsch* trial, *L'Orient,* June 22, 1962. Suspicions of British complicity were heightened when the government expelled the British editor of the English-language paper *Beirut,* whose publishing house also printed the party organ of Camille Chamoun. *Arab World Opinion,* January 24, 1962. There were also unconfirmed reports that a British warship was cruising off the Lebanese coast. Kamal Jumblat

charged that the British Middle East Center for Arabic Studies at Shimlan in Mount Lebanon was a spy center and that former President Chamoun had visited it before the coup.

[11] "The causes of the *Putsch* arise entirely out of the internal political situation. They do not come, contrary to the statement in the indictment, from any idea foreign to Lebanon. Our goal was to bring about moderately leftist reforms and the rebirth of society, to introduce social justice and authentic democracy, to raise the standard of living in every region of the country. We wanted to deliver the poor from misery, want, and disease." Trial testimony, *L'Orient,* June 20, 1962.

[12] Trial testimony, *L'Orient,* June 17, 1962.

[13] "L'Acte d'Accusation dans l'Affaire du Complot PPS du 31 Decembre 1961," *L'Orient,* May 10, 1962.

[14] For example, on the eve of the 1949 P.P.S. crisis, the Kataeb gave a dinner in honor of Dr. Anis Saghir, Chief of the Najjadeh. *Le Jour,* June 9, 1949.

[15] Interview with Adnan Hakim, June 11, 1962.

[16] It even gives grudging approval to what the party chief of its rival, the Kataeb, has done as Minister of Public Works. Interview with Ramadan Lawand, June 9, 1962.

[17] Suleiman, *op. cit.,* pp. 174–81. Some members of the Muslim Brotherhood, however, were arrested for illegal political activity in 1966.

[18] *Ibid.,* pp. 182–5.

[19] *Ibid.,* pp. 57–62 ff., which corrects W. Z. Laqueur, *Communism and Nationalism in the Middle East* (New York: Praeger, 1956), on several points.

[20] Suleiman, *op. cit.,* pp. 65–6.

[21] Khaled Bakdash, *La Charte National du Parti Communiste en Syrie et au Liban* (Beirut: Saout ul-Chaab, 1944), pp. 9 ff.

[22] *Ibid.,* p. 43, which cites Joseph Stalin, *Marxism and the National and Colonial Question,* and pp. 45–6, Articles VII, X, XIII, XV, XVI, XVII, XIX.

[23] *Ibid.,* pp. 23–5.

[24] The party leader, Farjallah Helou (no close relation to Charles Helou), received more than 10,000 votes in Mount Lebanon, which, although the vote was less than one-third that of the winners, was still better than the electoral showing of Shaykh Selim al-Khoury's Neo-Destour list—nine men were elected out of seventeen candidates. Helou also did almost as well as other such party representatives in Mount Lebanon as Elias Rababi of the Kataeb and Assaad Ashkar of the P.P.S.

[25] George and Mokdessi, *op. cit.,* p. 76.

[26] Size estimates are from a labor leader. See also Samir Khalaf, *Managerial Ideology and Industrial Conflict in Lebanon* (Unpublished doctoral dissertation, Princeton University, 1963), p. 259. Two unions in the Federation of Labor Unions of North Lebanon are also Communist dominated.

[27] *Ibid.,* pp. 73–5. In 1955, 208 disputes were brought before the Conciliation Board of Beirut, part of the Ministry of Labor and Social Affairs; in 1960 the board handled 1,015 disputes. There were four strikes in 1955 and thirty-four in 1960. It might be noted that 1960 was an unusually bad year and that the number of strikes declined until 1964.

[28] *The New York Times,* May 26, 1947, p. 7.

[29] Iskandar Riachi, *Qabl wa-ba'd* (Beirut: Maktabat al-'arfān, 1953), pp. 95–9. *Cf.* Camille Chamoun, *Crise au Moyen-Orient* (Paris: Gallimard, 1963), pp. 390–3.

[30] Interview, July 17, 1965.

[31] "I personally believe, besides, that Asia—this land of Christ, of Muhammad, of Confucius, and of Buddha—has something original to give to the world, something other than bourgeois or dialectical materialism, than a dictatorship of race, continent, or class. It is, in addition, something other than a formula of simple compromise, which is a trap, a continued injustice, and a disgrace. This unique contribution is a conception of total social harmony that must be converted into reality." Kamal Jumblat, *Citoyen Libre et Peuple Heureux* (Beirut: Dār al-Kachaff, n.d.), pp. 5–6.

[32] Interview with Nassim Majdalani, July 24, 1962.

[33] A party officer (also in 1962) claimed a membership of 15,000 or 16,000, which he said was comparable to the membership of the Kataeb. Such discrepancies indicate the sizable margin of error in quantitative data on Lebanese politics.

[34] A former member of the P.S.P., Jibran Majdalani, who subsequently became an important figure in the Lebanese branch of the Baath party, joined the P.S.P. "unofficially" before the Khoury regime was ousted and "officially" after President Chamoun's election. He stated that he had not heard of the Baath at that time and that he saw the P.S.P. as the only alternative for a young socialist and nationalist. He and his fellow defectors attributed many of their grievances with the P.S.P. to its leader's quixotic and arbitrary command. Interview, July 12, 1965.

[35] In 1953 Jumblat said that his opposition to the proposed Western defense pact had prompted a foreign intelligence service to attempt to bribe him to desist. *L'Orient,* July 15, 1963.

[36] Interview with Nassim Majdalani, July 24, 1962. Nassim Majdalani, the banker, should not be confused with his distant relative, Jibran Majdalani, the lawyer and Baathist leader.

[37] In 1962 Jumblat, as a member of the government, found himself in the unfamiliar position of supporting the regime instead of attacking it. Although the content of the Chehab program did not approach his own socialist goals, he felt that it was, in Lebanese terms, a big step in the right direction. Interview, May 2, 1962. Two years later Jumblat strongly supported the unsuccessful attempt to renew Chehab's mandate.

[38] Kamal Jumblat, *Démocratie Nouvelle* [Lectures Delivered Between 1950 and 1955] (Beirut: n.d.), pp. 8, 9.

[39] *Ibid.,* pp. 21–3. Jumblat rejects simple majoritarian theories that exalt the ignorant masses. He believes that the elite owes its legitimacy not to an assembly of *bavards* but to its natural obligation to develop civilization and a better life. "C'est donc à un ordre social qui permette la révélation des véritables Chefs—à tous les échelons de la collectivité—c'est à dire, à un ordre qui assurera la meilleure organisation possible et l'efficience maxime de l'Economique, du Social, du Politique, c'est à un ordre semblable que nous devons nous rapporter pour réaliser la véritable Démocratie Sociale" (p. 22).

["It is then to a social order that permits the appearance of genuine leadership, at every level of the community, that is, to an order that will assure the best possible organization and maximum efficiency in the economy, in society, in the polity—it is to such an order that we must attach ourselves, in our effort to realize genuine social democracy."]

[40] "Political democracy is an effort to apply Reason to all the relations between man and man that can arise in society . . . democracy is then a work of intelligence, of science, that is to say, of wisdom." *Ibid.,* pp. 46–7.

[41] Jumblat, *op. cit.,* pp. 12–31.

Among the more specific policies the P.S.P. has advocated for achieving these ends are the following:

—a judiciary and bureaucracy independent of politics
—strengthening the power of the executive
—an electoral law that makes voting obligatory, reduces the size of electoral districts, and establishes judicial supervision of the elections
—the simplification and decentralization of the administration, with promotions on the basis of merit
—establishment of obligatory medical assistance facilities in public institutions and private organizations employing more than ten people
—medical assistance on a cooperative or syndicate basis with state aid
—improvement of all techniques of production
—lowering living costs by reducing indirect taxes, stabilizing and increasing real purchasing power
—suppression and confiscation of excess profits
—creation of a favorable climate for foreign investment
—harmonization of the relations between the factors of production by the nationalization of all institutions that have a "collective character" or special importance; dividing great landholdings into small parcels for the peasants; adapting a system of cooperatives.

[42] Interview with Kamal Jumblat, July 17, 1965.

[43] Jumblat, *Démocratie Nouvelle,* pp. 79–87.

[44] Interviews with Kamal Jumblat, May 2, 1962, and July 17, 1965.

[45] It is regrettable that Riad Sulh, the most prominent non-Christian politician of Lebanon, left no memoirs. See the reminiscences of his daughter Alia Sulh in *Le Jour* (Summer and Autumn 1965).

[46] Interview with Sami Sulh, August 2, 1965.

[47] Majzoub, *op. cit.,* pp. 106–7.

[48] Ali Bazzi, nominally a member of the National Appeal, won a Shiite seat from South Lebanon in 1957, but his victory and subsequent re-election were the result primarily of his own efforts and not of help from the Sulhs.

[49] Interview with Takieddine Sulh, May 30, 1962. He recalls a discussion with Michel Aflaq of the Baath, who told him that the youth is rallying to Arab socialism; Sulh replied that the National Appeal would attract them after they had grown up.

[50] Interview with Munah Sulh, May 30, 1962.

[51] George and Mokdessi, *op. cit.,* pp. 47–9.

[52] Hazem Zaki Nuseibeh, *The Ideas of Arab Nationalism* (Ithaca: Cornell University Press, 1957), analyzes the origins and alternative forms of Arab

nationalism in general. Samir Ahmad in "Nasser's Arab Socialism: Its Place in World Ideologies" (Unpublished paper, Harvard University Center for International Affairs, February 1965) describes the philosophy upon which the Arab nationalist movement draws heavily.

53 For detailed accounts of these demonstrations, see *L'Orient,* March 20–21, 1965.

54 Such, for example, was the case with the National Bloc.

55 "In Lebanon, we are seeking at present to spread our doctrine, until the day when the majority of Lebanese have come to believe in the idea of Arab nationalism. Only then will our real work begin, work that we shall undertake by all the democratic methods." George and Mokdessi, *op. cit.,* p. 50.

56 See, for example, the articles on this subject by Muhammad Kishaly in the Arab nationalist weekly, *al-Ḥuriyyah,* June 14 and 21, 1965.

57 Chamoun, *op. cit.,* pp. 234–5.

58 *Ibid.,* pp. 317–24, 349–53.

59 Michel Aflaq, *Fī sabīl al-ba'th* [*In Behalf of the Renaissance*] (Beirut: Dār al-ṭalī'ah, 1959). A comprehensive description of Baath theory is outside the scope of this study, but an excellent analysis appears in Suleiman, *op. cit.,* pp. 121–55. See *Middle East Journal,* 13 (Spring 1959), 195–200, for an English translation of the Baath Constitution. See also George and Mokdessi, *op. cit.,* pp. 31–2; and Gordon H. Torrey and John F. Devlin, "Arab Socialism," *Journal of International Affairs,* 19, No. 1 (1965), 47–62.

60 George and Mokdessi, *op. cit.,* pp. 29, 32.

61 A leader in an Arab nationalist club interviewed in 1962 admitted that, although the Arab nationalists could provide a few general principles, the Baath was the source of the best theory. Some members of this club were torn between commitment to President Nasser and to the intellectually challenging and militant Baath. A Lebanese Arab nationalist newspaperman interviewed in 1965 argued that, although Nasser may not yet have achieved the best socialism, he is on the road to socialism and has contributed more to the Arab nation through the Egyptian experience than has Baathist theorizing. Furthermore, he charged that the Baathists themselves do not agree on the kind of socialism that ought to be introduced.

62 Interview with Jibran Majdalani, July 12, 1965. Jumblat, he said, is essentially a Druze leader; otherwise he is indefinable.

63 Interview with Jibran Majdalani, July 21, 1965.

64 See, for example, "On Renewing the Lebanese Left and Uniting It," *al-Hurriyyah,* August 30, 1965, pp. 14–5. The Moscow-oriented Communists spell out their position in a pamphlet, by a "socialist struggler," *On Some Elementary Understandings for the Problems of Unifying the Socialist Forces* (Beirut: 1965?).

65 See, for example, Mohsen Ibrahim in *al-Ḥuriyyah,* July 12, 1965.

66 For an account, see *al-Akhbār* (Beirut Communist weekly), July 25, 1965. Speakers included prominent representatives of the Arab nationalists, the Communists, and the Progressive Socialist Party.

67 One such rally, at the Druze village of Btichnay, prompted the conservative notables to sponsor a counterrally at which socialism was denounced. See Kamal Jumblat in *al-Anbā',* October 9, 1965, and Michel Abujaoudeh's commentary in *al-Nahār.*

PART THREE

Institutional Performance

CHAPTER · 6

Trends in Representation

Like the frail sapling in a strong wind, the Lebanese political system bends under the pressures of environmental change, too flexible to break yet not rooted deeply enough to stand. The secret of its precarious survival is its very institutional weakness. This weakness precludes complete political stagnation and requires incessant, though superficial, change. At the same time, however, it retards the rapid development of those aspects of political modernization—like broadly based parties; a rationalized, efficient bureaucracy; and secular, programatic, and centralized policy making—that might well destroy the system of traditional balances. Lebanon has in this way avoided, at least for the moment, the dilemma posed by its changing environment. The result has been an apparently stable short-run equilibrium, for the independent Lebanese Republic has endured for a full generation. In the long run, however, this equilibrium may be unstable. Social modernization and regional ferment demand political innovation, as well as adaptation, and those very aspects of political modernization that are retarded by institutional weakness are the keys to innovation. Lebanese politics is too complex, however, to be fitted easily into mutually exclusive dichotomous categories like "stagnant-dynamic," "weak-strong," and "traditional-modern"; and existing theory provides little guidance in analyzing short-run and long-run processes or stable and unstable equilibria. Therefore, if Lebanese political performance is to be analyzed adequately, it is necessary to go beyond classifying it in "either-or" terms and to attempt to show *how much* and *what kind* of real development are taking place within the rigid institutional framework imposed by Lebanon's fragmented political culture.

211

How, precisely, has the Republic thus far avoided the perils of complete immobilism and destructive dynamism? It has done so partly because its representative institutions function but do not function very well. If there were no genuine representative institutions in the Republic, it would surely lapse into primordial strife; but if these institutions represented all the political tendencies existing in Lebanon in all their intensity, national life would be hardly less chaotic. Instead, Lebanon's representative institutions, exemplified in this chapter by the electoral process, are highly restrictive, yet they show a certain limited expansion in representation over time. This chapter explores the narrow flexibility exhibited in the electoral process and assesses its long-term prospects.

The functioning of the electoral process in Lebanon is marred by official pressures, corruption, high campaign costs, lack of serious debate, and absence of an organized party system. In terms of Lebanon's future these are serious defects. Yet with all these flaws, and perhaps because of them, the electoral process contributes to the country's short-term political tranquillity. Tranquillity requires that the traditional elements be given reasonable security, and the electoral process helps to meet this need by guaranteeing places to the notables who represent these elements. Every Parliament and Cabinet is a complex microcosm of the families, clans, regional interests, sects, and economic interests that have traditionally claimed to represent the people of Lebanon. The electoral process thus institutionalizes traditional pluralism and excludes those who would destroy this pluralism. Anyone who has observed the transformation of Lebanese society in recent years, however, must be disturbed by a growing isolation of the politically relevant population from the formal representative institutions. The nontraditional groups and the unorganized, well-educated stratum are still generally excluded from "normal" political participation (through the representative institutions). Although they may perhaps be dangerous when they are included, they are an even greater threat when they are excluded.

THE ELECTORAL MECHANISM

The contemporary Lebanese political culture (described in Chapter 1) requires a fixed sectarian ratio of deputies in Parliament in order to control sectarianism as a dimension of electoral competition. In the same spirit, regions and districts are allocated enough seats to represent them "fairly" in the Chamber and also to reflect the sectarian balance within the constituency of each district. The device for accomplishing this double basis of representation is the list system. Usually, but not always, competing lists of candidates will be formed for each district. These lists will be composed of candidates for the various sectarian seats at stake in a particular district. In general—but there are important exceptions—lists are formed by the most powerful notable from the majority sect of each region. The dynamics of local politics drive this notable to find as co-listers for the minority sect seats those who will attract the largest possible share of votes from those communities. The potential co-listers, in turn, if they are ambitious, want to affiliate with the most powerful notable of the majority sect. Typically, there is thus a kind of mutual coattail effect both in the formation of a list and in its performance on election day: The leader, especially if he is not all-powerful in the dominant sect (he usually does not have such an advantage) is grateful for the minority support his co-listers may attract, and the lesser notables who cannot be confident of winning even with the solid support of their sect need the majority votes a strong notable can attract.

This arrangement has two important consequences for system maintenance. It imposes a necessity to organize politically. In the absence of strong parties, the notables of the area who are most powerful locally and who have the most extensive clientele have an advantage. The list system, especially in the early years of independence, has been a kind of gearbox, harmonizing a national political system imposed by the French with the complexities of traditional pluralism. The national political organizations, such as they are, consist mainly of notables and their followings, especially in North Lebanon, South Lebanon, and the Biqa—they are a traditionalist substitute for parties in establishment politics. The list system in these areas also encourages a pattern of stable and competitive bifactionalism. As long as the primary electoral organization is the interlocking client group, the list system performs tolerably well as an instrument of peaceful change.

The second consequence of the list system is the encouragement of sectarian moderation. Although it is generally true that the major sects are generally concentrated in particular regions, there is enough geographical intermingling to permit the kind of districting that creates politically significant minorities, given the fact that there already is what amounts to proportional representation by sect. In heavily Maronite Jbeil, for example, a substantial Shiite minority tempers Christian extremism; in North Lebanon, Greek Orthodox enclaves must figure in electoral calculations; in southern Mount Lebanon, Druzes and Christians are sufficiently mixed to force even such bitter enemies as Kamal Jumblat (Druze) and Camille Chamoun (Maronite) to wage their struggles on a nonsectarian basis. The list system gives security and political influence to the Maronites, Greek Orthodox, and Catholic minorities in South Lebanon and the Biqa and to the Sunnite enclaves in Mount Lebanon and the Biqa. In short, the list system imposes moderation by equipping sectarian enclaves with political power. This arrangement has kept people reasonably happy and secure.

The list system has also two basic disadvantages. Because it harnesses traditional notables and their cliques to the state apparatus, this electoral mechanism raises a barrier to the expanding politically relevant elite. It cannot integrate many of the increasingly popular movements into the formal governmental structures. Some of the examples that follow show why individuals who cannot or will not associate with a traditional list fail to break into the establishment. Furthermore, because the list system perpetuates and reinforces the local power of notables, it is extremely difficult to establish such less archaic political organizations as parties. The individual who wants to create a strong parliamentary party is faced with a frustrating chicken-egg problem: For success under the present circumstances, a party must include the same notables it seeks to displace. It is only the liberal benevolence of some of the leaders that permits the introduction of policy problems into a governmental apparatus whose function is mainly the adjustment of competing factions.

The second disadvantage is that the mechanism that encourages sectarian moderation does so by exploiting sectarian tension. Sectarian moderation in election campaigns is the product of latent fears as to the consequences of immoderation. In the short run the consequence is the risk of losing the election; in the long run it is the threat of massive disorder. Under these circumstances the sectarian distribution creates a strategic situation analogous to a system of exchanging hostages or mutual deterrence in international politics. The tangible benefits of this arrangement are visible in the Lebanon of the 1960s: The country has prosperity, tranquillity, and charm. The drawback is less visible but no less tangible: Sectarian identity is perpetuated and positive national unity correspondingly hindered by the list system. In normal times this is not a great disadvantage— it is certainly preferable to the insecurities that the abolition of fixed proportions would breed—but, when crises arise, as they do all too frequently in the twentieth-century Middle East, the old antagonisms can reappear in a very ugly manner.

The electoral system exhibits the problem of the Lebanese political system in general: the incapacity for significant change in a highly delicate balance of power. That this delicacy imposes structural rigidity is apparent in Tables 11 and 12. The first depicts the distribution of seats by religious sect.

TABLE 11

DISTRIBUTION OF PARLIAMENTARY SEATS
BY SECT, 1947–1964

Sect	1947	1951	1953	1957	1960	1964
Maronite	18	23	13	20	30	30
Greek Orthodox	6	8	5	7	11	11
Greek Catholic	3	5	3	4	6	6
Armenian Orthodox	2	3	2	3	4	4
Minorities	1	3	1	2	3	3
Sunnite	11	16	9	14	20	20
Shiite	10	14	8	12	19	19
Druze	4	5	3	4	6	6
Totals						
Christian	30	42	24	36	54	54
Non-Christian	25	35	20	30	45	45
Grand Total	55	77	44	66	99	99

The proportion of parliamentary seats allotted to each sect remains constant over time. More important, the distribution between Christians and non-Christians is always six to five, respectively. Maronites receive about 30 per cent of all the seats and Sunnites 20 per cent. These proportions are roughly those that prevailed in the legislatures under the Mandate and were established by the census of 1932. When Dr. Ayoub Tabet attempted to increase the proportion of Christian deputies in the Parliament of 1943, he precipitated a serious crisis that resulted in his removal by the reluctant French and the restoration of an acceptable ratio after strong diplomatic pressure from the British.[1]

No President since then has sought to tamper with the propor-

tions, recognizing that to do so raises the whole problem of Lebanon's national identity. Nor has any ruler had the temerity to abolish sectarian representation altogether. Change of this sort has been
ruled out, even though, as Chapter 2 suggested, the proportion of
Christians to non-Christians in the population today is probably no
longer six to five. Each province still retains roughly the same share
of seats, as Table 12 indicates. There is nothing particularly note-

TABLE 12

DISTRIBUTION OF PARLIAMENTARY SEATS AND DISTRICTS
BY REGION, 1947–1964

	1947		1951		1953		1957		1960		1964	
Region	*S**	*D†*	*S*	*D*	*S*	*D*	*S*	*D*	*S*	*D*	*S*	*D*
Beirut	9	1	13	1	7	5	11	2	16	3	16	3
Mount Lebanon	17	1	23	3	14	9	20	6	30	6	30	6
North Lebanon	12	1	16	3	9	8	14	7	20	7	20	7
South Lebanon	10	1	14	1	8	7	11	7	18	7	18	7
Biqa	7	1	11	1	6	4	10	3	15	3	15	3
Total	55	5	77	9	44	33	66	25	99	26	99	26

* S = seats.
† D = districts.

worthy about such constancy except that two decades of migration
to Beirut have brought about a relative overrepresentation of the
rural areas. Because regional particularisms are still intense, there
has been no serious attempt to make any adjustments in the proportion. Such then are the structural rigidities in the Lebanese electoral
system.

There has, however, been one structural modification during the
independence period—the only one, indeed, that the situation permits. This change, like the few other important political changes
that have occurred, originated with the President of the Republic.
Each of Lebanon's three independence Presidents enlarged the Parliament but always maintained the sectarian-regional proportions.

The simplest aspect of the change can be seen in Table 12. In
the period from 1947 to 1964, the Parliament increased in size
from fifty-five to ninety members. Although the number of
seats has not risen steadily, the number of identifiable factions competing for them definitely has, as will be demonstrated shortly. The

1947 elections, like the 1943 French-"supervised" elections, were carried out under the system of the "Grand List," in which each of Lebanon's five provinces was a single constituency. For example, all the voters in South Lebanon would elect a slate of ten representatives that would, by law, include six Shiites, one Sunnite, one Maronite, one Greek Catholic, and one Greek Orthodox. Victory in an electoral district the size of an entire province, with its diversity of sects and big families, stimulated the formation of coalitions of local notables, because the immediate parochial clienteles of individual notables would not provide enough support to win. The support of other notables and of voters of the other sects was necessary to win a particular seat. The most influential notables of a province were thus impelled to organize multisectarian slates that they hoped would win support from all the traditional groupings in the province. Organizing such lists required substantial sums of money as well as influence. Obtaining membership on a powerful notable's list could be crucial to an individual's chances of victory, and it required, of course, a certain loyalty to the organizer of the list. Under this arrangement, a few notables—mainly landlords—wielded influence beyond their immediate neighborhoods, and sectarian harmony was promoted. The Grand List system permitted a small number of skilled leaders to consolidate Lebanon's shaky independence. It also fostered electoral corruption because the notables were more powerful in their domains than the government was; indeed, the more powerful notables could heavily influence the government officials in charge of the elections. Electoral corruption, furthermore, contributed to general administrative corruption, insofar as it promoted the oligarchical tendencies of the system. This corruption, in turn, along with thwarted ambitions among some of the leaders, stimulated the opposition. In order to reduce the relative strength of his parliamentary opposition and to bring in more supporters, President Khoury raised membership in the 1951 Parliament to seventy-seven and abandoned the Grand List in Mount Lebanon in favor of several smaller electoral districts. President Khoury thus retained an overwhelming parliamentary majority and reduced the scope of his opponents' influence simultaneously. A year later, when these measures proved inadequate and President Khoury had been evicted from the Presidency, the new President, Camille Chamoun, undertook the boldest electoral experiment of the time by abandoning the Grand List system altogether and replacing it with thirty-three small districts, of which twenty-two were for single members.

FIGURE 3. *The President Prepares Some Changes in the Cabinet and Chamber of Deputies.*

This move reduced parliamentary membership to forty-four, and, in President Chamoun's words, "la qualité remplaçait la quantité." [2]

President Chamoun's stated intention was to weaken the feudal stranglehold on the political system and to end the grave electoral abuses of the past. His unstated intention was to increase the power of the President. The immediate results were mixed. Instead of weeding out the most influential feudal leaders, he merely sacrificed their less powerful colleagues, but he did succeed in dislodging the remnants of the Constitutional Bloc. Four years later, when it was time to elect a new Parliament, President Chamoun had accumulated a set of problems arising both from the Suez crisis and from his tactless domestic politics. Chamoun's awareness of the growing animosity of his enemies (both members and affiliates of the old Constitutional Bloc) was at least as important a factor in the President's decision to push through another electoral law as was any general wish for reform. Under the new law, the number of deputies was increased to sixty-six, and the newly elected Parliament was not only overwhelmingly Chamounian but also purged of the President's traditional enemies. The lines of the new districts had been carefully drawn. Several leaders from South Lebanon, Mount Lebanon, and Beirut, gerrymandered out of their customary seats, were conspicuous by their absence. These traditional leaders could not be eliminated so abruptly, however, particularly when the President, in the opinion of many, had violated the National Pact by associating too closely with the West. President Chamoun's strong-arm electoral tactics in 1957 contributed substantially to the crisis of 1958.

When the civil war was over, the previous political status quo was re-established; but the new President, Fuad Chehab, continued the expansion of Parliament. He raised the membership to ninety-nine (the number of districts was twenty-six), but the new law did not squeeze out any of the important establishment figures or tamper with the sectarian balance. Instead, organized party representation increased in numbers and the social composition of the membership broadened somewhat. As suggested earlier, General Chehab may have reasoned that the bigger Parliament is, the more unwieldy it becomes, and the less trouble it gives: Let the representation of local interests and new (but respectable) elements increase and at the same time bring a sizable number of the traditional leaders into the Cabinet and in so doing satisfy as many people as possible.

All three of postwar Lebanon's Presidents expanded the Parliament as a representative institution, each for practical political purposes. There was a common result in each case: The electoral process became more fragmented and the pattern of political organizations more complex.

INCREASING POPULAR INVOLVEMENT

The limited flexibility in the Lebanese electoral process is demonstrated not only by the limited attempts at formal structural expansion but also by the trends in voting participation, entry of new men, and competitiveness. Regular elections and increasing voting participation are indicative of institutionalized mass participation, though not necessarily of general stability. The whole electorate may vote, but, if the same men keep getting re-elected or if the turnover rate is very high, the high voting rates may simply be signs of unrest, particularly in light of restrictive or corrupt electoral procedures. It is thus necessary to consider how often new men get in and to examine electoral contests for competitiveness. Because of Lebanon's religious and socioeconomic cleavages, it is also important to view the three trends in terms of religious and regional-economic divisions.

Voting Participation

There is communal ritual in a Lebanese election campaign, and voting statistics cannot adequately portray the popular involvement it engenders. A few examples, however, may be helpful. Candidates in the rural areas must spend large amounts of money to transport voters who normally live in Beirut back to the villages where they are registered. The candidates travel in caravans of cars, and each candidate—in the American fashion—tries to shake as many hands as possible. Frequently he borrows a large house in a village and receives local notables and citizens, supplying, of course, a cup of coffee to each visitor. In return for support, the candidate promises more government aid for the village—new pavement for the road, a telephone line, improvements in the electric supply, water-purification programs. Distribution of government largesse is the basic "issue" in a Lebanese parliamentary campaign. In Beirut, the technique is similar, though somewhat more mechanized. The buildings are plastered with posters; illuminated portraits gaze down on crowded intersections; banners bearing slogans are hung above the roadways. Especially inventive candidates have even hired airplanes to distribute leaflets and display banners. In the parliamentary elections of 1943, 1947, and 1951, election day was chaotic, but President Chamoun in 1953 instituted the practice of holding elections on successive Sundays in the various districts in order to give the government more time to mobilize its security forces in case of violence. Opposition candidates have complained that the concentration of governmental and military influence, ostensibly to prevent violence, is a form of intimidation, but the practice has been strengthened with time. The elections since the 1958 crisis have been carried out in the more unruly districts of the North and Biqa under the watchful supervision of gendarmes and soldiers.

Whereas organized political parties play a distinctly minor role in the electoral process, candidates take full advantage of the highly developed traditional organizations as a means of furthering their interests. In order to gain the backing of these organizations, the candidate must cultivate the support of village priests or *shaykhs,* heads of municipalities, *mukhtars,* and the heads of important families. It is a complicated and delicate business, for the candidate inevitably finds himself drawn into local and personal rivalries. Corruption, nepotism, and favoritism are the preferred charges chronically leveled at deputies. In all probability, Lebanese deputies are no more avaricious than legislators elsewhere, but they do incur a bewildering variety of obligations on the road to Parliament. At least one deputy has a large filing cabinet packed with pending complaints, biographical data on constituents, and reports on projects affecting his district. Letters from constituents are relatively rare, because legislators are generally easier to reach personally. Fence mending is probably the principal occupation of Lebanese deputies, but candidates also rely on less visible means to win votes. In the traditional areas, both urban and rural, both Christian and non-Christian, the candidate must somehow engage the services of local strong men who have the power to deliver a certain number of votes or withhold them. These "election keys," like the ward bosses in old-fashioned American urban machines, do not provide their services without prospect of some benefit, financial or otherwise, in return. Traditional leaders, even the most Europeanized, also engage squads of young men to assist their campaigns, to act as bodyguards, and to keep order if the opponents' men should cause disturbances. Disturbances, indeed, are frequent in Lebanese election campaigns and have shown no sign of disappearing; and it is not uncommon to read that one of a boss's men has been beaten up or wounded—sometimes killed—by men of the other side.

An impressive increase in the number of people voting between 1943 and 1964 suggests that the electoral process has engaged a growing segment of the population and has acquainted most adult Lebanese with orderly democratic processes. In the parliamentary elections of spring 1964, Lebanese voters went to the polls in record numbers. Voting turnout increased by 14 per cent over the totals registered in the 1960 elections. This trend is by no means recent: The voting population has been expanding rapidly since 1943, as Table 13 shows.[3] Table 14 indicates that the voting increase trend does not simply reflect the growth of population in general. Whereas

TABLE 13

VOTING PARTICIPATION IN SEVEN PARLIAMENTARY ELECTIONS

Province	1943	1947	1951	1953	1957	1960	1964	Average Annual Increase 1943–1964
Beirut	11,429	21,599	21,998	51,660	65,500	71,436	42,637	1.065
Mountain	43,323	53,138	61,932	124,977	124,787	167,107	178,266	1.070
North	29,675	32,893	48,645	90,082	100,246	110,093	168,073	1.086
South	24,394	29,179	35,814	75,107	83,832	99,512	116,435	1.077
Biqa	20,807	31,134	31,010	48,106	71,895	73,716	89,775	1.072
National	129,628	167,943	199,389	389,932	445,260	521,864	595,186	1.075

Official figures were reported in *L'Orient*, April 8, 1951; June 7, July 13, 20, 27, 1953; May 8, 1960; April 15, 28, May 4, 1964; and in *Le Jour*, May 27, June 3, 1947.

TABLE 14

VOTERS AS PERCENTAGE OF ESTIMATED TOTAL ADULT POPULATION, 1943–1964 *

1943	1947	1951	1953	1957	1960	1964
26.4	29.7	38.5	60.0	60.8	66.0	66.7

* The percentages are only rough approximations because the population estimates are themselves only educated guesses. According to the Institut de Formation en Vue du Développement (IRFED) population-age profile, 48 per cent of the population is over twenty years old, and these calculations are based on this figure.

Republic of Lebanon Ministry of Planning, *Besoins et Possibilités de Développement du Liban,* I (Beirut: 1960–1961), 48.

the population increased by just over two-thirds between 1943 and 1964, the number of voters increased more than 4.5 times.[4]

The rate of voter increase is not smooth. In 1953 there was an increase of some 190,000 voters over the 199,000 who voted in 1951—the voting population had nearly doubled. Whereas approximately 15 per cent of the entire population voted in 1951, about 29 per cent voted two years later. This voting explosion was a direct result of President Chamoun's electoral law of November 6, 1952. In addition to the redistricting already described, this law gave the vote to women, made voting compulsory for men, and instituted the secret ballot. Although the Chamoun regime later disappointed many reformers and although the broadened suffrage has yet to be exploited fully—women are still reluctant to go to the polls—it did take a decisive step toward expanding the electoral base of the country's political institutions. The enlarged electorate is accompanied by an increased number of factions, a differentiation of rivalries, and a diminution of the once-tight control exercised by the notables and officials.

When the voting-participation trend is broken down by region, a familiar yet curious pattern emerges. The voting-increase rate of the "backward" rural areas between 1943 and 1964 exceeds that of Beirut and Mount Lebanon, according to the logarithmic calculations presented in Table 13. North Lebanon has the highest increase rate, followed by South Lebanon and the Biqa; Mount Lebanon places fourth, followed by Beirut. This trend is particularly clear in the post-1952 period of universal suffrage, as Table 15 indicates. One might have expected a positive correlation between voting participation figures and the level of socioeconomic development,

TABLE 15

OVER-ALL PERCENTAGE INCREASES IN VOTING
BY REGION, 1953–1964

Beirut	Mountain	North	South	Biqa	National
− 17.4 *	42.6	64.4	56.3	86.6	52.6

* Beirut shows a net decrease in the number of voters for the 1953–1964 period. For the 1953–1960 period, however, it shows an increase of 38.3 per cent. See Note 3, p. 258.

but this is obviously not the case in Lebanon. Quite the contrary; the "backward" districts exceed the economically developed areas in the absolute rate of increase, even though they are losing population to the Greater Beirut area. It will be shown shortly that the backward areas also exhibit the greatest relative shifts in elite composition as well. The statistics suggest that the "other" Lebanon is undergoing a popular political awakening. Some of this new activity is channeled into the election process, but it is questionable that all of it is absorbed by this mechanism.

Mount Lebanon and especially Beirut—the areas with high social mobilization levels—do not participate to the same extent. The low level of electoral participation in Beirut is a cause for concern, for it is there that newly politicized lower and middle classes are concentrated. These groups have not made a very great impression on the electoral process. This ominous situation is partially explained by the fact that many Beirutis are registered in their home towns and villages and thus vote outside the city. Some of the electoral apathy also results from the cosmopolitan and cynical character of this modern urban area. Traditional social organizations are relatively weaker than in the rural areas, and modern urban machines are just beginning to appear. Neither of these explanations eliminates the problem that an enormous number of urban Lebanese do not participate in the institutionalized politics that the electoral system, above all, is supposed to provide. Many of the inhabitants of Greater Beirut, of course, cannot vote; they are Syrian laborers, Palestinian refugees, or Europeans. But this fact is no reason to believe that the limited base of participation in the region has no serious consequences. Impressions and interviews suggest that in many parts of the urban core area there is disdain and even contempt for the electoral process. In Beirut, the "new men" (as William Polk calls them) cannot come to power via traditional family means because urban political success depends on money and traditional organization outside the family.[5] At the same time communal particularism still hampers the development of nontraditional machines.

The voting figures show that the increasingly politicized Lebanese participate more and more in the formal political system. The figures do not show, however, whether or not these people are also increasingly committed to that system. The trend is thus not necessarily a predictor of short-run stability: The increasing voting participation of 1953 and 1957 did little to prevent the crisis of 1958. The most the voting figures can show is that the present order is not entirely stagnant in the face of demographic and social change. Furthermore, regional voting figures reveal differential rates of increase. Beirut, the urbanized and developed area, scores poorly. Institutionalized mass participation there is relatively weak. Yet the highly socially mobilized people in this area ought to be highly participant. On the other hand, in the outlying areas, where political life is dependent on the actions of a landed oligarchy, mass participation is increasing. This participation may be indicative of more than blind obedience to local chieftains. If so, it suggests that the increase is most pronounced where, in terms of systemic stability, it is least desirable.

COMPETITIVENESS

A competitive electoral process is one sign of a healthy pluralistic system because it indicates flexibility and responsiveness. A trend toward increasing competitiveness suggests that a process of institutionalized change is developing. It also poses the question whether or not "too much" competition imposes strains on stability.

For reasons already explored it is exceptionally important in Lebanon that there be some degree of free play among the various interests: For the traditional groups it is the only satisfactory assurance of security. Electoral contests in Lebanon have become steadily more competitive during the two decades since independence. Although this fact does not say anything about the kind of choice offered to the voters (it is still rather limited) it does show that Lebanon's political structure is flexible enough to support a significant, though rarely unified, opposition. Lebanon's moderately competitive electoral process connects the country's political culture of traditional pluralism with its formal political system. In light of the shift toward increasing voter participation and broadened recruitment of candidates, the trend toward greater competition is particularly significant.

Methodology

Calculations were made for 276 contests in the six parliamentary elections between 1947 and 1964. "Contest" was defined on a sectarian basis: A contest constituted the campaign for the seat or seats allotted to a particular sect in a particular district. If in a particular district there were four seats at stake, of which one was allotted to a Greek Orthodox, one to a Maronite, and two to Sunnite Muslims, then by this definition there were three contests. Competitiveness was determined by calculating the percentage of the total vote that the winner or winners in each sectarian contest received. A score of 100 per cent indicates that there was no opposition or no election—or that the opposition received no votes whatever. Such a race is noncompetitive. A score of less than 50 per cent—reflecting a plurality but not a majority—is evidence not only of competition but also of the fact that there were more than two aspirants for each seat in the contest. It cannot be assumed that, if the winner's percentage of the vote was low, then his political position was correspondingly weak because the opposition might be fragmented among many candidates; the winners of a contest who received only 40 per cent of the vote, with the rest being divided among six isolated candidates, might in fact be stronger than the winners in another district who received 60 per cent against a unified opposition. But in all cases a score of 60 per cent or less indicates a "definitely competitive" situation.

The System as a Whole

Table 16 indicates that the Lebanese system as a whole is moderately competitive by the criterion established: The mean percentage of winners for all 276 contests was 62.6 per cent. Of course, judged by the standards of an American presidential election, a winner with 62.6 per cent of the vote has won by a landslide, but, in Lebanon's comparatively minuscule constituencies, a winner by this proportion may have enjoyed a margin of fewer than 2,000 votes. With margins this small a winner can hardly afford to remain indifferent to his constituency if he wants to be re-elected.

The national mean for each of the six elections is compared in

TABLE 16

MEAN PERCENTAGES OF TOTAL VOTES RECEIVED BY WINNERS
IN SIX PARLIAMENTARY ELECTIONS

1947	*1951*	*1953*	*1957*	*1960*	*1964*	*Mean for 6 Elections*
80.0	60.1	62.2	60.5	59.5	61.1	62.6

Table 16. Two interesting points emerge. First, there is a significant increase in competitiveness after 1947. The elections of that year—the first conducted without the presence of foreign troops—were notoriously corrupt, and they aroused serious opposition to Bechara al-Khoury and Riad Sulh, two of the "founding fathers." The 80 per cent that the regime's candidates averaged in winning that election suggests a distinctly noncompetitive situation. The high degree of competitiveness four years later (60.1 per cent) indicates that the Khoury regime, even though its supporters took a decisive majority of the parliamentary seats, was losing its authoritarian grip and that the electoral process was capable of at least registering opposition tendencies. The mean stabilizes after 1951, but the increase in competitiveness does not cease. In fact, as Table 17 indicates,

TABLE 17

PERCENTAGE OF PARLIAMENTARY ELECTORAL CONTESTS IN
WHICH THE WINNERS RECEIVED LESS THAN 60 PER CENT
OF TOTAL VOTE

1947	*1951*	*1953*	*1957*	*1960*	*1964*
43.3	56.4	54.5	59.6	65.0	71.7

the percentage of competitive contests has steadily risen. Table 17 records the percentage of contests in each election that fell into what we have defined as a "definitely competitive" category. With the slight exception of the 1953 election, there is a steady increase in the percentage of competitive contests. The spread of competition is particularly impressive because there has been a growing number of contests to fill newly created seats.

The second interesting fact is that the mean percentage has hovered so consistently at approximately 60 per cent since 1951. Even though these elections span three presidential regimes, two near revolutions, one acute crisis, and two attempted *Putsches,* there is remarkable stability in voting behavior. This stability indicates a certain separation between the electoral process and national politics, a separation that, though casting doubt on the relevance of elections to important issues, is functional in that the constant figure is about 60 per cent and not, let us say, 35 or 85 per cent. The lower figure would indicate that most candidates had won by only simple pluralities. Such an outcome would suggest that most winners do not have a very substantial popular backing and that the political culture is more highly fragmented than it actually is. A high figure, as already suggested, would indicate a weak opposition of any kind. An increasing proportion of winners, then, consistently wins by a clear but not overwhelming majority; and the fact that it happens in the absence of an organized party system renders it an even more impressive indicator of basic stability.

Competitiveness by Region

All the regions show a reasonably high degree of competition in their electoral contests. Mount Lebanon, long the most advanced area, not surprisingly shows the most consistently high competition. But South Lebanon, whose general level of development is very low, is a close second. Then come the Biqa, North Lebanon, and Beirut, the least competitive of all. The rank order of these five regions is curious. One might have expected to find a correlation between the degree of competitiveness and the standard of living, on the assumption that the higher the living standard (particularly the level of education), the more independent the voter and the more active his political life. In the advanced areas there would thus be fewer safe seats. When one compares the regional rankings on socioeconomic development with the rankings on competitiveness, however, one does not find such a simple correlation.

Mount Lebanon seems to support the correlation hypothesis; it scores in first place on both scales. This region in particular was superior in educational facilities during and immediately after the Mandate, when most current voters were of school age. At the other end of the development scale, North Lebanon seems also to support the idea; and the Biqa has the middle rank on both scales. Beirut and South Lebanon, however, present glaring discrepancies. In the late 1950s Beirut and Mount Lebanon shared first place in development, far exceeding the other regions, but on the competition scale the two could not be farther apart. Beirut's competitiveness score is very poor—just as its voting-participation score is very poor. It is difficult to explain this performance merely by the fact that Beirut is urban, whereas Mount Lebanon is suburban and rural; the city of Tripoli is urban too, yet it exhibits a competitive mean that is only a shade above the national mean and 3.8 per cent below the mean for all of the North. Perhaps the answer lies in the fact that Beirut is cosmopolitan and highly diverse in the sectarian, economic, and cultural dimensions, whereas Tripoli is provincial, largely Sunnite, and less diversified. In Beirut politics is just another activity, but in Tripoli it galvanizes the whole town. For Lebanon, neither urbanization nor development is a good predictor of competitiveness.[6]

With time, all the regions have experienced increasingly competitive contests. Most dramatic is the trend in the Biqa, where pluralism has blossomed and traditional seigneurs find it increasingly difficult to maintain their dominance. South Lebanon is also the scene of consistently close struggles. There, competitiveness has arisen out of the stable bifactionalism of the Assaad family organization and its unified opponents, but increased competitiveness also reflects the dispersion of power and rivalry among a younger generation of highly educated Shiites. North Lebanon remains the stronghold of landed proprietors and clan bosses—both Sunnite and Maronite—against whom effective opposition has yet to arise. As for Beirut, its competitive performance was best in the topsy-turvy elections of 1953, when the redistricting destroyed old spheres of influence. Beirut's poor showing in 1964 is the result of the successful efforts of the Kataeb to build a modern political machine in the Christian district: It had frightened away or absorbed the token opposition before election day.

Competitiveness and Sectarianism

Because sectarianism is an abiding aspect of Lebanese politics, it is worth inquiring if there is any relationship between it and competitiveness. Is politics more competitive and thus more democratic in the absence of sectarianism? Because sectarianism is the rule throughout the country this is not an easy question to answer; but crude guidance can be obtained by comparing the competitiveness of single-sect and multisect districts. There were no single-sect districts in 1947 and 1951, but the election law of 1952 did away almost entirely with the multisectarian list system and created instead thirty-three electoral districts, of which twenty-two were single-member (and therefore single-sect). Calculations (on the same basis as the previous discussion) show no significant difference between the single-sect and the double-sect districts in terms of competitiveness; the former averaged 62.8 per cent, only a shade above the national average of 62.2 per cent. The 1957 electoral law reduced the number of electoral districts to twenty-five, of which eight were single-member (and single-sect) and five were multimember single-sect. The thirteen single-sect districts averaged 67.7 per cent, somewhat less competitive than the national average of 60.5. In the 1960 elections a new high in over-all competitiveness was achieved, with an average of 59.5 per cent for the sixty constituency contests; the average for the ten single-sect districts was 59.1. In the 1964 elections, in which the 1960 district boundaries were retained, the single-sect districts averaged 57.9 per cent, compared with the general average of 61.1. It can be concluded, therefore, that there was no important difference in competitiveness in single-sect and multisect districts in the four elections in which there was a basis for comparison. The absence of sectarianism does not seem to promote competitiveness, and multisect districts are not necessarily more competitive than others.

Although the degree of competition is not affected by the number of sects in the district, it is still possible that some sects are more competitive than others. Our general knowledge about the socio-economic differences between Muslims and Christians suggests that Christian electoral contests might be more competitive than non-Christian contests because the Christians have had greater general exposure to Western influences. There are two ways to test the accuracy of this notion. First, one may compare Christian single-sect (single-member and multimember) districts with non-Christian districts, assuming that the minority sect populations in those districts are insignificant. One can also make a more general investigation and compare the closeness of all sectarian contests, including those in multisect districts. The second comparison is less discriminating than is the first because members of all sects vote for each sectarian seat in multisect districts. The data show, however, that individuals in multisect districts do not consistently vote straight tickets (in some contests candidates run independently of any list) and that the votes cast for the winning Maronite do not always equal the votes cast for the winning Sunnite, even when both are on the same list. Variations in competitiveness between different sectarian contests within a single district may reflect differences in the political behavior of the sects. If the

Christian contests are consistently and strikingly more competitive in those situations for which we can make a comparison, then there is something to the original hypothesis.

The notion of superior Christian competitiveness, however, is clearly disproved by the first test, a comparison of fifty-four single-sect district contests in the elections of 1953, 1957, 1960, and 1964. The all-Muslim contests are more competitive than are the all-Christian contests, with average percentages of 57.7 and 66.3, respectively. (The percentage, as before, is the share of the total vote in a given contest going to the winner or winners.) The percentage for Sunnites in twelve contests is 55.0 and for Shiites in eighteen contests 61.2, whereas the percentage for Maronites in sixteen contests is 63.3, for Greek Orthodox in four contests 74.7, for Protestants in one contest 35.9, and for Armenian Orthodox in three contests 80.6.

The second test groups all 276 contests in the six parliamentary elections by sect, and in this case there appears to be no significant difference in competitiveness among them. The average share of the total vote going to the winner in 147 contests for Christian seats is 62.6 per cent, whereas the average percentage for non-Christians is 60.2. Of the Christian sects the Maronites average 62.2 per cent, the Greek Catholics 62.1 per cent, the Greek Orthodox 60.8 per cent, and the Armenian Orthodox 71.7 per cent. Of the non-Christian sects the Sunnites average 61.3 per cent, the Shiites 59.9 per cent, and the Druzes 68.2 per cent. As far as the two tests are valid, sectarian peculiarities have no predictable influence on competitiveness.

ORGANIZATIONAL DEVELOPMENT

Lebanese political life, complex to begin with, is becoming increasingly complex over time in terms of organization. This trend is a highly important one for the student of political change. Increasing organizational differentiation is at least a preliminary step in political modernization. If such differentiation leads in turn to institutionalization, the system's capabilities, in terms of flexibility, stability, broadened political recruitment, and administrative efficiency, are enhanced. Without institutionalization, on the other hand, differentiation can lead to disintegration. The electoral process offers an excellent example of the increasing group differentiation in Lebanese politics. To describe this process most effectively, an overview of the trends during six parliamentary elections of the first two decades may be helpful.

Lebanon owes some of its moderate political success to its ability to institutionalize the rivalry of factions. In Lebanese politics the faction—a nonideological coalition of notables, their families, and their clienteles—is the unit upon which other more complex forms like caucuses (which are collections of factions bound together by some external political goal) and organized parties are built. One of the most successful institutions for combining traditional factions of Lebanon into a reasonably coherent political unit was the amirate, or principality, ruled by an *amir,* a local hereditary prince. But in the twentieth century an amirate is generally—though not universally—regarded as an archaic form. Since the Mandate, republican institutions have served as a framework for regulating factional rivalry. These institutions have been strengthened by the National Pact of 1943. The subsequent decades have seen the routinization of factional politics within this framework.

Factional Proliferation

To describe factional proliferation in the electoral process adequately, it is necessary to impose categories and generalizations on a field that does not lend itself easily to such academic niceties.

Lebanese factions have been classified in one of four categories of increasing complexity: individuals, cliques (or lists, which is the form in which they appear on the electoral scene), caucuses, and parties.[7] "Individuals" run independently of a list, caucus, or party; they campaign on their own merits or espouse their own programs. The individual may be extremely enlightened or respected, but organizationally he is primitive because he relies only upon an informal support group among his family and friends. Scarcely less primitive in the organizational sense is the "clique" or list, which is a coalition of notables gathered together to win an election. Because of the nature of Lebanon's electoral system, each notable must rely on the others to pull the whole list to victory. Although members of lists invariably speak of policies and platforms, their basic appeal is entirely parochial, and lists win mainly because the voters think that they will do most for the area. As late as 1964, some two-thirds of the parliamentary membership was composed of deputies who ran either as individuals or as members of lists. "Caucus groups" are primitive parties: They command a slightly higher ranking in complexity because they are organized to institute national programs and they have slightly broader geographical membership than lists have. In independent Lebanon there have been only two major caucus groups, the Constitutionalists (Destour) and the National Bloc, as well as a smattering of minor ones like the Nida al-Qawmi, and the Hay'at al-Watania. Because they are somewhat more nationally (rather than privately) oriented and rationalized organizationally than are the cliques, the caucuses require a special place, though their real organizational strength has proved less durable than has that of certain such stable cliques as the Assaad list of South Lebanon. Finally, there is the most elaborate form of organization, the norm in most developed political systems of the world but in Lebanon a rarity: the organized political party. Counted as organized parties—even though they may lack the degree of organization as well as some other important characteristics of Western parties, like a national base and a secular outlook—are the Kataeb, the Tashnaq, the P.P.S., the P.S.P., the Communist Party, the Arab nationalists, the Baath, the Najjadeh, and the Islamic Liberation Party. In speaking of the nonestablishment organizations it was noted that only a handful of the outsiders or counterelite have been elected to Parliament or named to the Cabinet. The fact that party men are rarely included in the institutions of government does not mean that the parties are unimportant. Nor does it mean that there is not a more visible party activity outside the Chamber: There is. For reasons that should now be apparent, it has been very hard for parties to break into Parliament. It is thus all the more important for the observer to note carefully the attempts—both successes and failures —of parties to gain access to Lebanese institutions. The criteria used for classifying individuals as party members and for noting the representation of parties in parliamentary contests (even where it is nearly hidden in traditional forms), are therefore generous. An attempt has been made to compare the contestants in seven parliamentary contests, in 1943–1964, by employing the four-category classification already described.

The actual classification process is cumulative rather than mutually exclusive; that is, certain lists in certain elections are also caucus groups, and the same organizations have been classified with each label. Certain lists may contain members of one or more political parties; these lists are also classified separately. An individual may be classified both as an individual and as the representative of a party. Furthermore, a caucus group is listed for every list of candidates it fields: The Destour was thus counted three times in the 1951 election because it ran lists in Metn, Chouf, and Kisrwan. In order to introduce a bit more sophistication, all contestants in all categories have been cross-classified as organizationally "strong" or "weak." [8]

The General Trend

There is a distinct trend toward group differentiation. The increase in the number of seats that are contested in each election is, of course, some indication that the electoral process has become more complex. There is more to it, however, and to represent the complexity more adequately a simple weighting system has been devised, which allots points to each organization according to the following system:

Individuals Weak:	1	Caucuses Weak:	3
Individuals Strong:	2	Caucuses Strong:	4
Lists Weak:	2	Parties Weak:	4
Lists Strong:	3	Parties Strong:	5

Every electoral grouping in every district in seven elections from 1943 through 1964 has been scored. The number of groups of all types observed and the gross scores for each election are reported in Table 18, which may be taken as a general summary

TABLE 18

SUMMARY OF THE TREND IN GROUP DIFFERENTIATION
IN SEVEN ELECTIONS

	1943	1947	1951	1953	1957	1960	1964
Number of groups	15	32	52	104	104	148	132
Total score	47	83	127	243	237	357	345
Ratio score: group	3.13:1	2.59:1	2.44:1	2.34:1	2.28:1	2.41:1	2.64:1
Number of seats	55	55	77	44	66	99	99

of the trend in group differentiation. Whereas the number of parliamentary seats increases by 80 per cent, the number of groups that play in the electoral game increases by 880 per cent from 1943 to 1964. If 1960 is taken as the latest point of comparison, the rate of increase in the number of groups is, of course, even higher. When the groups are weighted in terms of the classification described previously, the rate of increase is also impressive: 732 per cent. It is significant, however, that this increase in "weight" does not exceed the rate of increase in the number of groups, even though the more complex groupings are highly weighted and generously classified. It seems clear that fragmentation has occurred somewhat more rapidly than has institutionalization—the development of cohesive groupings—in the electoral system. For example, although there were only fifteen distinct groupings present in the 1943 elections, nearly all were strong lists; the ratio of weighted score to number of groups was 3:1. But twenty-one years later the group structure as a whole was somewhat less complex, the ratio being 2.6:1, even though the raw number of groups had vastly increased. When the total group composition is examined, the reason for the decreasing ratio becomes apparent: The increased number of more primitive, lower-scoring groups has almost exactly offset the scoring gains created by the greater weight given to each new, more complex group. Indeed, if the total weighted score is compared with the number of groups, as in Table 18, the ratio hovers consistently around 2.5:1. The conclusion is clear: Simple differentiation of groups has occurred over time as the Parliament has been enlarged and the number of districts increased, but the share of the more complex groups in this expanding arena, although it has expanded absolutely, has remained constant relative to the shares of other types of groups.

Caucuses and Organized Parties

Let us look specifically at the appearances of caucus and organized party representation in the electoral arena. The number of such groups (both strong and weak) in each of the seven elections is shown in Table 19.

Two conclusions may be drawn from the data in Table 19. The locus of organized electoral politics is overwhelmingly the Beirut–Mount Lebanon area, which has the highest social mobilization and yet relatively poor voting participation. The appearance of more complex forms has also shown an upward trend. The rate of appearance of such forms accelerated after the fall of Bechara al-Khoury in 1952 and increased sharply again after the accession of General Chehab in 1958. Still, as we have seen, the rate of increase of the more complex group forms is absolute, not rela-

TABLE 19

CAUCUS AND ORGANIZED PARTY REPRESENTATION IN PARLIAMENTARY ELECTIONS

NUMBER OF GROUPS

Caucus	1943	1947	1951	1953	1957	1960	1964
Beirut-Mount Lebanon	2	3	5	6	6	13	12
North-South-Biqa	0	0	0	0	0	1	3
Party							
Beirut-Mount Lebanon	3	6	6	12	12	12	12
North-South-Biqa	0	1	0	2	3	5	8
Total	5	10	11	20	21	31	35

tive, and it only mirrors the increased differentiation of all competitive groups, including individuals and lists. Furthermore, few of the party groups have ever won seats, and, though Table 19 suggests that there is a degree of openness in the process, it also shows that the process screens out new elements. The Communists have run a few candidates in every election since 1943 and never won a seat; the P.P.S. entered the Chamber officially as late as 1957 (though they seem to have supported their ex-member Ghassan Tueni, who was elected in 1951 and 1953); and the Kataeb did not succeed in electing a deputy until 1953. Only the Armenian Tashnaq has consistently returned candidates to the Chamber. The major caucus groups have fared no better. The Destour virtually disappears as a discrete organization after 1952, though a number of important leaders continue to claim affiliation with the old Khoury machine; and the National Bloc, excluded from power under Khoury, re-emerges in 1953, though virtually indistinguishable—except in the sophistication of its leaders—from the traditional lists.

Strong and Weak Organizations

The hypothesis that political development means stronger institutions does not necessarily mean that these institutions must be closer to modern Western rationalistic types. One could argue convincingly that a trend toward stronger traditional organizations serves the same ends of political stability and even national development. With this qualification in mind, the group structure in the electoral process has been broken down in terms of strong and weak institutions (Table 20).

TABLE 20

INCIDENCE OF STRONG ORGANIZATIONS IN LEBANESE
ELECTION CAMPAIGNS*

Region	WEIGHTED PERCENTAGE OF STRONG INDIVIDUALS, LISTS, CAUCUSES, AND PARTIES OUT OF TOTAL SCORES						
	1943	*1947*	*1951*	*1953*	*1957*	*1960*	*1964*
Beirut-Mount Lebanon	43.7	25.8	58.2	56.9	38.3	62.7	56.9
North-South-Biqa	100.0	80.0	91.6	76.1	74.0	72.3	71.3
National	61.7	42.2	67.7	64.2	54.0	66.1	64.1

* Calculations are percentage of total group *scores* accounted for by strong groups of all types. By weighting the scores as described in the text, an attempt has been made to count more heavily the appearance of, for example, a strong party as opposed to a strong list.

Table 20 indicates that the national level of group strength in the electoral process has generally remained constant, suggesting that there has been no relative decline of strong (cohesive and successful) organizations. The rural areas appear consistently more highly organized than the Beirut–Mount Lebanon area (especially Beirut): There are fewer loose coalitions in the rural picture. The developed areas are showing a slight tendency toward higher organization over time, whereas organizational strength in the rural areas is declining somewhat; there was, in short, a distinct tendency toward convergence by 1964. In organizational complexity the two Lebanons are becoming more alike: Organizations in Beirut and Mount Lebanon are tightening up; in North Lebanon, South Lebanon, and the Biqa they are loosening. Nevertheless, in 1964, as in 1943, the strong list—composed of notables generally without modern political party affiliations—remained the dominant form of organization, especially in the rural areas; and with a handful of rare exceptions its dominance has not been challenged by non-traditional organizations.

PARLIAMENTARY MEMBERSHIP

As the politically relevant stratum has increased in size, new sources of power have been created, new philosophies have been articulated, and new expectations have been created concerning public institutions. Are the formal representative institutions opening up to a new political generation? If in fact they are, one might expect to observe increasing numbers of new men in Parliament; shifts in the membership away from the old men toward the post-Ottoman, and indeed post-Mandate, generations; shifts away from the traditional elite occupational bases of land and law; and shifts toward more deputies and ministers with modern political orientation—affiliation with caucuses and organized parties and not just with traditional cliques. An examination of the parliamentary and Cabinet membership in the independence period will indicate whether or not such trends are actually occurring.

The Chamber of Deputies warrants first consideration. Although this institution may not actually govern Lebanon, its members still play an important part in keeping the delicate political situation in order. As the principal mediator between the rulers and the ruled, the Lebanese Parliament—like all legislatures—must represent the real political forces in the country to some extent if the system is to remain coherent. A brief description of precisely who the Lebanese Chamber of Deputies represents and of the extent to which its representational base is changing with Lebanon's changing society will indicate how well the Chamber fulfills its prime function.

The cohesion of Lebanon's parliamentary elite is apparent at a glance. Interlocking relationships based on marriage, education, region, sect, and occupational interests make it very difficult to single out distinct types within the elite. The typical Lebanese deputy is about fifty years old, bilingual, and university educated, usually in the French tradition. He probably holds a law degree, but, even if he actually practices law as a profession, he is not prevented from engaging in banking, business, and above all politics. The typical deputy calls himself an "independent," thus making political distinctions hard to draw. At least 85 per cent of the elite are affiliated with a traditional political bloc or faction, and at least 95 per cent do not belong to a modern political party.

With certain exceptions, the prevailing political attitudes cluster well to the right of center in American terms.

The New-Entry Rate

The number and percentage of newcomers in each of the seven Parliaments are presented in Table 21. The significance of the

TABLE 21

NEW ENTRANTS IN SEVEN LEBANESE PARLIAMENTS*

	1943	1947	1951	1953	1957	1960	1964
Number	31	22	45	12	26	52	29
Percentage	52.6	40.0	56.3	27.3	39.4	52.0	29.3

* A new entrant is a man appearing for the first time in any Lebanese Parliament, including those during the French Mandate. The percentages are calculated against total membership figures that do not quite coincide with the number of seats, owing to occasional mid-term replacements.

turnover rates may be briefly stated. They are very high compared to older and more mature parliamentary systems. The percentage of new entrants in the British House of Commons, for example, ranged between 2.1 per cent and 11.1 per cent in the period 1950–1959.[9] The Lebanese rate has fluctuated between 27 and 56 per cent in the same period. Lebanon is thus more similar to its neighbor Syria, whose new-entry rates in the same period fluctuated between 42 and 79 per cent.[10] The Lebanese new-entry rate also fluctuates widely and unpredictably over time. For all the homogeneity of its members, then, there is incessant change in the Lebanese parliamentary elite, a symptom of the system's fluidity. This constant fluctuation in membership hinders the effectiveness of Parliament by impairing consistency in legislation and breeds a tangible public cynicism. The more the Parliament changes the more it stagnates, people say; and they console themselves with the thought that less change would be even worse. Given this legislative merry-go-round it at first seems strange that Lebanon's radicals should complain that the turnover rates are too low; what they are demanding, of course, is an infusion of modernists and reformers, not just the sons of the old bosses.

These rates of turnover are not spread evenly throughout the Chamber. Key positions like committee chairmanships are monopolized by a band of parliamentary veterans who are perennially returned from their safe districts. Thirty-five of these perennials have sat in an average of 4.6 (out of 7) Parliaments; or, putting it another way, nearly one-third of the seats available have been occupied by 14 per cent of all the deputies elected to those 7 Parliaments. Legislative power is thus monopolized by a few, rendering the apparent change even less meaningful than it might otherwise seem.

Age

The Parliamentary elite of the 1960s is older than that of the 1940s. The mean age has risen from forty-six in the 1943 Parliament to fifty in the 1964 Parliament.[11] Of course, this dimension of change is not dramatic and in fact can be interpreted as a sign that the electoral processes are producing a more mature elite. In the United States 86th Congress, which might be considered mature, the members averaged 51.9 years of age.[12] Furthermore, it is an obvious but important fact that a greater percentage of deputies have been born in "modern" times. If one should arbitrarily choose a birth date of 1910 as the dividing line between the men raised in a traditional era and those raised in the post-Ottoman world, one would find that the post-Ottoman deputies accounted for 10.3 per cent of the 1943 Parliament and that the percentage has increased steadily through 1964, when post-Ottoman deputies accounted for 64.3 per cent of the Chamber's membership. Such qualifications, although they may put the age change in better perspective, do not impress the younger generation, whose formative years are not only post-Ottoman but also postcolonial and who see access to Lebanon's establishment blocked by "old" men, old in both age and outlook. Half the Lebanese population is under 20 years of age; even the somewhat more youthful entrance age of parliamentary newcomers (44.9 years) seems antique by comparison.

Educational Level

The high educational level of the deputies is impressive and testifies to the exclusive nature of the parliamentary establishment. About 63 per cent of all the new men elected between 1943 and 1964 held higher degrees, and most of the rest had secondary schooling.[13] The Beirut–Mount Lebanon deputies were somewhat more highly educated than were those from North Lebanon, South Lebanon, and the Biqa: Of the deputies elected from the two modernized areas, 81.2 and 73.2 per cent had higher degrees, whereas the percentages of such deputies from the three outlying areas were 45.8, 62.8, and 46.4, respectively. The Christian deputies were 66.9 per cent university educated, compared with 55.9 per cent for the non-Christian deputies. The Greek Catholics were the most highly educated Christian sect, and the Sunnites were the most highly educated non-Christian sect. The levels remained relatively constant over time among all regions and sects.

Occupational Background

Stronger evidence for a shift in elite composition may be found by studying the occupational backgrounds of Lebanese deputies. At first glance the seven independence Parliaments all look alike in occupational terms: They are aggregations of wealthy landowners, lawyers, businessmen, and well-to-do professionals; and, indeed, this picture is approximately correct for either the 1943 or the 1964 Parliament.[14] Consistently absent are small businessmen, laborers, small farmers, peasants, and women.[15] In the entire roster of 251 deputies from 1943 through 1964, there were only 9 who come from such groups.

Within the elite occupations represented by parliamentary deputies there is a shift away from the traditional and parochial and toward the achievement oriented and sophisticated, as Table 22 shows. The landed proprietors have declined almost by half in relative terms, although their numerical representation remains fairly constant. At the other end of the elite occupational spectrum, professionals (doctors, teachers, engineers, civil servants, salaried employees, and a few full-time politicians) have increased both numerically and relatively. The shift is a muted echo of the more dramatic diversification of power in Lebanese society. This trend is a hopeful indication that the establishment is slightly more receptive than it used to be to politicians who rise outside the traditional prestige occupations of land, law, and finance.

Because Lebanon has in effect a presidential system, there is some point in comparing the parliamentary elite composition in the three presidential regimes of the independence period. At the same time, one may compare the parliamentary-elite composition of areas of high and low social mobilization (Beirut–Mount Lebanon and North Lebanon, South Lebanon, and the Biqa, respectively). This comparison is made in Table 23. The number of landlords fell off most sharply between the Khoury and the Chamoun regimes, both in absolute and relative terms. Under General Chehab, the

TABLE 22

OCCUPATIONS OF DEPUTIES*

Occupation	1943 PARLIAMENT		1947 PARLIAMENT		1951 PARLIAMENT		1953 PARLIAMENT		1957 PARLIAMENT		1960 PARLIAMENT		1964 PARLIAMENT	
	No.	Percentage of Total Membership	No.	Percentage of Total Membership	No.	Percentage of Total Membership	No.	Percentage of Total Membership	No.	Percentage of Total Membership	No.	Percentage of Total Membership	No.	Percentage of Total Membership
Land	31	52.5	29	52.7	36	45.0	18	40.9	22	33.3	26	27.0	28	28.3
Law	23	39.0	17	30.9	29	36.2	20	45.4	26	39.4	27	27.0	30	30.3
Business	19	32.2	14	25.4	28	35.0	12	27.3	12	18.2	27	27.0	31	31.3
Professional	15	25.4	15	27.3	23	28.7	13	29.5	19	28.8	43	43.0	42	42.3
Total No. of Deputies	59		55		80		44		66		100		99	

* Percentages exceed 100, and numbers exceed the actual number of deputies because many deputies have more than one occupation.

Library of Parliament; Ahmad Haidar, *Al-dawlah al-lubnāniyyah* [*The Lebanese State*] (Beirut: Nijmeh, 1954); *L'Orient*; Bureau des Documentations Libanaises et Arabes; and *Who's Who in Lebanon, 1963–64* (Beirut: Editions Publitec, 1964). I have presented these data in cruder form in "The Electoral Process and Political Development in Lebanon," *Middle East Journal*, 20 (Winter 1966), 173–86; there I allowed a deputy only one occupation. As additional biographical information accumulated, this practice appeared increasingly arbitrary, even though it produced the same trends evident here but more sharply.

TABLE 23

PARLIAMENTARY ELITE BY REGIME, REGION, AND OCCUPATION, 1943–1964

Occupation	Province	BECHARA AL-KHOURY 1943, 1947, 1951			CAMILLE CHAMOUN 1953, 1957			FUAD CHEHAB 1960, 1964		
		Total Positions	*No.*	*Percentage of Deputies from Region*	*Total Positions*	*No.*	*Percentage of Deputies from Region*	*Total Positions*	*No.*	*Percentage of Deputies from Region*
Land	Beirut-ML *	93	28	30.1	52	10	19.2	93	11	11.8
	NL †-SL §-Bq **	102	68	66.6	58	30	51.7	106	43	40.6
Law	Beirut-ML	93	38	40.8	52	27	51.9	93	36	38.7
	NL-SL-Bq	102	31	30.4	58	19	32.7	106	21	19.8
Business	Beirut-ML	93	39	41.9	52	15	28.8	93	28	30.1
	NL-SL-Bq	102	22	21.6	58	17	29.5	106	30	28.3
Professional	Beirut-ML	93	38	40.9	52	20	38.5	93	44	47.3
	NL-SL-Bq	102	15	14.7	58	12	20.7	106	41	38.7

* ML = Mount Lebanon.
† NL = North Lebanon.
§ SL = South Lebanon.
** Bq = Biqa.

relative decline in the number of landlords continued, though the absolute number increased somewhat. It is notable that landlords retained 40 per cent of the rural positions even under the Chehab regime. The number of lawyers declined relatively during all regimes but rose in absolute terms in the Chehab regime, whereas the number of businessmen diminished over time in the Beirut–Mount Lebanon area and slightly increased in the outlying regions. The number of professionals increased generally but relatively faster in North Lebanon, South Lebanon, and the Biqa.

Table 23 indicates that the occupational shift is not uniform by region. Beirut and Mount Lebanon have elected many fewer landlords to the seven parliaments than have the outlying regions, averaging 23.9 per cent and 19.1 per cent respectively, compared with percentages of 52.8, 48.7, and 59.2 in North Lebanon, South Lebanon, and the Biqa. The rate of decline in the number of landlords has been much higher in the outlying areas, however, and the relative rise in the number of professionals has been much greater there. Beirut and Mount Lebanon thus seem to exhibit greater consistency in the occupational affiliations of the candidates they elect than do the rural districts. This finding is perhaps an ominous one, for one might expect the area of high social mobilization to show more change than the relatively quiet hinterland. If the hinterland is not really as quiet as it seems, then its relative neglect ought to be ended. The lawyers and businessmen were slightly more concentrated among the deputies in the Beirut–Mount Lebanon area than in the other three provinces.

There are also notable occupational differences between the Christian and the non-Christian deputies. Non-Christian landlord representation declined much faster than did Christian landlord representation between 1943 and 1967. The percentage of Christian deputies who are lawyers has declined, whereas law as an occupational base among non-Christian deputies has somewhat increased, reflecting no doubt the fact that the legal profession has become more accessible to non-Christians in recent years. There is no significant shift in the business and finance representation: For Christians this base remains consistently more important than for Sunnites, Shiites, and Druzes.[16] Interestingly, the rate of increase of deputies from the professions is roughly the same for Christians and non-Christians. The nonlegal professions seem thus to have about equal political relevance for the elite of both religions, in clear contrast to land (which is more important for Muslims than for Christians) and law and business (which are better political bases for Christians than for non-Christians). By looking at the distribution over time it is possible to plot the changing recruitment patterns within the two communities. Among the Christians through 1957 law and business are the chief occupational bases from which deputies are recruited, but in 1960 and 1964 the nonlegal professions take first place by a narrow margin. Through 1957 the greatest number of non-Christian deputies was in the landowner category (although in the small Parliament of 1953 there was an equal number of lawyers), but in 1960 the steadily increasing category of professionals became the largest occupational group. The 1958 crisis has proved to be a kind of watershed in the recruitment process for Christian and non-Christian deputies alike. These trends can be more clearly shown by comparing the occupational composition of new deputies over time by religion. As might be expected, among the non-Christian newcomers the number of landlords is declining even faster than among all non-Christians in particular parliaments. From the beginning of independence, the professions have provided a better base for election to Parliament for non-Christians than for Christians. The percentage of Christians and non-Christians who are lawyers has become nearly equal, though in 1943 law was primarily a means to power for Christians.

Finally, let us compare the occupational shifts in the two major sects, Maronite Christians and Sunnite Muslims, the two most politically important religious communities. During the Khoury regime land and the nonlegal professions were the dominant political backgrounds among the Sunnite deputies, whereas by 1964 there was a fairly even distribution among all four occupational groups, because land had declined as the other three advanced. Maronites have retained throughout the period a consistent and substantial landed representation in the Chamber, despite the near absence of feudalism in Mount Lebanon. There are, of course, concentrations of Maronites in all the outlying regions, particularly North Lebanon. The Maronites, too, have exhibited an increasingly even distribution of occupational origin, marked by the relative decline in the number of lawyers and the rise in the number of nonlegal professionals. This gradual equalization of occupational categories in the two major sects may be taken as an indication of the slight broadening of access to Parliament during the independence period.

Political Orientation

The great majority of Lebanon's parliamentary deputies have no political orientation beyond the list or clique that got them elected. Nevertheless, there is some indication that the proportion of deputies with more sophisticated political orientation has been increasing since about 1949, when the Khoury machine began to deteriorate rapidly. As noted earlier, it is difficult in Lebanon to specify when a traditional clique has metamorphosed into a more modern political organization. It is similarly difficult to decide whether a deputy's political orientation, regardless of his opinions, is archaic or modern. To reveal this political orientation, the membership of the seven independence parliaments has been evaluated (in Table 24) against

TABLE 24

PERCENTAGE OF DEPUTIES WITH "MODERN" ORIENTATION,
1943–1964 *

PARLIAMENT

Standard of Classification	1943	1947	1951	1953	1957	1960	1964
Generous							
Number	15	6	22	11	13	35	30
Percentage	27.3	10.9	28.8	25.0	19.7	35.3	30.3
Restrictive							
Number	2	2	9	6	7	23	20
Percentage	3.6	3.6	11.7	13.6	10.6	23.2	20.2
Number of deputies	55	55	77	44	66	99	99

* The classification, particularly in the early Parliaments, is difficult because the caucus memberships shifted a good deal. I have tried to include as Destourians only those consistently associated with Bechara al-Khoury and his group and have excluded some (in 1947, 1953, and 1957 especially) who had gone off in other directions. The "restrictive" listing is less arbitrary and includes individuals who were party members, were supported by parties, or were fairly clearly affiliated with organized parties. For example, I counted Ghassan Tueni in 1951 and 1953 as a P.P.S. candidate, even though he was no longer an actual member of the P.P.S., and I counted Naim Mughabghab in 1957 as an affiliate of the P.P.S., even though he was not their candidate. I did count Kamal Jumblat with the National Bloc in 1943, though he bolted during the crisis with France three months later. I did not count him in 1947, but I have counted him as head of the P.S.P. from 1951 onwards. This classification is generally consistent with that of Michael W. Suleiman, *Political Parties in Lebanon* (Ithaca: Cornell University Press, 1967), p. 265.

two standards of political orientation, one generous and the other restrictive in its definition of a nontraditional political affiliation. The generous standard assumes that any deputy who is (or was, even for a brief period) affiliated with a caucus group or organized party should be counted as one of the "modern" group.[17] The restrictive standard admits to the modern group only those deputies affiliated with an organized party and excludes notables identified with the old caucus groups. According to the generous classification, roughly one-third of the deputies have held affiliations beyond the strictly parochial at some time during the two decades, but there is no discernible trend. The figures reflect the country's basic political structure: Beirut and Mount Lebanon have supported an active caucus politics, which has been concerned mainly with the questions of national independence and the interpretation of the National Pact; in the traditional rural areas nonmodern regional cliques and client groups remain the dominant forms. Beirut and Mount Lebanon supply nearly all the deputies that are included as modern under either the generous or the restrictive classification. Furthermore, the overwhelming majority of the modern deputies are Christians. The restrictive classification reveals a trend toward increasing representation of the modern deputies. According to this classification, these affiliates of organized parties come from even more diverse sectarian and geographical backgrounds than do the deputies who are considered modern according to the generous classification: There are proportionally fewer deputies who are Christian and fewer who come from the Beirut–Mount Lebanon area, even though these deputies still account for the bulk of the "restrictively modern" type. This weak trend is indicative of a certain broadening of the electoral process, but it should not be overstressed: The fact remains that in the middle 1960s fewer than one fourth of the Lebanese deputies have party affiliations.

Barriers to Innovation and Adjustment

Lebanon's electoral trends are cause for what W. S. Gilbert might have called "modified rapture." The sectarian list system keeps primordial conflicts under control. Voting participation increases, and elections occur regularly, suggesting a degree of successful institutionalization. Electoral competition shows moderate improvement over time without producing either chaos or stalemate. The trend toward factional proliferation suggests the development of a more complex and stable system. As for the parliamentary elite, it shows both continuity and change. Furthermore, the contemporary Lebanese electoral process is thoroughly rooted in Lebanon's communal structure. Every deputy has a vast network of poor cousins who feel a special attachment to their successful namesake and who in fact often do benefit from his position. One might not believe that these traditional points of access still exist unless he had seen numerous deputies receiving rooms full of constituents. The parliamentary elite is by no means as unresponsive to public wishes as the exclusive composition of its membership might imply.

Nevertheless, this happy picture is flawed. The limited effectiveness and the dysfunctional aspects of the electoral system have already been discussed. The electoral process, furthermore, actually perpetuates rather than resolves Lebanon's political dilemma. Two facts should be amply clear from the preceding discussion. First, the institutionalization of traditional pluralism is essential to the stability that in turn is necessary for national development. Second, whereas the electoral and parliamentary institutions carry out the institutionalization functions associated with stability, they do not do so very well. As mechanisms for conflict resolution among the establishment notables they perform a difficult task with considerable success, but as devices for recruiting and integrating a growing nontraditional political stratum they leave much to be desired, notwithstanding the limited trends toward adjustment and broadening in this area. There are three formidable barriers to greater innovation and adjustment: the exclusion of organized, nontraditional politicians, deeply ingrained corruption, and high election costs.

Exclusion of Organized, Nontraditional Politicians

The only aspect of Lebanese society that is badly represented in Parliament is the political element. Paradoxical as such a statement may appear, it points up a very real weakness in the system. Just as Lebanese society has become more complex, so has its politically active stratum become stronger and more highly differentiated. It is true that there is a trend toward the increasing representation of "modern" political types, but the discussion of Table 24 indicated that this trend is rather feeble. One might have thought that the shift away from a large representation of landlords in favor of professionals would be accompanied by an increas-

ing politicization of the Chamber and especially a strengthening of
"progressive" political ideas. Even if the occupational shift were
to succeed in transforming Parliament, however, it would be impossible to predict its political orientation. The fact is that there is no
correlation between socioeconomic background and political opinion
in the Chamber or cabinet. A feudal landlord is the founder and
mainstay of the Progressive Socialist Party, and he has been supported by lawyers and bankers. The most conservative deputies
are doctors. Lawyers are found supporting all causes. Whatever
increase there has been in the number of deputies with modern
political ideas and affiliations, it does not seem to be related to
the change in the occupational backgrounds of the new men.

Perhaps it is unfair to condemn an institution for excluding what
in fact does not exist. Lebanon may have "parties," but it does not
have a party system. The structural and environmental conditions
of the parliamentary and electoral mechanisms are, to say the
least, not conducive to the development of rationalized party organizations. All parties that are represented owe their survival to
traditional appeals to some extent. Members of the middle-class
intelligentsia find association with such parties self-defeating, yet
without organized support they cannot break into politics. Their
lack of representation in Parliament only contributes to the weakness of that institution in the total system and therefore the weakness of the total system itself. Two examples may clarify the
problems that members of the modern stratum face in the electoral
process.

In one case, a young Druze university professor was a candidate
in the 1960 election. The professor, whose father was a businessman, had taken a doctorate in the United States. He ran as an
independent in Aley, a town just above Beirut. In his own analysis, this man had to run on the basis of his ideas and skills as a professor, for he did not have the influence of an *amir* or a *bey* and was
not extraordinarily rich, nor did he wish to compromise his principles by joining the clique of an established notable. Unfortunately
for his chances, Aley is in the electoral territory of Amir Majid
Arslan, who represents the Yazbaki faction of the Druze sect. A
list supported by Kamal Jumblat, leader of the rival Druze faction and head of the Progressive Socialist Party, was also competing. Although the town of Aley itself is Christian, the surrounding
area is mostly Yazbaki Druze. Under such circumstances it was
unlikely that an independent, especially a Druze, could win; for

the majority of the Druzes would support Amir Majid on traditional grounds, and the remainder would be pulled into the camp of Kamal Bey. Because both Majid Arslan and Kamal Jumblat are powerful traditional leaders and exert strong "coattail" effects and because both were putting up Christian candidates as well (the Arslan list had important support from former President Camille Chamoun), it was unlikely that a Druze independent could pull enough of the Christian vote to win. The results were more favorable than the professor expected, but he still lost badly. Whereas all the candidates on the Arslan list won, polling between 8,000 and 16,400 votes each, and the Jumblat-P.S.P. candidates received between 6,900 and 8,400 each, the professor won 4,674 votes. Most of these votes, he suspected, were from the younger and better-educated groups, and not more than 1,000 of them were Druze. Why did the professor run under such unfavorable circumstances? Part of his motivation was simply ambition; he also wanted to further the interests of the Druze community. Finally, as he put it, he wanted to "give something to his country." In particular, he wanted to strengthen the civil service and reduce the patronage power of the deputies. Reflecting on the campaign after his defeat, he decided that one of his mistakes had been not to run on a list. The only alternative was to run as an individual. Instead of adapting traditional means for a reformist end, the professor had tried to organize an independent campaign and lost. If there had been a nontraditional party or organization to put up a list of like-minded progressive candidates, he might have won.

The second case is the campaign for a Sunnite seat in Beirut's second district in 1964, and the candidate was a highly articulate, well-educated, Sunnite Muslim. He may be described as a "Lebanese progressive" and was one of the bright young men who had been recruited into public service to undertake President Chehab's modernization of the state. As an editor, he was a strong defender of the army against charges from conservative Christian notables that it was interfering in politics. His campaign was planned long in advance of the election, and he worked assiduously to build up his reputation as a modernist but one who did not want to upset the political status quo. Some years before the 1964 elections he had attempted unsuccessfully to organize a political party. In 1964, it was the lack of a party organization that ensured his defeat.

Beirut's second district, after the redistricting of 1960, was a small "catch-all" district, which elected a Shiite, a minority Christian, and a Sunnite deputy. The first and third districts, on the other hand, were in effect reserved for the Kataeb-dominated Christian leaders and the more influential Sunnite notables respectively. There were no lists in the second district, although there were very weak associations among some of the candidates, and the district was mostly Christian but not heavily Maronite. In the previous election, Beirut's second district had returned three progressives, including a member of the Progressive Socialist Party and a member of the Najjadeh. Because the traditional and sectarian factors were somewhat weaker there than elsewhere, it seemed a sensible district from which a rising modern politician might seek election. Traditional factors, however, still proved strong enough to defeat the modernist Sunnite candidate. He had been opposed by "Papa" Sami Sulh, a man who was once one of the top Sunnite leaders but who had lost a great deal of influence among Sunnites through his association with President Chamoun. Among the minority groups, especially the Christians, however, he was still regarded with affection, especially in comparison to the other Sunnite candidates. The young modernist was also opposed by Adnan Hakim, chief of the Najjadeh, the pan-Islamic political party, a man not greatly beloved by Christians. Compared with his rivals the newcomer was a moderate, secular progressive. In this election, however, secular progressivism was no match for traditional personalities and even fragmentary alliances. Sami Sulh won with 5,403 votes; Hakim was a close second with 5,337; and the newcomer received 2,339. It is probable that Sulh won most of the Christian votes and Hakim most of the Sunnite votes, leaving the newcomer with no substantial body of support. Actually, the outcome was slightly more complex. Sami Sulh had allied informally with the old Shiite notable, Rashid Beydoun. Beydoun, in turn, had associated with the candidate running for the seat allotted jointly to all the sects that were too small for separate representation, Farid Jibran, who was allied with the Druze leader, Kamal Jumblat. Sulh, through clever alliances, thus attracted to himself a share of the entire non-Sunnite —Shiite and Druze—vote in the district, as well as the Christian vote. Hakim and his former co-lister Mohsen Slim, a Shiite also known for his radical views, found to their dismay that radicalism was no longer popular in the second district and that people apparently preferred the old, dependable, and harmless candidates. This shift in opinion also doubtless hurt the moderate progressive candidate. The backing of an organized party might have enabled this "new man" to overcome his electoral obstacles; lacking such a coherent organization, he did not have a chance.

Corruption and Coercion

Corruption is a distinctive feature of the Lebanese political system.[18] It takes many forms, from vote buying to fairly severe intimidation. Corrupt practices may be seen as a kind of degenerate substitute for rationalized political organization; both the regime and the opposition resort to them in an attempt to control opposition factions. Both also find corruption a useful tool in breaking the grip of incumbents who are not likely to be turned out of office by the "free" workings of the ballot box. Useful as it is to short-run system maintenance, corruption is dysfunctional to Lebanon's political modernization in the long run. Prolonged experience with governmental corruption contributes significantly to the popular cynicism and disillusionment that deprive the political institutions of legitimacy. We shall give a few examples to demonstrate the accuracy of this conclusion.

Vote buying is certainly a normal electoral practice in Lebanon, particularly in the highly competitive districts where victory may hinge on a few hundred votes. The low incomes of most voters stimulate the practice, and a vicious circle of cynicism perpetuates it. A poor man who sells his vote for L£100 (U.S. $33) can feed himself for perhaps one month. Several well-known politicians (interviewed in 1962 and 1965) admitted quite freely to allocating certain amounts for vote buying. They regretted the necessity but argued that it was standard practice in their districts. One complained that the price of votes has been going up rapidly in recent years, but then so has the income of politicians. In any case, the practice is still widespread, particularly in Zahleh and parts of Beirut, both developed, Westernized areas.

Negative pressures are also common: They range from hiring away all the taxis to keep an opponent's supporters from the polls to murdering political opponents. In this kind of behavior, as in bribery, the Lebanese were well tutored by the French. Mandate elections were not noted for their purity.[19] The last election held under Mandate auspices (1943) was described by a participant, one of the veterans of Lebanese politics, as among the worst he had ever encountered in terms of official interference and pressures.[20] The elections of May 25, 1947, however, stand above all the others before or since as a model for ingenious corruption. The spirit of that campaign is best illustrated by the following excerpt from a Beirut magazine article, entitled "How to Choose Your Deputies: Necessary, Precise Instructions":

—Every voter who is on the list can participate—dead or alive.
—Voters may cast more than one ballot, depending on the situation.
—You don't have to carry your Lebanese identity card because all Arabs are brothers.
—The ballot box can have more than one opening; it is best if it has two —one for deposits and one for withdrawals.
—No voter may cast more than 10 ballots.
—Never say who won or lost—even if one man is 10 times ahead of the other—until an official declaration is made.[21]

After the balloting, which was dubbed, "the operation of May 25th," the opposition National Bloc charged: "By means of negotiations, intimidation, and all sorts of intervention the Government has succeeded in destroying the opposition in many districts or in forcing the candidates to withdraw." [22] Lists of registered voters had not been sent to the village councils on time. In some cases the location of the polling place was not revealed until election day, and then it was inaccessible. The date of the election itself was not announced far in advance. There was ballot box stuffing, minor violence in the polling areas, and interference by election officials, gendarmerie, police, and *mukhtars*. Three days before the election a National Bloc meeting in Jbeil was broken up by police and its speaker, Raymond Edde, was arrested. The opposition press claimed that the government had forged 30,000 new identity cards and was also using the identity cards of 3,700 Armenians repatriated to the Soviet Union. In his memoirs, President Khoury concedes that some irregularities occurred, especially in Mount Lebanon, but he claims that they did not affect the results significantly.[23]

Although in no subsequent election have there been such brazen violations as in the 1947 vote, neither have they all been free of various sorts of coercion. Every election and its aftermath produces conflict ranging from simple threats to violence and murder. In 1953, for example, a landed political boss from North Lebanon, Muhammad Abboud, was gunned down in broad daylight in Beirut, the victim of a political feud with his cousin. The 1957 elections were carried out with unmistakable government interference as the interior situation deteriorated.[24] Opposition groups had to obtain permission from the Ministry of Defense to hold public meetings;

candidates were forbidden to speak outside their own districts. The opposition announced it would defy the government restrictions on public meetings, and it staged a big rally on May 30. Violence broke out, and the army moved in to restore order; two people were killed, and a number were injured, including one of the major leaders, Saeb Salam.

In another incident, an opposition P.S.P. candidate in Beirut recalls that he was labeled a communist and that the government jailed his followers every time he held a public meeting because the Communist Party was outlawed. On election day itself, he recalls, the government resorted to numerous devices to harry the opposition. Every candidate was supposed to supply an observer for each of Beirut's 250 polling places; on the night before the election 160 of this candidate's observers were arrested. Intimidation of voters reached new heights of ingenuity.[25] Following the balloting in Mount Lebanon on June 16, 1957, the two "neutrals" who had been added to the Cabinet to ensure fair elections resigned.[26] Shortly after that election, the combination of family feuds with national politics resulted in the massacre of seventeen Maronites in a church near Zagharta; ten members of the (pro-Chamoun) Duaihy family and seven from the rival (anti-Chamoun) clans of Frangieh and Moawad were killed.

After the 1958 crisis and during the Chehab regime, violence continued to be a hazard of parliamentary life. When a pro-Jumblat mob assassinated a pro-Chamoun deputy, Naim Mughabghab, in July 1959, he was replaced by a pro-Jumblat deputy. Chehab's regime was also marred by other assaults on certain opposition deputies and journalists. The 1960 and 1964 elections were accompanied by the usual irregularities, but a new factor was present. The military appeared to be taking more than professional interest in the outcome of certain campaigns. The National Bloc leader, Raymond Edde—a man long accustomed to governmental pressures—accused the army of trying to arrange his defeat in Jbeil in the 1960 and 1964 general elections and in the by-election of 1965.

All in all, bribery, coercion, and other forms of corruption are quite common in the electoral process, and nobody is very surprised when new instances are pointed out. There can be no doubt, however, that they have tended to hinder the legitimization of government in general—the civil service and the courts as well as

Parliament and the military—and encouraged a cynicism that is dysfunctional for political modernization.

High Campaign Costs

The cost of running for Parliament—exorbitant in relation to the living standard—can best be illustrated by some figures. In the first place, the annual per capita income was about $400 in the early 1960s, and only 3 per cent of the work force had an annual income exceeding $3,300. A candidate in recent years has been obliged to make a $1,000 deposit in order to run at all, and it is refundable only if he receives at least 20 per cent of the total vote. This requirement alone—in the absence of strong political parties that might contribute a deposit for nonelite candidates—militates against the candidacy of the newly politicized professionals, not to mention the ordinary people. Lebanon's folklore hero, a shrewd old mountain peasant named Abu Khalil, could never be elected to Parliament unless the market for his apples greatly improved. The registration fee is only the first barrier to nonestablishment candidacies. Campaign expenses alone make Lebanese elections among the most expensive in the world, calculated on a per capita basis. Assuming conservatively that each of the 267 candidates who took part in the 1960 elections spent about L£40,000, the whole election may have cost candidates about L£10,680,000. This figure comes to a per capita campaign cost of L£5.34, or about $1.78, for every Lebanese citizen in a population of 2 million, and it may be compared with Alexander Heard's estimate for the per capita expenditure in election campaigns in the United States ($0.90), West Germany ($0.25), Italy ($0.50), and Israel (more than $5.00).[27] A more sophisticated but still conservative calculation for the same election gives a total of L£16,635,000, which comes to L£8.32 ($2.77) per capita.[28] A deputy from Aley reported he spent L£100,000 both in 1957 and 1960; a major Beirut notable reported spending L£70,000 to finance his election to Parliament. Independent estimates suggest that these figures are on the low side. Other individual deputies in 1960 were said to have spent sums varying from L£12,000, to L£800,000.[29] By 1964, election costs seemed to have risen appreciably. One major Beirut list reportedly spent between L£1 million and L£1.5 million during the 1964 campaign and two independent notables L£1 million between them. A veteran election reporter estimated that individual candidates in Beirut were spending about L£120,000 on the average.[30] Whatever figures one prefers, one can only conclude that people in the middle- and lower-income groups cannot run for office in Lebanon without outside assistance, and outside assistance can only come from either the patricians or from foreign sources as long as there are no organized, mass-based parties. Why are elections so expensive? Although vote buying and other corrupt practices are common, legitimate expenses alone are still heavy. In the rural areas a major outlay is hiring caravans of cars to "whistle stop" in the numerous villages. On election day itself, it is customary for the candidates to provide taxi service for the voters to the polling place. Because a great many provincial voters live in Beirut, these costs can be heavy. Other expenses include posters, badges, rental fees for public halls, and refreshments.[31] High costs as well as the web of tradition thus exclude from the parliamentary elite representatives of the newly politicized elements in Lebanon.

CONCLUSION

A shortage of politicians is nothing to complain about in the opinion of most Lebanese. The majority of the Lebanese citizens feel that all politicians are bad. If Parliament and Cabinet are to perform the essential representative function in Lebanon's political system, however, the more politicians—good or bad—in the establishment, the better. President Chehab reportedly decided that Lebanese political life could be most quickly improved by putting as many of the traditional leaders in the Cabinet as possible, even if they didn't speak to each other, because their presence would increase general stability. Chehab felt that, under a strong presidential system, the accompanying tendency to *immobilisme* would not impair policy making. The same lesson could be applied to the new political elements. As modernization progresses the entire Lebanese population—educated and uneducated alike—is confronting serious new problems and learning new doctrines. If a serious economic crisis in Lebanon promotes social unrest, a system whose representative institutions are inaccessible to new social forces is in danger. One does not need to argue that the unemployed liberal-arts major is a potential revolutionary—though the history of the P.P.S. in Lebanon and its two attempted *coups d'état* supports such an argument—to make the point. An increasing number of educated Lebanese see the need for change and have the skills to attack the new problems but find no way to gain access to the institutions of public power. An increasing number of the poor and less educated have become more sensitive to Lebanon's political shortcomings than to its political benefits. If the disparities between the formal representative institutions and the real political environment are not alleviated, one may anticipate worse instability in the future. There are, as has been indicated, some signs of institutional adjustment. Under the best of foreseeable circumstances, however, this adjustment will be very limited. The burdens of adaptation and innovation are thus thrust upon the institutions of policy making.

NOTES

[1] The incident is described in detail in the dispatches of the U.S. Diplomatic Agent in Beirut, George Wadsworth, in U.S. Department of State, *Foreign Relations of the United States, 1943,* IV (Washington, D.C.: U.S. Government Printing Office, 1964), 976–80.

[2] Camille Chamoun, *Crise au Moyen-Orient* (Paris: Gallimard, 1963), p. 248.

[3] The percentage of voter turnout for 1964 would have been even higher if there had been a formal vote in Beirut's First District, where 33,574 people voted in 1960. In that district the list headed by Pierre Gemayel and the Kataeb was so strongly entrenched that there was no opposition. It was therefore decided that voting would be an empty and expensive formality.

[4] The reported proportion of actual voters to eligible voters, however, is somewhat lower (53.3 per cent in 1964) than the proportion of voters to estimated population. This paradox suggests that population increases are underestimated (confirming a suspicion raised in Chapter 2) or that registration figures are inflated, a situation owing in part to the retention on the registration rolls of emigrants, who cannot cast absentee ballots. As emigrants have come mainly from Beirut and Mount Lebanon, this point would help to explain the particularly small voter-to-registrant ratio in those districts. The rate of increase in voting participation is therefore a datum of uncertain reliability.

[5] William R. Polk, "Social Modernization: The New Men," in Georgiana G. Stevens (ed.), *The United States and the Middle East* (Englewood Cliffs, N.J.: Prentice-Hall, 1964), pp. 30–52.

[6] *Cf.* Republic of Lebanon Ministry of Planning, *Besoins et Possibilités du Développement du Liban,* II (Beirut: 1960–1961), 81 (hereafter cited as *IRFED Report*); and Chapter 2 of this book.

[7] Although not entirely suitable for present purposes, the classifications of Maurice Duverger, *Political Parties* (New York: Wiley, 1959) chaps. 1, 2; and Hisham Sharabi, *Government and Politics of the Middle East in the Twentieth Century* (Princeton: Van Nostrand, 1962), chap. 20, are helpful.

[8] It has been difficult to adhere to very rigorous criteria in making such distinctions because the conditions within electoral districts vary a good deal. In general, an individual is placed in the "strong" category if he receives more than about 2,500 votes and in the "weak" category if he receives fewer. Individuals who receive only a handful of votes are generally excluded. Lists are regarded as strong if they are cohesive—that is, all the members obtain roughly the same number of votes—and if they are broadly competitive with the winning list (which is usually classified as strong itself). The same rule applies to caucuses, though there can be weak caucus representation when one member of a caucus group appears on a list. A contestant (list or individual) earns a strong party rating if the party dominates the list or if the individual as party member is strong; a weak party classification is assigned to party members who are primarily benefiting from association with a traditional clique and to those who do poorly.

[9] Philip W. Buck, *Amateurs and Professionals in British Politics, 1918–*

1959 (Chicago: University of Chicago Press, 1963), pp. 137–8. In 1945, however, 40 per cent of the members were new entrants.

[10] R. Bayly Winder, "Syrian Deputies and Cabinet Ministers, 1919–1959," *Middle East Journal,* 16, No. 4 (1962), 422. Winder remarks, "Again the theory that underdeveloped countries without stable party systems will produce very rapid turnover in elected representation is borne out." In Turkey, however, despite an apparently stable party system, the new-entry rate for the same period was also high, ranging between 32 and 81 per cent. Frederick W. Frey, *The Turkish Political Elite* (Cambridge, Mass.: Massachusetts Institute of Technology Press, 1965), p. 164. The age of the particular political system seems to explain the difference most satisfactorily.

[11] According to data received from the former Librarian of Parliament. The mean age of the thirty-five new entrants in the 1943 Parliament, however, was virtually the same as that for the twenty-eight new entrants in 1964: They were 44.9 and 44.3 years respectively.

[12] *The New York Times,* January 3, 1965, p. 46.

[13] The education figures were compiled from several sources, including the Library of Parliament, the newspaper *L'Orient,* the Bureau des Documentations Libanaises et Arabes, and *Who's Who in Lebanon, 1963–64* (Beirut: Publitec, 1964). The percentage of deputies with higher education is probably a conservative figure, because it was assumed that individuals for whom no higher education was reported had therefore received none.

[14] For that matter, it is an accurate picture of all the Mandate legislatures. According to Ahmad Haidar's classification, about 70 per cent of all the Mandate parliaments were composed of landlords and lawyers, and the other 30 per cent were businessmen and professionals, mainly doctors. *Al-dawlah al-lubnāniyyah* [*The Lebanese State*] (Beirut: Nijmeh, 1954).

[15] The exception was Mrs. Myrna Bustani al-Khazen, who was elected to fill the seat vacated by her father, Emile Bustani, who died in a plane crash in April 1963. Her election was uncontested, and she did not stand for re-election in 1964.

[16] This fact reflects the prevailing domination of business and finance by Christians. A check of the *Recueil Documentaire sur les Sociétés en Activité au Liban* (Beirut: Bureau des Documentations Libanaises et Arabes, 1957) revealed that thirty-six deputies of the independence era were associated with one or more of the 230 large companies surveyed and that twenty-six of them were Christian. The Christian domination of big business and finance is well documented by Yusif Sayigh, *Entrepreneurs of Lebanon* (Cambridge, Mass.: Harvard University Press, 1962), p. 69; he reports that only one-sixth of his sample of 207 business leaders were Muslims and that the Muslims were particularly weak in industry, finance, and services.

[17] "Modern" is a potentially misleading label. A large number of the deputies who do not belong to a caucus or organized party and who indeed pride themselves on their "independence" are not only enlightened but are also in some cases even progressive. It should be recalled that we are at this point analyzing not attitudes but the ties that link the parliamentary establishment with the expanding elite outside.

[18] In a well-known Beirut story, a British diplomat remarks to his French rival: "My poor fellow, you pay millions to buy the voters; then we pay thousands and buy the deputies."

[19] Iskandar Riachi, *Qabl wa-ba'd* (Beirut: Maktabat al-'arfān, 1953), chaps. 3, 15, and *passim*.

[20] Interview with Henry Pharaon, August 12, 1965. Press censorship, especially of articles dealing with the Mount Lebanon campaign, is indicative of the irregular proceedings. *Le Jour*, August 21–31, 1943.

[21] *al-Ḍabbūr*, April 28, 1947, p. 5.

[22] *The Black Book of the 1947 Lebanese Elections* (New York: Phoenicia, 1947), translated from the Arabic original, p. 9. The tract was originally published by the opposition National Bloc.

[23] Bechara al-Khoury, *Haqā'iq lubnāniyyah* [*Lebanese Truths*], II (Beirut: Awrāq lubnāniyyah, 1961), 41. Khoury said that the election officers responsible had taken lessons from the French. His supporter, Michel Chiha, wrote that these elections were a considerable improvement over 1943 ". . . avaient compté parmi les plus brutales, les plus odieuses que le Liban ait connues." *Le Jour*, May 27, 1947.

[24] Camille Chamoun, *Crise au Moyen-Orient* (Paris: Gallimard, 1963), pp. 383–5, categorically denies such reports. Calling the elections calm and fair, he attacks pro-Nasser "mercenaries of the pen" for making untrue allegations.

[25] One observer, a member of the anti-Chamoun front, recalled that the government intimidated women voters by stationing prostitutes in front of the polling places. They obstructed women trying to vote; when the women's husbands tried to protect them, they were attacked in turn by toughs stationed nearby. If the husbands resisted the toughs, then the security agents also present would arrest the husbands.

[26] *L'Orient*, June 18, 1957. In their letter of resignation, they stated rather cryptically, "malgré le fait que les opérations électorales, du point de vue administratif, se sont déroulées d'une manière précise et correcte, nous regrettons que l'atmosphère générale et certaines implications ne nous encouragent pas à continuer notre mission."

[". . . (I)n spite of the fact that electoral procedures, from the administrative point of view, were managed in a precise and correct manner, we regret that the general atmosphere and certain implications do not encourage us to continue our mission."]

[27] Alexander Heard, *The Costs of Democracy* (Chapel Hill: University of North Carolina Press, 1960), pp. 373–4.

[28] This estimate is based on figures supplied by a former Minister of National Economy, who said that a major list usually spends around L£300,000 and that a serious independent candidate spends only slightly less. I reduced his estimate for major independent candidates to L£100,000 and estimated that candidates obtaining fewer than 2,000 votes probably spent about L£15,000. In 1960, there were forty-three electoral lists, thirty-four major independent candidates, and forty-nine minor independent candidates. The lists spent a total of L£12,900,000, the major independents L£3,400,000, and the minor

independents L£335,000. The total is L£16,635,000, and the per capita cost is L£8.32.

[29] Figures reported in interviews conducted in 1962.

[30] Christian Merville in *L'Orient,* April 28, 1964. Taxi fares and other logistical problems probably made rural campaigns even more expensive.

[31] *Ibid.* Merville estimated that one-sixth of the typical candidate's campaign chest in 1964 went for press publicity, another sixth for illuminated signs and posters (of which L£6,000 went to the Electricity Office, L£10,000 to store owners, and L£4,000 to poster artists), an eighth for streamers and banners, a fifth for campaign offices in various districts, and the bulk—one-third—for taxis, coffee, and other refreshments. The figures do not include funds allocated for vote buying.

CHAPTER · 7

Presidential Power: The Struggle to Dominate

The Presidency is the critical institution in Lebanon's precariously balanced political system. The Presidency most clearly mirrors the Lebanese dilemma, for it is at once the system's greatest asset and its greatest liability. Only the President can provide the dynamism that a rapidly changing country requires. As we have seen, alternative institutions like the party system and the Chamber of Deputies are too weak organizationally to supply this dynamism. It is precisely this possible dynamism, however, that makes the President the greatest threat to Lebanon's pluralistic balance, even though the maintenance of this balance requires the constant help of the President. Each of independent Lebanon's first three Presidents was condemned for being ineffectual, and each was condemned for being dictatorial. Each President lacked the power to govern the country properly and worked incessantly to develop this power. Domestic and external cross pressures plus inadequately developed intermediate and nontraditional organizations—parties, interest groups, political clubs, and autonomous local governments—made these efforts to develop a power base seem heavy handed. The same circumstances that require increasing Presidential authority make the President increasingly authoritarian because there are no sufficiently institutionalized power bases to check Presidential power. In the Lebanese context, dictatorship inevitably leads to crisis. Yet the President cannot escape his predicament by refusing to act, much as he might prefer such a solution; nothing could be more dangerous to volatile, modernizing Lebanon than a weak President.

The crucial test for the Lebanese Republic is whether or not it can build a Presidency that is not only powerful enough to make and

262

implement wise policies but is also one that can function without destroying traditional pluralism. It is by no means certain that this task can be accomplished. The record of the Republic's first three Presidents suggests that, although it may be possible, it is certainly very difficult.

The Lebanese Presidents have employed three strategies to build their power. They have systematically enlarged the administrative apparatus, a governmental domain over which they have had virtually unlimited control. Not until the Chehab regime was a civil-service board created, and it reflects legislative rather than Presidential influence over the administration. In enlarging the administration, they have enhanced their bargaining power vis-à-vis local and primordial interests, through the allocation of patronage. Administrative development has also served as an instrument of social justice, particularly since 1958; the Chehab regime was distinguished by its emphasis on using administrative apparatus to serve the interests of the poor, non-Christian, and rural groups to a greater extent than the earlier regimes had done. The second Presidential strategy has been strictly political. Lebanese Presidents have been both adroit and aggressive in their attempts (against considerable odds) to build a Presidential coalition among the notables. But the Presidents have increasingly attempted to use a third strategy. They have bypassed the notables to build their own power among other groups. It is the Presidents who have given some influence to the nonpolitical professionals, who have pulled nonparliamentarians into cabinets and administration, who have tried to win the support of some organized groups outside the establishment, and who have developed followings among the ordinary people.

Each of the first three Presidents after 1943 developed his own style for handling the special problems of his time. President Bechara al-Khoury's overriding task was to secure national independence. He began his term with no army and only a rudimentary administration, and he had to face the uncertainties of international politics and the domestic crises brought about by the conclusion of World War II and Lebanon's newly won independence. Lacking solid institutional power, he employed his formidable personal influence and negotiating skill to keep the fragile state intact. President Camille Chamoun was a fighter. He was challenged from inside and outside the state, and he had to develop new bases of power. Ultimately his efforts to build influence as a major Arab leader foundered, the notables he recruited lacked adequate traditional support, and the organized groups he relied on in the 1958 crisis (the **P.P.S.** and the Kataeb) were neutralized by equally well-organized opposition from other groups, but the expansion of administration begun by Chamoun was considerable, and it gave his successor something to build on. President Fuad Chehab appears as a kind of political carpenter, repairing an edifice that had split apart and building on top of it the skeleton, at least, of a modern state.

THE KHOURY REGIME: EXPLOITING TRADITIONAL PLURALISM

The man who did most to achieve Lebanon's independence from France and to establish the viability of the new state was also, in the opinion of many, its most accomplished politician. Bechara al-Khoury, short in stature but commanding in presence, developed procedures for integrating Lebanon's semi-independent notables into the political system; and he accomplished it all at a time when the instruments of the state itself were only poorly developed. As an administrator Khoury was less than successful; indeed, it was his administrative failings that precipitated his removal in 1952. As a politician, however, he not only guided Lebanon through the painful process of disengagement from France and into harmony with the other new Arab states, but he also exploited the country's traditional pluralism to create a presidential party, the Constitutional Bloc (Destour), and a means for regularizing change. His main instrument was the device of cabinet change.

It is difficult at first to accept the idea that the cabinet-change process has contributed anything positive to Lebanese politics. There were, after all, thirty-six changes of government between September 1943 and July 1965. Collective responsibility for policy is a rule more honored in the breach than in the application because of the absence of a strong party system. Cabinet ministers rarely bring to their ministries appropriate technical qualifications and administrative leadership, and the administration is left to the supervision of civil servants who are hobbled by political pressures. Because the Lebanese Prime Minister lacks independence, authority, and tenure, he has been typically only *primus inter pares* and has been tactically inclined to avoid initiatives for fear of weakening his coalition. By conventional criteria, the Council of Ministers stands as one of the weakest institutions in Lebanese politics. Liberal critics never tire of pointing out its inadequacies in terms of the needs of a modern, rational political system.[1]

Although there is much truth in their criticism, it is important for purposes of analysis to consider the possibility that the process of cabinet change does serve an important function. During the Khoury regime the Lebanese state was little more than an uneasy federation of traditional chiefs commanding a bureaucracy pitifully inadequate for anything more than custodial functions—that is, maintaining a minimum of civil order—yet saddled with the need to curb inflation, to supply scarce wheat, to eliminate French control of vital services, and to put down communist-inspired labor unrest. Under these circumstances the first priority was to consolidate national independence. Starting with little more than the appeal of his strong personality, President Khoury institutionalized traditional rivalries in the cabinet process. He did so by including the major traditional power holders in the cabinet and thus giving them a stake in the system. In so doing, he maneuvered himself into the position of arbiter. He also gained necessary time to build up an administrative base, although he did so less to fulfill any popular demands for expanded government services than to expand his options as head of state. The primary criterion for evaluating Lebanese institutions in the first critical years is their contribution to basic stability and consolidation. Later on, other criteria such as efficiency, incorruptibility, and social justice assume greater importance. Khoury's use of the cabinet, an institution of Western liberal democracy, to achieve the first goal was masterly; his failure to adapt it to meet the other criteria eventually led his regime to political disaster. Under his successors the cabinet process continued to play the same important integrating role, but it had to be supplemented by new institutions and processes for the system to meet the other standards that were increasingly applied to it.

How did the cabinet process as used by President Khoury promote national solidarity? First, he used it to give important traditional leaders a stake in the state apparatus. This move was essential because of the initially weak formal position of the President and because the population was not yet politically oriented toward Beirut but had powerful ties to the various notables whose local positions were nearly invulnerable. Second, it kept the traditional power holders themselves in a reasonably stable equilibrium and discouraged overt rivalries through a ritual of change known to its critics as "musical chairs," by which portfolios were regularly redistributed in order that the many deserving notables be given an opportunity to support the regime actively. The musical-chairs process was—and is—an excellent means for keeping the notables involved in the success or failure of the government yet so unbalanced and disorganized that they could not easily combine against the President. President Khoury was emulated, but never surpassed, by his successors, who also rewarded notables who cooperated with the regime. Khoury understood the uses of patronage, and he took full advantage of the fact that every important politician in Lebanon has numerous clients to serve and debts to repay. Corruption was the inevitable price of cooperation.

Third, the cabinet functioned as a protective buffer for the President and the fragile national unity that he symbolized. In this respect, Khoury was much more successful with his cabinets than his successors were. Because during his term the nontraditional political infrastructure was relatively primitive, a cabinet of "giants"—acknowledged sectarian and financial leaders of national reputation and influence—conferred sufficient legitimacy on a government whose activity was relatively restricted. With the flowering of radical groups outside the establishment and the growing factionalism within it during the Chamoun regime, the cabinet became considerably less effective as a buffer. Under General Chehab, who hardly needed a buffer at all, the cabinet was not very important. Fourth, because the cabinet was weak in policy making and administration, the President had a free hand in making decisions. President Khoury was somewhat less effective in exploiting this possibility than his successors were, partly because the notables in his cabinets individually enjoyed considerable power and partly because he permitted certain members of his own entourage to build up their personal power in the administration.

President Khoury was greatly aided in his efforts to consolidate power by the legacy of the French Mandate. The Constitution gives the President sweeping power over Parliament and cabinet.[2] The President names a prime minister who in turn must form a cabinet that will hold the confidence of Parliament. In theory, both President and cabinet are responsible to the Parliament. In practice, however, the President plays a commanding role because he has the power to promulgate "urgent" and "double urgent" legislation by decree (Article 58);[3] to veto bills (Article 27); to dissolve the Parliament (Article 55); and to appoint and dismiss the Prime Minister and the cabinet (Article 53). As a result, it has always been the President, not the Parliament, who has brought down governments. Parliament is never in a position to withhold confidence from a cabinet that has the blessing of both President and Prime Minister because its own organization is primitive, based as it is on personal cliques and regional blocs, and because the President exerts powerful influence over the parliamentary election process. The President therefore has been able to manipulate the formation of cabinets as a means to keep the notables as a group in line, which leaves him a free hand to manage the country's affairs. Nor have prime ministers and cabinets been able to initiate legislative programs without presidential backing. This development has not pleased Sunnite politicians. Compared to the President, the Prime Minister has a tenure that is indeed precarious: A president has a fixed term of six years, whereas a government lasts for about 6.5 months; three men have been President in the first two decades of independence; during the same period there have been nine different prime ministers (not counting interim prime ministers), of whom only three remained in office for periods longer than fourteen months.[4]

Within four years President Khoury had developed his political superiority to such an extent that he could persuade Parliament without difficulty to amend the Constitution to permit him a second term. The Parliament, for reasons discussed earlier, was in no mood to resist his request. Although neither of Khoury's two immediate successors actually requested a renewal of their terms of office, there is no doubt that Parliament would have provided it had they done so.

In order to assess Bechara al-Khoury's performance as a consolidator of national power, to compare it with that of his successors, and to obtain a better idea of the development of the Presidency as an institution, it will be helpful to describe a typical case of cabinet change.

At the end of March 1946 the Cabinet of Sami Sulh had begun to disintegrate. The disintegration had been precipitated by rivalries within the Lebanese delegation in Paris negotiating the terms of the French troop withdrawal. One of the delegates was the popular Sunnite leader, Riad Sulh, anxious to use his role in negotiating the agreement as a means to return to power. Another delegate was Yussef Salem (Greek Catholic), Sulh's friend and co-lister from South Lebanon, who was the Interior Minister; another was Hamid Frangieh, the Maronite Foreign Minister.[5] Salem was persuaded to quit his cabinet post upon his return to Beirut, ostensibly on the grounds that his plans for reform were being frustrated, and it was rumored that Frangieh would follow him.[6] The days of Sami Sulh's cabinet seemed numbered, and the two major opposition factions, both of which were dissatisfied with their weak cabinet representation, began maneuvers to gain control of the next government. The Destourians, led by Philippe Taqla, Wadih Naim, Farid Khazen, and Majid Arslan, were one of the competing factions. The other was the Independent Bloc, led by Abdel-Hamid Karami, Henri Pharaon, Ahmad al-Assaad, and Abdallah Yafi. At issue was the office of Prime Minister: The Destourians were willing to continue their alliance with the powerful Riad Sulh, whereas the Independents (who included two aspirants for the post of Prime Minister) were anxious to keep Riad Sulh out of office, as they were suspicious of his ultimate aims in foreign policy. Only a relative neutral like Sami Sulh could head a cabinet that would not completely alienate one of these two important factions. Sami Sulh could try to maintain his present cabinet, replace the defectors, and then go before Parliament for a vote of confidence, or he could take his amputated Council of Ministers before Parliament immediately. Because he preferred the first alternative, he began to search for replacements to fill the empty positions. At that point, sectarian and regional factors came into play. To fill the vacancies created by Frangieh and Salem, it was necessary to find a Maronite notable from Mount Lebanon and a Greek Catholic, preferably from the Biqa. The two most prominent candidates were Philippe Taqla (Greek Catholic) and Yussef Istaphan (Maronite). Taqla, however, would not join a cabinet unless his Destour colleague, Majid Arslan (Druze), was also made a minister; but Sami Sulh could not include Amir Majid without displacing the incumbent Druze, Dr. Jamil Talhouk. Such a move would upset the Druze followers of Kamal Jumblat. Kamal Jumblat, meanwhile, was on the verge of throwing his support to the Karami-Pharaon Independents, if that faction would promise to stand behind a strong reform program. Furthermore, because Gabriel Murr, the Greek Orthodox Public Works Minister, was also in sympathy with the Jumblat group, to replace Talhouk would be to risk Murr's resignation. There was also opposition to Istaphan's appointment, which would alienate the Abdel-Hamid Karami faction; it might then retaliate by pulling out the Justice Minister, Saadi Munla (Sunnite of Tripoli), and perhaps three other ministers as well. Sami Sulh could have then started all over again, but solution would hardly have been easier. On April 9, however, Sulh's cabinet was reprieved when Philippe Taqla agreed to join as the Greek Catholic representative without insisting on a portfolio for Majid Arslan and President Khoury persuaded Hamid Frangieh not to resign.[7]

These repairs only postponed the crisis for a few weeks however. The negotiations with France had been handled satisfactorily, but the government's handling of the domestic situation was under incessant attack from a disorganized but growing opposition of notables. Riad Sulh and his associates were anxious to return to Lebanon, but the other opposition group, the Independents, led by Abdel-Hamid Karami and Henri Pharaon, would not accept a cabinet with Riad Sulh as Prime Minister. There were also sharp differences between Karami and Pharaon themselves over the kind of electoral reforms that they wanted the government to undertake. Karami strongly advocated a single-member system based on the Lebanese administrative districts, and Pharaon, whose own influence was greatly enhanced by the "Grand List," based on the larger geographic divisions of the five provinces, opposed it. Seeking to improve his position, Karami changed the name of his group from the Independents to the Reform Bloc. By this maneuver, he gained the support of a number of powerful leaders, some of whom were known for their reformist ideas.[8] These notables, acting in a "nonpartisan" manner, presented President Khoury with a petition that charged, among other things, that the domestic situation required a complete overhaul, including a reduction of the administrative apparatus and expenditures; the creation of coherent, trained administrative and military cadres; an office for auditing administrative accounts; a new electoral law; modern social legislation; and a campaign against unemployment.[9] President Khoury was also attacked by the opposing faction. Yussef Salem, a friend of Riad Sulh, continued his efforts to undermine the cabinet by publicly prophesying that Lebanon would be ruined if public and private expenditures did not decrease. With the more than 20,000 workers once dependent upon the Allied armies now unemployed and the termination of the foreign military expenditures that had been running to $40 million annually during World War II, a stronger government than that of Sami Sulh was necessary.[10]

On May 9 a new crisis was precipitated, when Majid Arslan, a close ally of Khoury in the Destour and a hero of the Lebanese resistance in 1943, made a violent attack on the notables' petition. This act prodded his traditional Druze rival Jumblat, one of the signers, into retorting that Arslan was a traitor. A duel was narrowly averted.[11] A week later the campaign against Sami Sulh's cabinet reached its climax. Ranged against Sulh and his ministers were Riad Sulh and his friends, Habib Abuchahla, Yussef Salem, Hamid Frangieh, Kazem Khalil, and Adel Osseiran, and the six deputies of Khoury's own grouping, the Destour.[12] The other opposition group, the reformist coalition, still divided by the problem of electoral districting, included at that point Abdel-Hamid Karami, Henri Pharaon, Alfred Naccache, Kamal Jumblat, Saeb Salam, Saadi Munla, and Abdallah Yafi. Meanwhile, President Khoury, whose followers wanted to remove Sami Sulh from the prime ministership, acted as a supposedly neutral mediator and listened patiently to the complaints of various notables and waited for the government to fall. On May 17 the three ministerial allies of the Karami group, Jamil Talhouk, Saadi Munla, and Ahmad Assaad, submitted their resignations, and Sami Sulh's cabinet collapsed.[13]

The process of forming a Lebanese cabinet is hardly less Byzantine than that of destroying one; but, although President Khoury could simply bide his time and wait for the accumulation of rivalries to undermine the government, he had to use his power positively to put a new one together. This tedious task was made easier by the fact that the opposition was chronically so divided that individual notables could usually be tempted to forget their old affiliations in return for a portfolio. Khoury writes that he offered his friend Riad Sulh the post of Minister of State but that Riad would accept only on the condition that Khoury also admit a num-

FIGURE 4. *Prime Minister (Left) and President.*

ber of his friends.[14] Although the reformists agreed on their opposition to a cabinet controlled by Riad Sulh and his friends, they could not reach a compromise on the reforms they wished to undertake. When President Khoury consulted with Abdel-Hamid Karami and ingenuously asked him to submit the program his group supported, Karami could therefore only temporize and report that the majority of his group did not yet agree with the group's written platform.[15] The reform faction could not even agree on a candidate for Prime Minister among its Sunnite members. Some observers believed that a cabinet of "giants," consisting of Riad Sulh, Pharaon, Karami (as Prime Minister), Camille Chamoun (who immediately left his diplomatic post in London), Habib Abuchahla, and Ahmad al-Assaad, would emerge. Even had Riad Sulh been content to play second fiddle to Karami or had Pharaon been willing to sit in the same cabinet with Riad Sulh or had Habib Abuchahla been prepared to work with Pharaon or had Khoury himself been interested in accepting Camille Chamoun, there still would have been the question of selecting the Druze representative. Riad Sulh and the Destour insisted that Majid Arslan participate in any cabinet with them, but Karami's Reform Bloc and other reformists preferred the more socially conscious Jumblat. It would not be possible to do without a prominent Druze in any Lebanese cabinet, and it was equally unthinkable that Jumblat and Arslan could both be appointed in light of their recent battle in Parliament.

The deadlock gave the President considerable leverage. Khoury used it with his customary skill to form a cabinet that effectively

blunted the formidable offensive of the reformists. For the office of Prime Minister he suggested Saadi Munla, who was not the strongest leader in the reformist faction.[16] Khoury then put together a cabinet containing three associates of the reformists (Munla, Yussef Hraoui, and Saeb Salam) but excluding such major reform figures as Karami, Pharaon, Naccache, and Jumblat. Furthermore, Khoury neutralized the three reformists by also including four allies or friends of Riad Sulh and the Destour: Emile Lahoud, Philippe Taqla, Majid Arslan, and Ahmad Husseini. President Khoury had deflected the reformist thrust by creating a weak cabinet. When this cabinet fell apart seven months later, the domestic situation had become so disorganized that a cabinet of "giants" was an urgent necessity. On December 14, 1946, seven days after Munla's cabinet had collapsed, President Khoury and Riad Sulh put together a new and stronger combination, initiating a five-year period of ministerial continuity.[17]

Such was the style of cabinet politics during the Khoury regime. The President exploited traditional rivalries with consummate skill, turning the inherent weakness of the new state to his advantage. In this difficult task he had the good fortune and good sense to be associated with an outstanding Sunnite leader, Riad Sulh. As long as Sulh was in tandem with Khoury, the underlying sectarian tension was low—probably lower than before or since—for most Sunnites felt that they were being strongly represented by an Arab nationalist of great stature. Sulh's positive contribution to this state of affairs was expressed by President Khoury's leading press critic, Georges Naccache, in the following terms:

> Pourquoi nous sommes riadistes? Parce que, compte tenu de ses qualités et de ses défauts—des changes et des risques qu'il exprime —M. Riad Sulh se situe, dans le nouvel équilibre libanais, au centre même de tout notre système politique. A quoi tient le privilège? Moins peut-être au génie propre et aux vertus du personnage qu'à un ensemble d'éléments qui ont joué et continuent de jouer en sa faveur. Sa personalité, son passé, sa position intérieure, ses relations internationales—tout le jeu subtil enfin des impondérables qui se cristallisent autour de lui—contribuent à faire de ce personnage un personnage nécessaire.[18]

With time, however, the Khoury-Sulh style proved increasingly difficult to maintain. Not only was it impossible to satisfy all the demands of the notables, but it was also impossible to avoid ultimately alienating them by superficially successful clever maneuvers. Still, the President might well have served out his second term—in spite of the domestic corruption, the Palestine problem, and the radicalization of politics—had he been able to maintain his alliance with Riad Sulh. Their separation and then Sulh's assassination in July 1951 eroded Khoury's support among the Sunnite masses. Lacking protection from the Sunnite notables he had so cleverly excluded in the past, Khoury lasted for only fourteen months before the inexorable factionalism of Lebanese politics brought upon him a cabinet crisis that he could not solve.

The Chamoun Regime: Adjusting to the New Radicalism

Before 1952 Lebanese politics was like chess, and the President was a master player facing a divided opposition on the institutional chessboard; for six years after 1952, it was closer to war, and the President was a commander trying desperately to eliminate his opponents from the field. In the cabinet crises of the 1950s, popular reform, socialism, Arab nationalism, relations with the West, and sectarian strife figured to an extent unknown during Khoury's regime. One crude indicator of President Chamoun's difficulties is the fact that the governments during his tenure average only six months in duration, compared with a figure of nine months for cabinets during the previous regime.[19]

As a politician, President Chamoun was admirably suited for carrying on presidential politics in the style of his predecessor. He belonged to President Khoury's generation of liberal nationalists; he was only six years younger and had been raised in the same milieu. He too had suffered at the hands of the Turks; he too had a legal background; and he too was, from the moment of his entrance into politics in 1929, a Maronite who aspired to a prominent role.[20] As a member of the new political elite under the Mandate, Chamoun must have learned a great deal about factional politics both from the French and his own colleagues and rivals. From the moment he entered national politics he was a popular figure in Mount Lebanon, and particularly around his home town of Deir al-Qamar. As a Destourian he identified himself with the most progressive stand on national independence, but as a personality he always preferred to associate the Destour with himself rather than himself with the Destour. This individualism, so characteristic of Lebanese politics, had by 1943 forced Chamoun into direct, though still covert, rivalry with Khoury. In fact, Chamoun was for a time the only candidate for President in 1943; his candidacy had been used as a "compromise" between Bechara al-Khoury and Emile Edde.[21]

With a strong local following of his own and the backing of British diplomats, the ambitious Chamoun was, from 1943 on, a more serious rival to President Khoury than anybody from outside the Constitutional Bloc. Posted to London in August 1944 under French pressure, Chamoun's political isolation was a blessing in disguise, for it kept him free of the growing corruption surrounding the new regime's attempt to develop an indigenous administration.[22] Camille Chamoun permanently returned to Lebanon early in 1947 at a politically auspicious moment. Opposition groups both inside and outside the establishment were beginning to exert pressures on the Khoury regime: The Syrian National Party (P.P.S.), to whom Chamoun in his capacity as Interior Minister had issued a license in 1944, was about to welcome home its founder, Antoun Saadeh, and to launch a campaign against the government; the communists had made greater inroads in the labor movement than before or since; Kamal Jumblat was casting about for a means of reforming the state, and Khoury believed that he was playing a highly destructive role both inside the government and outside it; Emile Edde, though certainly no friend of Chamoun, shared his interest in a change of regime; and Abdel-Hamid Karami remained impatient to see the end of a regime that, in his words, exploited Lebanon as if it were a family fief. All these domestic complaints had as background the Palestine struggle, then drawing to a climax. Chamoun had distinguished himself for diplomatic service against the Zionist movement through his activities in London and as one of the most important spokesmen for the Arabs at the United Nations. This service added to Chamoun's political luster, assured him of support from Arab nationalists and Muslims, and offset to some extent his reputation as a man of the British; a year later, when the war had been lost, he was one of the few Arab politicians to survive with reputation intact. By spring 1947, the regime's unpopularity must have been apparent to a politician with Khoury's astuteness; the 1947 elections were thus particularly important. Chamoun partially succeeded in splitting the Destour in Mount Lebanon by insisting that he would never run on the same list with the President's brother, but the Khoury machine still retained enough control of the situation to engineer a constitutional amendment and the re-election of the President a year later.[23]

The crisis that forced President Khoury to step down halfway through his second term brought Camille Chamoun to the Presidency. As one of the leaders of the Socialist National Front, Chamoun had been instrumental in mobilizing the opposition to Khoury. His only opponent, Hamid Frangieh, withdrew before the election.[24] By then, however, the tide of reformist opinion and the undercurrent of Arab nationalist unrest that had contributed to Khoury's success had already begun to turn against him. In addition to the classic game of cabinet politics, Chamoun thus had to struggle with the notables of the Socialist National Front who had put him in power, because he would neither go to the extremes they advocated nor share power with them. His predecessor had completed a full term before having to worry about these assorted radicals. Furthermore, whereas President Khoury had kept his lines of communication open both to the Arab states and to the West, President Chamoun found it an impossible task, largely because of the introduction of the Cold War into the Arab world with the decline of British influence, American efforts to establish a Middle Eastern NATO, the flareup of the Palestine problem, and the Soviet Union's arms deals with Egypt and Syria. By splitting the Arab world and Lebanon itself into pro-Western and anti-Western blocs the United States and Britain presented Chamoun with a dilemma: Lebanese commitment to either side would be interpreted as a violation of the National Pact by the other, and representatives of each side within Lebanon were powerful enough to destroy the Lebanese equilibrium. The political institutions of the state were put to this test during Chamoun's term, and the surprising fact is that they contained the forces of crisis until the last four months, despite a series of tactical errors on the part of the President.

Reformist Pressures and Presidential Response

President Khoury had come to power with a mandate to complete Lebanese independence and to build an efficient administration. His success in the first task is incontestable; not only did he ease the French out with skill, speed, and reasonable amity, but he also established a system of political relationships that institutionalized establishment rivalries. In the second task he failed, and administrative corruption became so flagrant that the fragmented opposition succeeded in combining temporarily to force the President out. President Chamoun came to power indebted to these reformers. He thus could not simply play the cabinet game of his predecessor; on the other hand, he could not opt out of cabinet politics, however distasteful they may have seemed, because the cabinet process was the only orderly way of handling the various rivalries and also an important instrument for building his own power. Just as the wish for independence had strengthened the Presidency during Khoury's first term, so did the need for reform give President Chamoun a potential means of support. Although completing independence was to the interest of all the establishment, reforming the government and administration was not; in fact, a substantial bloc of ex-Destourians and other friends of the old regime looked upon reform with outright dismay. The radical groups that had been so important in Chamoun's election quickly proved to be too extreme for his taste in their demands for power and policy changes.

Faced with a very difficult situation at his accession to power, President Chamoun thus lost the support both of the reform movement and the traditional politicians. Scarcely a year after his inauguration, when the first ramifications of the Cold War conflict hit Lebanon, the President's domestic weakness forced him into hostile defensive maneuvers and encouraged his foreign and domestic enemies to acts of greater boldness. Chamoun did not overcome the problems that faced him, and his determination to strengthen the Presidency only aggravated them. In fact, the combination of this attempt to increase Presidential power and the inability to achieve basic reforms helped bring about the strange alliance of feudal bosses and progressive elements that opposed him in 1958. His partial success led to national disaster.

To illustrate the *immobilisme* resulting from the collision of the radical progressives and the traditional elements, it is only necessary to examine President Chamoun's first attempts to establish cabinets. The President had been in office scarcely a week when it became clear that the most radical of the leftists—the Kamal Jumblat group, recent allies of Chamoun in deposing President Khoury—wanted nothing less than control of the next cabinet. It also sought promises for reforms that went far beyond what Chamoun or the non-leftists in the reform coalition—not to mention the majority of former loyalists in Parliament—would accept. Jumblat's Socialist National

Front demanded the nationalization of important industries, redistribution of the large land estates among tenant farmers, a social-security program, and the use of surplus public funds for social and economic projects.[25] Chamoun first tapped Dr. Abdallah Yafi as the logical first choice for Prime Minister. Yafi had a liberal reputation, and he had been jettisoned a year before as President Khoury's Prime Minister by the faction of the Destour headed by the President's brother. Yafi, however, could not form a cabinet acceptable both to Chamoun and to the old Parliament, in which the S.N.F. would hold five seats. Other leaders also demanded seats: Ahmad al-Assaad, South Lebanon's political boss, for example, insisted that his relation Sabri Hamadeh—a loyal friend of the Destour—be included, but Jumblat would not accept any prominent members of the old ruling establishment.[26]

Chamoun then turned to another relatively neutral Sunnite, Saadi Munla of Tripoli, who had been associated with the late Abdel-Hamid Karami; but he too found the S.N.F. intractable, even though he offered a program that promised administrative reform, electoral reform at the parliamentary and municipal levels, and a liberal press law. When Munla also failed to form a cabinet, Chamoun called upon Abdel-Hamid Karami's son Rashid, who was known to be more strongly committed to reform and to solidarity with the Arab world than the others were; but because Rashid Karami's proposed cabinet was manned exclusively by opposition members, it was vetoed in advance by the pro-Khoury parliamentary majority. Furthermore, the right wing of the reform coalition, led by Pierre Edde of the National Bloc, was unwilling to participate in the same government with a radical socialist like Abdallah Hajj of the S.N.F.[27] Finally, when nerves were stretched to the breaking point, President Chamoun called in Amir Khaled Chehab, the venerable veteran of Mandate politics and an early associate of the Destour. Khaled Chehab succeeded in forming a four-man cabinet of nonparliamentarians, and he obtained sweeping decree powers from the Parliament.[28] The reformists spoke in behalf of antisectarianism, compulsory voting, investigating the income sources of deputies, women's suffrage, a new census, and land reform. The new government declared that it intended to reform the electoral law on the basis of small, single-member districts; liberalize the press law; give the vote to women; reform the judiciary; and decentralize and reform the administration. This bold move threw both the old Destourians and the radicals off balance, and the cabinet was ultimately approved by sixty-five to one, with two abstentions.[29]

Presidential response to the calls for reform was vigorous in intent, if not in execution. Nicknamed "the government of the decree laws," Amir Khaled's regime, with President Chamoun's vigorous backing, issued some ninety different decrees in the field of administrative reform alone during its six-month exercise of emergency powers.[30] President Chamoun singles out this administrative reform as one of the most important accomplishments of the Khaled Chehab cabinet because it simplified and clearly defined the functions and responsibilities of all civil servants.[31] The other important accomplishments were the judicial reform, which, Chamoun claims, finally gave Lebanon an independent judiciary; the liberalization of the press law, which under the Khoury regime had been used to detain opposition journalists and to shut down their newspapers; and the electoral reform.[32]

Whatever the real merits of Chamoun's first reform effort—they will be discussed shortly—the political results were hardly encouraging. The general reshuffling of general directors and administrative streamlining was regarded with dismay by those whose traditional access to the bureaucracy had been cut off, whereas the extreme left found the whole operation insufficiently comprehensive. Only two weeks after the cabinet had been installed, one deputy accused the government of dragging its feet.[33] A parliamentary interpellation on the government's administrative policy on February 19, 1953, was highly critical of the administrative reform, even though confidence was again granted to the Khaled Chehab cabinet; the S.N.F. was also reportedly becoming restive.[34] Outside Parliament the new political alignment caused even bigger disturbances. In South Lebanon clashes occurred between partisans of the S.N.F. progressives and the followers of Ahmad al-Assaad at Taybeh and Kab-Elias, and al-Assaad also accused members of Jumblat's P.S.P. of trying to kill him.[35] Another fight broke out between the partisans of Kamal Jumblat and followers of Majid Arslan.[36] The reform effort seemed to be exacerbating rather than reducing political conflict. Sectarian strife also threatened, and the Hay'at al-Watania joined with Sunnite organizations in Saida and Tripoli to complain that Sunnites were not getting a proper share of new appointments in the administrative reshuffle. At the same time, three of the leading Sunnite establishment figures, Sami Sulh, Abdallah Yafi, and Saeb Salam, called for a constitutional amendment to limit the President's powers and create a Muslim Vice-Presidency.[37]

In addition to these complications, other problems created by a movement for economic unity with Syria virtually paralyzed the government, and the task of actually pushing through the reforms was left to President Chamoun. By the end of February the notables, traditional and reformist, who had been excluded from power, were hovering like vultures over the Khaled Chehab government, plotting in classic fashion the composition of its successor. Khaled Chehab resigned on April 29, fourteen days after the expiration of his cabinet's emergency powers, after severe attacks both from old Destourians and radical leftists in Parliament.[38] President Chamoun's political honeymoon—if it can be called that—was over; the experience showed President Chamoun that reform without the notables was difficult, and it also showed that government without the politicians was impossible. The President learned from this experience and turned to an experienced establishment Sunnite, Saeb Salam, to form the next cabinet; the struggle of traditional rivals and progressive factions began again. Druze against Druze; Destour against National Bloc; Arab nationalist against Lebanese conservative; nonsectarians against clerical interference; divisions within radical factions—all the familiar conflicts were still present. It is not surprising that Chamoun realized immediately that he would have to have another parliament in order to establish stable rule.

The new Parliament, even though it had been elected under the Chamoun reform law, did not make President Chamoun's second reform campaign any easier or more successful than the first one because, even though it contained a few new faces, it was still composed of notables pursuing parochial and private interests. The second reform drive was launched during autumn 1954 in an atmosphere charged with foreign and sectarian tensions—additional complications in a situation already complicated enough with traditional and social-justice demands. Neither the new Parliament nor Chamoun's own polished demeanor had mollified the hard-core opposition. Sunnites of the establishment were increasingly critical of the President's ambivalence on foreign policy; Destourians were regrouping to undo the reforms already enacted; the Hay'at al-Watania and Najjadeh were pressing for a census; and a Committee of Political Parties, created in February 1954, was attempting to coordinate the opposition.[39] Although the S.N.F. had suffered major defections the year before, when Emile Bustani, Dicran

Tosbath, and Ghassan Tueni had declined to support Jumblat's assaults on President Chamoun, its hard core continued to oppose the President, and the National Bloc refused to give the regime unqualified support. On September 16, 1954, President Chamoun called on Sami Sulh to form a government, after the efforts of Abdallah Yafi, who had been Prime Minister in the two previous weak governments, had failed. Again, the cabinet was granted emergency-decree powers for a limited period. Under the new reform program, one American and two Dutch administration experts were brought in, a civil-service board was established, and the groundwork was laid for a national school of public administration.[40] As before, unfortunately, the reform only excited more political opposition than support. By the end of May 1955 the new decree laws were the object of sustained attacks by Raymond and Pierre Edde of the National Bloc; Hamid Frangieh, Chamoun's defeated Presidential rival; and Abdallah Yafi, recently Chamoun's Prime Minister.[41] On a single day in July, four newspapers, ranging in political orientation from the far right to the far left, attacked the government's "inane" reform efforts.[42] The cabinet itself, after barely exceeding the six-month average life span, was beginning to disintegrate: At the end of May the Justice Minister, Charles Helou, quit during a debate on the decree laws, taking with him the support of moderate financiers and ex-Destourians, and in July a dispute over the appointment of an ambassador to Paris necessitated a major reshuffle of the Sulh cabinet.[43] The conflict over the appointment, however, was merely the surface manifestation of a deeper rift involving the direction of foreign policy, just as the demands of Sunnites and Shiites for a more favorable sectarian distribution of administrative posts reflected a more fundamental discontent with the over-all power arrangements.[44]

Meanwhile, there had been an outbreak of sectarian conflict: A series of incidents in 1953 and 1954 aroused tensions not felt in Lebanon since the Mandate.[45] Sectarian tensions were also related to the demands for closer economic unity with Syria, championed by notables like Rashid Karami of Tripoli, and, as the British-American design for the Middle East became apparent, sectarian conflicts also prompted demands from some Sunnite quarters for a broader and more militant unity against Western imperialism. As political complications increased, President Chamoun's ability to carry out reforms declined. Subsequent evaluations of his reform efforts agree that they produced more change than progress. A study published in *L'Orient* in October 1958 cited the two reform experiments as "unfortunate" because they were too short to do much good (one lasted six months, the other three).[46] Experts in public administration from the American University of Beirut reached a similar conclusion, noting that there had been no systematic investigation of the administrative problem and that asking high bureaucrats to prepare reform proposals for their own departments was not the most objective means of determining reform priorities.[47] Furthermore, the basic problems—excessively formalized procedures and a lack of well-trained and adequately paid civil servants—had not been successfully attacked. Despite the failure of these reforms, the demand for them from the younger notables excluded from full power during the Khoury regime—incoherent as it sometimes was—gave the President an opportunity to try to extend his authority dramatically and to develop the bureaucracy as his instrument of power. His nationalization of several important utilities is a case in point. President Fuad Chehab had clearly learned some political lessons from his predecessor when he undertook his own administrative-reform program, which, as Chapter 8 suggests, further strengthened the Presidency.

External Pressures and Presidential Response

The great bulk of President Chamoun's attention was devoted to foreign affairs and their domestic consequences.[48] Part of this preoccupation derived from his own background as a diplomat in London and New York, when he spoke for all the Arab states during World War II and the Palestine crisis, and from a personal orientation more cosmopolitan than that of either his predecessor or his successor. Even before the series of regional crises that shook Lebanon, the new President was already making visits to the Arab heads of state. He accepted congratulations in Cairo, Riyadh, Baghdad, and Amman, and he visited Brazil, Argentina, Uruguay —with their large colonies of Lebanese immigrants—and Spain, Italy, Greece, Turkey, and Iran.[49] This auspicious beginning was soon marred when the Arab states began to split into two hostile blocs. The collapse of Colonel Adib Shishakly's dictatorship in Syria on February 25, 1954, which soon brought radicals like the Baathists into influential positions there, demonstrated that the conflicting external interests in that time of turmoil in the Arab world were a constant threat to every regime in the area. On April 2, 1954, Turkey and Pakistan signed an agreement that proved to be the first step toward the Baghdad Pact, and on January 12, 1955, the keystone of that pact was laid when Turkey and Iraq announced a similar agreement and invited other states in the area to join in the common defense. The United States and Great Britain seemed to be having great success with their "Northern Tier" strategy for containing the Soviet Union.[50]

The reaction of the new military regime in Egypt to this latest attempt to "organize the area" in defense of Western interests was unmistakably hostile. Cairo launched a diplomatic and propaganda campaign against the new alignment with the West. The Egyptian government was especially harsh with Britain, which Cairo believed was using this method to regain the influence it had signed away only three months earlier in the Suez Evacuation Agreement.[51] Syria, the scene of a tense struggle between pro-Iraq and leftist-nationalist elements, slipped into the Egyptian orbit during February and March, with the timely assistance of the Soviet Union, which had promised arms and protection to both countries.[52] The announcement of the Soviet-Egyptian arms deal in September 1955 revealed the weakness of the Northern Tier as a strategic concept and dealt a severe blow to what British and American statesmen considered their vital interests. On the regional scene, meanwhile, the increasing savagery of Israeli raids against Egypt and Syria in the Gaza Strip in February 1955 and hostile Turkish maneuvers against Syria intensified the atmosphere of crisis.

The pressures on Lebanon were enormous. Because the Lebanese population was split between commitment to the West and loyalty to the Arab world, the intrusion of the Cold War into the area rendered a mere continuation of the simple friendship policies of the Khoury regime totally inadequate. President Chamoun's attempt to moderate Egyptian distaste for the Baghdad Pact, the West, and alliances in general was unsuccessful.[53] Chamoun does not mention that he ever tried to dissuade Great Britain, Iraq, or Turkey from making alliances; instead he takes a mildly approving stand:

Le Pacte de Bagdad, utile, peut-être, à la défense des frontières septentrionales de l'Irak, ne m'avait inspiré aucun intérêt particulier. Je souhaitais cependant voir les Arabes sortir du cercle étroit dans lequel ils continuaient de vouloir s'enfermer, et s'ouvrir à la coopération politique, économique et militaire avec des Etats voisins tels que le Pakistan, l'Iran et la Turquie.[54]

Conceivably, had President Chamoun elected to adhere to the kind of strict nonalignment for which he was reproving President Nasser, Lebanon might have avoided the Western entanglement from which the crisis of 1958 emerged. His refusal to align Lebanon with the Egyptian-Syrian-Saudi Arabian pact of March 2, 1955, which had been created to counter the Turko-Iraqi treaty, made it appear that Lebanon was indeed following a policy of impartiality. The Cairo bloc, however, interpreted the Lebanese abstention as an act of hostility, thus demonstrating the difficulties in convincing others of one's honorable intentions. President Chamoun followed this apparent rebuff with a gesture that appeared to turn Lebanon publicly toward the West, although—again—no formal commitments were made.

At the beginning of April 1955, on the eve of the Bandung Conference, President Chamoun and Prime Minister Sami Sulh paid a visit to Turkey and concluded their stay by issuing a joint statement that proclaimed the perfect harmony of the policies of the two countries.[55] If the President was pursuing a policy of neutrality, this statement certainly did not have a neutral tone in the opinion of many Lebanese. Instead, it appeared to be a gesture of approval for the Baghdad Pact; a slap at Syria, which was at the time in serious conflict with Turkey; and a gesture of defiance to President Nasser, whose diplomatic coup in the Soviet arms deal had captured the imagination of the entire Arab world. Four prominent Muslim notables—Abdallah Yafi, Saeb Salam, Sabri Hamadeh, and Ahmad al-Assaad—announced that they would boycott the ceremonies marking the return of Chamoun and Sulh on a Turkish yacht.[56] The suspicions of the pro-Cairo bloc in Lebanon that the Chamoun regime was drifting toward the West could only have been confirmed when Colonel Adnan Malki, the Syrian army's most important Baathist and pro-Nasser officer, was assassinated on April 22 by a member of the P.P.S. An army purge drove Syrian P.P.S. members to take refuge in Lebanon. Chamoun, who had given the party a license in 1944, who had tolerated its reorganizing in Lebanon, and who shared its distaste for the forces who were against the Baghdad Pact, refused to grant the Syrian government's demands for extradition. In May Sami Sulh declared in Parliament, in reply to anti-Baghdad Pact speeches, that it would be foolish for Lebanon to help isolate Iraq, a counterweight to Egyptian pressures and an important trading partner.

President Chamoun's reasons for not joining the Baghdad Pact but instead opting for a pro-Western neutrality toward it are not difficult to imagine. In terms of the logic of the Lebanese National Pact, friendship with the West and part of the Arab world seemed preferable to friendship with another part of the Arab world and the Soviet bloc. Lebanon's economic and social links with the United States were numerous and important; Lebanese Christians had a deep cultural and spiritual affinity for Europe; and President Chamoun's own dealings with the British had left him with a frank admiration for their character as a people. Even more important, perhaps, was Chamoun's growing realization that President Nasser was on the verge of becoming too powerful, and therefore too dangerous, in the area. Indeed, his hatred and fear of Nasser are reminiscent of those of Sir Anthony Eden's but perhaps more understandable. As a professional diplomat, Chamoun could see very clearly that Lebanon would ultimately have to orient its policies to harmonize with those of whatever "great power" emerged in Arab regional politics, and he may have reasoned that Lebanon could not long survive if that power were firmly anti-Western.

Although Chamoun was sensitive to the international implications of the Middle East power struggle, he cared less about the limitations that the domestic situation places on the Lebanese President's conduct of foreign policy. Unlike Bechara al-Khoury, who was patient and successful in dealing with his notables, President Chamoun had enormous difficulties in trying to establish a solid power base. Because he had been put into power by a complex coalition of notables and nascent radical groups that was plagued with contradictions and rivalries, Chamoun hardly had the opportunity to utilize the "natural" power structure of Lebanon. A brief survey of cabinet politics in the year preceding the Suez crisis will reveal some of the turmoil that President Chamoun faced.

The events of the first half of 1955 placed increasingly heavy strains on the cabinet of Sami Sulh, the least pan-Arab in orientation of all the candidates for Prime Minister. The foreign situation hindered the reform attempt of Chamoun and the Prime Minister, and reform, as a political tactic, failed to divert parliamentary attention from the struggles taking place outside Lebanese boundaries. Despite a partial cabinet reshuffle in July, which replaced the staunch old independent, former President Alfred Naccache, as Foreign Minister with the Cairo-oriented Hamid Frangieh, the opposition was unsatisfied. The Baghdad Pact had become an issue with powerful emotional impact, and a simple cabinet reshuffle was insufficient to counter it. Frangieh lost no time in bringing down the cabinet by resigning early in September. Frangieh, it will be recalled, had clashed with Chamoun nine years previously in Paris during the troop-evacuation negotiations, when both were maneuvering for the Presidency; then in 1952 he had lost to Chamoun. In that contest one of Chamoun's advantages had been his influence and sympathies with the Arab world, whereas Frangieh's reputation at that time was only local in scope. Now the positions were reversed: Frangieh was the leading Maronite pro-Egyptian spokesman, bidding perhaps for non-Christian support in the next Presidential election; Chamoun, saddled with his own responsibilities and a conflicting Western orientation, appeared to be playing a more equivocal role.[57] For a week after the resignations, Chamoun backed Sami Sulh's efforts to assemble another coalition, but the opposition, more than usually united by the polarization in the Arab world, insisted on a prime minister friendly to Cairo. The two candidates that commanded the most support were Saeb Salam of Beirut and Rashid Karami of Tripoli, both of whom were outspoken sympathizers with the Cairo bloc, and Chamoun reportedly was not enthusiastic about either one. Finally Chamoun designated Rashid Karami as the new Prime Minister.

Karami promptly declared that he would observe Hamid Frangieh's informal agreement with Nasser that stated that Lebanon was against imperialist military pacts.[58] This announcement put the Prime Minister somewhat out of step with the President. Chamoun, however, had little room for maneuver because his strength vis-à-vis the opposition was much less potent than the monopoly of power that the Khoury machine had exercised at its height. The opposition had a powerful and popular foreign issue, in addition to the incessant patronage squabbles that increasingly discredited the Chamoun regime. Since 1953 opponents of the regime had also been grouped in a common front composed of such dignitaries as Hussein Oueini, who enjoyed good relations with the government of Saudi Arabia; the notables of the ex-Destour, now nominally reorganized as the Democratic Party and quietly supported by the deposed President from his villa at Kaslik; Ahmad al-Assaad, who particularly resented President Chamoun's support for a rival, Kazem Khalil; Kamal Jumblat, leading the hard-core elements of the old S.N.F. and the powerful P.S.P.; the Sunnite businessmen of the Hay'at al-Watania; and radical Arab nationalists in the various clubs around the American University of Beirut and in the coastal towns. The small Communist Party, too, supported the enemies of the Baghdad Pact but could not play a major role because it was vigorously persecuted by the government. President Chamoun's support, on the other hand, had not crystallized to the same extent, partly because his "natural" allies in this situation were the conservative Lebanese nationalists who included four potential rivals for the Presidency. The two most direct competitors, Raymond Edde and Pierre Gemayel (of the National Bloc and the Kataeb, respectively) were unwilling to commit themselves fully to the President. The new Maronite Patriarch, Butros-Boulos Meouchi, who succeeded the conservative Antoun Arida, was still an unknown quantity, as was the Commander of the Army, General Fuad Chehab, who had already been head of state for a brief period. President Chamoun, therefore, recruited several newcomers to the cabinet to provide a counterweight to the Prime Minister. But the events of the fall and winter—the Soviet-Egyptian arms agreement, the Egyptian-Syrian military treaty, the Israeli assault on Syria at Lake Tiberias—only increased the pressures on Lebanon to demonstrate its commitment. Lebanon was offered membership in both the Iraqi-Turk and the Egyptian-Syrian military pacts. Although Prime Minister Karami declared himself favorable to the latter,[59] President Chamoun, mindful of the other half of the nation, reportedly declared that Lebanon would like to conclude a military pact with Syria, as long as the interests of other Arab countries like Iraq were not jeopardized by it.[60]

The domestic ramifications of the Cold War did not work entirely to Chamoun's disadvantage. Negotiations with the Iraq Petroleum Company (I.P.C.) over transit fees gave the President an opportunity to show that Lebanon could be tough with a British firm; and, because the Prime Minister's constituency was Tripoli, where the I.P.C. refinery is located, President Chamoun had a means for controlling Karami, whose prestige was on the line in the negotiations. Furthermore, the President's followers in the cabinet provided another check on the Prime Minister; and, when seven of them resigned suddenly in January 1956 over a rumor that Karami was about to redistribute administrative posts in favor of Muslims, Presidential intervention was necessary to persuade them to stay on. Through astute manipulation of his institutional powers, Chamoun had managed, through Karami, to make a gesture of support for the Syrian-Saudi Arabian-Egyptian bloc without a firm commitment; at the same time he used the conservatives to keep Karami in check, and finally on March 15 he let the cabinet fall over one of many domestic problems.[61]

President Chamoun's exploitation of local particularisms is evident in his appointment of two of Karami's Beirut rivals, Abdallah Yafi and Saeb Salam, as Prime Minister and Minister of State, respectively, in the next cabinet. Yafi's cabinet caved in after only two months and two weeks; its demise was precipitated by complaints about the handling of reconstruction efforts in the wake of an earthquake in March. The new cabinet differed little in composition from its predecessors, and the only notable casualty was Emile Bustani, the Public Works and Planning Minister, who lost his portfolio, although he kept his job as head of the Earthquake Reconstruction Office. So far, President Chamoun had exploited the parliamentary game to keep the domestic scene under control while waiting for the regional crisis to go away. Instead, however, it exploded in the chain reaction of events beginning with the withdrawal of Western aid for the Aswan High Dam Project (July 18, 1956), the nationalization of the Suez Canal (July 26), and the Anglo-French-Israeli invasion of Egypt (October 29). A crucial test for Lebanese policy and President Chamoun's diplomacy was at hand.

The situation would have been difficult even if relations between Lebanon and Egypt were not strained. As we have seen, however, the pro-Cairo elements found Chamoun's foreign policy wanting, even though it was formally correct. As for Chamoun, he was well aware, by July 1956, that political disruptions were being produced in Lebanon by Cairo: "La politique nassérienne de dislocation nationale avait, depuis 1955, fait ses ravages dans les milieux libanais. Sous le couvert de la lutte engagée contre le Pacte de Bagdad, les dirigeants du Caïre commençaient à encourager une opposition systématique contre les pouvoirs établis. . . ." [62] These clear manifestations of Egyptian interference produced countermanifestations in the form of demonstrations and petitions that affirmed strict Lebanese sovereignty and deepened the growing crack in national unity so carefully nurtured after independence. President Chamoun quickly sent a message of support after the nationalization of the Suez Canal, and made a public address in which he reiterated that Lebanon stood behind what was clearly a legitimate exercise of Egyptian sovereignty, even if the action did have a "brusque aspect." He also reassured Britain and France that Egypt knew that its own interests lay in developing the Canal rather than in restricting its use.[63] This position, however, could hardly be called one of enthusiastic approval, and the Egyptians were displeased. Lebanese conservatives, however, were relieved at the restrained character of the response. At the same time that the London Conference was attempting to relieve the Suez crisis and the French, British, and Israelis were planning their invasion, the Lebanese cabinet was negotiating with the proprietors of two oil carriers, the Trans-Arabian Pipeline and the Iraq Petroleum Company, whose installations terminate at Saida and Tripoli respectively. For thirteen months the negotiations over revised transit fees had been going on, and the two Lebanese negotiators, first Rashid Karami and then Saeb Salam, had suffered a loss of prestige among their nationalist followings because of their inability to obtain the companies' agreement to substantially higher fees. The companies had not hesitated to use diplomatic pressures and threats to fire employees; the I.P.C. even threatened to move its entire operation to Banyas in Syria. By late October the Yafi cabinet and Saeb Salam, the special negotiator, were in considerable difficulty because of their failure to strike a better bargain, and the opposition press was predicting the cabinet's collapse when President Chamoun returned from a visit to Iran, the newest adherent to the Baghdad Pact.[64] Egypt's nationalization of the Canal Company can only have added both to the Arab nationalist zeal and to the discomfiture of such notables as Yafi and Salam, whose own commitment and popularity increasingly reflected Cairo's brilliance.

Within hours of the Israeli invasion President Chamoun, anticipating the position into which the opposition would try to force him, called a conference of all Arab heads of state in Beirut to decide on concerted action. Aside from the merits of such a conference in terms of the crisis itself, the move was a shrewdly conceived device for demonstrating Lebanon's commitment to a cause that could bridge the gap at least temporarily between Baghdad and Cairo. It emphasized Lebanon's useful role as a mediator, without attachment to any particular Arab faction. This initiative also served as an instrument for parrying criticism of Lebanon's reluctance to break diplomatic relations with Britain and France.

Breaking diplomatic relations with the two countries most responsible for the Lebanese Republic's existence was not a pleasant move for President Chamoun to contemplate. Only a few months earlier he had been quoted as saying: "Our time will come. The

Russians and Egyptians are busy among the people. We will not be able to resist without strong support from the West." [65] Yet he well knew that such a gesture would be demanded, and it is reasonable to suppose that he too was indignant at the tripartite collusion and aggression. A source close to the President reports that Chamoun actually took the initiative, while the bombs were falling, in urging that all the Arab countries break relations at the very least.[66] Lebanon would not even insist that the Arab states be unanimous in this policy, although a unified approach would certainly be more effective. Chamoun ultimately went all the way with the pro-Cairo group, leaving the Sunnite opposition with little to complain about. Chamoun's escape clause lay in his reasonable proposal that Lebanon could not act alone, vulnerable as it was to pressures from all sides. Events moved so swiftly that Lebanon was luckily spared the necessity of substantive action.

The Egyptian decision to withdraw in view of the overwhelming superiority of the tripartite invasion force ruled out a military response on the part of the other Arab states.[67] For Lebanon the immediate concern was defensive, and President Chamoun promptly named General Fuad Chehab as military governor and imposed martial law. By the time the conference of Arab heads of state convened on November 13, the fighting was over, and the main objective of the Arabs, President Chamoun now states, was then to secure the removal of Israeli forces from Egyptian territory. This end would not be served if all the Arab states broke off relations with Britain and France.[68] A resolution written by President Chamoun was unanimously adopted on November 15. It called upon the Great Powers to implement the United Nations Security Council resolution that called for a withdrawal of the Anglo-French-Israeli forces and the separate consideration of the problems of the Suez Canal and the recent aggression. The heads of state also declared their support for the Algerian people in their struggle for independence and saluted President Nasser and the Egyptian people for their patriotic spirit.[69]

The proposal for a joint unified Arab military command discussed at this conference established the precedent for the one set up eight years later, though it had little effect on the resolution of the crisis.[70] As a stratagem in the Lebanese political context, the proposal succeeded to some extent in taking the wind out of the sails of the opposition, a process begun by Chamoun's cool handling of the question of breaking diplomatic relations. In the first days of the crisis Chamoun had been pressured by Salam and Yafi to break relations. Their veiled threat to resign over that issue was forgotten during the conference itself, according to Chamoun; but the day after the conference ended, to Chamoun's "great astonishment," they did resign, bringing down the entire government.[71] From the point of view of Yafi and Salam, however, President Chamoun had hedged dishonorably during the crisis. They felt that the least Lebanon might have done was to break relations with England and France; and, when the government failed to do so, they felt that it was no longer honorable to be associated with the Chamoun regime. Resignation was the only choice.[72] Chamoun's agile maneuvering had made it difficult for his domestic enemies to oppose him successfully over the Suez crisis. The fall of Yafi's cabinet could be interpreted as a victory for the regime, insofar as it had adroitly weakened and shaken off the pro-Cairo faction with a minimum of strain. On the other hand, the anti-Westerners could claim that their withdrawal had weakened and embarrassed the President and revealed his true, proimperialist colors. Chamoun seems clearly to have been the short-run winner; he succeeded in maintaining the political initiative throughout. As the editorialist for *L'Orient*—no friend of the regime at that time—put it: "Le Chef de l'Etat est devenu tout le Législatif et tout l'Executif; et cela est tellement vrai que l'on s'aperçoit, chaque fois qu'il s'absente, que tous les pouvoirs sont absents avec lui. . . ." [73]

In the long run, victory went to the pro-Cairo bloc, and Chamoun's surface brilliance as a politician dimmed. Camille Chamoun did enlarge the scope and influence of the Presidency through his initiatives and activism. His strong personality dominated local politics and society. Up until the spring 1957 elections and under extremely difficult circumstances, he made the Presidency more than an umpire between opposing forces and gave it a degree of dynamism. After that date, as Lebanon slid toward anarchy, his initiatives threatened the traditional structures, and his dynamism took on dictatorial overtones. Hindsight shows that he did not succeed in building for the Presidency a solid, reliable, and universalistic base of support. Consequently, like his predecessor, he spent energies that might have been used more constructively for other purposes to balance factions against one another and thus to stave off the demands of a disorganized but growing opposition.

NOTES

[1] Among them are René Ajjiouri of *L'Orient,* Bassem al-Jisr of *al-Jarīda,* Ruchdi Maalouf of *al-Ṣafā,* and Ghassan Tueni of *al-Nahār.*

[2] The French, not unreasonably, assumed that they could always control the selection of the President. They may therefore have regarded a powerful Presidency as a useful adjunct to their control over the vital administrative and security agencies of the state.

[3] American University of Beirut Department of Political Studies and Public Administration, *The Lebanese Constitution: A Reference Edition in English Translation* (Beirut: Khayat's, 1960).

[4] These three were Riad Sulh, who headed four governments consecutively from December 1946 to February 1951; Sami Sulh, who headed three between November 1956 and September 1958; and Rashid Karami, who headed two consecutively during the period from September 1958 to May 1960 and another one from October 1961 through February 1964, by far the longest-lived government since independence in 1943.

[5] The fourth delegate was Camille Chamoun, then Lebanon's minister in London and—although a Destourian—a potential rival of Khoury for the Presidency. Chamoun criticized the other three members of the mission for bowing to French intransigence (he obviously hoped such criticism would discredit President Khoury), and he was especially critical of Frangieh, another rival for the Presidency. See Camille Chamoun, *Crise au Moyen-Orient* (Paris: Gallimard, 1963), pp. 175–9.

[6] *L'Orient,* April 6, 1946. Bechara al-Khoury, *Haqā'iq lubnāniyyah* [*Lebanese Truths*], II (Beirut: Awrāq lubnāniyyah, 1961), 233, reports that Salem explained his resignation on the grounds that he knew Sami Sulh's government was sinking fast and did not want to go down with it. Frangieh was unhappy because Chamoun, through General Spears' contacts in Lebanon, had been attacking him behind his back.

[7] *L'Orient,* April 10, 1946; Khoury, *op. cit.,* II, 236–7.

[8] Khoury, *op. cit,* II, 237. Among these leaders were Yussef Karam (Maronite, North Lebanon), Muhammad Abboud (Sunnite, North Lebanon), Omar Beyham (Sunnite, Beirut), Omar Daouk (Sunnite, Beirut), Habib Trad (Greek Orthodox, Beirut), Nuhad Arslan (Druze, Mount Lebanon), Alfred Naccache (Maronite, Beirut), and Kamal Jumblat (Druze, Mount Lebanon).

[9] *L'Orient,* May 8, 1946.

[10] *Ibid.,* May 5, 1946.

[11] *Ibid.,* May 10, 1946. Khoury denies that he instigated Arslan's speech. Khoury, *op. cit.,* II, 238.

[12] *L'Orient,* May 16, 1946.

[13] Khoury, *op. cit.,* II, 239.

[14] *Ibid.,* p. 240.

[15] Karami's program consisted of the following points: first, to modify the constitution to make a stronger executive department; second, to redraw the electoral districts along district lines, rather than by province, and to guarantee free elections; third, to abolish the Ministry of Supply; fourth, to reorganize

the Sûreté Générale; fifth, to reduce the bureaucracy; sixth, to create an accounting department and a civil-service board; seventh, to develop new educational programs; eighth, to invite foreign experts to study Lebanon's financial and agricultural problems; and, ninth, to change the administration of foreign affairs. See *L'Orient,* May 22, 1946. By 1964, the second, third, fourth, sixth, and eighth points had been accomplished.

[16] Khoury, *op. cit.,* II, 240.

[17] The followers of Sami Sulh were persuaded to participate in the same Cabinet with Sabri Hamadeh; the Pharaon group was to participate with Hamid Frangieh and Riad Sulh himself, Pharaon to relinquish his claim to the Ministry of the Interior, Arslan and Jumblat to serve together, and the Shiites to accept representation of only one portfolio. The second Maronite portfolio finally went to Camille Chamoun because, as Chamoun suggests, his great popularity in Mount Lebanon was essential for the Destour in the forthcoming parliamentary elections. Camille Chamoun, *op. cit.,* p. 198.

[18] "Why are we Riadists? Because, taking into account his virtues and his defects—of the changes and risks that he represents—we find that Mr. Riad Sulh is, in the new Lebanese equilibrium, at the center of our entire political system. To what does he owe the privilege? Less perhaps to his own genius or to the virtues of his character than to a combination of elements that have acted and continue to act in his favor. His personality, his past, his domestic position, his international relationships—in fact, the whole subtle play of imponderables that crystallize around him—contribute to making him an indispensable leader." *L'Orient,* December 15, 1946.

[19] This figure excludes the three short-lived cabinets following Sami Sulh's dramatic resignation on September 9, 1952. If they were included, the figure would still be 7.8 months, well above the figure for the Chamoun era.

[20] Chamoun, *op. cit.,* pp. 78–9, describes his first political victory in the campaign for the Chamber of Deputies in 1929 and the political ambition it inspired.

[21] According to Chamoun, *op. cit.,* pp. 107–8, Emile Edde, who sensed defeat, proposed to withdraw his candidature if Khoury would withdraw his; Edde suggested Chamoun's name as one of three he would find acceptable. Edde then withdrew his proposal because he believed that he had mustered sufficient support from the Délégation-Générale to win. At a meeting of the Destour, Khoury offered to leave Chamoun's name in as the party's candidate, but Chamoun declined and promised Khoury his total support. In order to deceive the French, however, Chamoun suggested that the party leave his name, whereupon the French—who considered Chamoun the man of the British— promptly withdrew their support from Edde in exchange for the Destour withdrawing its support from Chamoun. Bechara al-Khoury thus became the compromise candidate. Khoury, *op. cit.,* I, 257–65, tells a different story. He claims that he had a clear majority several days before the election. Edde saw that his rival was about to win and therefore declared that he (Edde) would withdraw in favor of any of four men, not including Khoury, one of whom was Chamoun. When informed by the British General Spears of this maneuver, Khoury immediately called the bluff, declaring his readiness to forfeit in favor of Chamoun if Edde would also withdraw. The French, fearing that

Chamoun, "the man of the British," might win as the compromise candidate, were furious and threatened to tell General de Gaulle. Khoury believes that Edde hoped that De Gaulle would annul or prevent the election. Finally, Edde was prevailed upon not to retire in favor of Chamoun and Khoury's candidacy was reopened. Chamoun was visibly unhappy at the turn of events and would not formally withdraw his own candidacy but pledged "his" votes to Khoury instead.

[22] Chamoun, *op. cit.,* pp. 124–5, writes that, through his quick thinking as Minister of the Interior, he saved the regime from an attempted coup that resulted from the election of the antigovernment candidate in a North Lebanon by-election in April 1944. This effort prompted the French to send him away.

[23] Chamoun, *op. cit.,* pp. 198–9. Chamoun writes that the irregularities of the campaign provoked his break with President Khoury, which, however, did not become public until the latter announced his intention to seek a second term in May 1948. When Parliament actually re-elected the President on May 29, Chamoun resigned his post as Minister of Finance and formally entered the opposition. Chamoun, *op. cit.,* pp. 232–3.

[24] Chamoun, *op. cit.,* p. 243, writes that Frangieh was supported by the clergy, financial circles, and several foreign interests (including, presumably, France).

[25] *Daily Star* (Beirut), September 30, 1952. See also Yusif El-Khalil, *The Socialist Parties in Syria and Lebanon* (Unpublished doctoral dissertation, American University of Beirut, 1962), p. 169. These demands were the more extreme items of a ten-point program, and other sections were ultimately implemented.

[26] *Daily Star,* September 26 and 27, 1952.

[27] *Ibid.,* October 1, 1952.

[28] Khaled Chehab had been a member of the 1922 Representative Council.

[29] *Daily Star,* October 10, 1952. Sami Sulh, the Prime Minister whose resignation precipitated the original crisis, voted against the government, whereas two former friends of the Destour, Selim al-Khazen and Charles Helou (the future President), abstained.

[30] These decrees were intended to create new administrative cadres in all ministries and departments. A new personnel law was issued; the judicial system was revised; new accounting and auditing procedures were introduced; and the Board of Economic Planning and Development was created. Furthermore, about 600 contract employees were fired. Ralph E. Crow and Adnan Iskandar, "Administrative Reform in Lebanon, 1958–1959," *International Review of Administrative Sciences,* No. 3 (1961), pp. 293–307.

[31] Chamoun, *op. cit.,* p. 247. He does not claim that this codification actually eradicated the corruption that was rampant throughout the apparatus and especially in the Ministry of Public Works.

[32] *Ibid.,* p. 248.

[33] Deputy Kabouli Zaouk complained about the "snail's pace" of reforms. *Daily Star,* October 24, 1952.

[34] *L'Orient,* February 20, 1953.

[35] *Ibid.,* February 24, 1953.

[36] *Ibid.,* February 27, 1953.

[37] *Ibid.,* March 14, 1953. Simultaneously, a serious public dispute was going on as the result of an "Islamic Congress" and the countermanifesto of Christian notables, which had been the result of suggestions for closer economic unity with Syria.

[38] See, for example, *ibid.,* April 22, 1953, for an account of a parliamentary debate in which the old Destourian Emile Lahoud accused the government of replacing tens of bureaucrats with hundreds and of mismanaging affairs in the Ministry of Education. The Destourians sought without success to have the decree laws annulled.

[39] Its members were Joseph Chader of the Kataeb, Nassim Majdalani of the Progressive Socialist Party, Takieddine Sulh of the National Appeal, and Habib Rebeiz of the Hay'at al-Watania. *Ibid.,* February 10, 1954.

[40] Crow and Iskandar, *op. cit.,* Pt. I.

[41] *L'Orient,* May 28, 1955.

[42] They were *al-Nahār* (rightist, pro-P.P.S.), *al-'Amal* (the Kataeb journal), *al-Hayāt* (pro-British), and *al-Dyār* (leftist).

[43] *L'Orient,* July 9, 1954, commented: "La crise ministerielle la plus scandaleuse que le Liban ait jamais connue s'est ouverte hier. Une misérable querelle autour de l'attribution d'une Ambassade a fini par emporter tout un Gouvernement. . . ."

["The most scandalous ministerial crisis that Lebanon has ever known began yesterday. A wretched quarrel over the award of an ambassadorship ended by overturning a whole government. . . ."]

[44] It was at this point that Pierre Gemayel of the Kataeb shot back at the Muslims who were demanding more positions by stating: "Ne craignent-ils pas qu'ils réclament, par exemple, l'égalité devant les charges destinées à alimenter la tresorerie de l'Etat? Il est en effet établi que les Chrétiens paient un peu plus de quatre-vingt pour cent des impôts alors que le Musulmans n'en acquittent que vingt pour cent."

["Aren't they afraid that they will achieve, for example, equality in payments to feed the state treasury? It is an established fact that the Christians pay a little more than 80 per cent of the taxes, whereas the Muslims contribute only 20 per cent."]

Ibid., July 10, 1955.

[45] For example, there were the flurry of excitement in March 1953 over the Islamic Congress and its Christian counterpart and the "Chakar affair" of summer 1954, which concerned the distribution of a pamphlet insulting to the Prophet Muhammad. See Chapter 3 of this book and *L'Orient,* March 14–20, 1953, and July 30–August 2, 1954.

[46] *L'Orient,* October 18, 1958.

[47] George Grassmuck and Kamal Salibi, *Reformed Administration in Lebanon* (Beirut: Catholic Press, 1964), pp. 18–9. Adnan Iskandar, *Bureaucracy in Lebanon* (Beirut: American University, 1964), p. 136, comments that, although Chamoun showed more concern for reform than his predecessor had, his efforts were "superficial and unsuccessful" and "did not result in overall significant changes in the administrative machinery."

[48] Approximately 78 per cent of President Chamoun's account of his regime

(143 of 186 pages, not counting his description of the 1958 crisis), *op. cit.*, is devoted to foreign affairs.

[49] *Ibid.*, pp. 254–60.

[50] For a detailed analysis, see Charles D. Cremeans, *The Arabs and the World* (New York: Praeger, 1963), pp. 137–48.

[51] For a discussion of the Egyptian policy, see Erskine Childers, *The Road to Suez* (London: MacGibbon & Kee, 1962), pp. 111 ff.

[52] Patrick Seale, *The Struggle for Syria* (London: Oxford, 1965), pp. 220–37. For a complete account, see also chaps. 15, 18. Syria became the first Arab country to receive Soviet arms when it received a small shipment of tanks in 1954. *Ibid.*, pp. 232–4.

[53] The text of his message and of the Egyptian responses is in Chamoun, *op. cit.*, pp. 267–8.

[54] "The Baghdad Pact, useful perhaps in the defense of the northern borders of Iraq, had not aroused in me any particular interest. I wanted, however, to see the Arabs break out of the tight circle in which they still wanted to confine themselves and to open themselves to political, economic, and military cooperation with such neighboring states as Pakistan, Iran, and Turkey." *Ibid.*, p. 266.

[55] According to Chamoun, *op. cit.*, p. 272, he had originally been invited to Turkey in October 1954, when there had been "no question" of the Turko-Iraqi treaty; the dictates of protocol fixed the precise date. He writes that the idea of Lebanon's joining the Baghdad Pact was brought up during the talks but that he rejected it, saying that Lebanon could not cavalierly disregard Arab public opinion (p. 276).

[56] *Arab World Opinion,* April 6 and 12, 1955.

[57] Chamoun, *op. cit.*, p. 281, suggests that Frangieh's behavior was motivated by narrow political considerations and that there was no valid reason for his resignation. Frangieh's pretext—if it really was a pretext—was the alleged irregular exemption of certain companies from their income taxes by the previous Minister of Finance. *L'Orient,* September 5 and 7, 1955. Hamid Frangieh was shortly afterward incapacitated by illness and withdrew from politics.

[58] *L'Orient,* September 8–21, 1955. *Arab World Opinion,* September 27, 1955.

[59] *L'Orient,* October 20 and 28, 1955.

[60] *Arab World Opinion,* January 3, 1956. The Syrian Defense Minister called this outlook a "negative attitude."

[61] *L'Orient,* March 15 and 16, 1956. The particular issue was a proposal for subsidizing private schools, which Karami and Minister of Finance Jamil Mikkawi (both Sunnites) opposed, though the Minister of Education, a Maronite, supported it.

[62] "The Nasserian policy of national dislocation had since 1955 created disturbances in Lebanese quarters. Under cover of the struggle against the Baghdad Pact, the Cairo leaders began to encourage a systematic opposition to the established authorities. . . ." Chamoun, *op. cit.*, p. 281. He charges that the Egyptian embassy in Beirut was a center for subversion and propaganda

and that shops in certain sections of Beirut and in Saida and Tripoli had begun to display portraits of President Nasser.

[63] The text of this message is in Chamoun, *op. cit.,* pp. 282–3.

[64] *L'Orient,* October 24, 1956.

[65] A Turkish Foreign Office official reported that Chamoun made this statement after John Bagot Glubb's dismissal in Jordan; quoted in Terence Robertson, *Crisis: The Inside Story of the Suez Conspiracy* (New York: Atheneum, 1965), pp. 44–5.

[66] Emile Bustani, in *al-Hayāt,* April 24, 1957, wrote that he was present in council with the President, along with Ministers Yafi, Salam, and Selim Lahoud, when Chamoun made this statement.

[67] Seale, *op. cit.,* p. 262, reports that the Egyptians restrained Syrian officers from retaliating because they feared an Anglo-French invasion of Syria. The British bombing, which began on the evening of October 31, persuaded the Egyptian command to withdraw on all fronts. Childers, *op. cit.,* pp. 292–3.

[68] Chamoun, *op. cit.,* pp. 302–5. Lebanon was the only Arab state in the area that did not break relations with either country. Saudi Arabia and Syria followed Egypt in breaking with both, whereas Iraq and Jordan broke only with France.

[69] *Ibid.,* pp. 311–3.

[70] The conference is not even mentioned in the studies of the Suez crisis by Terence Robertson, *op. cit.;* Herman Finer, *Dulles Over Suez* (Chicago: Quadrangle, 1964); and Erskine Childers, *op. cit.*

[71] Chamoun, *op. cit.,* p. 314.

[72] Interview with Abdallah Yafi, July 1, 1965. Yafi also recalls that he had suggested the idea of a conference to Chamoun in the first place.

[73] "The Chief of State has become the sole legislator and the entire executive; that statement is so true that it seems, each time that he is away, that all power has gone with him. . . ." *L'Orient,* June 17, 1956.

CHAPTER · 8

Presidential Power: The Attempt to Modernize

The 1958 crisis, the watershed in the politics of independent Lebanon, brought into the Presidency General Fuad Chehab, Commander of the Army. President Chehab's background and personality, his attitude toward politics, his conception of the Presidency, and, finally, his performance as President set him apart from his two predecessors. President Chehab made it his mission, once a degree of national reconciliation had been achieved, to modernize the state. During the six years of the General's rule the Presidency grew in power and made substantial changes in the traditional political practices; but, when it was all over, the question remained whether or not Lebanon could ever break out of its political stalemate.

The Chehab regime sought to modernize the Lebanese system in three ways. First, Chehab attempted to circumvent traditional politics without, however, disturbing "normal" political life; he drew heavily on "new men" in the professions and the army. Second, the President undertook the transformation of the state administration on a larger scale than any attempted before and with somewhat greater success. Third, there was a significant elaboration of the prevailing political doctrine to encompass radical demands for social justice without sacrificing the dogma of a "free economy" and political sectarianism. For the first time the Presidency became the source of a national political philosophy and the term "Chehabism" entered the political lexicon.[1] Chehabism—Lebanon's equivalent of the New Deal—was basically a moderate welfare ideology tailored to the Lebanese situation.

A New Political Style

Under normal circumstances the Lebanese system would never have drawn a man of General Chehab's background or temperament to the Presidency. Politics in Lebanon is a game that primarily attracts cosmopolitan lawyers and bankers. General Chehab, on the other hand, belonged to a profession held in low esteem by the establishment. Military service, as one of the notables put it, is the last refuge for those who cannot succeed in business or the respectable professions. As a fighting machine the Lebanese army is virtually untested, unable to boast of either decisive victories or heroic defeats.[2] It therefore commands little prestige among the middle or upper classes. Furthermore, General Chehab did not have the personality of a typical successful Lebanese politician. Whereas the prototype politician, as described earlier, is a sophisticated political broker, extravagant in manner and quite at home in the labyrinth of Lebanese politics, the General was reserved, straightforward, and somewhat disdainful of the political game.[3] To his admirers he was also distinguished from most of the politicians for his honesty, his methodical leadership, and his selfless devotion to the interests of Lebanon. Lebanese radicals of all persuasions were drawn to General Chehab because he appeared to share with them a wish for order and clarity in political life, whatever the substantive goals might be.

President Chehab was born in 1903 in the Kisrwan district of Mount Lebanon, and entered the military service when he was nineteen years old.[4] He belonged to one of Lebanon's most famous families and was distantly related to Amir Bashir III who ruled briefly after the Egyptian withdrawal in 1840. He attended village schools and the Collège des Frères Maristes in Jounieh. In 1921 he was admitted to the Damascus Military Academy and left it two years later as a sublieutenant in the Mixed Troops in the service of the Mandate. Chehab became a lieutenant in 1929 and a captain in 1930 and was then sent to France for further military training. Between 1931 and 1937 he commanded the garrison at Rachaya. After another year in France he returned to Lebanon at the beginning of World War II. After Lebanon fell under British-Gaullist control, Chehab was charged with organizing detachments of the Troupes Spéciales du Levant for service in Libya, Tunisia, Italy, and France. Already a lieutenant-colonel in 1944, he was made a general in 1945 and Commander in Chief of the Troupes Spéciales in Lebanon. When the Lebanese army was created in 1946, Chehab was its first commander. One of his main interests as commander was developing a modern, scientifically oriented, and professional organization.[5] He inspired unusual respect and devotion; he reportedly insisted on passing on each promotion personally and knew a great many of his men by name. The General was more successful in modernizing the army than the politicians were in modernizing their political organizations. General Chehab's "nonpolitical" characteristics, far from constituting a barrier to personal power, were an asset that brought him more widespread popularity than he could have enjoyed by belonging to one—or indeed all—of Lebanon's political parties.

The General's rise as a politician was a function of Lebanon's political divisions. Specifically, it resulted from the cyclical collisions between radical and establishment elements, with the outcome of each conflict dependent on how, or whether or not, Chehab used the coercive powers of the state. A series of emergencies between 1948 and 1958 placed Presidents Khoury and Chamoun in a position in which they had to call for Chehab's assistance. In most developed states the power of the head of state over the commander of the army is clear, and for the military man to disobey a civilian command is treason; but in Lebanon the Constitution is ambiguous on the nature of this relationship.[6] The constitutional vagueness only reflects the real situation: The army, formally a nonsectarian organization, was devoted to its founder and commander, and the commander saw his primary obligation as the preserver of the state before all other commitments. The Presidents requested rather than commanded his cooperation. On a number of occasions during both regimes General Chehab did cooperate, notably during the abortive P.P.S. coup of 1949 and the Suez crisis of 1956; but, as indicated in Chapter 3, his refusal to aid the Presidents in 1952 and 1958 greatly altered the course of events and made him a powerful political figure. The turmoil of the 1958 civil war and the American intervention in Lebanon brought Chehab to the Presidency. His conspicuous lack of involvement in the deepening crisis, at the same time others were discrediting themselves through partisan participation, made him the only figure who could possibly stabilize the system. General Chehab did not have to plot a coup or proclaim a revolution to achieve power. It was unnecessary: The opportunity was thrust upon him. On July 31, 1958 the reluctant General was elected President by a vote of forty-eight to seven.[7]

As long as General Chehab was exercising negative influence, he was undisturbed by the normal political activity; but, when he was elected President, he was required to alter the scope, base, and style of his power. Chehab was compelled even more than his predecessors to dominate the traditional political system. In the first place, the traditional system had been torn apart by the 1958 crisis, particularly the events of September and October, and the establishment seemed incapable of restoring national unity by itself. In the second place, Chehab needed to fulfill the expectations of his supporters among the insurgents that he would reform the state and adhere to a more pro-Arab interpretation of the National Pact than had President Chamoun. For these reasons it would no longer be possible simply to ignore the politicians; Chehab set about trying to control them. His strategy was to build on the alliance of the rural, largely non-Christian landowners and progressive forces that had supported the insurgents and to temper it with a considerable injection of younger, non-political types—professional men, who would serve the purposes of promoting nonpartisanship and of improving the administration. They would also owe their loyalty directly to the President.

Chehab's first cabinet, formed September 24, 1958, was composed largely of moderates, progressives, and technicians, but it left the Chamoun partisans completely excluded. This exclusion proved to be a mistake, and fighting, precipitated by a nasty incident (the kidnaping and apparent murder of a Christian journalist of the Kataeb's party newspaper), broke out again, and the Kataeb manned the barricades. On October 15, in an extremely tense atmosphere, Chehab formed a new cabinet that made no pretenses to normality. Two important (if reluctant) supporters of the Chamoun government, Raymond Edde and Pierre Gemayel, both Maronite, were paired with two Sunnite insurgent leaders, Hussein Oueini and Rashid Karami, and Karami again was Prime Minister. This time, however, the President insisted that the cabinet be given wide emergency powers; and for a year he used them to restore normal order in the country. When Raymond Edde left this government in October 1959, as the result of his conflict with the Army and Pierre Gemayel, the cabinet was enlarged to resemble very closly the cabinet of September 1958; all the five new entrants represented moderate-to-progressive tendencies.[8] The next cabinet was deliberately made even more neutral, because its job was to preside over the 1960 parliamentary elections. To this point all of Chehab's cabinets had deviated from the norm in the political game either because of their high proportion of neutrals and new faces or because of the problems surrounding the emergency. By both means Chehab had circumvented the traditional role of both the Parliament and cabinet.

The 1960 election, however, marked a turning point in this tactic. Pro-Chehab, pro-insurgent deputies overwhelmingly outnumbered the little band of Chamounians and Edde supporters that had been returned from Mount Lebanon. With this considerable institutional support, President Chehab evidently decided the normalization of political life was then in order. His first postelection cabinet, headed by Saeb Salam, contained no less than eighteen ministers, allowing even greater scope for personal, regional, and sectarian rivalries to flourish harmlessly. As if to make sure of his hold, President Chehab, without warning, submitted his resignation on July 20, 1960, and declared that his mission of national reconstruction was over.[9] The consternation in political circles and throughout the state generally was so acute that Chehab was persuaded by an imploring Parliament to retract his resignation, which he did a few hours later. The crisis gave the President a powerful vote of confidence. It demonstrated not only his apparent indispensability but also the relative impotence of the other institutions of government.

During the remainder of his term, Chehab enjoyed a secure political position based on the cooperation of the following elements: the Kataeb, which found a meeting ground with the other groups in a common desire for moderate social improvements and which also wanted power; the Armenian Tashnaq; the Assaad bloc in South Lebanon; the Jumblat-P.S.P. bloc in the Chouf and parts of Beirut and the Biqa; the Destour; the Sunnite notables of Beirut, Tripoli, and Saida (although their support was not uniform); and various "giants" of outlying regions, like Sleiman Frangieh (brother of Chamoun's rival), René Moawad, Fuad Ghusn, and Sabri Hamadeh. These groups combined to make up a majority bloc and were consistently opposed by the much smaller group of opponents of the regime. It was by no means a disciplined bloc, however, and Chehab had to deal with the same traditional rivalries that had troubled Khoury and Chamoun. Chehab's position was much stronger, however, and he ruled undisturbed, even though the notables had resumed their rivalries. The regime was not much affected by the quarrels between Saeb Salam, Sabri Hamadeh, and Kamel al-Assaad. The fights between Camille Chamoun's new National Liberal Party and Jumblat's P.S.P. or the personal rivalry between Pierre Gemayel and Raymond Edde were not real problems for the regime. The enlarged cabinets of the Chehab regime gave the President and his Prime Minister greater maneuverability and simultaneously reduced the cabinet-wrecking capacities of the numerous factions. Cabinets averaged 10 men during the Chehab regime, compared with 8.8 men under Chamoun and 6.9 men under Khoury. Chehab governments also lasted longer, averaging 10.3 months. Rashid Karami was Prime Minister most often, alternating with Saeb Salam, compared with the greater variety of Sunnites employed by Chamoun and Khoury. Government under Chehab operated more smoothly than it had since the days of Riad Sulh.

There were, of course, problems. The only Chehab cabinet not to win overwhelming parliamentary approval was Saeb Salam's second cabinet of May 20, 1961, when Salam cut his former government from eighteen members to eight, which displeased a great many former insurgents close to his rival, Rashid Karami.[10] Karami's triumph over Salam came at the end of October 1961, when the Prime Minister found his cabinet disintegrating around him. In a classic maneuver, Kamal Jumblat, then a minister in Salam's cabinet, quarreled with Salam over a high bureaucratic appointment and launched a personal attack against Salam himself; in a bill of accusations strongly reminiscent of his assault on Khoury and Riad Sulh in 1947, he condemned the Salam government for everything from encouraging tobacco smuggling to refusing to recognize Communist China.[11] By resigning in "principle" yet remaining in office to torment the government, Jumblat for a time accomplished the remarkable feat of being both inside and outside the government simultaneously. When Salam insisted that President Chehab remove Jumblat, the President failed to use his superior position as umpire and did nothing, and another cabinet fell of its own weight. Karami, whose relations with the President were better than Salam's were, was also, according to some accounts, more willing to use his position to help the President bring about his reform program. According to others, Salam's frequent complaints about army intervention in administrative appointments were the decisive factor in the fall of his cabinet. On the whole, then, President Chehab restored the old political game to a semblance of its earlier "health," and, although he had to pay the usual price in influence peddling and inefficiency, it gave him the stability he wanted and freed his energy for the task of national development.

The major political innovation of the Chehab regime was the creation of a personal political organization quite unconnected with the traditional political system. A group of men, who owed their loyalty entirely to the President, acted as his agents within the bureaucracy and carried on the President's campaign to create an orderly and capable administration. Prominent within this top circle of advisers was the President's Chief of Cabinet, Elias Sarkis (Maronite); Père Louis-Joseph Lebret, a French Jesuit priest; and Intendant Jean Lay, a particularly close associate. Lay, an engineer and former French colonel in the Mandate service, quickly gained a reputation as the regime's *éminence grise*. His presence at meetings of the Council of Ministers and constant contacts with high officials irritated more than one non-Chehabist politician.[12] Among the other civilians in this privileged circle were the technical adviser in the President's office, Chafic Muharram (Sunnite), and Georges Haimari, head of the Customs Council and adviser to several Presidents. The President also recruited a number of younger, "progressive" intellectuals and professionals for middle-rank administrative jobs and the new agencies that he created; many of these men were brought in from outside the administration on a contract basis and at higher salaries than ordinary officials received. They, too, had direct loyalty to the President. These appointments seem to have both injected greater skill and initiative into the new administrative ventures and assured more direct presidential control.

The complexion of the President's inner group was predominantly military, however. A select group of officers, some of them trained in the United States and all extremely loyal to General Chehab as a person, were reportedly closer to him than were most of the politicians.[13] Beside this top echelon there was also a group of younger officers, captains and majors in their thirties, who were getting a taste of politics for the first time. These officers had come mostly from the lower middle class and had gone through the *deuxième partie* of the baccalauréat program (at age nineteen), after which they had attended the Army Staff College for four years. Some then went on to universities to study law and the liberal arts or enrolled at military schools in France and the United States. According to one well-placed Lebanese observer, these younger officers had no concrete political affiliations, but they shared in general a certain contempt for the politicians, "aristocrats born with silver spoons in their mouths," and a vague desire for "social justice." This attitude put them somewhat left of center in Lebanese terms but well to the right of Marxist or communist beliefs.

Whereas the army served an increasingly important political function as a deterrent to radicals and troublemakers, it also became a new instrument for carrying out the President's program. President Khoury had directed his political energies to manipulating the traditional system; President Chamoun had tried to replace it; but President Chehab, after he had enlarged the traditional arena a bit, proceeded to ignore it and to build up an organization that would exert a systematic and controlling influence in the bureaucracy, so that he could go on about the business of modernizing the country economically, socially, and politically. Had Chehab been moved by the examples of Charles de Gaulle and Gamal Abdel Nasser? The similarities between him and these two other officers in politics are striking. Chehab shared with them an attitude of distaste for civilian politicians, which he acquired during his military training in France. As De Gaulle was repelled by the incompetence of French politicians during the 1930s and Nasser was indignant at the decadence of Egyptian politics under King Farouk, so too Chehab may have felt a certain contempt for the corruption and lack of direction in Lebanon's political life. As De Gaulle and Nasser seem to have served as obvious models for General Chehab, so they may also have exerted direct political influence on the Lebanese General; during his regime he successfully cultivated warm, though discreet, relations with Paris and Cairo.[14]

The extent of army intervention in politics is very difficult to judge, especially because the press was forbidden to print news about activities of the military, other than official releases, on security grounds.[15] Well-placed and responsible individuals, however, spoke of officers applying pressure in the appointment of provincial governors and directors-general of ministries and benefiting from the allocation of certain public-works contracts. In this connection, there was some indication of intervention in the activities of the Finance Ministry over budgetary matters. A respected opposition editor claimed that the standard of living of officers had increased spectacularly under the Chehab regime. Army officers allegedly received preferential treatment when they applied for loans from the government-sponsored Agriculture and Industrial Credit Bank. Opponents of the regime claimed that good connections with the army would help one to obtain a license, to settle a dispute, or to obtain a govern-

ment job. Identical allegations had been raised against the two preceding regimes and even against the regimes of the Mandate era.

The political activities of the officers, however, were not restricted to the administrative field. Although the army applied only
selective pressures during the 1960 elections, its presence was everywhere, and the Lebanese voter—long sensitive to signs that indicated
which candidates the regime preferred—could draw his own conclusions. This degree of official pressure was certainly not unusual
for Lebanon. After the attempted coup by the P.P.S. at the end of
1961—during which several high officers close to Chehab, including
Lieutenant-Colonel Yussef Shmayet, Lieutenant-Colonel Abdel-
Kader Chehab (commander of the Beirut garrison), Lieutenant-
Colonel Toufic Jalbout, and Major François Genadry were successfully kidnaped—the army reacted with Draconian efficiency. At
least 6,000 people were arrested, the passports of six prominent
political figures—including former President Chamoun—were re-
voked, and in the public trial that followed the names of Chamoun
and Raymond Edde were mentioned in connection with the plot,
though no formal allegations were made. Thereafter, the army's surveillance of the political scene greatly increased. Enemies of the
regime found themselves the objects of intimidations that included
slashings, shootings, lawsuits, and business pressures. Editors became
aware that the regime was extremely sensitive to criticism. The 1964
elections for the Parliament that would elect (or re-elect) the President were marked by several important instances of military interference, even more than in 1960. In Akkar, a region of tough feudal
rivalries, the army reportedly backed Bashir Osman against Sleiman
al-Ali. Four years earlier the army had been neutral, and al-Ali had
beaten Osman, but in the intervening period Osman had allegedly
curried favor with the army.[16] In Baalbek-Hermel there were obvious
intimations that Sabri Hamadeh was not in favor; in Beirut Takieddine Sulh was. In Jbeil, where Raymond Edde, the army's chief
civilian opponent, thought he was assured of victory, certain elements
of the army exerted pressure, and he lost by a narrow margin. In the
Chouf President Chamoun was at first reported to have won, but a
delayed vote count indicated that he had lost after a campaign
marked by some official harassment. In Tripoli the army was out in
force on election day, which may have reminded the voters that
Rashid Karami was the President's favorite Prime Minister. Whether
or not these selective interventions were crucial in eliminating from
Parliament two potential presidential rivals and in ensuring the

success of key regime supporters is hard to say, but the results and the rumors were enough to convince many people that there might be some truth in Raymond Edde's well-publicized charges of army interference.

In the maneuvering that preceded the Presidential elections, the army scarcely hid its support for Chehab's re-election; on July 20, the fourth anniversary of the President's attempted resignation, the Defense Ministry was strung with lights like a Christmas tree, and the streets were festooned with banners, proclaiming homage to Chehab, which had been placed there at the request of the army. Some friends of the regime thought that the officers had overplayed their hand by appearing so obviously to interfere against Chehab's opponents and by identifying so openly with the Chehabist bloc in Parliament; these moves alarmed such important actors in the traditional politics as the Maronite Patriarch, certain influential bankers, and the Shiite notables in South Lebanon. There was not even complete agreement within the army on this degree of involvement, and at least one important faction, headed by a Christian officer, opposed interference in Edde's campaign.

The officers' active participation in politics was deeply resented by traditional politicians of all political tendencies. One of them remarked that, although scandal and corruption had certainly been present during previous regimes, at least it had been possible at that time to protest publicly and use the established institutions—imperfect as they were—to bring about changes; but, when the military prohibited free expression, it smothered one of the most important self-correcting devices in the Lebanese system. To notables who held this opinion, the failure of the campaign in 1964 to amend the Constitution and renew President Chehab's term saved liberal democracy in Lebanon. The other side argued that political modernization required the stronger leadership that Chehab and the military provided at the top.

Apologists for the regime pointed out, fairly enough, that intervention by the President's group in administrative appointments and decisions has been the norm rather than the exception. The fact that some of President Chehab's agents were officers was not inherently sinister: Like his predecessors, he was only using his trusted friends and associates, and they happened to be mainly military men. The politicians were unhappy, according to the Chehabists, because the officers had deprived them of patronage. The Chehabists also emphasize that the attempted coup by the P.P.S. had been a traumatic experience for the military; the kidnapings of officers had sharply reduced the tolerance and restraint that the military had long exercised in politics. Is it not understandable, they asked, that the officers, who are only human, should have showed their feelings? [17] Furthermore, the officer corps shared General Chehab's concern for modernizing the state without delay and had become impatient with what they considered the petty inefficiency of the normal political process. A high Defense Ministry official put the case bluntly. We don't think much of the politicians, he said, and the army only puts up with their petty squabbling because it is patient. Military men, therefore, were reluctant to accept the refusal of Chehab to press for another term but hoped that his successor would carry on his policies.

General Chehab certainly wished to preserve liberal democracy in Lebanon, but the divisions reopened by the 1958 crisis, the Arab "cold war" between "radical" and "conservative" regimes, and the growing domestic demands for "social justice" placed him in a difficult position. If he relied entirely on the traditional system of conflict resolution, he might have been confronted with another popular crisis. In the face of an expanding politicized population, which was laced through with radical groups, weak government would invite discontent and rebellion, and rebellion would lead to foreign intervention and sectarian strife as it had in 1958. On the other hand, to establish the political base for strong government required introducing new elements into the political scene; and the officer corps, although it had as many sectarian divisions as any other public institution, was, by virtue of its unifying mission for Lebanon and its disciplined professionalism, the least divided by sectarian suspicion and the best organized group for rational action. More important, the army was the only group that the new President could trust. Military influence within the government, however, clashed with Lebanon's traditional *laissez-faire* politics. General Chehab restrained his officers through his self-effacing example, and he felt that the traditional balancing function of the parliamentary institutions should not be impaired. There is no doubt, however, that he severely damaged the prestige of these institutions on several occasions. Nonetheless, the Lebanese situation placed restraints on General Chehab. Direct military government may have been possible, but its consequences might have been severely destabilizing. By attempting to focus national attention on development and social justice, Chehab tried to divert Lebanese from their traditional political parochialisms and to find a common goal above sectarian and nationalistic conflict. Although he was far from successful, the fact that Chehab could maintain a coalition that included the Kataeb, the Destour, the Tripoli bloc, Kamal Jumblat, Kamel al-Assaad, and a number of the "nonpolitical" professionals is a significant testament to his prowess as a politician. Chehab provided the impetus for a moderate social-democratic grouping, which, if ever realized, could provide his successors with a stable and dynamic structure for combating Lebanon's political troubles.

THE EXPANSION OF GOVERNMENT

A drastic expansion of government accompanied the Chehab regime's effort to rationalize the political process. Tables 25 through 28 provide an overview of this expansion. They show that, although considerable growth took place during the two preceding regimes, there was a marked acceleration in administrative development after General Chehab became President. As these figures reflect, the 1958 crisis appeared as a grim warning that the burdens on the Lebanese political system were exceeding its capabilities; hence the heavy emphasis of the Chehab regime to promote social justice through national development.

As Table 25 indicates, governmental expenditures as a percentage

TABLE 25

EXPENDITURES IN THE ORDINARY BUDGET AS A PERCENTAGE OF GROSS NATIONAL PRODUCT, SELECTED YEARS, 1950–1964

Year	1950	1956	1958	1961	1964
Percentage	8.1	11.4	13.7	14.5	23.2

Republic of Lebanon Ministry of Planning, *Besoins et Possibilités de Développement du Liban*, I (Beirut: 1960–1961), 80; and Republic of Lebanon Ministry of Finance, *Fadlakat mashrū' mawāzanat 'ām 1966 [Résumé of the 1966 Budget Project]* (Beirut: 1965), p. 7.

of national product have risen steadily. The increase was especially sharp during the years of the Chehab regime. By the early 1960s this percentage had reached the level of several Western countries. When the trend of expenditures in the budget itself is examined (Table 26), ordinary budget expenditures in 1964 are found to be

TABLE 26

EXPENDITURES IN THE ORDINARY BUDGET, 1944–1966

	Year	Actual Expenditure (Lebanese pounds)
Khoury regime	1944	27,666,573
	1945	35,920,893
	1946	51,993,915
	1947	60,722,427
	1948	70,076,517
	1949	83,401,986
	1950	84,521,928
	1951	90,051,120
	1952	88,509,851
Chamoun regime	1953	96,308,968
	1954	111,182,939
	1955	132,376,965
	1956	161,348,024
	1957	192,466,137
	1958	181,622,338
Chehab regime	1959	198,571,296
	1960	243,087,753
	1961	269,260,306
	1962	415,278,121
	1963	430,284,750
	1964	473,016,000*
Helou regime	1965	514,790,000*
	1966	585,300,000*

* Totals approved by Parliament.

Republic of Lebanon Ministry of Finance, *Qata' al-hisāb, 1951–1963* [*Closed Accounts*] (Beirut: 1964); Sleiman Gemayel, *Evolution du Budget Libanais* (Beirut: 1962), p. 70; Republic of Lebanon Ministry of Finance, *Fadlakat mashrū' mawāzanat 'ām 1966* [*Résumé of the 1966 Budget Project*] (Beirut: 1965), p. 175.

approximately seventeen times those in 1944. The development of specific services over time and as a proportion of the total ordinary budget is roughly portrayed by Table 27. Public works, defense, and education had the highest priority throughout a period characterized by generally high growth in government services. Public works took an especially high percentage of the budget in the later period. They also share the highest growth rates during the early 1950s. In the later period public works are matched by the percentages for propa-

TABLE 27

COMPARISON OF SELECTED ORDINARY BUDGET EXPENDITURES, 1951, 1957, AND 1964 *

Expenditure Category	1951	Percentage of Total	1957	Percentage of Total	Percentage Increase, 1951–1957	1964	Percentage of Total	Percentage Increase, 1957–1964
Total budget	90,051	–	192,466	–	214	473,016	–	246
Education	9,763	10.7	21,220	11.0	217	59,451	12.6	280
Public works	15,485	17.2	31,735	16.5	205	143,331	30.3	452
Public health	4,582	5.1	7,680	3.9	168	13,703	2.9	178
Labor and social affairs	none	–	2,676	1.4	–	12,702	2.7	475
Interior	11,951	13.3	21,025	10.9	176	42,965	9.8	204
Defense	17,986	19.9	39,065	20.3	217	76,624	16.2	196
Agriculture	4,859	5.4	8,040	4.2	165	15,475	3.3	192
Information	none	–	944	.5	–	9,678	2.0	1,025

* Figures are in millions of Lebanese pounds (L£3 equals approximately $1.00).

Republic of Lebanon Ministry of Finance, *Closed Accounts* (Beirut: 1951, 1957, 1964); and Republic of Lebanon Ministry of Finance, *Résumé of the 1966 Budget Project* (Beirut: 1965), p. 71; Raja S. Himadeh, *The Fiscal System of Lebanon* (Beirut: Khayat's, 1961), pp. 12–3.

ganda and labor and social affairs as the regime embarks on modernization.

Outside the ordinary budget there has been an important increase in governmental direction of special services—mostly in the areas of water supply and electricity—since 1951. In that year the Beirut Water Company was nationalized, and in 1954 the government took over the functions of the privately owned Beirut Electricity and Tramway Company and established the Common Electricity and Transport Service. It also initiated the Litani River development project. These agencies are the most important in a series of new autonomous authorities whose financial growth is shown in Table 28.

TABLE 28

EXPENDITURES OF AUTONOMOUS AUTHORITIES, SELECTED YEARS, 1957–1964

Year	Expenditure*
1957	69,912,000
1959	79,311,193
1960	148,274,360
1962	189,968,240
1964	225,145,000

* In Lebanese pounds.

Raja S. Himadeh, *The Fiscal System of Lebanon* (Beirut: Khayat's, 1961), p. 21; Republic of Lebanon Ministry of Finance, *Résumé of the 1966 Budget Project* (Beirut: 1965), pp. 90, 153.

In terms of employed manpower, development is also substantial. The 1933 budget went to support a government of only 3,600 bureaucrats, of whom 1,600 were in the police. The Department of Public Works employed 80, the Department of Public Instruction 391, and the Department of Public Health and Assistance 47.[18] The number of civil servants in 1947, not counting police, was 5,421, in 1953 it was 14,800, and in 1958 a budget study showed that the civil service included 17,562 employees.[19] The Ministry of Public Works then numbered 1,088 and the Ministry of Education 5,370. The Chehab administrative reform of 1959 reportedly raised this figure by 1,700 positions.[20] Officials are extremely reluctant to divulge more recent figures on government employment, but one source outside the government placed the 1966 total at 26,000, and an authoritative source within the government gave a figure of 30,000. Two experts surveying the development of government in 1955 stated that "government and its administration are Lebanon's biggest business and perhaps her largest responsibility of the time." [21] They could hardly have anticipated just how big it would become in the following decade.

The military forces too have increased markedly, both in numbers and in fighting capacity. According to President Chamoun, the army numbered about 6,000 men in 1952, and by 1956–1957 its ranks included more than 10,000 men.[22] During the regime of General Chehab it grew to 15,000, and some of its rather antique equipment was modernized. The Lebanese army, incessantly denigrated by many Lebanese, is probably a better fighting force than they think. Unlike neighboring forces, it is a professional, not a conscript, army. Furthermore, its officer corps is well trained and has never been diminished in numbers or effectiveness by political purges, as have the officer corps of the Syrian and Jordanian armies, for example.

Whether or not the Chehab presidency succeeded in rationalizing the political process is questionable, but nobody doubts that it challenged prevailing conceptions of the role of the state itself. After 1958 Lebanon gave up the guidance of Herbert Spencer for that of John Maynard Keynes and tried to lay the foundations for a significant transformation of the state economic system. Under Chehab's tutelage this effort had three aspects. It involved, first of all, an attempt to engage in comprehensive planning and thus to give the state an active role in social and economic development. Administrative reform was the second aspect of the Chehab program, and although it was not new in conception, it was innovative in application. The third feature was the creation and implementation of new programs, ranging from reforestation to social security. President Chehab described his goals in the following words:

> Animé de cet esprit nouveau, celui d'organiser les rapports sociaux sur des assises modernes, l'Etat s'efforce de résoudre les problèmes sociaux d'une manière qui permette de renforcer chez les Libanais la croyance, déjà enracinée en eux, qu'un pays qui veut se moderniser et développer sa vie économique et sociale peut y parvenir par la voie démocratique.[23]

The origins of this "new spirit" lie in the turmoil of the 1958 crisis. One of the President's associates declared that the new regime was inspired by the following simple analysis: The fundamental causes of the 1958 crisis were socioeconomic, arising from the crystallizing discontent in Lebanon's own underdeveloped areas. According to this analysis, only a spark is necessary to set off an explosion that could eventually take on religious coloration and lead to the ruin of the state. In 1958 there had been several sparks; there could be more at any time. The first priority of the state, therefore, must be not only the maintenance of short-term stability or simply the promotion of economic prosperity; it must also be the promotion of basic equality among the different regions and sects. Muslims, in particular, must be persuaded that they too have a stake in Lebanon; a Lebanese patriotism (*liwa' lil-watan*) must be created. Giving non-Christians a greater share of administrative posts and substantially improving basic services, the Chehabists argued, will encourage Muslim loyalty. This equalitarian, materialistic approach was bred by the concern of the Chehab modernists for the fragility of Lebanon's "negative consensus."

Planning

The basic thrust of the Chehab regime's three programs was not new to Lebanon, but their magnitude far exceeded previous efforts, especially in the planning programs. A Planning Council had been established during the Chamoun regime in 1953, and a Ministry of General Planning was created in 1954. Despite its ministerial status, planning remained a small-scale operation until 1962. The budget for the Ministry's first year amounted to only L£236,000 (about $78,000), and four years later it was only L£367,000 ($122,000); this figure was about enough to pay for the salaries of eighteen civil servants, a small statistical office, liaison operations with other ministries, a planning council, and a control agency overseeing fuel companies, mines, public lands, fairs, and exhibitions. The Chehab decree laws of 1959 stripped the Ministry of several of these functions and provided for its reorganization. In May 1962 the Ministry was reorganized again. By that time it possessed a staff of 209 civil servants. The Ministry's budget in 1964 was L£2,409,000 ($803,000).[24]

President Chehab was not content, however, to rely solely upon the Planning Ministry for guidance. In March 1959 the President arranged with Père Louis-Joseph Lebret, then Director of the French Centre Nationale de Recherche Scientifique and head of the Institut International de Recherches et de Formation en vue de Développement Intégral et Harmonisé (IRFED), to bring to Lebanon a research team that would study the country's development problems and make fundamental recommendations. The IRFED mission, which included eleven French experts and thirty-two Lebanese technicians, was nominally established under the auspices of the Planning Ministry, but it had direct responsibility to the Presidency as well. Several of the programs of the Chehab regime, which will be described later, were inspired directly by the IRFED mission. The acid reaction to IRFED among the President's opponents demonstrates that the implementation of "développement intégral et harmonisé" paid political dividends as well; critics charged that IRFED was a state within a state and that it was attempting to impose "Vatican socialism" on the free economy.

The IRFED diagnosis discusses many of the socioeconomic problems that have been described in Chapter 3, and its suggestions form the core of the Chehabist approach to Lebanon's weaknesses. Its recommendations are a model of Gallic rationality and comprehensiveness. The first phase of IRFED's operations was a systematic inventory of the needs and resources of the country encompassed in a two-volume report published in 1961.[25] The second phase was the creation of a long-term plan (*le plan perspectif*) and a middle-range, four-to-six-year plan.[26] The directors of IRFED then subdivided their subject chronologically and functionally. They argued that there are four phases of national planning: elaboration, in which the necessary plans and subplans are drawn up and specialists hired; decision, in which the number of acceptable projects and subplans is reduced and choices are made between various alternatives for chosen ends; execution, in which the ministries and regional authorities put into effect the plans selected during the second phase; and, finally, the phase of successive adjustments, in which the execution of the plans is adapted to unforeseen changes and unforeseeable situations. After the completion of the initial survey, the IRFED group began to make subplans that would eventually harmonize with one another in conformity with *le plan perspectif* in the following areas: hydraulic engineering, roads, transport, ports, airports, energy, agriculture, industrial and handicraft orientation, education (including culture and sports), applied research, and tourism. These plans in turn would be subdivided regionally by province and municipality and generally into the areas of integrated financing, zoning, and administration at the national level.

Whereas long-term planning and investment in large projects long antedated the arrival of IRFED on the Lebanese administrative scene, these earlier efforts were considerably more restricted in scale than development under Chehab. A Development Works Fund had been established in 1944 and had spent more than L£200,646,000 by 1958.[27] Much of this money had been allocated for the construction of the Beirut International Airport and for water projects. In 1954 ten-year development plans for water and electricity were initiated. It was not until 1962, however, that general planning was given the prominent position it continues to enjoy. In that year, five-year plans in irrigation, programs to provide drinking water, electricity, roads (excluding Beirut and Tripoli), and antiquities were initiated, totaling about L£205 million.[28] In July 1963 IRFED took a giant step by proposing a L£3 billion five-year plan for 1964–1968, a figure about 1.5 times the country's total Gross National Product in 1963. The plan required Lebanon to obtain a L£300 million loan from Kuwait.[29] The advisers of the Chehab regime obviously hoped that the President could offset some of the disadvantages of the Lebanese political system by programing long-term development. Although these activities may have been a far cry from Arab socialism, they were not a very close approximation of Lebanese *laissez-faire*.

More Administrative Reform

That such rational planning could be implemented in Lebanon's free-wheeling economic and political milieu struck some Anglo-Saxon observers as unlikely. To carry out the plans depended not only on neutralizing the political field—which President Chehab accomplished over the opposition of many notables—but also and even more on building an administrative apparatus capable of such a formidable task. Past experiences did not augur well for such an undertaking: The Khoury regime had fallen largely because of administrative corruption, and the reform efforts of President Chamoun had aroused a storm of opposition. It seemed almost beyond the government's power to sustain the growing number of essential services, much less to undertake new ones. On the eve of General Chehab's inauguration, a respected editor wrote:

> Il est impossible de dire qui est chargé de surveiller la nourriture présentée dans un grand hotel de la montagne: la municipalité locale? le Commissariat du Tourisme? le Service de la Répression des Fraudes? ou le Ministre de la Santé? Quand on ouvre une nouvelle artère dans la capitale, on n'a pas fini de l'asphalter que le Service des Eaux, ceux des

égouts, de l'électricité, et du téléphone viennent chacun à son tour éventre la chaussée pour y installer leurs cables ou leurs tuyaux. . . .[30]

Within three months after he took office, President Chehab had asked for and received sweeping reform powers for a six-month period, in order to carry out his administrative reforms. Racing the clock, the regime issued 162 decrees on June 3, 1959, which called for the overhauling of virtually every branch of the bureaucracy.[31] The decrees were designed to facilitate decentralization, define duties and responsibilities more precisely, cut red tape in working procedures, improve central control as a means to reduce corruption, and revise recruitment procedures to improve the quality of civil servants.[32] A Central Committee for Administrative Reform, composed of high civil servants and private individuals, was established to supervise the implementation of the decree laws. It was given three months to accomplish this Herculean task; two years later, entangled in politics, it was not finished.

The earliest evaluations of the reforms were highly critical. The newspaper *L'Orient,* a strong supporter of the regime, remarked: ". . . [J]amais les services publiques n'ont été plus désorganisés et les formalités plus lentes que depuis le promulgation des fameux décret-lois de 1959; jamais les agents de l'état n'ont pris moins d'initiatives." [33] Two experts in public administration criticized the reform because it had failed to decentralize thoroughly; because it had been, like its predecessors, carried out as a "bootstrap" operation without sufficient expert guidance; because it had been rushed

FIGURE 5. *Administrative Reform.*

through too quickly; and because it had failed to reduce the excessive emphasis on red tape.[34] Another specialist wrote in 1961 that the low standards of public services (health and education) were not offset by the additional expenditures being made in those fields: "The standard of public social services is so low that money grants equivalent to what is spent on these services can probably increase efficiency more than the health and education services offered by the Government can do." [35] With the perspective of four years, two other experts made the following assessment:

> In practice the operation could not be and was not as well coordinated as in theory and in plan. The reform proposals which did come to the central committee were often the products of pressure rather than of measured, coordinated thinking; and they may have embodied the earlier convictions, if not the interests, of those who were already ensconced in the public service.[36]

Friends of the regime appeared to share this view; the Minister of State for Administrative Reform thought that the reform had been rather effective at the higher levels but had failed to have much impact at the lower levels of administration, where the general public has most of its contact with the bureaucracy.[37] Another prominent defender of the regime thought that the reform was only beginning to have an effect when President Chehab's term expired. The final judgment, however, was made in effect by President Chehab's successor, Charles Helou; following the traditional custom, he began an administrative reform of his own.

Despite its failings in terms of its ambitious goals, the reform still made several advances. It laid the basis for combating the single most serious weakness in the apparatus: the poor quality of personnel. A Civil Service Council was established to rationalize the recruitment process; although it ran into predictable difficulties with rival and older governmental agencies and with politicians who saw in it a threat to their patronage powers, it has made substantial progress since it began operating late in 1959.[38] A related outgrowth of the reforms was the National Institute of Public Administration, established by a French expert to provide administrative training in conjunction with the Civil Service Council. Nevertheless, private business continues to draw off the top talent, and government posts—although they offer considerable security—still do not pay well.

The reform also extended central control over programs and allocations. The effectiveness of the Central Inspection Agency was augmented by giving preaudit powers to its Court of Accounts and adding an organization for research and guidance to the Agency. Although these modifications conflicted somewhat with the goals of decentralization and cutting red tape, they were useful in making possible better supervision of the tremendous expansion of administrative activities. The reform, in addition, provided for a significant enlargement of the powers of the Prime Minister. The Court of Accounts, the Central Inspection Agency, and the Civil Service Council were placed under his direct jurisdiction, and the budget for the Prime Minister's office climbed between 1960 and 1964 from L£3,493,000 to L£9,618,000. Furthermore, when Rashid Karami was Prime Minister—a position he held during most of the Chehab regime—he not only enjoyed a close working relationship with a powerful President, but he also took the Finance Ministry portfolio for himself, thus greatly enhancing his influence.[39] The Prime Minister's new power was probably beneficial, in that it improved executive efficiency and gave the restive Muslim community an additional increment in the sectarian balance of power. Limited as these reforms may have been, Lebanese administration did make a significant step forward in efficiency.

There was also a shift in the sectarian composition of the bureaucracy that gave non-Christians near parity with Christians in top positions. One Chehabist remarked that, although every modern person would like to be rid of sectarianism in administration for good, it is impossible at the moment. The regime did the next best thing: It adopted a fifty-fifty rule for the distribution of high posts. Although it is difficult to show accurately the extent of this erosion of Christian predominance, the figures in Table 29 suggest that the non-Christians have made relative gains. Except for provincial administrator, all categories show a perceptible decline in the percentage of Christians that averages about 9 per cent.[40]

New Programs

The Chehab regime scored its most spectacular political and administrative gains in actual implementation of programs. Much of the popular appeal of Chehabism was due to the expansion of water, electrical, and road service to areas that had previously been deprived of these benefits. The year 1962 was the turning point in this transformation: In that year public expenditures rose from L£269 million to L£415 million; the ordinary budget ran a deficit for the first time; and government expenditures as a percentage of national income jumped from 14.5 per cent to 22.2 per cent. If the expenditures in both the ordinary budget and the budgets of the independent agencies are included, the percentage of the national income was 33.6, a figure that compares favorably with those in such developed nations as Belgium, Japan, Italy, Denmark, Canada, and the United States.[41] Total ordinary budget outlays in 1964, the last year of the Chehab regime, were nearly 2.5 times greater than the biggest budget of the Chamoun regime; and expenditures in the independent authorities (which mainly supervised electricity and water development) had risen by 322 per cent.[42] Between 1945 and 1962, one authority has argued, the Lebanese state actually manufactured a mild deflationary condition, without knowing it, by following almost mercantilist financial policies.[43] The cost of sound-money policies has been unbalanced economic development: Services of various kinds account for two-thirds of Lebanese Gross National Product in the 1960s; agriculture and industry share the other third. After 1962 President Chehab and his cautious successor Charles Helou sought to alleviate long-standing deficiencies in the socio-economic infrastructure.

Their efforts took several forms. The enormous expansion in public-works projects was the most noticeable. The budget of the Ministry of Public Works increased 4.5 times between 1957 and 1965, far exceeding the budget of the other major ministries both

TABLE 29

BALANCE OF SECTS IN ADMINISTRATION

Office	Year	CHRISTIAN							NONCHRISTIAN				Grand Total	Percentage Christian
		M*	GC	GO	Lat.	Prot.	AC	Total	S	SH	D	Total		
Directors-general and heads of services	1946†	6	–	3	–	–	–	9	5	–	1	6	15	60
	1962	11	2	8	–	–	1	22	12	1	4	17	40	55
Administrators of districts	1946	1	1	1	–	–	–	3	1	–	1	2	5	60
	1962	1	1	1	–	–	–	3	1	–	1	2	5	60
High magistrate positions	1946	2	–	–	–	–	–	2	1	–	–	1	3	67
	1962	4	1	1	1	–	–	7	5	–	1	6	13	54
High diplomatic positions	1946	5	–	2	–	–	–	7	3	1	–	4	11	64
	1962	6	4	2	–	–	1§	13	11	1	1	13	26	50
Total	1946	14	1	6	0	0	0	21	10	1	2	13	34	62
	1962	22	8	12	1	0	2	45	29	2	7	38	84	53

* Abbreviations: M = Maronite, GC = Greek Catholic, GO = Greek Orthodox, Lat. = Roman Catholic, Prot. = Protestant, AC = Armenian Catholic, S = Sunnite, SH = Shiite, D = Druze
† The 1946 and 1962 samples are not necessarily comparable in any statistical sense, but they may be useful for rough generalizations.
§ Armenian Orthodox.

The 1946 figures are from Pierre Rondot, *Les Institutions Politiques du Liban* (Paris: Imprimerie Nationale, 1947), p. 89. The 1962 figures are from a list of government officials provided by the American Embassy, Beirut.

in absolute size and relative gains. Massive road-building efforts and comprehensive projects for redevelopment in the Beirut area were undertaken.[44] The Kataeb, in particular, benefited from this policy because its chief, Pierre Gemayel, had control of this choice portfolio, as did the builders, contractors, and property owners affected by these grand projects. One of the most important elements of the Public Works Ministry was the engineering section headed by the city planner Michel Ecochard. Ecochard's group, like several others scattered throughout the bureaucracy, enjoyed good access to the development-minded President. The various water and electricity agencies also expanded during the Chehab and Helou regimes (most of them had only been brought under public control during the Chamoun presidency). In 1964, of the seventy-one independent authorities, the most important financially were the Common Electricity and Transport Authority, the National Litani [River] Authority, the National Reconstruction Authority, the State Railroad, the Office of Social Development, and the Beirut Water Authority.[45] A French-owned company until the government took it over in 1954, the Electricity Authority's budget quadrupled between the last "normal" year of the Chamoun regime and the last year of the Chehab regime.

Other executive agencies appeared. A special word should be said about Lebanon's U.S. $77 million hydroelectric and irrigation project, the Litani River scheme. The National Litani Authority, established in August 1954 and financed initially with a U.S. $27 million loan from the World Bank, began in 1957 to build a complex of dams, tunnels, and generating stations that are expected to supply 124 million kilowatt hours of electricity annually. In 1964 the nearly completed project supplied one-seventh the electric power of Beirut—89,332,000 kilowatt hours.[46] Perhaps more important in terms of the Chehabist policy of rural development was its capacity to irrigate 40,000 new hectares (approximately 98,800 acres) in poverty-stricken South Lebanon. The National Reconstruction Authority was established after the severe earthquake of March 1956 to rebuild the devastated areas; it is financed by special surtaxes and continues to be used for these emergencies. The Office of Social Development became the specialized institution for distributing public assistance through private charities and sends teams of social workers into the more remote rural areas. This agency was originally linked with the IRFED mission and loosely associated with the Ministry of Labor and Social Affairs.

Education

The regime tried to strengthen the inadequate public education facilities both quantitatively and qualitatively. The percentage of students in government schools showed a moderate increase: Only 31 per cent of the primary and secondary students in 1959 attended government schools, but by 1964 42 per cent attended these schools. At the secondary level alone, the government schools' share of the enrollment rose from 23 per cent in 1955–1956 to 34 per cent in 1963–1964. A five-year plan for education, which envisaged the construction of 620 new schools, mostly in rural areas, was launched in 1965. Committees reviewed the curriculum, which had been modeled after the French system, in response to pressures to diversify the program above the elementary level and thus to give more scope for technical and vocational courses. Some educators urged more and better training in the social sciences.

Although the Chehab regime was aware of the importance of education, its reform efforts were hindered by familiar political problems. The inefficiency of the government made improvement painfully slow. Competition from the private schools, with their better salaries and working conditions, drew off the better teachers. At the same time the private schools, responding to the law of supply and demand, raised their fees, further intensifying the need for expanded government education. Despite a basic curriculum for all schools, public and private, there was no doubt that the educational system remained an important perpetuator of sectarian distinctions. Curriculum reform in history teaching, for example, is particularly difficult because Muslim educators stress the necessity of emphasizing the Arab cultural heritage, whereas Catholic educators are reluctant to reduce their concentration on Western European civilization.

One of the most imaginative innovations of the Chehab regime was the Green Plan, a program for land reclamation and development designed to help curb the migration to the cities and improve the techniques of agricultural production by providing heavy equipment and easy loans to farmers.[47] Established in 1963, the organization began work in July 1964 with a ten-year budget of L£70 million and an administrative staff of seventy. Like other Chehab development projects the Green Plan was not under the direct supervision of any ministry but was only loosely associated with the Agriculture Ministry. Its loans and credits are channeled through the government-sponsored Agricultural and Industrial Credit Bank. By the end of its first working year the Green Plan reported that it had completed twelve small reclamation projects, mostly in South Lebanon, and that twenty-eight more were in progress. A drive through South Lebanon revealed bulldozers from the Green Plan terracing and clearing stony, barren plots, but it also impressed observers with the magnitude of the task: The rural stagnation was obvious. If Beirut is a lure, the uncertainties of the border situation, the tightness of the market for rural products, the intractability of the land, and the limited resources of even a socially conscious government are factors that also explain the depressed nature of this area.

The Chehab regime also established a central bank when the currency-issuing functions of the Banque de Syrie et du Liban expired in 1964. The new bank typified the changing position of the state in economic life. Until the establishment of the central bank, the state was deprived of an essential instrument of monetary policy. As one student of the subject wrote: "The private banks do their business the way they like and the government, except in periods of crisis, does not interfere in the banking activities and thus under normal conditions the government's influence is almost negligible." [48] In theory the new central bank could extend easy credit and increase the volume of money in hard times and contract the money supply during periods of inflation, policies that were not compatible with the wishes of private banking interests. In fact, however, it did not exercise such initiatives at first, partly because of limited rediscounting capacity and partly because it lacked important information about the state of the economy. In its first annual report, the governor of the central bank, Philippe Taqla, an old Destourian and a banker himself, complained of the inadequacy of statistics, particularly those concerning labor costs, revenues in general, and the changing cost of living. Such information, he remarked, is indispensable for both intelligent state and intelligent private action.[49] During the 1966 Intra Bank crisis, the Central Bank remained conspicuously aloof. Although another important piece of the machinery of a modern state had been added, its operational capabilities remained uncertain.

Probably the most ambitious of all the projects was the social-security scheme. Article 54 of the Labor Law of 1946—the most significant legislation of the Khoury regime—explicitly envisaged a social-security code.[50] The gestation period for this project had been leisurely. Attempts to pass relevant legislation in 1952 and in 1956 had never gotten past the drafting stage. Scarcely two months after General Chehab took office in 1958, however, the Council of Ministers formed a committee to design a social-security project.[51] A draft was drawn up on the basis of studies made in the Ministries of Finance and Social Affairs; during 1959 and 1960 this draft was circulated among various business, political, and labor groups for comment: The Kataeb was particularly active in its elaboration at this stage. Late in 1962 an amended draft law was approved by the Council of Ministers and sent to the Parliament for study. There it remained until autumn of the following year. On September 26, 1963, the President promulgated the law by decree, and on May 1, 1965, after delays caused by sectarian disputes over the appointment of a director, the first stage of the project went into effect. The system was intended, when fully operational, to provide for medical and maternity insurance, insurance for job-related accidents and sickness, a system of family allowances, and end-of-service indemnities. The main instrument of the scheme, the Social Security Treasury, took its place among the ranks of special organizations added to the state by the regime. The Social Security Treasury was backed by the government for 25 per cent of its funds, with the remainder supplied by employers and employees, and it was designed to be financially and administratively independent, although it was placed under the surveillance of the Ministry of Social Affairs.[52]

Not one of the notables or politicians interviewed by this writer doubted that Lebanon needs a social-security system badly; most, however, expressed doubts that the state is capable of administering such a complex program. Some experts were critical of the program itself, pointing out the inadequate statistical information, the excessive burdens placed on small employers and their employees, and the insufficient governmental participation.[53] There were also the deeper problems of political rectitude and popular attitudes: Could the Social Security Treasury guarantee that retirement pensions and medical assistance would be given? Was the government capable of operating a social-security system without corruption or scandal? Could employers and employees be persuaded or compelled to subscribe part of their wages and income to a social-security program? A history of administrative scandal and inefficiency has not given the Lebanese people great confidence in the abilities of their government. On the other hand, proponents of the project argued that there is no other choice for Lebanon; even a scheme poorly run at first is preferable to none at all. They also argued that the scale of the operation in comparison to those operating reasonably well elsewhere was very small, and that the Lebanese do not lack talent and the ability to learn. For Lebanon, social security, they argued, is especially advantageous because of its redistributive and integrative possibilities.[54]

Lebanon's Political Future: Capabilities Versus Loads

Chehab's term expired in the summer of 1964 with a great many projects started but few completed. *Chehabisme* had restored the prosperous pre-1958 status quo but had failed, despite a determined effort, to resolve the Lebanese political dilemma. To General Chehab's successor, Charles Helou, fell the task of walking the tightrope.

In some ways President Helou was eminently qualified to carry on the attempt to modernize. He was, for example, well prepared for handling the sectarian problem, because he had been Ambassador to the Vatican from 1947 to 1949 and during that time he had helped to persuade the Pope to deny diplomatic recognition to Israel. In 1958 his leadership of the Third Force, which was in moderate opposition to the Chamoun regime, entitled him to the blessings of the Muslim communities and to acceptance by the radical insurgents. As a journalist, a tourism director, and a protégé of the banker Michel Chiha, Helou possessed the connections and skill in dealing with people that are particularly helpful for the President in Lebanon. Most important, he had no powerful enemies.

Not only was Helou well qualified, but his election was, for Lebanon, a model of orderly succession. For the first time since independence the Presidency changed hands without the accompaniment of a general strike or foreign intervention. Renewal of the President's term was again an issue, but this time the crisis revolved around the President's refusal to accept a second term. The election of Charles Helou was also remarkable because the Parliament showed a modicum of autonomy vis-à-vis the President when a thirty-three-man bloc of deputies from South Lebanon deserted the majority that wanted to re-elect Chehab. Contrary to the expectations of some observers, the army did not intervene to name a successor to General Chehab, nor did the embassies of the United States and the United

Arab Republic play an active role in the selection process. Although his enemies doubted it until the last moment, General Chehab proved that he did not harbor further political ambitions and that he did not regard himself or any other chosen officer as indispensable. A major and expected obstruction to restoring civilian rule thus failed to materialize. The new President began his tenure with a vigor that undoubtedly surprised some of his supporters. He lost little time in taking up questions of municipal reform, public housing, taxation, and administrative housecleaning.

Despite his qualifications and intentions, President Helou was to a large extent the prisoner of a situation that imposed narrow limits on executive power. Any assessment of the Presidency or of the Republic's future requires an analysis of this situation. The situation may be viewed in terms of the capabilities of a political system to handle the loads placed upon it. President Helou's success or failure, as well as the long-range survival or disappearance of Lebanon itself, is largely a function of these capabilities and loads.

The new President came to office with the disadvantage that afflicts all Lebanese Presidents: the lack of a permanent, organized power base. Charles Helou's position in this respect was weaker than that of his predecessors because he lacked even their rudimentary organizational backing. Furthermore, as a dark-horse, compromise candidate, he could not enjoy the full confidence of either the Chamoun or the Chehab partisans. Helou's immediate predecessor bullied deputies into supporting reform legislation simply by getting angry. When a notable complained that Chehab's Civil

FIGURE 6. *A Fateful Choice for the President.*

Service Council was choking off patronage, the General bluntly informed him that the President was not the notables' electoral agent. Such behavior was less easy for the more vulnerable Helou, but even the strongest Lebanese President could be frustrated by parochial legislators and administrators. Lebanon's tendency toward political stagnation, in the absence of a modern party structure, makes it difficult for the President to innovate in policy formulation and implementation. Despite some favorable developments among the ruling establishment, the radical outsiders, the electoral process, and the Presidency itself, the capacity of the system for rational policy making and execution remains limited indeed.

Meager capabilities only multiply the effect of the loads imposed on the system by its diverse and generally adverse environment. The burdens arising out of Lebanon's heterogeneous, primordial political culture and its rapid social mobilization and the problems imposed by international and regional political conflict were discussed in Part One. Their implications have been recognized by President Helou, who has written:

> It is no longer possible in the second half of the twentieth century for any government to follow a policy of laisser-faire. . . . This laisser-faire doctrine is now rejected because individuals do not always know their best interest and even if they knew, they are not always able to achieve it. . . . The Lebanese Government has the responsibility of establishing the basic conditions and facilities which help the Lebanese people to produce more and improve their living conditions.

Its main task is to establish the infrastructure of development and provide the fundamental conditions needed by the enterprising Lebanese people.[55]

As if in deference to Lebanon's free enterprise norm, Helou adds, "The Lebanese businessman is more enterprising and is a much better manager than his government." Social mobilization has set the terms of the country's major internal problems: the need for rural development, expansion of urban facilities, low-cost public housing, the establishment and efficient collection of more progressive income taxes, and the development of new jobs in all sectors. This set of tasks is a formidable one for an administrative apparatus as small and weak as Lebanon's. Parochial and transnational sentiments render these tasks even more difficult. Sectarianism and conflicting national loyalties divert time and resources from national development and hamper administrative efficiency.

In light of these persistent problems, it was hardly surprising that President Helou's administrative reform quickly lost momentum and his political stance became defensive rather than innovative. When a prominent Beirut editor was assassinated in 1966—a casualty of the Arab cold war—the Lebanese government could not prosecute the case vigorously, for fear of damaging its relations with neighboring Arab states implicated in the affair. The liquidity crisis in the country's largest bank in the same year showed not only that Lebanese prosperity is paper thin but also that the regime lacked the capacity to prevent it, even though its newly created Central Bank had been established to ensure general financial stability. Israel's defeat of Syria, Jordan, and the U.A.R. in the war of June 1967 added new burdens to Lebanon's economy, sectarian relations, and foreign policy and challenged the power structure itself. The dangers of political immobility seemed fully as serious as those inherent in political modernization.

Lebanon's democratic institutions—defective as they are—have been the factor most responsible for the precarious viability of the state during its first two decades of independence. Democratic procedures have turned the disintegrative aspects of this fragmented political culture to functional uses. The flexibility of representative institutions permits limited change within strictly defined limits. Governments come and go, coalitions form and disintegrate, administrative activity increases, regular free elections are held, and vast amounts of political steam are dissipated. Nothing very startling happens in this process, which is precisely the reason for its success in promoting stability. The trends surveyed here suggest, however, that problems that the system previously ignored, smothered, or "solved" only in token fashion cannot be put off indefinitely. Lebanon's political institutions work rather well when there is little to be done, but as the work load increases the defects that once were tolerable become dangerous liabilities. If this analysis is correct, the Lebanese system can reduce its fundamental weaknesses by becoming more democratic than it now is. The one innovation that would decisively improve Lebanon's prospects for future stability, development, and social justice is the development of a country-wide, left-of-center social-democratic party. A popular, progressive party would give the representation processes added legitimacy and make the President stronger. It could recruit into legitimate and useful activity the growing number of educated and mobilized people who are disillusioned with the exclusive character of the present system. It could also create new lines of loyalty and identity between the outlying areas and the regime.

The call for stronger parties in Lebanon is hardly new; in doctoral dissertations, the press, and political debates the desirability of such organizations is generally accepted, if only because parties are characteristic of all politically advanced countries. Lebanese politicians of varying tendencies have been trying (and generally failing) to establish viable parties for years. Efforts to organize coherent national parties have been wrecked by local particularisms, especially the sectarian loyalties. Existing parties, sincere as their protestations to national loyalty may be, cannot shake off sectarian or personal coloration and thus fail as integrating devices. As long as sectarianism remains embedded in the mentality of the people, runs the familiar argument, a rationalized party or party system will be impossible. There are, however, several reasons for thinking that the idea is more feasible than it once was. First, there is evidence to suggest that an increasing proportion of the population, especially in the educated middle class, can be mobilized into legitimate, open, and routinized political activity, particularly if the appeal were moderate and progressive. Second, the sectarian problem might be managed not by merely avoiding it—the method employed by all the past and present parties—but rather by explicit acceptance of the fact that sectarianism is going to remain a potent force for the foreseeable future. If Parliament and the bureaucracy can be integrated through a precise allocation of positions according to a formula, it is possible that a political party's directorate can be organized the same way: 50 per cent Christian, 50 per cent non-Christian. A party might even follow the example of guild socialism and allow specific quotas for occupational groups as well. Instead of being nonsectarian, the party would be avowedly multisectarian. Instead of destroying traditional channels, it would exploit them. Third, a party of this sort might succeed if it could be organized from the beginning in a nonparochial manner. In particular, its leaders would have to devise means to permit the less affluent to run in parliamentary elections without the support of rich landlords or bankers. Although it would be fruitless to expect that popular regional leaders would not attract membership because of parochial ties, it might be possible to avoid the mistakes of the early 1950s, when recruitment of the newly politicized middle class became bogged down in traditional client politics. In short, an organizational effort far more elaborate than any yet attempted in Lebanon would be necessary. If such a social-democratic party actually took root, it is conceivable that it would set in motion similar forces among the factional forces of a more conservative tendency. Such a development would go a long way toward institutionalizing the elements newly sensitized to politics and could greatly enhance the performance of the executive agencies.

The Lebanese Republic is a remarkably adaptive political system whose hope of survival lies in creative exploitation of its defects. This study has attempted to show how, within limits, Lebanon parries the forces of parochialism, transnationalism, and uneven social change. Ingenious as the system is, however, it faces a future that is dependent on the precarious balance of loads and capabilities. Lebanon's political capabilities have developed substantially over the first two decades of independence: The system has become more liberal, more open to citizen participation, more legitimate, and more capable of executive action. Its limited democratic structures have performed surprisingly well as the adjustment mechanism for traditional pluralism. The fact that Lebanon has survived at all under these circumstances, with only one disastrous crisis in two decades, is sufficient testimony to the fact that its political system has developed an important measure of flexibility and complexity. The critical question, however, remains: Are the loads on this system increasing even faster than its capabilities? The evidence presented here, although incomplete, suggests that they are. Lebanon's historic problems are not disappearing: Parochialism if anything is aggravated by social change. The prospects for domestic prosperity and tranquillity are dubious in the light of demographic trends and a weak productive sector. Radicalism, partially a function of continuing ferment in the Arab world as a whole, finds no legitimate place in Lebanese politics; and the system has failed to develop a responsible leftist opposition. Despite the National Pact, Arab nationalism and regional rivalries continue to pose a certain threat to the Lebanese entity, and Great Power competition continues to involve the people in the area. Lebanon is too strategically situated to escape embroilment in these conflicts. At the risk of underestimating Lebanese ingenuity, it must be concluded that the Republic's political future will be stormy.

NOTES

[1] See Georges Naccache, *Chéhabisme: Un Nouveau Style* (Beirut: Cénacle Libanaise, 1961).

[2] In the Palestine war, Chehab commanded a minuscule Lebanese force in operations that were mainly defensive in character. Actual Lebanese engagement in Palestine itself was confined mainly to volunteers fighting under the command of Fawzi al-Kaoukji. See *Le Jour,* May 19–26, 1948.

[3] As the notables tend to look down on the army, so the officers also do not hold politicians in very high esteem. Since the Palestine engagement, the younger officers in Lebanon, as in every other Arab country that fought in that war, have blamed the civilian politicians for the defeat. The acute sensitivity of the Lebanese army to press comment—ostensibly on grounds of security—is one indication of the latent bad feelings.

[4] The biographical data are from the Bureau des Documentations Libanaises et Arabes, Beirut.

[5] Chehab's concern for modernizing the army is indicated by this extract from an article he wrote for the army's magazine, *al-Jundī al-lubnānī* [*The Lebanese Soldier*] in August 1946 (p. 3): "It has not been the custom that the head of the Army talks to followers in newspapers and magazines. But *The Lebanese Soldier* is not a stranger in our midst. It is from us and to us. That is why I saw that through it I should direct to the officers and men encouragement for taking it as a stage for increasing their education and to slake their thirst for knowledge and to shorten the distances between them and the outside world. . . . Educating the Lebanese soldier in the research, technical, methodological, historical, and scientific . . . subjects . . . helps the growth of general education in explaining the things that are connected with military affairs."

[6] The Commander in Chief is appointed by cabinet decree; has complete control over all military forces, including the Deuxième Bureau; and is nominally responsible to the Minister of Defense. Parliament has no powers of supervision or investigation of the military, and the President is not given explicit superior military command. There is implicitly such a grant of command, perhaps, in the Presidential obligation to defend national sovereignty.

[7] See Chapter 3 of this book and Fahim I. Qubain, *Crisis in Lebanon* (Washington, D.C.: Middle East Institute, 1961), pp. 154–6. The seven votes went to Raymond Edde. There was one abstention. Ten pro-Chamoun deputies did not attend the session.

[8] Philippe Taqla was an old Destourian; Ali Bazzi was a former member of the National Appeal and a moderate Arab nationalist; Maurice Zouein was an independent and a respected Maronite notable who leaned in the direction of Raymond Edde; Fuad Butros was a Beirut lawyer close to the Kataeb; and Fuad Najjar was a Druze agricultural expert whose views were closer to those of Jumblat than to those of Arslan.

[9] *L'Orient,* July 21, 1960.

[10] For the vote, see *L'Orient,* May 21, 1961.

[11] *L'Orient,* October 19 and 21, 1961.

[12] During the Khoury regime, an analogous position had, for a time, been filled by the President's brother. General Chehab kept his immediate family out of politics.

[13] This group included Lieutenant Colonel Yussef Shmayet (Druze), Chief of Staff; Major Toufic Jalbout (Greek Orthodox), Director of General Security; Lieutenant Colonel Antoine Saad (Maronite), Chief of Army Intelligence; Major François Genadry, assistant to Lieutenant Colonel Shmayet; and Captains Ahmad al-Hajj and Munir Sardouk (both Sunnite), the President's aides.

[14] Given the Lebanese context, Chehab could hardly be expected to advertise any admiration he might have felt for Nasser's domestic policy. Although Chehab's programs for "social justice" were far milder than Nasser's "Arab socialism," he shared with the Egyptian a desire to use the state for developing the society.

[15] The primary instruments of the alleged interference were the Deuxième Bureau of the army, responsible for military intelligence, and the branches of the Ministry of Interior that were responsible for general security and internal security, which embraced the police, gendarmerie, and district general-security departments. For a description of these agencies, see George Grassmuck and Kamal Salibi, *Reformed Administration in Lebanon* (Beirut: Catholic Press, 1964), pp. 48–51.

[16] This development was a continuation of the bitter feud that resulted in the slaying of Muhammad Abboud, one of President Khoury's old associates, in 1953. See also Chapter 7 of this book. Abboud's father engaged Osman to carry on the struggle, and in 1964 Osman apparently found the military willing to help him.

[17] Charles Rizk, "Le Régime Politique Libanais" (Unpublished doctoral dissertation, University of Paris, 1964), p. 156.

[18] Grassmuck and Salibi, *A Manual of Lebanese Administration* (Beirut: American University, 1955), p. 8.

[19] Sleiman Gemayel, *Evolution du Budget Libanais* (Paris: Librairie Generale de Droit et de Jurisprudence, 1962), pp. 44, 48. The latter figure includes the internal security forces of the Ministry of Interior. It is useful to recall, however, that size is relative; the total Lebanese civil-service manpower in 1958 was a bit less than half that of the New York City Transit Authority.

[20] Ralph Crow and Adnan Iskandar, "Administrative Reform in Lebanon, 1958–1959," *International Review of Administrative Sciences*, 27, No. 3 (1961), 293–307.

[21] Grassmuck and Salibi, *A Manual of Lebanese Administration*, p. 17.

[22] Camille Chamoun, *Crise au Moyen-Orient* (Paris: Gallimard, 1963), p. 407. The army was large enough, he suggests, to have crushed the insurgents, if its commander had wished to do so.

[23] "Animated by this new spirit, that of organizing social cooperation on modern foundations, the state is forced to resolve social problems in a way that allows it to reinforce among the Lebanese the belief, already rooted in them, that a country seeking to modernize and to develop its economic and social life can do so by democratic means." President Chehab's Independence Day Address, 1962; quoted in *L'Orient*, November 22, 1962.

24 Jean Chami, "Le Ministère du Plan Fait Peau Neuve," *L'Orient,* May 31, 1962. See also Grassmuck and Salibi, *Reformed Administration in Lebanon,* pp. 78–80.

25 Republic of Lebanon Ministry of Planning, *Besoins et Possibilités de Développement du Liban* (Beirut: 1960–1961).

26 Jean Chami, "L'IRFED Assura, Pendant 2 Ans, la Direction des Etudes et de le Planification," *L'Orient,* June 1, 1962. For a critical evaluation of the IRFED mission's recommendations, see Georges G. Corm, *Politique Economique et Planification au Liban, 1953–1963* (Beirut: Universelle, 1964), pp. 126–7.

27 Raja Himadeh, *The Fiscal System of Lebanon* (Beirut: Khayat's, 1961), pp. 97–8.

28 Republic of Lebanon Decree No. 6844 (1961).

29 Corm, "Bilan des Finances Publiques Libanaises: 1945–1965," *Le Commerce du Levant,* March 3, 1965, p. 11.

30 "It is impossible to say who is responsible for inspecting the food served in a large mountain hotel: the local municipality? the Commissariat of Tourism? the Fraud Control Service? or the Ministry of Health? When a new street is opened in the capital, hardly has the asphalt been laid before the Water, Sewer, Electricity and Telephone Services come, each in its turn, to tear it up, in order to install their cables or their pipes. . . ." *L'Orient,* October 22, 1958.

31 Lebanese Republic, *Les Décrets Législatifs de la Réforme* (Bureau des Documentations Libanaises et Arabes, 1959) (mimeo).

32 Crow and Iskandar, *op. cit.,* pp. 301–4.

33 ". . . [N]ever have public services been more disorganized and bureaucracy more sluggish than since the problem of the famous decree laws of 1959; never have public officials taken less initiative." *L'Orient,* May 16, 1960.

34 Crow and Iskandar, *op. cit.,* pp. 304–7.

35 Himadeh, *op. cit.,* p. 112.

36 Grassmuck and Salibi, *Reformed Administration in Lebanon,* pp. 22–3.

37 Interview with Khatchik Babikian, June 27, 1964.

38 Adnan Iskandar, *Bureaucracy in Lebanon,* Social Science Series, No. 22 (Beirut: American University of Beirut Publications of the Faculty of Arts and Sciences, 1964), pp. 128–34. See also Shaykh Farid Dahdah, *Report of the President of the Civil Service Council* (Beirut: 1963).

39 Rizk, *op. cit.,* p. 167.

40 See also Crow, "Religious Sectarianism in the Lebanese Political System," *Journal of Politics,* 24 (August 1962), 489–520; Halim Fayyad, "Sectarianism and the Lebanese Administration" (Unpublished master's thesis, American University of Beirut, 1956). Fayyad reports (p. 69) the sectarian affiliations of eighteen Directors and Inspectors-General in 1942. Thirteen of the eighteen, or 72 per cent, were Christian.

41 Comparisons from Bruce Russett *et al., World Handbook of Political and Social Indicators* (New Haven: Yale University Press, 1964), p. 65. Of the forty-one countries for which data were available, Lebanon would rank between the thirteenth and fourteenth and in the fourth case decile and fourth range decile. Figures for Lebanon are from Ministry of Finance, *Résumé,* pp. 7, 71.

[42] Ministry of Finance, *Résumé,* pp. 90, 153; Himadeh, *op. cit.,* p. 21.

[43] Georges Corm, "Bilan des Finances Publiques Libanaises," pp. 10–3.

[44] Among the larger projects are the construction of the coastal superhighway that links Saida, Beirut, and Tripoli; the improvement of the mountain approach roads to Beirut; and the enlargement of the ports of Beirut and Tripoli.

[45] For comparative budget figures, see Ministry of Finance, *Résumé,* pp. 90, 153.

[46] *L'Orient,* May 30, 1962; *Le Jour,* June 18, 1965.

[47] The texts of decrees and a description of the operations are found in its publication, *Plan Vert* (Beirut: 1965). For an evaluation, see Henry Yacoub, "Plan Vert a un An," *L'Orient,* August 3 and 4, 1965.

[48] Yahya Ahmed Mahmassani, *A Central Bank for Lebanon* (Beirut: Feghali, 1961), pp. 28–9.

[49] "Le Premier Rapport Annuel de la Banque du Liban," *Le Commerce du Levant,* August 11, 1965, p. 1.

[50] Article 54 states, "Until such time that legislation is enacted for social security, the employer shall pay to the worker . . . a dismissal indemnity equivalent to the wage for one month for each year of service and one-half month if the period of service is less than one year." (English translation courtesy of the American Embassy, Beirut.)

[51] *L'Orient,* November 19, 1958.

[52] Social Security Code, Decree No. 13,955 of September 26, 1963, published in *The Official Gazette* of September 30, 1963. For further descriptions, see *L'Orient,* November 25 and 26, 1958, and February 17, March 15, and May 10, 1965; and Iskandar, *Social Security for Lebanon* (Beirut: Dār al-ṭalī‘ah, 1962), pp. 57–63.

[53] Iskandar, pp. 56–76. Also see Elias Saba, "Social Security in Lebanon: A Blessing or a Curse?" *Middle East Forum,* 37, No. 4 (1961), 27–31.

[54] See, for example, le Père le Génissel, "La Sécurité Sociale au Liban: Est-Elle Souhaitable? Est-Elle Possible?" *La Revue Sociale,* No. 2 (February 1961), pp. 5–11. "La sécurité sociale produit une certaine rédistribution de la richesse et, partout où elle est acceptée de bon coeur, développe un sentiment de solidarité sociale qui influe beaucoup sur la cohésion de la communauté nationale." (p. 5)

["Social security produces a certain redistribution of the wealth and, wherever it is accepted in good part, develops a sense of social solidarity that has a strong influence on the cohesion of the national community."]

[55] Charles Helou, "Lebanon's Development Policy," *Middle East Forum,* 41, No. 2 (1965), 5–6.

Bibliography

GENERAL

ALMOND, GABRIEL A. "A Developmental Approach to Political Systems," *World Politics,* 17, No. 2 (1965), 183–214.

ALMOND, GABRIEL A., and JAMES S. COLEMAN (eds.). *The Politics of the Developing Areas.* Princeton: Princeton University Press, 1960.

BERGER, MORROE. *The Arab World Today.* Garden City, N.Y.: Doubleday, 1962.

BINDER, LEONARD. *Iran: Political Development in a Changing Society.* Berkeley: University of California Press, 1961.

———. "Prolegomena to the Comparative Study of Middle Eastern Governments," *American Political Science Review,* 51, No. 3 (1957), 651–68.

———. *Religion and Politics in Pakistan.* Berkeley: University of California Press, 1961.

CUTRIGHT, PHILLIPS. "National Political Development: Measurement and Analysis," *American Sociological Review,* 28, No. 2 (1963), 253–64.

DAHL, ROBERT A. *Who Governs? Democracy and Power in an American City.* New Haven: Yale University Press, 1961.

DAVIES, JAMES C. "Toward a Theory of Revolution," *American Sociological Review,* 27, No. 1 (1962), 5–19.

DEUTSCH, KARL W. *Nationalism and Social Communication: An Inquiry into the Foundations of Nationality.* New York: Wiley, 1953.

———. *The Nerves of Government.* New York: Free Press, 1963.

———. "Social Mobilization and Political Development," *American Political Science Review,* 55, No. 3 (1961), 493–514.

DUVERGER, MAURICE. *Political Parties.* New York: Wiley, 1959.

EISENSTADT, S. N. "Modernization and the Conditions of Sustained Growth," *World Politics,* 16, No. 4 (1964), 576–94.

EMERSON, RUPERT. *From Empire to Nation.* Cambridge, Mass.: Harvard University Press, 1960.

FINER, HERMAN. *Dulles Over Suez.* Chicago: Quadrangle, 1964.

FRIEDRICH, CARL J. "Political Pathology," *Political Quarterly,* 37, No. 1 (January–March 1966), 70–85.

HALPERN, MANFRED. *The Politics of Social Change in the Middle East and North Africa.* Princeton: Princeton University Press, 1963.

HUNTINGTON, SAMUEL P. "Political Development and Political Decay," *World Politics,* 17, No. 3 (1965), 386–430.

———. "Political Modernization: America vs. Europe," *World Politics,* 18, No. 3 (1966), 378–414.

LANDAU, MARTIN. "On the Use of Metaphor in Political Analysis," *Social Research,* 28, No. 3 (1961), 331–53.

LERNER, DANIEL. *The Passing of Traditional Society: Modernizing the Middle East.* New York: Free Press, 1958.

LEVY, MARION J., JR. "Patterns (Structures) of Modernization and Political Development," *Annals of the American Academy of Political and Social Science,* 348 (March 1965), 29–40.

LIPSET, SEYMOUR MARTIN. *Political Man: The Social Bases of Politics.* Garden City, N.Y.: Doubleday, 1960.

MERRIAM, CHARLES E. *The Role of Politics in Social Change.* New York: New York University Press, 1936.

ORGANSKI, A. F. K. *The Stages of Political Development.* New York: Knopf, 1965.

PACKENHAM, ROBERT A. "Approaches to the Study of Political Development," *World Politics,* 17, No. 1 (1964), 108–20.

PARSONS, TALCOTT, and EDWARD A. SHILS (eds.). *Toward a General Theory of Action.* Cambridge, Mass.: Harvard University Press, 1951.

POLK, WILLIAM R. "Social Modernization: The New Men," in Georgianna G. Stevens (ed.). *The United States and the Middle East.* Englewood Cliffs, N.J.: Prentice-Hall, 1964, chap. 2.

PYE, LUCIEN W. "The Concept of Political Development," *The Annals,* 348 (March 1965), 1–13.

———. *Politics, Personality, and Nation Building: Burma's Search for Identity.* New Haven: Yale University Press, 1962.

PYE, LUCIEN W., and SIDNEY VERBA (eds.). *Political Culture and Political Development.* Princeton: Princeton University Press, 1965.

RUSSETT, BRUCE M., H. R. ALKER, JR., K. W. DEUTSCH, and H. D. LASSWELL. *World Handbook of Political and Social Indicators.* New Haven: Yale University Press, 1964.

SHANNON, L. W. (ed.). *Underdeveloped Areas.* New York: Harper, 1957.

SILVERT, K. H. (ed.). *Expectant Peoples: Nationalism and Development.* New York: Random House, 1963.

WALTZ, KENNETH N. "Political Philosophy and the Study of International Relations," in W. T. R. Fox (ed.), *Theoretical Aspects of International Relations.* Notre Dame, Ind.: University of Notre Dame Press, 1959, pp. 51–67.

WEINER, MYRON. "Political Integration and Political Development," *The Annals of the American Academy of Political and Social Science,* 348 (March 1965), 52–64.

WILLNER, ANN RUTH. "The Underdeveloped Study of Political Development," *World Politics,* 16, No. 3 (1964), 468–82.

LEBANON

Books

ABOU, SELIM. *Le Bilinguisme Arabe-Français au Liban*. Paris: Presses Universitaires, 1962.

ABOUCHDID, EUGÉNIE ELIE. *Thirty Years of Lebanon and Syria: 1917–1947*. Beirut: Sader-Rihani, 1948.

ALEM, JEAN-PIERRE. *Le Liban*. Paris: Presses Universitaires, 1963.

ANTONIUS, GEORGE. *The Arab Awakening: The Story of the Arab National Movement*. London: Hamilton, 1938.

BAALBAKI, LEILA. *Anā aḥyā [I Live]*. Beirut: Dār majalat al-shiʿr-maktabat al-ʿaṣriyyah, 1963.

BINDER, LEONARD (ed.). *Politics in Lebanon*. New York: Wiley, 1966.

BUSTANI, EMILE. *March Arabesque*. London: Hale, 1961.

CAMPBELL, J. C. *Defense of the Middle East*. Rev. ed. New York: Praeger, 1960.

CATROUX, (GÉNÉRAL) GEORGES. *Dans la Bataille de la Méditerranée*. Paris: Julliard, 1949.

———. *Deux Missions en Moyen-Orient, 1919–1922*. Paris: Plon, 1958.

CHAMOUN, CAMILLE. *Crise au Moyen-Orient*. Paris: Gallimard, 1963.

CHIHA, MICHEL. *Politique Intérieure*. Beirut: Trident, 1964.

CHURCHILL, (COLONEL) CHARLES H. *The Druzes and Maronites under Turkish Rule, 1840–1860*. London: Quarith, 1862.

———. *Mount Lebanon: A Ten Years' Residence, from 1842 to 1852*. 3 vols. London: Saunders & Otley, 1853.

COON, CARLETON S. *Caravan*. New York: Holt, 1951.

DE GAULLE, CHARLES. *Mémoires de Guerre*. Paris: Plon, 1956.

EVANS, LAURENCE. *United States Policy and the Partition of Turkey, 1914–1924*. Baltimore: Johns Hopkins Press, 1965.

FISHER, S. N. (ed.). *Social Forces in the Middle East*. Ithaca: Cornell University Press, 1955.

GEORGE, LUCIEN, and TOUFIC MOKDESSI. *Les Partis Libanais en 1959*. Beirut: L'Orient-al-Jaryda, 1959.

HADDAD, GEORGE. *Fifty Years of Modern Syria and Lebanon*. Beirut: Dar al-Hayat, 1950.

HITTI, PHILIP K. *Lebanon in History: From Earliest Times to the Present*. London: Macmillan, 1957.

HOURANI, ALBERT. *Arabic Thought in the Liberal Age, 1798–1939*. London: Oxford, 1962.

———. *Minorities in the Arab World*. London: Oxford, 1947.

———. *Syria and Lebanon: A Political Essay*. London: Oxford, 1946.

HOWARD, HARRY N. *The King-Crane Commission: An American Inquiry into the Middle East*. Beirut: Khayat's, 1963.

KHALIL, MUHAMMAD. *The Arab States and the Arab League*. 2 vols. Beirut: Khayat's, 1962.

AL-KHOURY, BECHARA. *Ḥaqāʾiq lubnāniyyah* [*Lebanese Truths*]. 3 vols. Beirut: Awrāq lubnāniyyah, 1961.

KIRK, GEORGE. *The Middle East in the War*. London: Oxford, 1952.

KOHN, HANS. *Nationalism and Imperialism in the Hither East*. New York: Harcourt, 1932.

LAQUEUR, WALTER Z. *Communism and Nationalism in the Middle East*. New York: Praeger, 1957.

———— (ed.). *The Middle East in Transition*. New York: Praeger, 1958.

LAWRENCE, T. E. *The Seven Pillars of Wisdom*. Garden City, N.Y.: Doubleday, 1936.

LONGRIGG, STEPHEN HEMSLEY. *Syria and Lebanon under French Mandate*. London: Oxford, 1958.

LYAUTEY, PIERRE. *Liban Moderne*. Paris: Julliard, 1964.

MACCALLUM, ELIZABETH P. *The Nationalist Crusade in Syria*. New York: Foreign Policy Association, 1928.

MARRIOTT, J. A. R. *The Eastern Question*. 4th ed. Oxford: Clarendon, 1940.

MATTHEWS, R. D., and MATTA AKRAWI. *Education in Arab Countries of the Near East*. Washington, D.C.: American Council on Education, 1949.

MEO, LEILA. *Lebanon: Improbable Nation*. Bloomington: Indiana University Press, 1965.

MEYER, A. J. *Middle Eastern Capitalism: Nine Essays*. Cambridge, Mass.: Harvard University Press, 1959.

MILLER, RICHARD I. *Dag Hammarskjöld and Crisis Diplomacy*. New York: Pyramid, 1961.

NANTET, JACQUES. *Histoire du Liban*. Paris: Minuit, 1963.

NIMEH, WILLIAM. *History of the Lebanon*. Mexico City: Editora Nacional, 1954.

NUSEIBEH, HAZEM ZAKI. *The Ideas of Arab Nationalism*. Ithaca: Cornell University Press, 1956.

PEARSE, RICHARD. *Three Years in the Levant*. New York: Macmillan, 1949.

PHARAON, HENRI. *Au Service du Liban et son Unité*. Beirut: Le Jour, 1959.

POLK, WILLIAM R. *The Opening of South Lebanon*. Cambridge, Mass.: Harvard University Press, 1963.

POUJADE, EUGÈNE. *Le Liban et la Syrie, 1845–1860*. 3d ed. Paris: Lévy, 1867.

PUAUX, GABRIEL. *Deux Années au Levant*. Paris: Hachette, 1952.

QUBAIN, FAHIM I. *Crisis in Lebanon*. Washington, D.C.: Middle East Institute, 1961.

RIACHI, ISKANDAR. *Qabl wa-baʿd* [*Before and After*]. Beirut: Maktabat al-ʿarfān, 1953.

————. *Ruʾasāʾ lubnān kamā ʿaraftuhum* [*Presidents of Lebanon as I Knew Them*]. Beirut: Maktabat al-tijārah, 1961.

RISTELHUEBER, RENÉ. *Les Traditions Françaises au Liban.* Paris: Alcan, 1925.

SALIBI, KAMAL. *The Modern History of Lebanon.* London: Weidenfeld, 1965.

SAYIGH, YUSIF A. *Entrepreneurs of Lebanon: The Role of the Business Leader in a Developing Economy.* Cambridge, Mass.: Harvard University Press, 1962.

SEALE, PATRICK. *The Struggle for Syria.* London: Oxford, 1965.

STEWART, DESMOND. *Turmoil in Beirut.* London: Wingate, 1959.

SULEIMAN, MICHAEL W. *Political Parties in Lebanon.* Ithaca: Cornell University Press, 1967.

SULH, SAMI. *Muḏakkirāt* [*Memoirs*]. Beirut: Maktabat al-fiqr al-ʿarabī, 1960.

THAYER, CHARLES W. *Diplomat.* New York: Harper, 1959.

TOYNBEE, ARNOLD J. *The Islamic World since the Peace Settlement.* London: Oxford, 1927.

ZEINE, ZEINE N. *The Struggle for Arab Independence.* Beirut: Khayat's, 1960.

ZIADEH, NICOLA A. *Syria and Lebanon.* London: Benn, 1957.

Articles

ALEM, JEAN-PIERRE. "Troubles Insurrectionnels au Liban," *Orient* (Paris), 2, No. 6 (1958), 37–47.

ARMSTRONG, LINCOLN, and RASHID BASHSHUR. "Ecological Patterns and Value Orientations in Lebanon," *Public Opinion Quarterly,* 22, No. 3 (1958), 406–15.

ASFOUR, EDMUND Y. "Industrial Development in Lebanon," *Middle East Economic Papers* (Beirut), 2 (1955), 1–16.

BAWARSHI, TEWFIQ. "The Lebanese Labour Scene," *Middle East Forum,* 39, No. 6 (1963), 21–4.

BOUTROS, FUAD. "Les Fondements de Notre Vie Nationale," *Les Conférences du Cénacle* (Beirut), 15th year, No. 12 (1961).

BOUTROS-GHALI, B. Y. "The Arab League: 1945–1955," *International Conciliation,* No. 498 (1954 [i.e., 1955]), pp. 387–448.

BRITT, GEORGE. "Lebanon's Popular Revolution," *Middle East Journal,* 7 (Winter 1953), 1–17.

CHURCHILL, CHARLES W. "Village Life of the Central Beqaʿ Valley of Lebanon," *Middle East Economic Papers* (1959), 1–48.

CORM, GEORGES. "Bilan des Finances Publiques Libanaises, 1945–1965," *Le Commerce du Levant* (March 3, 1965), pp. 10–3.

"Crise de la Jeunesse Libanaise," *Une Conférence du Cénacle Libanais* (Beirut: n.d.).

CROW, RALPH E. "Religious Sectarianism in the Lebanese Political System," *Journal of Politics,* 24, No. 3 (1962), 489–520.

CROW, RALPH, and ADNAN ISKANDAR. "Administrative Reform in Lebanon, 1958–1959," *International Review of Administrative Sciences,* 18, No. 3 (1961), 293–307.

FARIS, NABIH A. Review of Fahim I. Qubain's *Crisis in Lebanon,* in *Middle East Forum,* 38, No. 1 (1962), 32.

LE GÉNISSEL, LE PÈRE. "La Sécurité Sociale au Liban: Est-Elle Souhaitable? Est-Elle Possible?" *La Revue Sociale* (Beirut), No. 2 (February 1961), pp. 5–12.

GULICK, JOHN. "Old Values and New Institutions in a Lebanese City," *Human Organization,* 24, No. 1 (1965), 49–52.

HABACHI, RENÉ. "Liban 61," *Les Conférences du Cénacle* (Beirut), 15th year, No. 8 (1961).

HESS, C. G., JR., and H. L. BODMAN, JR. "Confessionalism and Feudality in Lebanese Politics," *Middle East Journal,* 8, No. 1 (1954), 10–26.

AL-HOSRI, SATI. "C'est au Liban Qu'est Née l'Idée Nationaliste," *L'Orient Littéraire* (Beirut), June 9, 1962.

HOTTINGER, ARNOLD. "Zuʿamāʾ and Parties in the Lebanese Crisis of 1958," *Middle East Journal,* 15, No. 2 (1961), 127–40.

HOURANI, ALBERT H. "The Decline of the West in the Middle East," *International Affairs,* 29 (January and April, 1953), 22–42; 156–84.

———. "Race, Religion, and Nation State in the Near East," in *A Vision of History* (Beirut: Khayat's, 1961), pp. 71–105.

———. "Twenty Years of Change," *Middle East Forum,* 32, No. 5 (1957), 7 ff.

HUDSON, BRADFORD B. (ed.). "Cross-Cultural Studies in the Arab Middle East and the United States: Studies of Young Adults," *Journal of Social Issues,* 15, No. 3 (1959), *passim.*

HUREWITZ, J. C. "Lebanese Democracy in Its International Setting," *Middle East Journal,* 17, No. 5 (1963), 487–506.

ISSAWI, CHARLES. "Economic and Social Foundations of Democracy in the Middle East," in W. Z. Laqueur (ed.), *The Middle East in Transition* (New York: Praeger, 1957), pp. 33–51.

K., G. E. "Elections in the Lebanese Republic," *World Today,* 8, No. 6 (1957), 260–5.

KERR, MALCOLM H. "Decision-Making in a Confessional Democracy," in Leonard Binder (ed.), *Politics in Lebanon* (New York: Wiley, 1966), pp. 187–212.

———. "Lebanese Views on the 1958 Crisis," *Middle East Journal,* 15, No. 2 (1961), 211–7.

———. "The 1960 Lebanese Parliamentary Elections," *Middle Eastern Affairs,* 11, No. 9 (1960), 266–75.

KHADDURI, MAJID. "The Army Officer: His Role in Middle East Politics," in S. N. Fisher (ed.), *Social Forces in the Middle East* (Ithaca: Cornell University Press, 1955), pp. 162–83.

KHALAF, SAMIR. "Industrial Conflict in Lebanon," *Human Organization,* 24, No. 1 (1965), 25–33.

KHURI, ZAHI N. "The Lebanese Press," *Middle East Forum,* 38, No. 2 (1962), 11–5.

KIRK, GEORGE E. "The Arab Awakening Reconsidered," *Middle Eastern Affairs,* 12, No. 6 (1962), 162–73.

LANDAU, JACOB. "Elections in Lebanon," *Western Political Quarterly,* 14, No. 1 (1961), Pt. I, 120–48.

———. "Peaceful Change in the Lebanon," *World Today,* 9 (April 1953), 162–73.

"Lebanon," special issue of *Middle East Forum,* Vol. 36, No. 5 (1960).

LENCZOWSKI, GEORGE. "Literature on the Clandestine Activities of Great Powers in the Middle East," *Middle East Journal,* 8, No. 2 (1954), 205–11.

LONGRIGG, STEPHEN H. "The Decline of the West in the Middle East: An Alternative View," *International Affairs,* 29, No. 3 (1953), 326–39.

MALIK, CHARLES. "The Near East: The Search for Truth," *Foreign Affairs,* 30, No. 2 (1952), 231–64.

MELIKIAN, LEVON H., and LUTFY N. DIAB. "Group Affiliations of University Students in the Arab Middle East," *Journal of Social Psychology,* 49 (May 1959), 145–9.

MOURAD, JEAN. "A la Recherche d'une Sécurité Sociale au Liban," *La Revue Sociale,* No. 2 (February 1961), pp. 1–15.

NACCACHE, GEORGES. "Un Nouveau Style: le Chéhabisme," *Les Conférences du Cénacle,* 15th year, No. 4 (1961).

NAJARIAN, PERGROUHI. "Adjustment in the Family and Patterns of Family Living," *Journal of Social Issues,* 15, No. 3 (1959), 28–44.

PATAI, RAPHAEL. "The Dynamics of Westernization in the Near East," *Middle East Journal,* 9, No. 1 (1955), 1–27.

———. "The Middle East as a Culture Area," *Middle East Journal,* 6, No. 1 (1952), 1–22.

PHARAON, HENRI. "Min mīthāq al-iskandariyyah ilā qiyām jami'at al-duwal al-'arabiyyah," "From the Alexandria Protocol to the Establishment of the League of Arab States," *Ṭayār wa-telegrāf* (Beirut), March 15–16, 1965.

POLK, WILLIAM R. "A Decade of Discovery: America in the Middle East, 1947–1958," in Albert H. Hourani (ed.), *Middle Eastern Affairs Number 2,* St. Antony's Papers, 11 (London: Chatto & Windus, 1961), pp. 49–80.

RONDOT, PIERRE. "Brèves Réflexions sur l'Evolution des Structures Libanaises," *Orient,* No. 14 (1960), pp. 27–32.

———. "L'Expérience du Collège Unique dans le Système Représentatif Libanais," *Revue Française de Science Politique,* 7, No. 1 (1957), 67–87.

———. "Les Nouveaux Problèmes de l'Etat Libanais," *Revue Française de Science Politique,* 4, No. 2 (1954), 326–55.

———. "Quelques Réflexions sur les Structures du Liban," *Orient,* 2, No. 6 (1958), 23–36.

———. "Les Structures Socio-Politiques de la Nation Libanaise," *Revue Française de Science Politique,* 4, No. 1 (1953), 80–104.

SABA, ELIAS. "Social Security in Lebanon," *Middle East Forum,* 37, No. 4 (1961), 27–31.

SALIBI, KAMAL. "Lebanon Since the Crisis of 1958," *World Today,* 17, No. 1 (1961), 32–42.

————. "Lebanon Under Fuad Chehab: 1958–1964," *Middle Eastern Studies,* 2, No. 3 (1966), 211–26.

————. "Six Aspects of Lebanon," *Middle East Forum,* 36, No. 2 (1960), 15–8.

SARAFIAN, VAHE A. "Ármenian Population Statistics and Armenian Political Realities Today," *Armenian Review,* 11, No. 1 (1958), 78–84.

SCHMIDT, H. D. "The Nazi Party in Palestine and the Levant: 1932–1939," *International Affairs,* 28 (October 1954), 460–9.

SHIBER, SABA GEORGE. "A Critical Glance at Greater Beirut," in Shiber, *Urban Form and Aesthetics.* Kuwait: 1961, pp. 77–91 (mimeo.).

"Social Change in the Arab World," special issue of *Middle East Forum,* Vol. 36, No. 1 (1960).

SOLTAU, IRENE C. "Social Responsibility in the Lebanon," *International Affairs,* 25, No. 3 (1949), 307–17.

SULH, ALIA (el-Solh). "Riad el-Solh: un Homme, une Légende," serialized in *Le Jour* (Beirut), Summer and Fall 1965.

TADMOR, GIDEON. "The Lebanese Elections," *Middle Eastern Affairs,* 2 (June–July 1951), 247–50.

TANNOUS, AFIF I. "Land Reform: Key to the Development and Stability of the Arab World," *Middle East Journal,* 5, No. 1 (1951), 1–20.

————. "The Village in the National Life of Lebanon," *Middle East Journal,* 3, No. 2 (1949), 151–64.

VAUMAS, ETIENNE DE. "La Répartition Confessionnelle au Liban et l'Equilibre de l'Etat Libanais," *Revue de Géographie Alpine* (Grenoble), 43, No. 3 (1955), 511–603.

WICKWAR, W. HARDY. "Patterns and Problems of Local Administration in the Middle East," *Middle East Journal,* 12, No. 3 (1958), 249–60.

WRIGHT, QUINCY. "The United States Intervention in the Lebanon," *American Journal of International Law,* 53, No. 1 (1959), 112–25.

ZEINE, ZEINE N. "Youth and Politics in the Near East," *World Today,* 7 (March 1951), 102–9.

ZIADEH, NICOLA A. "The Lebanese Elections, 1960," *Middle East Journal,* 14, No. 4 (1960), 367–81.

Monographs, Dissertations, and Reports

AMERICAN UNIVERSITIES FIELD STAFF. *Reports and Letters,* Southwest Asia Series, 1952–1958.

ARIDI, BASHIR A. *Parties and Politics in the Lebanese Society.* Unpublished doctoral dissertation, American University, Washington, D.C., 1955.

ASSOCIATION LIBANAISE DES SCIENCES POLITIQUES. *Presse, Radio, Télévision et Opinion Publique.* 3ème Congrès de Science Politique, Beirut, 1963 (mimeo.).

AYOUB, VICTOR FERRIS. *Political Structure of a Middle East Community: A Druze Village of Mount Lebanon.* Unpublished doctoral dissertation, Harvard University, 1955.

BADRE, A. Y. *The National Income of Lebanon.* 7 vols. Beirut: Economic Research Institute, American University of Beirut, 1953 (mimeo.).

BARROUD, ANTOINE. *La Situation Juridique des Journalistes au Liban.* Paris: Librairie Générale de Droit et Jurisprudence, 1965.

BELING, WILLARD A. *Pan-Arabism and Labor.* Harvard Middle Eastern Monograph Series, 4. Cambridge, Mass.: Harvard University Press, 1960.

BIKHAZI, SAMIAH JIBRAN. *The Lebanese Chamber of Deputies.* Unpublished master's thesis, American University of Beirut, 1962.

Bureau of Applied Social Research. *The Radio Audience of Lebanon.* New York, July 1951 (mimeo.).

Chamber of Commerce and Industry in Beirut. *Bayān bil-muʾasasāt al-tijāriyyah wal-sinā ʿiyyah wal-māliyyah* [*Catalogue of Commercial, Industrial, and Financial Institutions*]. Beirut: 1963.

CHÉHABE ED-DINE, SAID. *Géographie Humaine de Beyrouth.* Beirut: Calfat, 1960.

CHURCHILL, CHARLES W. *Beirut: A Socio-Economic Study.* Beirut: Dar al-Kitab, 1954.

Le Commerce du Levant. "1964 dans l'Economie Libanaise et Arabe," March 3, 1965.

———. "1965 dans l'Economie Libanaise et Arabe," March 5, 1966.

CROW, RALPH E. *Interest Groups in Lebanon.* Paper delivered at International Political Science Association Rome Congress, 1958 (mimeo.).

Federation of Non-governmental Organizations. *Directory of Voluntary Welfare Societies in Lebanon.* Beirut: Rihani, 1958.

FETTER, GEORGE C. *Attitudes Toward Selected Aspects of Rural Life and Technological Change Among Central Beqaʿa Farmers.* American University of Beirut Faculty of Agricultural Sciences Publication, 13. Beirut: 1961.

Ford Foundation (Beirut). *Report on the Activities of the Committee on Municipal Reform in Lebanon—the Development of the Congress of Lebanese Municipal Officials.* June 15, 1965.

FULLER, ANNE H. *Buarij: Portrait of a Lebanese Muslim Village.* Harvard Middle Eastern Monograph Series, 6. Cambridge, Mass.: Harvard University Press, 1961.

GEMAYEL, MAURICE. *La Planification Intégrale des Eaux Libanaises.* Beirut: St. Paul, 1951.

GEMAYEL, SLEIMAN M. *Evolution du Budget Libanais.* Université de St. Joseph [Beirut] Annales de la Faculté de Droit et des Sciences Economiques, 37. Paris: Librairie Générale de Droit et de Jurisprudence, 1962.

GRASSMUCK, GEORGE, and KAMAL SALIBI. *A Manual of Lebanese Administration.* Beirut: American University of Beirut Public Administration Department, 1955.

———. *Reformed Administration in Lebanon.* Beirut: Catholic Press, 1964.

GULICK, JOHN. *Social Structure and Culture Change in a Lebanese Village.* New York: Wenner-Gren, 1955.

HAIDAR, AHMAD. *Al-dawlah al-lubnāniyyah* [*The Lebanese State*]. Beirut: Nijmeh, 1954.

HARBY, MOHAMMED K. *Technical Education in the Arab States.* UNESCO Educational Studies and Documents, 53. Paris: UNESCO, 1965.

HARIK, ILIYA F. *Political Change in a Traditional Society: A Study of Institutional Conflict in the Iqṭāᶜ Political System of Mount Lebanon, 1711–1845.* Unpublished doctoral dissertation, University of Chicago, 1964.

HIGGINS, BENJAMIN. *Le Rapport Higgins sur l'Economie Libanaise.* Damascus: Bureau des Documentations Arabes, 1960 (mimeo.).

HIMADEH, RAJA S. *The Fiscal System of Lebanon.* Beirut: Khayat's, 1961.

HITTI, PHILIP K. *Origins of the Druze People and Religion.* New York: Columbia University Press, 1928.

HOURANI, BENJAMIN T. *Unionism in the Lebanese Labor Law of 1946.* Unpublished master's thesis, American University of Beirut, 1959.

ISKANDAR, ADNAN G. *Bureaucracy in Lebanon.* American University of Beirut Publications of the Faculty of Arts and Sciences Social Science Series, 22. Beirut: 1964.

ISKANDAR, MARWAN. *Social Security for Lebanon: An Economic Study.* Beirut: Dār al-ṭalī ᶜah, 1962.

KARAMI, NADIA and NAWWAF. *Al-ᶜālam al-ᶜarabī: tārīkh wa-rijāl* [*The Arab World: History and Men*]. Saida: Dayr al-mukhalliṣ, 1956.

KERR, MALCOLM H. *Lebanon in the Last Years of Feudalism, 1840–1868: A Contemporary Account by Anṭūn Ḍāhir al-ᶜAqīqi, and Other Documents.* American University of Beirut Publications of the Faculty of Arts and Sciences Oriental Series, 33. Beirut: 1959.

KHALAF, SAMIR GEORGE. *Managerial Ideology and Industrial Conflict in Lebanon.* Unpublished doctoral dissertation, Princeton University, 1963.

KHALAF, SAMIR, and EMILE SHWAYRI. *Family Firms and Industrial Development: The Lebanese Case.* Beirut: American University, 1965 (mimeo.).

MAHMASANI, YAHYA AHMED. *A Central Bank for Lebanon.* Beirut: Feghali, 1961.

MAJZOUB, MOHAMMED. *Le Liban et l'Orient Arabe, 1943–1956.* Aix-en-Provence: La Pensée Universitaire, 1956.

MAKDISI, NADIM K. *The Syrian National Party: A Case Study of the First Inroads of National Socialism in the Arab World.* Unpublished doctoral dissertation, American University, Washington, D.C., 1959.

MENASSA, GABRIEL. *Plan de Réconstruction de l'Economie Libanaise et de Réforme de l'Etat.* Beirut: L'Imprimerie Catholique, 1948.

NASR, GEORGE. *The Polity of the Lebanon, 1943–1952.* Paper submitted to Professor Walid Khalidi, American University of Beirut, 1961.

NASR, NAFHAT NASSIM. *The Presidency of Lebanon.* Unpublished master's thesis, American University of Beirut, 1960.

PATAI, RAPHAEL, *et al. The Republic of Lebanon.* Subcontractor's Monograph, 46. New Haven: Human Relations Area Files, 1956.

PROTHRO, EDWIN TERRY. *Child Rearing in the Lebanon.* Harvard Middle Eastern Monograph Series, 8. Cambridge, Mass.: Harvard University Press, 1961.

RAMSAUR, ERNEST E. *The Religions of Lebanon,* 1961 (mimeo.).

RIZK, CHARLES. *Le Régime Politique Libanais.* Unpublished doctoral dissertation, University of Paris, 1964.

RONDOT, PIERRE. *Les Institutions Politiques du Liban: des Communautés Traditionnelles à l'Etat Moderne.* Paris: Imprimerie Nationale, 1947.

RUSTOW, DANKWART. *Politics and Westernization in the Near East.* Princeton: Princeton University Center of International Studies, 1956.

SAADEH, MOUNIR R. *The Fifth Lebanese Legislative Assembly, 1943–1944.* Unpublished master's thesis, American University of Beirut, 1945.

SABA, ELIAS S. *The Foreign Exchange Systems of Lebanon and Syria, 1939–1957.* Beirut: American University, 1961.

SAGHIYYAH, FAKHRI G. *The Government of Dr. Ayoub Tabet, March to July 1943.* Unpublished master's thesis, American University of Beirut, 1961.

Semaines Sociales du Liban. *L'Economie Libanaise et le Progrès Social.* Beirut: Imprimerie Catholique, 1955.

SIKSEK, SIMON G., BASHIR J. DAOUK, and SAMI E. BAAKLINI. *Preliminary Assessment of Manpower Resources and Requirements in Lebanon.* Beirut: American University of Beirut Economic Research Institute, 1960.

TABBARAH, BAHIGE B. *Les Forces Politiques Actuelles au Liban.* Unpublished doctoral dissertation, University of Grenoble, 1956.

YAUKEY, DAVID. *Fertility Differences in a Modernizing Country.* Princeton: Princeton University Press, 1961.

Documents, Political Statements, and Reference Works

BAKDASH, KHALED. *La Charte Nationale du Parti Communiste en Syrie et au Liban.* Beirut: Saout ul-Chaab, 1944.

———. "Report of the Central Command of the Communist Party in Syria and Lebanon in January 1951," *Middle East Journal,* 7, No. 2 (1953), 206–21.

The Black Book of the Lebanese Elections of May 25, 1947. Translated from Arabic by George Akl, Abdo Ouadat, and Edward Hunein. New York: Phoenicia, 1947.

Congrès National Démocrate. *Rapport et Motion du Congrès National Démocrate,* held at Beirut, November 27, 1938.

Documents on Lebanese Politics, Jafet Library, American University of Beirut; a file of election handouts, party tracts, and political declarations from the Mandate period to the present.

EDDE, RAYMOND. *Nidāʾ ilā al-lubnāniyyāt wal-lubnāniyyīn li-munāsabat intikhābāt 12 tamūz 1953* [*Appeal to the Lebanese Women and Men on the Occasion of the Elections of 12 July 1953*]. Beirut, June 26, 1953.

———. "Ce que Je Reproche au Gouvernement," *Magazine* (Beirut weekly), June 27, 1963, pp. 20–1.

Great Britain Public Record Office, Correspondence Relating to the Affairs of Syria, 1860–1861; handwritten.

L'Indépendance du Liban: Documents 1919–1936. Collected and annotated by Ibrahim Maklouf. Beirut: Dar al-Ahad (1936?).

350 · BIBLIOGRAPHY

Institut de Formation en Vue de Développement. *Le Liban Face à son Développement*. Condensation of the IRFED study of 1960–61. Beirut: Catholic Press, 1963.

JUMBLAT, KAMAL. *Citoyen Libre et Peuple Heureux*. Beirut: Dar al-Kachaff, n.d.

———. *Démocratie Nouvelle*. Lectures, 1950–1955. Beirut: n.d.

———. *Ḥaqīqat ʿan al-thawrat al-lubnāniyyah [The Truth About the Lebanese Revolution]*. Beirut: Dār al-nashr al-ʿarabiyyah, 1959.

Kataeb Party (Ḥīzb al-katāʾib, Les Phalanges Libanaises). *Deuxième Congrès du Parti des Phalanges Libanaises*. Beirut: 1959.

———. *Bayān muhim [Important Declaration]*. Beirut: 1956.

———. *National Unity*. Press Conference of Pierre Gemayel. Beirut: n.d.

———. *Programme d'Action des Kataeb*. Adopted at the 6th Party Congress at Shtaura, September 27–29, 1963.

———. *Vingt-Cinq Ans au Service du Liban*. Beirut: 1961.

The Lebanese Constitution: Reference Edition in English Translation. Prepared by the American University of Beirut Department of Political Studies and Public Administration. Beirut: Khayat's, 1960.

The Lebanese League of Students. *Lebanon 1959*. Beirut: 1959.

The Lebanese Press Syndicate. Memorandum on "self-censorship." Beirut: 1962.

Lebanon, Republic of. Biographical Records of Deputies in the Lebanese Parliament, Library of the Chamber of Deputies.

———. *Les Décrets Législatifs de la Réforme*. 3 vols. Beirut: Bureau des Documentations Libanaises et Arabes, 1959.

———. *Nutrition Survey, February–April 1961*. Report by the Interdepartmental Committee on Nutrition for National Defense, U.S. Department of Defense and the Lebanese Government.

———. Ministry of Finance, *Faḏlakat mashrūʿmawāzanat ʿām 1966 [Résumé of the 1966 Budget Proposal]*. Beirut: 1965.

———. Ministry of General Planning, *Besoins et Possibilités de Développement du Liban*. Study made by the Institut de Recherche et de Formation en Vue de Développement (IRFED). 2 vols. Beirut, 1960–1961.

———. Ministry of General Planning, Central Directorate of Statistics, *Bulletin Statistique Mensuel*, from June 1963. Up to 1958, see Service de Statistiques, *Bulletin Trimestrial*.

———. Ministry of Labor and Social Affairs, *Enquête sur les Caractéristiques Démographiques et Sociales des Salaires au Liban*. Beirut: 1963.

———. Ministry of National Education, *Minhaj al-taʿlīm [Curriculum of Instruction]*. Beirut: n.d.

———. Ministry of National Education, Statistics on Primary and Secondary Schools and Teachers, Government and Private, 1955–1964.

National Bloc, Lebanese (*Al-kutlah al-waṭaniyyah al-lubnāniyyah*). *Niẓām al-ḥizb [Organization of the Party]*. Beirut: 1958.

———. *Baʿḍ al-maṭālib wal-mashārīʿ al-iṣlāḥiyyah [Some Demands and Projects for Improvement]* August 1957 (mimeo.).

————. *Minhāj* [*Program*]. Beirut: 1951?.

al-Nidā' (Communist newspaper) Editorial Board. *Naḥwa ṭarīq taqaddumī li-taṭawwur lubnān* [*Toward a Progressive Way to Develop Lebanon*] (Beirut: March 27, 1965).

"Pierre Gemayel dans la Petite Histoire," *Action Proche-Orient* (Beirut), 25th anniversary issue (1961), pp. 43–7.

Principles and Aims of the Syrian National Party: Interpreted by the Leader. Translated by Fakhri Maluf. U.S.A.: Fast Printing Service, 1943, 21 pp.

Progressive Socialist Party. (Al-ḥizb al-taqaddumī al-ishtirākī). *Ahdāfahu, shurūṭ al-intimā*', *ḥuqūq a'dā'ihi* [*Its Aims, Conditions for Membership, Rights of Members*]. Beirut: n.d.

————. *Al-ḍamān al-ṣihiyy fī lubnān* [*Health Security in Lebanon*]. Beirut: 1955.

————. *Mawqif min al-ḥarb al-bāridah, mashrū' Eisenhower, wa-takattul al-asyawī al-ifrīqī* [*Position on the Cold War, Eisenhower Doctrine, and Afro-Asian Bloc*]. Beirut: 1957?.

————. *Mīthāq* [*Covenant*]. Beirut: 1961.

Recueil des Archives Biographiques Permanentes du Monde Arabe. Damascus: Bureau des Documentations Syriennes et Arabes, 1962.

Recueil Documentaire sur les Sociétés en Activité au Liban. Beirut: Bureau des Documentations Libanaises et Arabes, 1957?.

United Nations. *Demographic Yearbook.* New York: 1960–1964.

————. *Statistical Yearbook.* New York: 1960–1964.

————. Department of Economic and Social Affairs, *Economic Developments in the Middle East.* New York: 1956–1957, 1959–1961.

————. Department of Economic and Social Affairs, *Report on the World Social Situation.* New York: 1961.

————. Educational, Scientific, and Cultural Organization (UNESCO), *Basic Facts and Figures.* Paris: 1960.

————. UNESCO, *World Communications.* Paris: 1964.

————. UNESCO, *World Illiteracy at Mid-Century.* Paris: 1957.

————. Food and Agriculture Organization (F.A.O.) Mediterranean Development Project, *Lebanon: Country Report.* Rome: 1959.

————. Observation Group in Lebanon (UNOGIL), Official Reports to the Secretary General, 1958, Documents S/4040, S/4051, S/4052, S/4069, S/4085, S/4100, and S/4114.

————. Relief and Works Agency for Palestine Refugees (U.N.R.W.A.), *Activities in Lebanon.* Beirut: April 1, 1961.

————. U.N.R.W.A., Annual Report of the Director, July 1, 1960–June 30, 1961, General Assembly *Official Reports,* 16th session, Supplement No. 14 (A/4861).

————. Security Council, *Official Records,* 1958, Meeting nos. 823–5, 827–8.

United States. Department of Commerce, *International Commerce,* Washington, D.C.: U.S. Government Printing Office, February 1, 1965.

————. Department of Commerce, Overseas Business Reports, *Market*

Factors in Lebanon (OBR 64–32). Washington, D.C.: U.S. Government Printing Office, March 1964.

————. Department of State, *1943, The Near East and Africa. (Foreign Relations of the United States,* Vol. IV.) Washington, D.C.: U.S. Government Printing Office, 1964.

————. Department of State, *Paris Peace Conference 1919. (Foreign Relations of the United States,* Vol. XII.) Washington, D.C.: U.S. Government Printing Office, 1947.

————. Operations Mission in Lebanon, *Economic Data for the Ekistic Programme of Lebanon.* Prepared by Doxiadis Associates, Consulting Engineers. Athens and Beirut: 1957.

————. Senate, *Foreign Aid Program.* Compilation of studies and surveys prepared under the direction of the Special Committee to study the Foreign Aid Program. (85th Cong., 1st sess.; Doc. 52.) Washington, D.C.: U.S. Government Printing Office, 1957.

————. Senate, Committees on Foreign Relations and Armed Forces, *The President's Proposal on the Middle East.* Hearings on the "Eisenhower Doctrine." (85th Cong., 1st sess.) Washington, D.C.: U.S. Government Printing Office, 1957.

Who's Who in Lebanon, 1963–1964. Beirut: Publitec, 1964.

YALE, WILLIAM. Papers. Yale University Library; papers relating to the dismemberment of the Ottoman Empire, 1917–1919.

Periodicals Consulted

Action Proche-Orient, journal of the Kataeb Party.

al-Akhbār, newspaper of the Communist Party.

al-Anbāʾ, newspaper of the Progressive Socialist Party.

Arab World Opinion, a daily English digest of Arab opinion and press reports.

Le Commerce du Levant, the leading Lebanese financial newspaper.

Daily Bulletin, published by the Republic of Lebanon Ministry of Information, Guidance, and Tourism.

The Daily Star, English-language newspaper.

The Eastern Times, 1943, long-defunct English-language newspaper.

al-Ḥawādith, Beirut political weekly.

al-Ḥurīyyah, Beirut political weekly.

al-Jarīdah al-rasmiyyah, The Official Gazette of the Republic of Lebanon.

Le Jour, Beirut daily originally published by Michel Chiha.

al-Jundī al-lubnānī [*The Lebanese Soldier*], military magazine, 1946–1948.

Lisān al-Ḥāl, Beirut daily.

al-Muḥarrir, Beirut daily.

al-Nahār, Beirut daily.

Ninth Army News, 1943, published by British Army Public Relations.

L'Orient, Beirut daily, of which Pierre Rondot has written, "Ce quotidien ne cesse de soumettre les institutions et les moeurs politiques libanaises à une critique aigue. . . ."

["This daily does not cease to subject Lebanese institutions and political customs to sharp criticism. . . ."]

(*Revue Française de Science Politique,* March 1954).

Le Réveil, Beirut daily, predecessor of *L'Orient.*

al-Ṣayyād, Beirut political weekly.

Index

Index

357

PUBLICATIONS WRITTEN UNDER THE AUSPICES OF THE CENTER FOR INTERNATIONAL AFFAIRS, HARVARD UNIVERSITY

Books

The Necessity for Choice, by Henry A. Kissinger, 1961. Harper & Bros.

Strategy and Arms Control, by Thomas C. Schelling and Morton H. Halperin, 1961. Twentieth Century Fund.

Rift and Revolt in Hungary, by Ferenc A. Váli, 1961. Harvard University Press.

United States Manufacturing Investment in Brazil, by Lincoln Gordon and Engelbert L. Grommers, 1962. Harvard Business School.

The Economy of Cyprus, by A. J. Meyer, with Simos Vassiliou (jointly with the Center for Middle Eastern Studies), 1962. Harvard University Press.

Entrepreneurs of Lebanon, by Yusif A. Sayigh (jointly with the Center for Middle Eastern Studies), 1962. Harvard University Press.

Communist China 1955–1959: Policy Documents with Analysis, with a Foreword by Robert R. Bowie and John K. Fairbank (jointly with the East Asian Research Center), 1962. Harvard University Press.

In Search of France, by Stanley Hoffmann, Charles P. Kindleberger, Laurence Wylie, Jesse R. Pitts, Jean-Baptiste Duroselle, and François Goguel, 1963. Harvard University Press.

Somali Nationalism, by Saadia Touval, 1963. Harvard University Press.

The Dilemma of Mexico's Development, by Raymond Vernon, 1963. Harvard University Press.

Limited War in the Nuclear Age, by Morton H. Halperin, 1963. John Wiley & Sons.

The Arms Debate, by Robert A. Levine, 1963. Harvard University Press.

Africans on the Land, by Montague Yudelman, 1964. Harvard University Press.

Counterinsurgency Warfare, by David Galula, 1964. Frederick A. Praeger.

People and Policy in the Middle East, by Max Weston Thornburg, 1964. W. W. Norton.

Shaping the Future, by Robert R. Bowie, 1964. Columbia University Press.

Foreign Aid and Foreign Policy, by Edward S. Mason (jointly with the Council on Foreign Relations), 1964. Harper & Row.

Public Policy and Private Enterprise in Mexico, by Miguel S. Wionczek, David H. Shelton, Calvin P. Blair, and Rafael Izquierdo. Edited by Raymond Vernon, 1964. Harvard University Press.

How Nations Negotiate, by Fred C. Iklé, 1964. Harper & Row.

China and the Bomb, by Morton H. Halperin (jointly with the East Asian Research Center), 1965. Frederick A. Praeger.

Democracy in Germany, by Fritz Erler (Jodidi Lectures), 1965. Harvard University Press.

The Troubled Partnership, by Henry A. Kissinger (jointly with the Council on Foreign Relations), 1965. McGraw-Hill Book Company.

The Rise of Nationalism in Central Africa, by Robert I. Rotberg, 1965. Harvard University Press.

Pan-Africanism and East African Integration, by Joseph S. Nye, Jr., 1965. Harvard University Press.

Communist China and Arms Control, by Morton H. Halperin and Dwight H. Perkins (jointly with the East Asian Research Center), 1965. Frederick A. Praeger.

Problems of National Strategy, ed. by Henry Kissinger, 1965. Frederick A. Praeger.

Deterrence Before Hiroshima: The Airpower Background of Modern Strategy, by George H. Quester, 1966. John Wiley & Sons.

Containing the Arms Race, by Jeremy J. Stone, 1966. M.I.T. Press.

Germany and the Atlantic Alliance: The Interaction of Strategy and Politics, by James L. Richardson, 1966. Harvard University Press.

Arms and Influence, by Thomas C. Schelling, 1966. Yale University Press.

Political Change in a West African State, by Martin L. Kilson, 1966. Harvard University Press.

Planning Without Facts: Lessons in Resource Allocation from Nigeria's Development, by Wolfgang F. Stolper, 1966. Harvard University Press.

Export Instability and Economic Development, by Alasdair I. MacBean, 1966. Harvard University Press.

The Soviet Bloc, by Zbigniew K. Brzezinski (jointly with the Russian Research Center), 1960. Harvard University Press. Revised edition, 1967.

Foreign Policy and Democratic Politics, by Kenneth N. Waltz (jointly with the Institute of War and Peace Studies, Columbia University), 1967. Little, Brown.

Contemporary Military Strategy, by Morton H. Halperin, 1967. Little, Brown.

Sino-Soviet Relations and Arms Control, ed. by Morton H. Halperin (jointly with the East Asian Research Center), 1967. M.I.T. Press.

Africa and United States Policy, by Rupert Emerson, 1967. Prentice-Hall.

Europe's Postwar Growth, by Charles P. Kindleberger, 1967. Harvard University Press.

The Rise and Decline of the Cold War, by Paul Seabury, 1967. Basic Books.

Student Politics, ed. by Seymour Martin Lipset, 1967. Basic Books.

Pakistan's Development: Social Goals and Private Incentives, by Gustav F. Papanek, 1967. Harvard University Press.

Strike a Blow and Die: A Narrative of Race Relations in Colonial Africa, by George Simeon Mwase. Edited and introduced by Robert I. Rotberg, 1967. Harvard University Press.

Aid, Influence, and Foreign Policy, by Joan M. Nelson, 1968. Macmillan.

International Regionalism, by Joseph S. Nye, 1968. Little, Brown.

The TFX Decision: McNamara and the Military, by Robert J. Art, 1968. Little, Brown.

Korea: The Politics of the Vortex, by Gregory Henderson, 1968. Harvard
    University Press.
*Political Development in Latin America: Instability, Violence, and Evo-
    lutionary Change,* by Martin Needler, 1968. Random House.

*Occasional Papers Published by the Center
for International Affairs*

1. *A Plan for Planning: The Need for a Better Method of Assisting Underdeveloped Countries on Their Economic Policies,* by Gustav F.
   Papanek, 1961. Out of print.
2. *The Flow of Resources from Rich to Poor,* by Alan D. Neale, 1961.
3. *Limited War: An Essay on the Development of the Theory and an
   Annotated Bibliography,* by Morton H. Halperin, 1962. Out of print.
4. *Reflections on the Failure of the First West Indian Federation,* by
   Hugh W. Springer, 1962. Out of print.
5. *On the Interaction of Opposing Forces Under Possible Arms Agreements,* by Glenn A. Kent, 1963.
6. *Europe's Northern Cap and the Soviet Union,* by Nils Örvik, 1963.
7. *Civil Administration in the Punjab: An Analysis of a State Government in India,* by E. N. Mangat Rai, 1963.
8. *On the Appropriate Size of a Development Program,* by Edward S.
   Mason, 1964.
9. *Self-Determination Revisited in the Era of Decolonization,* by Rupert
   Emerson, 1964.
10. *The Planning and Execution of Economic Development in Southeast
    Asia,* by Clair Wilcox, 1965.
11. *Pan-Africanism in Action,* by Albert Tevoedjre, 1965.
12. *Is China Turning In?* by Morton H. Halperin, 1965.
13. *Economic Development in India and Pakistan,* by Edward S. Mason,
    1966.
14. *The Role of the Military in Recent Turkish Politics,* by Ergun
    Özbudun, 1966.
15. *Economic Development and Individual Change: A Social-Psychological
    Study of the Comilla Experiment in Pakistan,* by Howard Schuman,
    1967.
16. *A Select Bibliography on Students, Politics, and Higher Education,*
    by Philip G. Altbach, 1967.
17. *Europe's Political Puzzle: A Study of the Fouchet Negotiations and
    the 1963 Veto,* by Alessandro Silj, 1967.
18. *The Cap and the Straits: Problems of Nordic Security,* by Jan Klen-
    berg, 1968.